ACKNOWLEDGEMENTS

This supplement to my previous work *Ātman: A Reconstruction of the Solar Cosmology of the Indo-Europeans* (Georg Olms, Hildesheim, 2005) focusses on the solar significance of the religious rituals of both the Japhetic Āryans and the Hamitic Sumerians, Egyptians and Indians. I hope that the reader will gain from it an adequate idea of the cosmological basis of these religions as well as of the intense concentration on the correspondence between the macrocosm and the human microcosm that characterises their various sacrificial, theurgic and gnostic systems. Taken together, these marks of the religious enlightenment of the ancient Indo-Europeans may indeed be considered to represent the highest spiritual evolution of mankind.

I should like to thank here Dr. Sylvia Stapelfeldt of the Fachbereichsbibliothek Südasien-, Tibet-, und Buddhismuskunde, Universität Wien, for her kind help with her collections during my several visits to the library. I must also thank the staff of the other libraries of the Universität Wien, and the Österreichische Nationalbibliothek, Wien, for their continual assistance. Finally, it is a pleasure to thank, once again, Prof. Ronald Sweet, Prof. Emeritus of the Department of Near Eastern Studies, University of Toronto, for his unfailing support.

Brno, 2011   Alexander Jacob

CONTENTS

ABBREVIATIONS

DED   *A Dravidian Etymological Dictionary*, ed. T. Burrow and M.B. Emeneau.
HW   *The Hindu World: An Encylopedic Survey of Hinduism*, ed. B. Walker.
EB   *Encyclopedia Britannica*
ERE   *Encyclopedia of Religion and Ethics*, ed. J. Hastings

AV	Atharva Veda
RV	Rgveda
KYV	Krishna [= Taittirīya] Yajur Veda
TS	Taittirīya Samhita
BP	Bhāgavata Purāna
BhavP	Bhavishya Purāna
BrvP	Brahmavaivarta Purāna
BrdP	Brahmānda Purāna
GP	Garuda Purāna
LP	Linga Purāna
MP	Matsya Purāna
SP	Skanda Purāna
ShP	Shiva Purāna
PP	Padma Purāna
VP	Vishnu Purāna
MBh	Mahābhārata
SB	Shatapatha Brāhmana
AB	Aitareya Brāhmana
GB	Gopatha Brāhmana
KB	Kaushītiki Brāhmana
TB	Taittirīya Brāhmana
BAU	Brhadāranyaka Upanishad

OEAG   *The Oxford Encyclopedia of Ancient Egypt*
LÄ   *Lexicon der Ägyptologie*

BD   *The Book of the Dead*, tr. E.A.W. Budge, London, 1895.
CT   *The Ancient Egyptian Coffin Texts*, tr. R.O. Faulkner.
UC   Petrie Museum of Egyptian Archaeology, University College, London.
ZÄS   *Zeitschrift für ägyptische Sprache und Altertumkunde*

RLA   *Reallexicon der Assyriologie*
AFO   *Archiv für Orientforschung*
ANET   *Ancient Near Eastern Texts Relating to the Old Testament*, ed. J.B. Pritchard.
BM   British Museum, Dept. of Western Asiatic Antiquities.
K   Kuyunjik Collection, British Museum.

CTH   *Catalogue des textes hittites*, by E. Laroche, Paris, 1971.
Kbo   *Keilschrifttexte aus Boghazköi*
KUB   *Keilschrifturkunden aus Boghazköi*
VAT   Vorderasiatische Abteilung, Tontafelsammlung, Staatliche Museen, Berlin.

"I am the Lord of Earth, the lord of the world,
the lord of the great creation ...
Brhaspati is the Brahman of the gods,
I am the Brahman of men."
(Āpastamba, *Shrautasūtra* I,3,18,3-4l)

PROLOGUE

In my recent work, *Ātman: A Reconstruction of the Solar Cosmology of the Indo-Europeans*,[1] I developed a synthetic view of the cosmology of the ancients which formed the basis of the mythologies of the Semites, Japhetites and Hamites. The historical thesis underlying this reconstruction is the unity of the original Noachidian race that branched out into the separate cultures of Egypt, Sumer, India and early Europe. In the present work I shall attempt to focus on the same solar cosmology as the source and significance of the principal rituals of these various peoples.

The concept of sacrifice is of primal importance in the religions of the ancient Indo-Europeans and yet it has been only partially understood, or sometimes quite misunderstood, both in the West and in India. The Indians and Iranians still conduct these sacrifices but mostly without a clear understanding of their magical symbolism and the cosmo-spiritual metamorphoses that they originally represented. Among western scholars, the role of sacrifice in the ancient religions outside the monotheistic framework has, especially recently, been misconstrued by modern empirical, sociological and phenomenological ways of thought. Jan Gonda's survey of the Vedic sacrifices in *Die Religionen Indiens* Bd. I (1960) remains a very clear-sighted account of ancient Indian sacrifices, while Madeleine Biardeau's *Le sacrifice dans l'inde ancienne* (1976) and Chapters 3 and 4 of H.W. Tull's *The Vedic Origins of Karma* (1989) dealing with the Agnicayana and Shmashānacayana rituals are also marked by profound understanding of Indian religion. Unfortunately, such studies apart, there have been other either superficial or misguided exercices that tend to distort the significance of sacrifices altogether. For example, Frits Staal, who actually recorded the performance of an Agnicayana[2]

---

[1] A. Jacob, *Ātman: A Reconstruction of the Solar Cosmology of the Indo-Europeans*, Hildesheim: Georg Olms, 2005.

[2] I have throughout this study used simplified transcriptional symbols to render the

ritual in India in his work, *Agni*, discusses in his next work, *Rules Without Meaning*, the focus on rules in Vedic ritual in such a phenomenological way that, while granting that the Shrauta Sūtras represent the only known "science" of ritual in the world, he insists that the rules that dominate the conduct of rituals have only a syntactic and no semantic significance. Thus, he concludes, the rituals are constituted of "rules without meaning", whereby he gives, willingly or unwillingly, the misleading impression that the rituals themselves are without meaning. In fact, the rituals were sacred dramatic events which were governed by equally sacred rules. The rigidity of the rules only demonstrates the extraordinary significance of the rituals which they regulate. The inadequacy of Staal's view is evidenced particularly in his discussion of mantras, which he believes can have no inherent meaning – though they, like the rules of ritual, may have a phonetic and syntactic signifance – since they are, according to him, constituted of meaningless syllabic utterances. But this is to ignore the value of sound in the formation of the cosmos according to the Vedic scriptures. For, as we shall see, the cosmos indeed began as Vāk (the Word, or Sound) and the gods are themselves most immediately represented – especially in the Tantric tradition – by the various sounds that constitute the bīja (seminal)-syllable mantras.[3] In ancient Egypt too, the entire creation was believed to have been created by the word of god, as Sauneron observed:

> The initial god, to create, had only to speak; and the beings or things evoked came from his voice. The word is ... in the Egyptian spirit ... the audible expression of the deepest essence of things; it remains what it was at the beginning of the world, a divine act which gave life to matter; in the articulation of the syllables resides the secret of the existence of the things evoked; to pronounce a word, a name ... is to act on the thing or being mentioned, it is to repeat the initial act of the creator.[4]

Another example of an anachronistic sociological interpretation of sacrifices is that of J.C. Heesterman in his recent study of ancient Indian sacrifice, *The Broken World of Sacrifice*,[5] where he has attempted to posit a distinction between sacrifice and ritual and maintains that the rituals of the Indians evolved from secular sacrifices which were originally life-and-

---

sounds of the various ancient languages cited in it.

[3]   See below p.290.

[4]   S. Sauneron, *The Priests of Ancient Egypt*, p.126.

[5]   J.C. Heesterman, *Broken World: An Essay on Ancient Indian Ritual*, Chicago: University of Chicago Press, 1993.

death contests between opposing social groups that were later stylised by the priestly caste for religious purposes. This is surprising considering that Heesterman's earlier work, *The Ancient Indian Royal Consecration*, notes with great clarity the ritual birth of the king as the cosmic deities Brahman and Sūrya during this ceremony as well as the king's subsequent ordering and infusion of the universe with his royal power.[6] In the later work, however, Heesterman declares that

> sacrifice, at least Vedic sacrifice, is from beginning to end a contest. It starts with the competition to be the actual sacrificer ... We also find, embedded in the more elaborate soma feasts such as the mahāvrata, a New Year's festival, or the royal rituals of rājasūya, vājapeya and aśvamedha, regular contests, albeit neatly packaged in the rules of the śrauta rituals ...

He goes on to suggest that

> The sacrificial arena ... does not require priestly expertise so much as skill and dexterity in the contest. It calls, in other words, for the consecrated warrior who challenges the sacrificer for brahmanhood and the goods of life. Being vowed to death the consecrated warrior is the sacrificer's necessary counterpart in the life-and-death contest of sacrifice.[7]

He thus maintains that

> The brahman officiant of the classical śrauta ritual derives from the consecrated challenger who may be called on to shoulder sacrificial death and from the ultimately successful embodiment of the brahman power. This tells us that the common brahman did not originate in the priesthood. His direct ancestor was the consecrated warrior vowed to death but hoping eventually to win through to his ultimate vindication. Briefly and crudely, before there were priests there were warriors.[8]

Heesterman seems to acknowledge the supreme power of the brāhman though he does not associate it with a class of men who may have always

---

[6] See J.C. Heesterman, *The Ancient Indian Royal Consecration*.

[7] See J.C. Heesterman, *Broken World*, p.185.

[8] *Ibid.*, p.186.

embodied this power, as the *Manusmrithi* for example does, but rather with the warriors themselves who must have had to acquire it through sacrificial contests. According to Heesterman, it was the ritualisation of the contest which served as the occasion for the rise of the brāhman priesthood, "the brahman being fixed in his expert concern with the ritualistic śruti."[9] Gradually this led to the internalisation of the ritual that superseded the priesthood itself, for it "produced the extrasocial figure of the renouncer who has established his sacrificial fire not in a fire temple but in himself, independent of the surrounding world."[10] Thus it was that, just as the original sacrificial contests were ritualised, so rituals were in turn internalised in various forms of asceticism.[11] The second part of this remark seems credible, but it fails to consider that the original sacrifices were themselves not mere contests but externalisations, or dramatisations, of the internal understanding of the intimate correspondence between the macrocosm and the microcosm that informed the entire ancient Indo-European religion. Besides, the evidence of the *Rāmāyana* (Uttara Kanda, Sec.87) suggests that asceticism was not an innovation in Brāhmanism but the very source of its first formulation.[12]

Heesterman's suggestion that brāhman priests were only warriors who began to specialise in rituals at a later stage in the development of Vedic culture also ignores the crucial Vedic myth of the Purusha (*RV* X,90) which clearly places the brāhman at the head of the cosmic creation. Indeed, Heesterman himself reveals that, according to the *Kāthaka Grhyasūtra* (VI,6,56,1) and the *Maitrāyani Samhita* I,8,7), a kshatriya is forbidden to perform the agnihotra "since he is engaged in improper and impure activities, he eats impure food, plunders and kills". Even if this is a relatively late text, the essential disdain on the part of brāhmans for kshatriyas is hard to understand if the former indeed were derived from the latter.

It may be recalled that A.M Hocart too had suggested that the divinisation of the kings was perhaps of greater antiquity than the veneration of priests.[13] The Egyptian and Sumerian king-lists, for instance, begin with divinities and merge imperceptibly into an enumeration of kings. According to Hocart, kings and priests were branches of the

---

[9]   *Ibid.*

[10] *Ibid.*

[11] *Ibid.*, p.82.

[12] See below p.156.

[13] See A.M. Hocart, *Kingship*, p.120.

same stem,[14] and priests were originally comparable to army leaders or commander-in-chiefs since both opened state proceedings, the former the peaceful ones and the latter the military. Thus, while kings patronised the sacrifices, it was the priests who actually carried them out. The role of the priests, argued Hocart, increased with the number of priests required for the administration of vassal states acquired by the king,[15] and gradually the priests sought to surpass the kings in social importance.[16] But this is to neglect the definite distinction made between the two offices in the Vedic literature and to the essential difference between the brahman power[17] and kshatra (sovereignty).

Hocart considered most of the brāhmanical rituals as being derived from the royal ones.[18] This is credible insofar as the divinisation that the various sacrifices aim at is best represented in the consecration of kings. However, as Hocart himself, unlike Heesterman, noted, all the rituals were basically creation rituals and derived from the creation myths.[19] And these creation myths could certainly not have been formulated without the spiritual insight into the creation of the cosmos that only yogic practice could have provided the ancient sages. Indeed, Heesterman's latest theory generally fails to understand the yogic bases of the knowledge of Brahman in the microcosm or in the macrocosm,[20] just as it ignores the cosmic dimension – derived from the original sacrifice of the cosmic Purusha – of all the brāhmanical sacrifices.[21]

Also, as Levi pointed out, the only contest evidenced at the birth of the sacrificial cult is the one between the gods and their opponents, the asuras, who were both created by Prajāpati.[22] The asuras first possessed the universe and had to be defeated by the gods. According to Levi, "Le sacrifice est, par excellence, le moyen de vaincre". The asuras, characterised by arrogance, are vanquished by the gods through their modesty and ascetic exertions (tapas, shrama).[23] Heesterman himself notes[24] that *JB*

---

[14] *Ibid.*, p.128.

[15] See A.M. Hocart, *Kings and Councillors*, p.195.

[16] See A.M. Hocart, *Kingship*, p.120.

[17] See below pp.20,237.

[18] See A.M. Hocart, *Kingship*, p.202.

[19] *Ibid.*, p.201.

[20] See below Ch.V.

[21] See below pp.158ff.

[22] S. Levi, *La doctrine du sacrifice*, pp.44ff.

[23] *Ibid.*, p.54.

[24] See J.C. Heesterman, *Broken World*, p.53.

II,69-70, points to a contest between Prajāpati and Mrtyu (Death) but
ignores the significance of the sacrifice of the Purusha as the means not
only of producing the material universe but also of overcoming this
mortal manifestation through various forms of sacrifice and ascesis. In
fact, Heesterman even makes a comparison of the sacrifice of the Purusha
with that of the Christ[25] but again does not understand the essential
spiritual similarity of the two as cosmic dramas that ensure immortality
through the restoration of a disintegrated god. As Gonda pointed out with
regard to the construction of the Vedic fire-altar,

> In building the great fireplace one restores and reintegrates Prajāpati,
> whose dismemberment had been the creation of the universe, and
> makes him whole and complete. At the same time and by means of
> the same ritual act, the sacrificer, who is identified with Prajāpati
> (cf. *Shatapatha Brāhmana* VII,4,15) constructs himself a new social
> personality and secures the continuance of his existence.[26]

Heesterman at one point gives the example of the first stotra (hymn) of
the soma sacrifice, the Bahishpavamāna, which is considered to be, as it
were, a vajra hurled at Death: "As long as this triple vajra moves day by day
along these [three] worlds, there will be no devāsura, no fight between the
gods and the asuras". He does not seem to perceive that this contest is one
focussed on the preservation of the solar light throughout the universe
(the three worlds) and that the ritual hymns are diffused through space
in order to combat time and mortality. Heesterman also notes a special
feature of the rituals wherein,

> while the fire is carried from the garhapatya to the eastern ahavaniya
> hearth, a chariot wheel is rolled in the same direction on the south
> side, and on the north side, a horse that was somewhat superfluously
> present in the drilling of the fire is equally led eastward to the
> ahavaniya. Indeed, one text, the Vaitāna Sūtra, puts them together
> again by having the fire carried on a chariot drawn by a horse.[27]

Heesterman fails to recognise the solar significance of any of these items.
He declares instead that "It can be shown that this rite of carrying the fire
forward was originally a raiding expedition".

[25] *Ibid.*, pp.45ff.

[26] See J. Gonda, *Prajāpati's Rise to Higher Rank*, p.16f.

[27] J.C. Heesterman, *ibid.*, p.66.

Again, in studying the Brahmaudana rite, Heesterman points to the three pieces of ashvattha wood stirred in the remainder of the ghee and the rice-mess left in the ritual vessel and then put into the brahmaudanika fire. He points to the Brāhmana texts of the *Black Yajur Veda* which explain this by referring to the myth of Aditi who became pregnant of the Ādityas by eating the remainder of the odana she had cooked. Thus the ghee is the semen, and the sticks the bones. The delay of a year between this rite and the setting up of the shrauta fires suggests a year-long pregnancy. As *TS* VI,2,8,4-5, declares, "In a year's time embryos are born full-grown, he installs [the fire] when it is full-grown". But having quoted this, Heesterman hastens to add, "The equation of the fire's gestation with Aditi's pregnancy and the birth of the Adityas seems forced". What is forced is indeed Heesterman's dismissal of the solar aspect of the rituals of the brāhmans in his increasingly secularist interpretation of them.

Similarly, E. Otto in his analysis of the sacrificial killing of a bull during the 'opening of the mouth' ceremony in ancient Egypt suggests that it was a relic of a more ancient hunting ritual. H. Roeder more perspicaciously maintains that the victim was originally not an animal but a man.[28] This is probably right, except that Roeder believes that the man was an enemy of the king and therefore the ritual a political one. Both Otto and Roeder disregard the clear liturgical references to the killing of Seth by Horus that are uttered during this ritual and the fact that this sacrifice is unequivocally a dramatic reenactment of the violence that attended Osiris's death at the hands of Seth and of his resurrection as Horus the Younger.

Given these dull interpretations of Indo-European sacrifice, it is advisable to disregard much of the modern sociologically- and hermeneutically-oriented scholarship and to investigate more carefully the soteriological aspects of the ancient Indo-European religions. The *Rgveda* X,130 indeed makes clear the primal significance of sacrifice as the means whereby the entire creation was brought into being:

1. The sacrifice drawn out with threads on every side, stretched by a hundred sacred ministers and one,—
This do these Fathers weave who hitherward are come: they sit beside the warp and cry, Weave forth, weave back.
2 The Man extends it and the Man unbinds it: even to this vault of heaven hath he outspun it.

---

[28]   See H. Roeder, "Mundöffnung und rituelle Feindtötung", p.47; cf., further, p.18f. below.

These pegs are fastened to the seat of worship: they made the Sāma-hymns their weaving shuttles.

...

6 So by this knowledge men were raised to Rshis, when ancient sacrifice sprang up, our Fathers.
With the mind's eye I think that I behold them who first performed this sacrificial worship.
7 They who were versed in ritual and metre,[29] in hymns and rules, were the Seven Godlike Rshis.
Viewing the path of those of old, the sages have taken up the reins like chariot-drivers.

The Man in verse 2 is the Purusha and the first sacrificers are said to be the Seven Sages, who, as we shall see, are the ancestors of the brāhmans,[30] so that the primacy of the latter is evident from the last lines.

Since the sacrifices included human and animal victims and, unlike civil or political executions, originally served an esoteric religious purpose, it would be helpful to begin with a consideration of some of the most ancient examples of sacrifice among the Indo-European tribes and to observe the role of the priesthood among them. As the Celts are presumably one of the oldest of Āryan tribes,[31] we may observe their religious rituals here briefly. The Celts are identifiable with the Cimmerians and the latter are said to be older than the Magog (Iranians) and the Madai (Medes). So it is possible that, if there was an original form of the Āryan sacrifices that was turned into the brāhmanical rituals among the Indians, it was similar, at least in some respects, to that of the Celts.

From the evidence of the Celtic religious practices, it is clear that the sacrifices were conducted in a sacred context and not in an agonic one, as Heesterman, for instance, would have us believe. The priestly caste of the Celts was divided into three orders, "bards", "vates" and "druids".[32] The bards were clearly the Celtic counterparts of the Indian Udgātr priests who chanted the sacred verses during the sacrifices.[33] The Vates were the counterparts of the Adhvaryu priests, since they were learned in natural philosophy and interpreted the sacrifices. The Druids themselves were the

---

[29] The rhythms of Vedic chants are those of the primal cosmic currents arising from the supreme soul, or Ātman, as Vāk (see below p.32).

[30] See below p.197.

[31] See below p.178.

[32] See S. Piggott, *The Druids*, p.92.

[33] See below p.249.

counterparts of the Brahman priests since they presided over the sacrifices and were both natural and moral philosophers. Of the Druids and the Vates, Diodorus Siculus, *Bibliotheca Historica* V,31,2-4 states that

> [The Celts] have highly-honoured philosophers and theologians [those who speak about the gods] called Druids. They also make use of seers, who are greatly respected. These seers, having great authority, use auguries and sacrifices to foresee the future. When seeking knowledge of great importance, they use a strange and unbelievable method: they choose a person for death and stab him or her in the chest above the diaphragm. By the convulsion of the victim's limbs and spurting of blood, they foretell the future, trusting in this ancient method. They do not sacrifice or ask favours from the Gods without a Druid present, as they believe sacrifice should be made only by those supposedly skilled in divine communication.

We note that the sacrifices among the Celts, according to Diodorus' account, tended to be human sacrifices and the Vates who officiated at them were versed in haruspicy, predicting the future from the victims' entrails, and perhaps in augury, divination from the flight of birds, as well.

The human sacrifices of the most ancient Indo-Europeans were originally related to the sacrifice of the Purusha which initiated the formation of the universe.[34] We know that the deity Brahman himself is called Eros in the Greek Orphic religion[35] and the Sanskritic term itself refers to the productive power of this deity.[36] Thus also is Brahman called Prajāpati or the Lord of created beings. In *SB* VI,I,2,13, Agni, who is said to have been created (i.e. in the second of his three births)[37] by Prajāpati, restores the latter, when he is exhausted by his creative exertions, by means of sacrifice.

These ancient Indo-European sacrifices were also viewed as a maintenance simultaneously of the cosmic organisation and of the social one. For instance, as Lincoln points out, among the Germanic tribes, only the Semnones, the noblest of the Suebi[38] (Swabians), were allowed to

---

[34] See below Ch.I.

[35] See below p.42.

[36] See below p.195.

[37] See below p.100.

[38] The Suebi were, according to Pliny, *Historia Naturalis*, 499, part of the Irminones or those who worshipped Irmin (from ON Jormunt, a name of Odin). Tacitus (*Germania*, 2) mentions Tuisco (Tvashtr) as the chief god of the Germans, and his son was Mannus (Manu). Mannus' three sons include the tutelary deities of the Ingaevones (devoted to

conduct the original sacrifice of Tuisto which involved dismemberment of the victim.[39] Among the ancient Romans too, in the Feriae Latinae which is described by Dionysus of Halicarnassus (4,49) as involving the sacrifice of a white bull and consumption of its meat, "a share in the ox" was considered to be "the concrete sign of their membership in the federation of Latin peoples".[40] The association in the Rigvedic Purushasūkta of the parts of the Purusha's body with the four castes, the head with the brāhman, the arms with the kshatriya, the thighs with the vaisya and the feet with the shūdra,[41] also makes clear the hierarchical ordering of ancient Āryan society and the superior position in it of the brāhman. Apart from the sociological evidence provided by the sacrifice, a careful study of the rituals of the Indo-Āryan folk in particular will show, moreover, that the superiority of the brāhman caste consists in its close identification with the creative brahman power that underlies all material phenomena and its consequent deep understanding of the creation.

The ultimate aim of the original sacrifices, modelled after the cosmic sacrifice of the Purusha, however, must have been the liberation of the self from the illusions of the material fabric in which it is entangled and the direction of the energy of man into the divine consciousness. This is indeed the principal aim of yogic ascesis as well, which is, as Heesterman has pointed out, an internalisation of the sacrifice. Since the primary purpose of a sacrifice is indeed that of self-sacrifice, the sacrifice of a human involved in the proto-Vedic Purushamedha[42] must originally have been conducted as a substitute for a sacrifice of the sacrificer himself, since the sacrificer is, in all Vedic sacrifices, identified with the victim. As Heesterman states, "self-sacrifice is an all-but-ubiquitous theme in the ritual brāhmana texts, the victim as well as the other offerings being regularly equated with the sacrificer".[43] That is why the victim in the

---

Freyr, since OE retains the compound Ingui-Frea), the Herminones (devoted to Wotan/Odin) and the Istaevones (who must have been devoted to Thor, since these three were the principal gods worshipped in the temple of Uppsala according to Adam of Bremen in his 11th c. *Gesta Hammaburgensis*).

[39]   See Tacitus, *Germania*, 39.

[40]   See Lincoln, *Myth, Cosmos and Society*, p.47

[41]   The Indic hierarchy is repeated in the Middle Persian Škend Gumānīg Wizār I,20-24, which declares with regard to the macroanthropos that "the head is like the priesthood, the hands like the warriorhood, the belly (or womb) like the commoners, and the feet like the artisanry" (see Lincoln, *ibid.*, p.146).

[42]   See below pp.219ff.

[43]   J.C. Heesterman, *Broken World*, p.173.

Purushamedha was originally exclusively a brāhman or a kshatriya,[44] since only these two castes were qualified to act as representatives of the Purusha and to conduct sacrifices.

At the same time, the sacrificial victim is always a male since only his energy can substitute for the phallic force of the Purusha that fills the universe with its life. We shall observe in our survey of the cosmological bases of sacrifices that the entire evolution of the material universe arises from repeated castrations, and preservations, of the divine phallus, first in the Ideal realm of the Purusha, then in the early cosmos of Brahman and, lastly, in the material universe, as the Tree of Life that arises from the underworld and extends to the heavens.[45] If what is most important in the Purusha is his phallic power, as is evident also in the Hesiodic account of the castration of Ouranos by Chronos,[46] it is probable that the sacrifice originally focussed on the victim's phallus, as we observe, for example, in the veneration of the penis of a slaughtered stallion among the ancient Nordic peoples.[47] Similarly, in the Equus October ceremony in ancient Rome a race-horse was slaughtered and its tail (standing no doubt for its penis) was brought to the regia.[48] In ancient Egypt, the castration of Re is represented as a self-castration. Hu, intellectual expression, and his consort, Sia, intuition, are said in a New Kingdom commentary on the *Book of the Dead* to be "the blood which fell from the phallus of Re, when he was going to mutilate himself".[49] Since the castration of Re corresponds to the castration of Anu in the Hurrian epic of the Kingship in Heaven, and the castration of Prajāpati by Shiva, we may assume that this event precedes the formation of the Cosmic Egg which, in the Purānas arises, from the seed of Prajāpati/Shiva. This may also have been the source of the practice noticed in some rituals of the Dionysiac religion that may have involved self-mutilation.[50]

Over time, however, the human victim was substituted with animals that equally represented the energy of the divine phallus, thus a horse or a bull, and finally with lesser animals such as sheep and goats. In all cases, however, the original significance of the sacrifice as a self-sacrifice is never forgotten, as many of the processes of the Vedic sacrifices as well

---

[44] See below p.219.

[45] See below p.79ff.

[46] See Hesiod, *Theogony*, I, 170ff.

[47] See below p.209f.

[48] See J. Mallory and D.Q. Adams, *Encyclopedia of Indo-European Culture*, p.330.

[49] See M.Sandman-Holmberg, *The God Ptah*, p.42.

[50] See below p.69.

as many of the accompanying Vedic chants reveal.[51] The spiritual purpose
of a sacrifice is indeed to control the sexual energy and convert it into
spiritual energy directed to the attainment of the ideal "sattvic" state of the
Purusha, that is, as the solar deity Vishnu.

It will be noted further that the phallic sacrifice of the ideal Purusha
is repeated in the manifest cosmos, for such a sacrifice is necessary for the
transference of the divine power to our solar system.[52] The second sacrifice
involves the destruction of Brahman/Prajāpati by his son Ganesha (Zeus/
Seth) and the swallowing of the divine phallus by the latter so that the
whole universe and its light moves into his body. Then Seth in turn is seen,
for instance in the Egyptian mouth-opening ritual, to have been castrated
or killed, for a bull representing Seth is slaughtered and its thigh is used to
revive the dead Osiris.[53] In the town of Saka, Seth as a bull undergoes self-
castration and, in the Pap. d'Orbiney, Seth (called Bata in Saka), castrates
himself in order apparently to avoid the sexual advances of his sister-in-
law, and then goes into exile in foreign lands.[54] This is clearly the source of
the rites of the Phrygian Attis rites mentioned in Lucian's *De Dea Syria*.[55]
In the mouth-opening cerermony performed on divine statues, too, the
"thigh" represents the divine genitals[56] – which, according to the Orphic
cosmogonies, Zeus (Seth) is said to have swallowed after they had been
severed from Ouranos by Zeus' father Chronos.[57] So it is not surprising
that Seth's genitals ("thigh") are brought forward to revive the moribund
Osiris with its life and light. According to the series entitled 'The
Contendings of Horus and Set', too, the conflicts between the two gods
include the violation of Horus the Younger by Seth and the castration of

---

[51] See below p.210.

[52] See below Ch.II.

[53] See below p.65.

[54] See H. te Velde, *Seth God of Confusion*, p.41.

[55] Attis was said to have been castrated by Cybele (the Phrygian counterpart of the Cretan
Rhea, consort of Cronos) (see Lucian, *De Dea Syria, The Syrian Goddess*, tr. H.W. Attridge
and R.A. Oden, Missoula, MT; Scholars Press, 1976, p.23). According to A.B. Cook (*Zeus*,
I:292ff.), Zeus, Pappas and Attis were Phrygian terms used for a god who, like Osiris, was
reborn as his son. For the relation between Attis, Adonis and Osiris, see *De Dea Syria*,
pp.13ff. Though not apparent, Attis' life resembles that of Dionysus, the sun-god who is
also killed and resurrected. When the cult was transferred to Rome, Cybele was celebrated
as Magna Mater deorum Idaea and the cult involved the famous taurobolium in which
initiates were drenched in the blood of a bull as a form of cleansing and rebirth.

[56] See below p.65.

[57] See below p.67.

Seth by Horus.[58] All these incidents focus on the importance of the divine phallus now as the life of the emerging universe as well as its light.

The transformations of the solar force that are recounted in the mythology are focussed within the fire that is worshipped in the Āryan rituals. Indeed, the Vedic texts reveal a more than scientific understanding both of the several forms of heat that pervade the human microcosm and of the different parts of the flames of external fire.[59] Such an understanding is clearly not a result of contests conducted among warriors but of the supernatural yogic discipline that informed the religion of the brāhmans and identifies them not just as wise men but indeed as "magicians". This is of course the reason why the term "magi" used for their Iranian counterparts has long been equated with "magicians".

The Indo-European sacrifice is important not only for the spiritual liberation of the sacrificer but also for the solar rebirth that it allows the sacrificer to undergo as a brāhman, or one who has realised the solar virtue of his soul, just as the death of Osiris is followed by his revival in our universe as the sun. In the Indian horse-sacrifice, ashvamedha, for instance, the horse represents the sun which has been lost and must be recovered. Thus *SB* XIII,3,1,1 declares:

> Prajâpati's eye swelled; it fell out: thence the horse was produced; and inasmuch as it swelled (ashvayat), that is the origin and nature of the horse (ashva). By means of the Asvamedha the gods restored it to its place; and verily he who performs the Asvamedha makes Prajâpati complete, and he (himself) becomes complete; and this, indeed, is the atonement for everything, the remedy for everything.

This is the same significance that attaches also to the Osirian funereal rites, especially the mouth-opening ritual.[60] For the assault on the solar force by Seth is referred to as the damage or robbing of the "Horus eye" [the sun] which must be restored to Horus the Elder/Osiris.

By performing a sacrifice the sacrificer is able not only to achieve a spiritual rebirth but thereby also to overcome death itself and achieve immortality. As Heesterman remarked, "In the sacrifice are summed up the two opposite poles of the cyclical rhythm of the cosmos, birth and

---

[58] *Book of the Dead,* Ch.113; see S. Mercer, *Horus Royal God of Egypt,* p.74; cf. H. Te Velde, *op.cit.,* p.58.

[59] See below p.211.

[60] See below p.276f.

death, ascension and descent, concentration and dispersion".[61] And indeed it is sacrifice which renders the gods themselves immortal, that is, by realising their essential self as immortals. According to *SB* XI,2,3,6, "In the beginning, indeed, the gods were mortal, and only when they had become possessed of the Brahman they were immortal." This was achieved through a focus on the vital fire within as well as without man.[62] As *SB* II,22,8ff makes clear, at first the gods noticed that Agni the fire alone was immortal and so they sought, through austerities and eulogies, to implant the fire within themselves and thus became immortal themselves. We see that the immortal self that is to be realised is primarily related to that of fire, Agni. The sacrifice is also a means of sustaining the immortality of the gods so that the latter may in turn bless the human sacrificer with boons such as rain, food, wealth, etc.

Ultimately, as *SB* XIV,32,1 declares, "the sacrifice is the self of all beings and of all gods". The sacrificer who performs the sacrifice to serve the external macrocosmic powers of the gods is called a devayājin. The sacrificer who is concerned exclusively with the self (ātman) is an ātmayājin (*SB* XI,2,6,13). And, as Heesterman points out,

> What distinguishes the self-sacrificer is his knowledge – the knowledge, that is, of the equivalence of ritual and self ... Thus he is freed from his mortal body, from evil, and construes with Rg-, Yajur-, and Sāmaveda and with oblations a transcendental body ... This transcendental body is no other than the ātman of the self-sacrificer, the erstwhile puruṣa who no longer undergoes sacrifice but has mastered and integrated it.[63]

This passage from Heesterman should indeed serve to counter his own theory regarding the secular origins of sacrifices and rituals as well as Staal's misleading discussion of the "meaningless" rules of rituals. Rather, the rituals of the Indo-European peoples, Āryan as well as Hamitic, were originally clearly soteriological in aim and based on the intimate correspondence between the cosmic Purusha and the human microcosm, the primacy of the solar force in the manifest universe, and the immortality and divinity of the soul. Of course, the correspondence between microcosm and macrocosm is not a literal one. For instance, in the frequent associations of the eye to the sun in the Vedic literature, it

---

[61] See J.C. Heesterman, "Reflections on the significance of the Daksina", p.245.

[62] See below pp.209ff.

[63] J.C. Heesterman, *Broken World*, p.215.

is the essence of the sun that is equal to the mystic eye.[64] Similarly, the sacrificer who recreates the universe in the Agnicayana ritual becomes immortal because he acquires during the sacrifice the essential self of the universe itself.[65] As Hocart pointed out, "The ancient ceremonies of creation and installation by putting into the consecrated person the essence, form,or double of the imperishable heavens, earth or middle air, provided him with an immortal soul".[66]

It is this sacred, and even magical, aspect of the Indo-European rituals that I shall focus on in the present study. One aspect of my study which may at first disconcert a reader who is not familiar with my previous book, *Ātman*, is the fact that I consider the mythologies of most of the ancient Near Eastern peoples as being based on a common solar cosmology. Especially for these readers I have provided, in chapters IV and VIII below, historical introductions to my studies of the Āryan and Hamitic rituals in order to suggest the possible links between apparently unrelated civilisations. In the Appendix I have added a collection of hymns that exemplify the principal stages of the development of the solar force that I discussed in detail in *Ātman* and have recapitulated in the first three chapters of the present work.[67]

---

[64] See Hocart, *Kingship*, p.200.

[65] *Ibid.*, p.201.

[66] *Ibid.*, p.235.

[67] I have not found it necessary to alter the scheme of my original reconstruction of the Indo-European cosmogony in any signficant detail since I first developed it seven years ago. In the historical part of the present study, however, I have revised my earlier view of the Japhetic Āryans as the youngest of the three branches of the Noachidian race and consider them now as representing an older spiritual tradition than that of the Hamites.

THE SOLAR FORCE

I.

THE FIRST SACRIFICE: PURUSHA

Since the sacrifices of the Indo-Europeans are based on the original sacrifice of the Ideal cosmic macroanthropos, Purusha, as well as on its repetitions in the manifest cosmos that result in the formation of the sun, it will be necessary to comprehend the spiritual significance of these cosmological sacrifices.[68] As in my previous work, *Ātman*, I combine here Āryan and Hamitic sources in my reconstruction of the original Indo-European cosmology since, although the prehistory of the cosmos is presented in clearest outlines in the Indic Purānic literature,[69] this account achieves a greater elaboration in the documents of ancient Egypt and Sumer that focus on the different stages of the development of the sun.

In the Indic *BP* III,xi,18-22, a day of the supreme Lord is calculated as equalling 1000 Chaturyugas, each Chaturyuga[70] being 12,000 divine

---

[68]   For a detailed analysis of the ancient Indo-European cosmology, see A. Jacob, *Ātman: A Reconstruction of the Solar Cosmology of the Indo-Europeans*, Hildesheim, Georg Olms Verlag, 2005.

[69]   Portions of the Purānas – which constitute the "Bible" of the Indo-Europeans – may indeed have been composed earlier than the Vedas, since the *BrdP* I,i,1,40-41 maintains that they were heard by Brahma before the Vedas. Purānas typically contain discussions of sarga (cosmogony), pratisarga (regeneration of the cosmos), manvantara (epochs of Manu), vamsha (ethnic genealogies) and vamshanucarita (royal genealogies). The cosmic Flood stories in the Puranas are to be found also in the Tamil 'Purānams', which copy the encyclopaedic genre of the Sanskrit models.

[70]   A chaturyuga is made up of four ages, Krita, Treta, Dvāpara and Kali, corresponding to a Golden, Silver, Bronze and Iron Age, in the course of which the divine virtue is gradually diminished. We now live in the fourth, degenerate, age (Kaliyuga) of the second kalpa called Padmakalpa.

years long (that is, years as prevalent in the realm of the gods),[71] or 4,380,000,000 terrestrial years.[72] After creating and sustaining the cosmos for this extraordinarily vast period of time (kalpa), comes the night in which the Lord "sleeps". This night is equally as long as the day of the Lord and is the period when the cosmos is dissolved into its original subtle constituents in the flood called Naimittika Pralaya (*BP* XII,4,3). According to the *BP*, the flood at the end of a cosmic age entails the total collapse of the cosmos, constituted of Heaven, Earth and the Mid-region, into the endless waters of the Abyss. During the flood, the Lord withdraws into this cosmic Ocean, within whose depths he reposes on the serpent Anantasesha (the eternal Sesha). Gradually waking, he begins to recreate the cosmos. The first kalpa was called Brahmakalpa (*BP* III,11,33ff.), since it was marked by the perfect light of Brahma,[73] and the second, after the cosmic cataclysm, is the present one, called Padmakalpa (the age of the lotus),[74] in which the divine light is transferred to the material universe.[75] Each kalpa is divided into fourteen "manvantaras" or ages of Manu, a Manu being the type of enlightened mankind.[76] Each manvantara lasts for 71 odd Chaturyugas, or 310,980,000 years (*BP* III,11,24) and is followed by a deluge lasting as long as a Krita Yuga, or 1,728,000 years (*Sūrya Siddhāntha*, I,18).

In the *BrdP*, the first form of the deity [at the beginning of a kalpa] is that of the supreme Soul, Ātman: "This entire dark world was pervaded by his Ātman" (I,i,3,12), with its three essential energies, or 'gunas', called Tamas, Rajas, and Sattva,[77] maintained in perfect balance. In the Vedas, *RV* X,129,1, the first hypostasis (Ātman/Hari of *BP*) is called the One,

---

[71] A divine day is as long as a terrestrial year.

[72] In the *BrdP* III,iv,229f., the night, which is equal to the day of Brahma is said to be 4,328,980,000 years long. The difference in reckoning between the various Purānas is thus slight.

[73] Brahma is the Purānic form of Brahman.

[74] According to *VP*, I,27-28, however, the first kalpa was called Padmakalpa (the kalpa of the Lotus) and the present one is called Varāhakalpa (the kalpa of the Boar).

[75] Current astrophysical theories suggest that the cosmos is roughly 14 billion years old whereas, according to the *BP*, the cosmos is approximately 13,140,000,000 years old (the first day and night of the Lord plus half of the second day). The latter is likely to be more accurate since it is not based on fallible empirical observation but on spiritual intuition.

[76] The names of the first six Manus of this kalpa are Swāyambhuva, Svarochisha, Uttama, Tāmasa, Raivata, Chakshusha (*BP* VIII,1), and those of the Manus following ours (called Shrāddhadeva/Vaivasvata) will be Savarni, Dakshasavarni, Brahmasavarni, Dharmasavarni, Rudrasavarni, Devasavarni, and Indrasavarni (*BP* VIII,13). For the Sumerian and Egyptian "kings" who correspond to the Indic Manus see below pp.96ff.

[77] See further below p.32.

which "breathless, breathed by its own nature: apart from it was nothing whatsoever". Although it is the only Existent, it is nevertheless surrounded by what is called a "Chaos" [Abyss] of dark and indistinct "water" (st.3), which, from the logic of the verse, must be still unformed.[78] This Soul or the One corresponds to the Egyptian Amun (who is also called Atmu, Soul)[79] and is the sole living Being, that which alone "breathes", in the earliest stages of the cosmos, just as Amun is the foundation of the Nun/Apsu.

RV X,129,4 goes on to state that from the One (Amun) arose Desire (Kāma), the "primal seed and germ of Spirit [Mind]". In AV III,21,4, Desire is used as an appellation of Agni, showing that Agni/Kāma is originally the desire of the One and the source of the ideal universe. That is why Agni is identifiable with Ātman as the very first form of the deity (Shiva). In AV XIX,52,1-3, the first hypostasis is said to be Desire (Kāma) itself, and it is said to have created Mind.[80] In RV X,90, further, it is stated: "Fervour [Tapas] creates Rta (the Sacred Order), and Truth"[81] and from these are produced first Night,[82] and then the Waters.[83] We have noted

---

[78] These primal entities correspond to the Egyptian Amun-Amunet, Nun-Nunet, Huh-Huhet, Kuk-Kuket (see K. Sethe, Amun) as well as the Hesiodic and Orphic Eros, Chaos, Earth and Tartarus (see Hesiod, Theogony, 116-120; cf. below p.54).

[79] Hu-Nefer papyrus, (see E.A.W. Budge, The Gods of the Egyptians, II:10,15). If the Egyptian Amun indeed represents a corruption of the Sanskritic 'ātman', then it must indicate the presence of an Indic priestly tradition in Egypt at a very early date, from at least the fifth dynasty, ca. 2500 B.C., when the worship of Amun is first attested. The Vedas do not give evidence of the worship of a god called, simply, Ātman. The concentration on the Ātman is peculiar, rather, to the Upanishads, and the Purānas, which latter are more comprehensive in their cosmogony than the Vedas.

[80] Here Mind is equivalent to the Ideal Man/Prajāpati/Brahman, though, at the stage of the Cosmic Man, the latter becomes identified with the Intellect rather than with the Mind, which is represented by the Moon (see below p.34).

[81] We may compare the mention of Amun-Amunet, Nun-Nunet, Atum-Routy, Shu-Tefnut in PT 301, pyr. 446-7 (K. Sethe, Amun, p.34f.; cf. S. Bickel, La Cosmogonie Egyptienne, p.28n.). This is not an ogdoad but, rather, an order of generations, whereby Amun is represented as the source of Nun, who fathers Atum, etc. Atum's consort Routy is perhaps linguistically cognate with Sanskrit Rta. Routy is represented as a pair of lionesses and identified also with Atum's children Shu and Tefnut in PT 447 (see 'Ruti' in LÄ V:321). It is not surprising therefore that Tefnut is regularly identified with Maat, the sacred order (for Routy's relation to Tefnut see S. Bickel, op.cit., p.190). Following the Vedic passage, Shu may particularly symbolise Truth, even as Tefnut symbolises Maat.

[82] In Hesiod's theogony, Night and Erebus are born of Chaos (Nun, Apsu). Night is also said to be the wife of An in Sumerian cosmology (Ebeling KAR I no.38, 9-23), which makes An the same as the Light of Dyaus and Night an aspect of the primal Earth, Prithvi/Ki/Antum.

[83] These Waters are not the formless cosmic streams of the Abyss/Chaos, but must refer

above, from RV X,129,1 that the Chaos itself was filled with the waters, so we may infer therefrom that the Waters produced after Night are now formed. Indeed, the Waters are ever moving and infused with Rta, so they are also ever striving for Truth.[84] Actually their name (apā) itself means "action or movement", so that in the *Nighantu*, it is given as a synonym of "karma".[85]

Purusha

The unmanifest deity begins to be gradually manifested when one of its three constituent energies, Tamas, Rajas, and Sattva, begins to predominate over the others.[86] The first manifest form of the deity caused by the disturbance of the balance of the essential energies is as an ideal macroanthropos. The Purusha is said in the *Katha Upanishad* to employ Prakrti, or Nature as the first agent of manifestation and this Praktri is the same as Ahamkara, or the Ego. All human yogic endeavour is thus directed to a destruction of the Ahamkara (as in the *Bhagavad Gita*, VI) and its desire in order to return to the Ideal state of the Purusha, called Vishnu.[87]

The Ideal Purusha is the intelligible form of the entire physical cosmos (*SB* XIV, 5,5,18). This ideal Purusha that is formed from the desire of the Lord is supposed to have issued from the Waters, Virāj (*AV* XIX, 6,9).[88] In the *RV* X,90 ('Purushasūkta'), however, while Purusha is said to have been born of Virāj, the latter too is born of the former, showing the close unity of the desiring Ātman and the energetic waves of Prakriti (Nature) that it uses to manifest itself. At *KYV* V,5,4, Agni is said to be born of the waters (considered also as the "wives" of Varuna) as Vāk, the Word, which

---

to the substance of Heaven, which is, in an Assyrian exegetical text, (see A. Livingstone, *Mystical and Mythological Explanatory Texts*, p.33) said to be constituted of waters ('ša me').

[84] See U. Choudhuri, *Indra and Varuna*, p.156.

[85] We have here an explanation of the identification of Rta with the later Hindu concepts of "karma" and "dharma".

[86] Cf. Shriram Sharma, *Scientific Basis of Yajnas*, Ch.20: "At the time of the Pralaya, Tamas ruled. The Lord did Ikshana which induced movement in Prakriti made of three gunas originally equipoised." From this Lord, or Yajna Purusha, emerged the manifest cosmos.

[87] See M. Biardeau, *op.cit.*, p.127.

[88] These waters are the counterpart of the Egyptian Nunet, the original substance of Heaven (see p.31n above).

appears at the stage of Virāj, the primal waters.[89] We shall see that Agni also rules speech in the body of the ideal Macroanthropos.[90]

The process of this primal, and entirely ideal, manifestation of the Lord (Hari) is recounted in the *BP* II,5. The Lord, desirous of creation arouses, out of his own power of illusion, Māya[91] – aided by Time (Kāla-Shiva) – the three forms of divine energy – Sattva, Rajas, and Tamas. We see already that Shiva, though representative of the destructive aspect of the deity, is indeed one of the primal agents of cosmic creation, as Time, and, as we shall see, also as the cosmic Ego.[92] In the *Shvetāsvatara Upanishad*, the Cosmic Man is indeed called "the omnipresent Shiva" (III,11), since he is the same as the supreme Soul, Ātman. The aim of the cosmic creation is not only the harmonious order of the physical universe but also its rise to self-consciousness (Intellect/Brahman).[93] When the divine energies are differentiated, the supreme soul assumes three forms, the sattvic aspect being represented by the perfect macroanthromorphic Vishnu, the rājasic by the luminous Brahma, and the tāmasic by the Shiva who will destroy the cosmos at the end of its cycle (*BrdP* I,i,4,5f.). This is a trinity that is "mutually interdependent; these do not become separated even for a moment" (*BrdP* I,i,4,11).

The first result of the disturbance of the equilibrium of the three divine energies during the earliest moments of the cosmic creation is the emergence of Mahat (The Great) from Nature (Prakritī/Pārvatī, consort of Shiva), combined of Rājas and Tāmas. It is from Mahat-tattva[=principle] that Ahamkāra (Cosmic Egoity), dominated entirely by Tamas, arises. In the *BrdP* III,iv,4,37 Ahamkāra is said to evolve from Mahat, and from the Ahamkāra arise the Bhūtas (elements) and the Indriyas (senses). The entire material universe is a result of the dull egoistic element of Ahamkāra.[94]

---

[89] This creative sound, or these sound-waves, must be related to the radio energy that has been observed emerging from the dark nucleus of a galaxy, the so-called "black hole" (*EB*, Macropedia, 16:635).

[90] See below p.34.

[91] For the Vaishnav and Shaivite Āgamic conceptions of Māya, see below Ch. XV.

[92] We note the creative aspect of Chronos also in the Orphic theogonies, and in the proto-Stoic cosmogony of Pherecydes (see below p.42).

[93] That is why the demon Vrtra that Indra famously battles in the Vedas is at once the demon of material restriction as well as of the unconscious (see J..Miller, *Vision*, pp.62,95,178). V.G. Rele, *Vedic Gods*, pp.56,103, observes the same contest between the unconscious and consciousness within the human microcosm.

[94] These primal cosmic elements of the *BrdP* reappear in the Sankhya philosophical doctrine of the Mahat, or The Great, as the first evolute from Prakriti. Pure sattvic

In the *BP*, from the Lord's power of imagination (illusion, Māyā) is formed first his heart, or spirit.[95] The heart gives rise to the Ego (Ahamkāra) (ruled by Rudra-Shiva, III,6,25), the Mind (which will be ruled by the Moon, II,10,30), the Intellect (to be ruled by Brahman) and prime matter.

From the highest form of Egoity (Ahamkara), that related to the sattvic level of energy,[96] arises Manas (Mind), whose presiding deity is the Moon, as also do the other gods who preside over the ten organs of knowledge and action. Manas is a characteristic of the Moon (*BP* III,6,24) and represents the emotional reservoir of the deity (*BP* II,10,32). It is thus located in the heart itself of the supreme deity.

From the rājasic level of Egoity of the supreme deity, on the other hand, arises Buddhi (Intellect) which is ruled by Brahman (*BP* III,6,23). From the 'space within his heart' arise the [ideal] faculties of sense, discernment and the physique. From the last three is formed the divine life-force or breath (Prāna). The five senses are related to the organs of knowledge – ears, tactile organ, nose, eyes, tongue – and the five forms of action to the organs responsible for speech, holding, walking, excreting and generating. The gods Dik [ears], Vāyu [nose], Sūrya [eyes], Varuna [tongue], and the Ashwins [skin] control the organs of knowledge, while Agni [speech], Indra [arms], Upendra (Vishnu) [legs], Mitra [excretion], and Prajāpati [generation] control the organs of action.

From the tāmasic Egoity, the dullest level of divine energy, emerges the prime matter of the universe, first as Ākāsha (Space) and its property

---

potentiality, Mahat is the principle of Manas and Buddhi.

The Ahamkāra or ego-sense is the second product of the evolution of Nature and is responsible for the self-sense in living beings.

Manas evolves from the sattvic aspect of the Ahamkara. The Pancha Tanmātras or five objects (color, sound, smell, taste, touch), which are the subtle form of the Pancha Mahābhūtas (see below), partake of all three gunas.

The Pancha jnāna indriyas or five sense organs (eyes, ears, nose, tongue and body) – are related to the sattvic aspect of Manas. The Pancha karma indriyas or five organs of action – the hands, legs, vocal apparatus, urino-genital organ and anus - evolve from the rājasic aspect of Manas.

The Pancha mahābhūtas, or five great substances – earth, water, fire, air and ether – are the gross form of the Tanmātras representing the tāmasic aspect of the "Ahamkara". These are the basis of the manifest universe.

[95]   The heart is the seat of the supreme deity's Māyā (Ātmamāyā; see *BP* II,10,30). We shall encounter the significance of the heart (Horus) and tongue (Thoth) of the deity also in the Heliopolitan cosmogony (see below p.62).

[96]   This may be one reason why the moon is called Gishnugal, the Great Light, in Sumer and Egypt (see below p.88). This level of divine energy corresponds to Nun as well as to Thoth (see below p.92).

Sound. From Ākāsha arises Vāyu (Wind), with Touch as its specific property, though, as an evolute, it contains also the properties of its preceding category, in this case, Sound. Vāyu then turns into Prāna (Life-breath). From Vāyu also arises Tejas (Fire) with its special property, form. From Tejas comes Ambhah (Water), with taste as its special property, and from Water, finally, Prithvī (Earth), with smell as its characteristic. Ākasha itself is descried in its various forms in the *Mandalabrāhmana Upanishad* IV thus:

> There are five (*viz.*): ākāś, parākāś, mahākāś, sūryākāś, and paramākāś. That which is of the nature of darkness, both in and out is the first ākāś. That which has the fire of the deluge, both in and out is truly mahākāś. That which has the brightness of the sun, both in and out is sūryākāś. That brightness which is indescribable, all-pervading and of the nature of unrivalled bliss is paramākāś.

In *AV* X,2 the entire Purusha is described as being formed by and infused with the creative force, Brahman.[97] The deity develops organs as a macroanthropos in order to give the gods, or the presiding geniuses of all knowledge and action, who have already been created, domains of personal influence (III,6,10).[98] From the incipient hunger and thirst of the materialising deity is formed the face, with the mouth forming first ruled by Agni. Vahni/Agni particularly rules the faculty of speech.[99] The principal organ of the mouth, the tongue, is presided over by Varuna (who, as we shall see, is the orginal form of Hari/Vishnu himself and counterpart of Enki/Osiris). Similarly are formed the nose, controlled by Vāyu (Wind), the eyes controlled by Sūrya (the Sun) the ears presided over by Dik, the skin ruled by Oshadhi [the Ashwins], the arms ruled by Indra, the generative organs ruled by Prajāpati, the excretory faculty ruled by Mitra, and the navel (the organ of transmigration) ruled by Yama (death) (II,10,15ff.). The organs of locomotion, the legs, are ruled by Vishnu, the most athletic solar force (III, 6,22).

According to the more metaphysical scheme of *SB* X,5,3 the original non-existent existent was Mind, which, desiring manifestation, created

---

[97] See Appendix p.327f below.

[98] For an interesting study of the operation of the Vedic deities within the central nervous system of the human microcosm see V.G. Rele, *op.cit.* For a more metaphysical understanding of the various gods, see Aurobindo Ghose, *The Secret of the Veda*, Sri Aurobindo Birth Centenary Library, vol.10, Pondicherry: Sri Aurobindo Ashram, 1971.

[99] In *RV* X,125 (Vāk Sūkta), Vāk, like Agni, is said to be born in the waters, and is the supreme lord who creates, and sustains the universe.

Speech, which in turn created Breath, which created the Eye, which created the Ear, which created Work, which created Fire.

In the *BP*, the macrocosmic manifestation of the primal lord, Vishnu/ Brahma, is described in terms related to the passions. From his own shadow (Night, related to the tāmasic quality mentioned above), Brahma [i.e. the Purusha, Nārāyana] is said to create Anger, Despair, Ignorance, Carnality and Concupiscence (III,20,18), while, from his bright form (Day, related to the sattvic quality), he creates the gods (22). The Manu's (prototypes of man in the several cosmic ages) arise from the Mind of the Purusha (49).[100] From his hips (related to the rājasic quality) arise the Asuras, marked by sexual desire (23), and then, from various other parts of his physical form, the Gandharvas, Apsaras, and demi-gods. The emergence of the "gross" form of the Lord follows that of His "subtle" form, constituted of the various orders of gods, Prajāpatis, Manus, Devas, Asuras, etc. (II,10,37ff.).

The formation of the deity as Purusha/Vishnu, the Ideal Man, is the result of the promptings of the divine 'heart' or spirit. This ideal Man, is, as we shall see, actually androgynous, since it is in his stomach that the Cosmic Egg develops that bears our manifest universe. In this, the second stage of creation,[101] the Supreme Lord activates these basic categories of Sattva, Rajas and Tamas, through his Maya, into the macrocosmic and microcosmic organisms of the universe. This results, macrocosmically, in the Cosmic Egg or womb from which the lord manifests himself as the Divine Light and Consciousness, Brahman.

Turning briefly to the *Paingala Upanishad* I,4ff., we find that the process of creation is viewed somewhat more differently than in the *BP*. The tāmasic consciousness produces Vishnu as the Cosmic Person who sustains the material universe. The macroanthropos (Vishnu) is here considered as the lowest state of the manifestation of the deity since the physical cosmos arises from his ideal body. The rājasic consciousness (associated with the creator, Brahman) results in the Hiranyagarbha (Cosmic Egg), which is partly spiritual and partly material. The sattvic consciousness of the divinity is itself said to constitute the "seed of the universe" [rather like the Desire of Ātman] which will ultimately result in the formation of the moon (bearing the seeds of animal life) and the sun (bearing the seeds of human life) in our system.[102]

---

[100] This points once again to the priority of the moon, the presiding deity of Manas, to the sun, whose son is but the seventh Manu, Vaivasvata.

[101] See below p.38.

[102] See below p.91.

In the *BP*, the divine Mind, which is the most spiritual aspect of the manifesting deity since it represents the highest level of divine energy, Sattva, is ruled by the Moon. The second aspect of the deity, his rājasic, is said to be dominated by Brahman, the creator of the manifest universe and the light that emerge from the Cosmic Egg.

According to the cosmogony of *SB* (VI,1,1,1), the first elements were the vital airs (prāna) (called rshis, or sages), which "desiring this [the existent universe] they perished by their exertion and their heat." From their death arise seven prānas, from which are formed seven Purushas, who coalesce into one. The Purusha, or Prajāpati, then creates by means of yogic tapas, the heat of the tapas producing first Brahman (representing the substance of heaven),[103] then foam (representing the substance of the mid-region) and, finally, earth.

In the *RV* X,90, Purushasūkta, the Purusha is described as first expanding "in all directions, to what eats and does not eat". The Lord as a Cosmic Man, Purusha, is thus finally of colossal proportions as is evident from the dimensions provided in *BP* II,6,36ff. There it is stated that our universe merely spans the distance between the heart and the waist of Purusha. From his hip downwards extend the underworlds of Earth and from his chest upwards the four divine worlds, Maharloka, Janaloka, Tapoloka and Satyaloka. In the *BP* III,6,26 it is stated that the head of the Purusha is Heaven, the feet Earth and the navel the Mid-region.

In *KYV* IV,6,2, too, the Purusha is described as encompassing the entire cosmic creation:

Then did the sky and earth extend
With eyes on every side, with a face on every side,
With hands on every side, with feet on every side.

From the Egyptian cosmogony which we shall note below we may assume that these "eyes", "face", "hands" and "feet" stand for gods,[104] who rule over the intellectual faculties of macrocosmic and microcosmic man. The sky and earth mentioned in the first line are not to be understood as our sky and earth but as the primordial Heaven and Earth informed by the gods.[105] That Purusha is replete with divine life is made clear by the identification of the birth of the gods with this early stage in the cosmic evolution.

---

[103] We see in this order of creation already the close relation between the Seven Sages and the brāhmans who represent Brahman (see below p.197).

[104] See below p.63.

[105] Cf. the Egyptian Tura hymn below p.62, where the primordial Man emerges before heaven and earth.

Since the intelligible being of the Purusha is constituted of the gods, he is sometimes equated with Indra, the chief of the gods – who is closely identified with Shiva.[106] Indeed, Indra, like Shiva, is sometimes (X,119) considered the supreme Self (Ātman) itself as well as the spirit within the sun.[107] In the *Aitareya Āranyaka* III,12; II,4, the metaphysical counterpart of Purusha is called Ātman (Soul), who is identifiable with Indra. Thus Indra represents the divine Self, and the self of the cosmos. Indra assumes multifarious forms through his Māya, or power of illusion. In *SB* VI,i,1,1-14, it is Indra, who as the Self of the deity, kindles the vital airs to form, indeed, seven cosmic men, purushas, who then combine into one.

According to the *BrdP*, the transformation of the Soul, Ātman, into Brahman, the self-conscious, enlightened form of the supreme deity, is accomplished through the power of intense yogic meditation (I,i,5,6). But the order of creation here is somewhat different. The first act of the macroanthropos is to recover Earth through the force of his "breath" which emerges from his nostrils in the form of the wind-god Vāyu assuming the shape of a "Boar". This is followed by the elemental creation beginning with the lower tāmasic and proceeding to the sattvic, the creation of the gods, of the "sages" who are intellectual creations of the deity, and, finally, of human life (I,i,5). Then the light of Brahman which develops in the ideal macroanthropos manifests itself materially as the light of the universe. This light is formed within the Cosmic Egg which develops in the ideal macroanthropos, Purusha.

The Sacrifice: Time and the Cosmic Egg

According to *SB* VI,1,2, the second phase of the cosmic creation is accomplished through a sacrifice in which the Purusha is the sacrificial victim. The Purusha brings forth as a result the manifest cosmos

---

[106] See below p.70. It has been suggested (for instance, by P. Kretschmer, "Indra und der hethitische Gott Indra", *Kleinasiatische Forschungen* I (1930), p.307) that the name Indra and the Iranian "andra" may be related to the Greek "aner"/man (the Vedic word for man, "nar" is clearly the original to which the Greek has added an initial euphonic "a"). However, Indra's name is more closely related to Vedic "ina" and "indriya" meaning strength as well as manliness (see V. Machek, ("Name und Herkunft", pp.146ff.). Hittite has a counterpart to this Vedic word in "innarawanza" (XVII 20 II 3, Bo 84 I 25) and its plural "innarawant" (IX 31 I 36 II 6=HT 1 I 29) (see E. Laroche, "Recherches", p.74). J. Przyluski ("Inara et Indra") also suggested that Inara, the Hittite counterpart of Indra, may derive from a root "nar" ("man"). V. Machek (*op.cit.*, p.146) objected that it is not certain that "nar" could be an abbreviated form of "inar". However, the Vedic "ina" may have given the name Inara, just as the Vedic "indriya" may be related to Indra.

[107] See *KYV* XIX,80-9, *RV* VIII,46,14.

constituted of the elements of earth, heavens and the mid-region, as well as its constitutents, the sun, moon, winds, humankind, and wild and domestic animals.[108]

Prajāpati or Brahman begins the second phase of this creative activity through three unions. The first union with earth, by means of Agni, results in a cosmic egg which becomes the mid-region (of the stars, also called "atmosphere") and wind. "That which was the embryo inside emerged as the wind ... and that which was the shell became the atmosphere". The second union is with the mid-region by means of the wind and this results in another egg the shell and embryo of which became the heavens and the sun. The third union with the heavens is effected by means of the sun and this results in the production of another egg. The shell and embryo of this egg became the quarters and the moon.

KYV V,6,4, relates that Prajāpati generated the earth in the form of a wind, Vāyu, which moved on the waters (Aditi) and implanted the fire in them. *KYV* VII,1,4 continues the account of Prajāpati's moving on the waters as wind, which represents the first incarnation of Vishnu, in the first Manvantara, as Vāyu:

> This was in the beginning the waters, the ocean. In it Prajāpati become the wind moved. He saw her, and becoming a boar he seized her. Her, become Vishvakarma, he wiped. She extended, she became the earth, and hence the earth is called the earth [lit. the extended].

The cosmic wind thus represents also the extensive power of the divine fire.[109] Vishvakarma is the expanded or fertilised Earth as daughter and consort of Vishvakarman/Tvashtr, who is the supreme Lord in his fabricative and formative aspect and, thus, an aspect of Vāyu. The primal cosmic matter is also polymorphous and dark. Vishvakarma as an early form of Earth is indeed represented as a Cow.

That Vāyu the spiritual force or wind working on the waters is a form of Ātman/Agni is made clear in *RV* III,29,11, where Agni is said to be the same as Mātarisvan (Vāyu): when he is "formed in his Mother; he hath, in his course, become the rapid flight of wind". The luminous quality of Vāyu is attested in the later manifestation of Vāyu in our incipient universe as the light of the Mid-region, just as Agni is the light of Earth and Āditya of Heaven, (*SB* VIII,iii,2,1). Further, in *KS* XIX,8 (9,16f.), Vāyu is called the "glow of the fire".

[108] See H.W. Tull, *The Vedic origins*, p.50.

[109] Cf. the notion of the extension of the sacrifice in *RV* X,130 (p.17 above).

Vāyu thus produces the first birth of Agni from Heaven, Dyaus, which is the substance of the Purusha. *SB* VI,7,4,3 recounts the first birth of this primal Agni from Vāyu in the following manner:

> 'From the sky Agni was first born;' —the sky, doubtless, is the breath, and from the breath he (Agni) was indeed first born,—

In the *SP*, when the resting god awakens, he begins to agitate the cosmic streams. Then, assuming the form of a boar (which, as we shall soon see, is a typical aspect of the wind-god),[110] he plunges into the Abyss, where, with his tusk, he extracts the substance of the previous cosmos, Earth, which had been dissolved by the cataclysm which ended the previous cosmic age (kalpa) Directly after the recovery of Earth, the macroanthropos Vishnu (i.e. the supreme lord called by his ultimate solar name) begins the task of cosmic recreation starting with the gods, fire, the moon and the sun. It is interesting that the "wind" which emerges as the breath of the Purusha and works on the primal waters is noted also by modern astrophysicists as the first gaseous agent of the formation of solar light in a hitherto darkened universe.[111]

Kāla

The first temporal movement in the cosmos is indeed initiated by the breath of the Lord, or the wind-god Vāyu. The elements of Earth and Heaven united in the Ideal Man are thus separated by the temporal aspect of the Ideal Man himself, Time (Chronos/Kumarbi/Enki). Since the breath of the Ideal Man arises in the form of a "rapidly moving wind", we may assume that it is the movement of the Wind that is responsible for the appearance of Time. Time may be considered to have not properly emerged until after the infusion of the divine breath/fire into the prime matter of Earth. We must also remember that Time operates on an entirely subconscious level since the Ideal Man does not achieve consciousness,

---

[110] The first incarnation of Vishnu as a boar corresponds to the first incarnation of Verethraghna in the Avesta. Among the Germans, the boar was sacred to Freyr, the ithyphallic god of the Vanir. Freyr is a son of Njordr, who may be related to the Earth-goddess Nerthus mentioned by Tacitus (*Germania*, 40). In the oath "So help me Freyr and Njordr and the almighty god" (see R. Simek, *Dictionary of Northern Mythology*, p.92) it is likely that Freyr represents the sun of Earth and the "almighty god" the solar force that rises from the universal Tree of Life (see below p.80).

[111] This is evident in the description of the first light of the universe offered by modern astrophysicists (see T. Folger, "The Real Big Bang", *Discover*, Dec.2002, p.43).

the divine light, until the latter emerges from the cosmic egg formed after the castration and impregnation of Heaven.

In the *Bundahishn* Ch.I, Zurvan (Time) is merely an aspect of Ahura Mazda, who corresponds to Brahman, since he inhabits eternally the region of infinite space called Light. Indeed, Ahura Mazda is also considered the father of the solar force, Mithra (who corresponds to the Hurrian Suwalliyat),[112] as well as of Atar (who corresponds to the Hurrian Teshup and Indic Brahmanaspati/Ganesha).[113] As such Ahura Mazda is identical to Shiva/Chronos/Zurvan as well, for Dyaus (Heaven) and Chronos are aspects of the same deity and the sacrifice of the Purusha is a self-sacrifice. In the Sassanian Pahlavi texts, Zurvan (Time, counterpart of Chronos) is considered the creator of both the twin forces of good and evil, Ahura Mazda and Angra Mainyu, who dwell in Heaven (the Boundless Light, symbolic of Brahman) and Earth (Darkness, symbolic of Ganesha/Seth, the Lord of Earth) respectively.[114]

The separation of the Heaven and Earth constituting the Ideal Man by Time is represented in some mythologies as a castration of Heaven's phallus, but this mutilation, is, as we shall see, as it were, a "self-sacrifice". The castration of the divine phallus causes its seed to impregnate the Cosmic Man himself resulting in the formation within his stomach of the egg from which the material matrix of the universe, Earth emerges in the form of a lotus suffused by the divine light of Brahman/An.

The supersession of the original Heaven is reflected in the early Greek cosomologies, as well as in the Hurrian, as a castration of Ouranos (Dyaus) by Chronos. Chronos' attack on Ouranos is an indication of an extremely violent nature that recurs in the character of his stormy son Zeus (Seth/Ganesha).[115] The Hesiodic Chronos is the daring son of Earth and Heaven who responds to his mother's desire to thwart his father's habit of hiding his offspring and not allowing them to become manifest. It is significant that Ouranos' hiding of his children is particularly described as "evil-doing" in Hesiod's *Theogony*, l.158, since Chronos is not the only villainous figure in the early drama of the cosmos. To aid his mother in her distress, Chronos undertakes to castrate Ouranos, whose anthropomorphic form in the Hesiodic account clearly identifies him with the Purusha himself.

---

[112] See below p.53.

[113] See below p.70.

[114] See R.C. Zaehner, *Teachings*, p.10.

[115] See below p.71.

In the Orphic cosmogonies, the Cosmic Egg is said to be formed by Chronos out of Aither and the Chasm,[116] Aither apparently corresponding to the Light of Ahura Mazda and the Chasm to Ahriman.[117] Chronos particularly forms Protogonos, or Phanes [Brahman] in the Cosmic Egg.[118] The proto-Stoic cosmogony of Pherecydes begins with Chronos [Time], Chthonie [Earth], and Zas [Heaven].[119] Chronos is said to "generate" fire, wind and water[120] in the five matrices of the gods from Chthonie and Zas.[121] Zas must therefore be identical to Aither and Chthonie to the Chasm.

The egg is surrounded by a serpent which breaks it by squeezing. In Epiphanius' account of Epicurus' cosmology, the serpent encircling the egg is itself constituted of wind.[122] The association of the egg with wind is also made clear in the description of Chronos' giving birth to "Eros and all the winds" in an Orphic poem quoted by Apollonius Rhodius.[123] In the cosmogonies of Hieronymus and Hellanicus, Chronos, who springs from the waters, produces the egg.[124] Again, though there is no reference to the formation of the divine light in a Cosmic Egg in Hesiod, in the Orphic account of Protogonos, Phanes is represented as being born of an egg.[125]

In the Hurrian epic of the Kingship in Heaven, Kumarbi is considered Anu's son,[126] and he destroys his father Anu so as to assume the rule of

---

[116] See M.L. West, *Orphic Poems*, p.70.

[117] See below p.59.

[118] *Ibid.*, p.178.

[119] H. Diels, *Doxographi Graeci*, Berlin, 1879, p.654; cf. Probus, *In Verg. Ecl.*6. Pherecydes calls 'Zas' Aither.

[120] Cf. the Assyrian exegetical text RA 62 52 17-8:
Girra: Anu: fire.
Primeval: Ea: water.
East wind: Enlil: wind.
(see A. Livingstone, *op. cit.*, p.74).

[121] The gods are called the fivefold race in the Vedas (*AV* VII,6,1) as well.

[122] See M.L. West, *op.cit.*, p.202.

[123] *Ibid.*, p.200. Eros is the same as Phanes/Brahman (see below p.54).

[124] See *ER* IV,126.

[125] See M.L. West, *op.cit.*, p.70.

[126] Kumār, in India, is the name of Shiva's solar son, Skanda/Muruga, who is the final ninth form of Agni, the first form being Rudra/Shiva himself. The other forms, according to *SB* VI,i,3, are Sarva, Pashupati, Ugra, Asani, Bhāva, Mahādeva and Ĩshana, who are embodied in the waters, plants, Vāyu, lightning, Parjanya (the rain-god), the moon and the sun respectively. In the *BrdP* I,ii,10, the identification of the forms of Agni/Shiva with

the primal cosmos. Kumarbi (Chronos) indeed castrates Anu (Heaven/ the ideal Cosmic Man) while dragging him down from Heaven. However, Anu succeeds later in fleeing to his natural abode, that is, Heaven. The manner of Kumarbi's castration of Anu is reminiscent of Chronos' in Hesiod:[127]

> After [Anu] Kumarbi rushed,
> and seized him, Anu, by his feet
> and pulled him down from the sky.
> He bit his loins[128]

According to *AV* XIX,53,8-9, both Prajāpati (here the creative form of the supreme deity, identical to the perfect light of Brahman who is "as it were the Mind", *KYV* II,6,6) and Fervour are said to be generated by Kāla, Time, who must be the same as the Desire (Agni) of *AV* XIX,52,1-3.[129] Desire and the Mind are then said to have created Heaven. Kāla is typically an epithet of Shiva, whose consort is called Kāli. Shiva/Enki as Time is thus closely allied to the Desire (Agni) of the supreme lord which serves as the prime motive force in the manifestation of the Deity. The erotic, as well as spiritual and ascetic, aspect of Shiva/Kāla is indeed clearly emphasised in the Shaivite mythologies.[130]

In Egypt, Time is posited at the stage of the appearance of Shu [Sumerian Enlil]: "[the Command of the supreme god] created Time – When Shu was there to raise the sky" (CT IV,325).[131] However, Plutarch (*De Iside et Osiride*, Ch.12), rightly considers Geb [Earth] and Nut

---

the universal phenomena is somewhat different. There, the first form of Shiva – who is the creation [or phallus] of Brahma – is Rudra, and is said to be embodied in the sun, the second, called Bhāva, in the waters, the third, called Sarva, in the earth, the fourth, called Īshana, in the wind (Vāyu), the fifth, called Pashupati, in the fire, the sixth, called Bhima (corresponding to Asani), in the ether, the seventh, called Ugra, in the initiated brāhman priest and the last, called Mahādeva, in the moon. The order of manifestations in the *SB* is more chronological than that of the *BrdP*, which represents them spatially in a series of concentric circles. For we note that the first and last forms, in the *BrdP* account, are constituted by the sun and moon respectively, the second and seventh by the waters and the Mind, the third and sixth by Earth and Heaven, the fourth and fifth by the Wind (Vāyu) and plantal life (Pashupati) – which latter is no doubt to be identified with Soma.

[127] See Hesiod, *Thegony*, ll.173ff.

[128] See H.G. Güterbock, "Hittite Mythology", p.156.

[129] See above p.31.

[130] See W. O'Flaherty, *Asceticism and Eroticism.*, Chs.IVff.

[131] See R.T. Rundle Clark, *Myth and Symbol*, p.76.

[Heaven] to be identical to Chronos and Rhea.[132] So Time is related to Earth as well. In Egypt, the counterpart of the episode of Prajāpati's seduction of his daughter is Re's impregnation of the cow Nut as the Bull of Heaven,[133] who, here, stands for Geb/Chronos, consort of Nut, Heaven.[134]

There are also references in the Egyptian literature to the "separation of Heaven from Earth and from the Abyss (Nun)".[135] Geb and Nut are sustained by the force of Shu after their separation by the latter. In the *Amduat*, the gigantic serpent called the "World-encircler" through whose coils the solar journey is undertaken in the underworld similarly represents Time.[136] The serpent is also the form taken by the Sumerian Enki/Okeanos surrounding Earth, showing the identity between Shu/Enlil and Enki.

The Lotus Earth

The principal elements of the Cosmic Egg formed in the Purusha after his castration are primal Earth, in the form of a lotus, and Brahman, the light of the cosmos. This light shines atop the material matrix of the manifest universe called Earth. The manifest universe itself is divided into Heaven, Earth and a Mid-region of the stars. In Egypt, the material matrix of the manifest universe is considered to arise in the form of a primeval "hill". This primeval hill which rises from the divine embryonic complex represents the phallic force [of Amun as Shu][137] and the core of the incipient physical universe. The hill is said to emerge particularly from the "navel" of the Lord.[138] The "primordial hill" and the "navel" represent the phallus and the womb of the supreme deity as macroanthropos. In Sumer,

---

[132] It should be noted that the male Geb, in Egyptian mythology, represents earth rather than heaven, as in Greek and Sumerian and Indian mythology.

[133] See E.O. James, *op.cit.*, p.177.

[134] See E.A.W. Budge, *op.cit.*, I:100.

[135] PT 627 pyr 1778 a-b (cf. S. Bickel, *op.cit.*, p.184).

[136] Cf. p.102 below.

[137] The phallic role of Shu is shared by the Sumerian Enlil, who is typically called 'the great mountain' (see pp.45,281 below).

[138] We note that the "navel" and "mountains" are equally regarded by Hebrew commentators as having been created before the heaven and earth and light (see A.J. Wensinck, *Ideas*, pp.17ff.). The rabbis, however, with typical Hebrew anthropo- and geocentrism, consider the 'mountains' as terrestrial forms, rather than as forms of the incipient universe.

Enlil, who is commonly called the "great mountain" (signifying the 'divine phallus') is accompanied by a consort, Ninlil, or Ninmah, who is later called Ninhursag, "Lady of the Base of the Mountain".[139] This suggests that Enlil and his consort are, like Shiva and Pārvati, the basis of the manifest universe which emerges in the form of a mountain.

In the Purānas, the lotus formation of Earth contains *in potentia* all the 'jīvas' (lives) of our system. The later division of Earth into seven "islands" (called continents in the Avestan literture) is due to the whirling action of the first form of the Divine Light, Priyavrata.[140] The seven islands are called Jambudweepa, Plakshadweepa, Shakadweepa, Shalmalidsweepa, Kushadweepa, Krounchadweepa and Pushkaradweepa and may refer to the planets since they are arranged concentrically around the innermost, Jambudweepa. Atop the lotus of Earth, the Lord manifests himself as Brahman, the light of Heaven (III,20,14ff.).

In the *PP* I,39,153-4, the lotus is said to be blazing like fire and equal to the "goddess earth" (I,40,4). Its "filaments" are said to be the mountains on the lotus-formed Earth, the central one of these mountains being Mt. Meru (*BP* V,16,7) which is situated at the very centre of the innermost "dweepa" (island) of Earth called Jambudweepa.[141] *BrdP* I,ii,15,18 declares that "it originated from the umbilical cord of Brahma [i.e. Purusha]", The sun arises from and is invisibly anchored to this mountain (*BP* V,21,7ff.; V,16,2).[142]

In *BP* III,10-12, the creation of the manifest universe within the "lotus" is depicted in considerable detail. The lotus on which Brahman rests is violently agitated by winds (Vāyu). He therefore subdues the wind and swallows the water around the lotus, whereupon his lotus-seat fills the entire sky (III,10,7). At this stage he decides to divide the lotus into the heaven, earth and mid-region of our universe. The divisions of earth are described in *BP* V,16, which details the "seven oceans" as well as "seven islands" [planets] of 'Earth'. In *BP* V,17,11 the outermost region of the

---

[139] See *Lugal e*, ll.394-5 (cf. J. van Dijk, *Inschriftenfunde*, II:101). In India, many phallic stones are represented erect in a base which represents the vulva.

[140] The seven islands of Earth are formed by Priyavrata, the son of the first Manu, Svāyambhuva Manu, when he rides in his chariot around Mt. Meru, which is at the very centre of Earth (*BP* V,16,5-7). This is reflected in the Hieronyman Orphic fragment (78) also, where Protogonos wheels round the world in his chariot to bring light to it (see M.L. West, *Orphic Poems*, p.214).

[141] In the *Bundahishn*, Ch.XII, Mt. Albûrz is described in the same cosmic terms as Mt. Meru, since it is said to be "around this earth and is connected with the sky" (3).

[142] In the *BrdP* I,ii,15,15ff., Mt. Meru is also called "Sumeru", which may well be the same as the Akkadian (hence proto-Dravidian) name for the land of Sumer, Šumeru.

central island, Jambudweepa, is called Bhāratvarsha and considered to be the only region in which lives may obtain merit or demerit through their karma (*BP* V,19.9ff.).[143] Bhāratvarsha is the name traditionally used to denote India. However, according to *Mbh*, Bhishma Parva, VI,11, Shakadweepa too has a mountain called Meru, followed by one called Malaya. Since Shakadweepa means the Saka or Scythian island, it seems that the names of the planets of the solar system were later employed for different continents on earth.[144] Shakadweepa is generally located in Central Asia, near Iran. The identification of Meru and Malaya on Shakadweepa as well as on Jambudweepa suggests that the original home of the Āryans may have been in Shakadweepa,[145] before the Indo-Āryans migrated to Jambudweepa and Bhāratvarsha.

In the Heliopolitan cosmology, Geb and Nut, who represent Earth and Heaven, are the first physical constituents of the Cosmic Egg, which, as we have seen, is formed by Geb himself. In the Egyptian *Book of Nut*, it is not Geb (Kronos) who swallows his offspring,[146] the "stars", but his consort the sky, Nut. Shu intervenes to allow the stars to be reborn in the Mid-region between Heaven and Earth.[147] The sun (that is, the solar force, Re/Agni) is thus free to move in the heavenly substance of Nut. We note here that the separation of Earth from Heaven is here attributed to Shu.[148] However, Osiris is equally credited with the separation of Nut and Geb,[149] since Osiris is the later solar form of Shu.[150] Osiris is also the god of Maat (Sum. me's), just as Shu is. Atum too is sometimes associated with the separation of Heaven from Earth, since he is but the same as Horus the

---

[143] The capacity of world-renunciation that informs the religion of the ancient Indo-European religions is thus considered to be reserved to the Indians.

[144] In the Avesta (for instance, Mihir Yasht [10], IV,15), the seven islands are termed "continents" (see p.122 below). In the Babylonian map of the universe dating from the eighth or seventh century (see W. Horowitz, "The Babylonian Map of the World", *Iraq*, 50 (1988), 147-66), the manifest universe is depicted as a land mass including all the known near eastern regions of Babylonia, Assyria, Elam, Urartu, and the Zagros, and surrounded by a river called "marattum", the "Bitter", which is probably the same as Okeanos surrounding Ge.

[145] Cf. the account of the Shakaldvipa brāhmans below p.199.

[146] As in Hesiod, ll.459ff.

[147] See E. Hornung, *Ancient Egyptian*, p.116.

[148] See S. Bickel, *op.cit.*, p.197f.; cf. E. Hornung, *ibid.*

[149] See E.A.W. Budge, *op.cit.*, II:100.

[150] It is interesting to note that Tushratta in his letter to the Egyptian Pharaoh (Kn 27, l.87, see H.-P. Adler, *Das akkadische*, p.221), calls on Amun and Teshup (Zeus/Seth) at the same time, indicating thereby the similarity of these two gods as well, since Seth is but the stormy aspect of Osiris (see p.45 below) and Osiris is a form of Shu/Amun.

Elder-Osiris.[151]

Geb emerges as the rising Earth from which the solar system universe is formed. This is the same as the primordial hill from which the solar force emerges, and this hill is encircled by the serpent Nehaher[152] (representing Time as well as Enki, the god of the ocean)[153] surrounding Earth in serpentine form. Geb is called the leader of the Ennead, that is, of all the gods.[154] Just as in the Purānic and Iranian cosmologies, in Egypt, Earth, or the solar system, is represented as an island (covered with reeds) that emerges from the primeval waters. This is most clearly evident in the records of the temple of Edfu, which also refer to the island or mound as a "lotus" formation in much the same manner as the Purānas do.[155] This island is supposedly produced by the insemination of the embryonic material called 'bnnt' by the "seed of Nun".[156] The first occurrence after the emergence of the island is the creation of form, ḏt, and the spiritual essences, 'ka's.[157] However, it is possible that the deities called "sages" preceded the formation of the island itself.[158] These sages assume the form of falcons in the waters ("wāᶜret") and foretell the creation of the cosmos.[159]

As in the Indic records, Earth emerges in the form of a Lotus, "the Great Lotus that issued from the pool in the Island of the Two Flames",[160] the "Province of the Beginning which initiated light".[161] The island is also called the Island of the Combat,[162] perhaps referring to the impending attack on the divine light Atum/Brahman by the storm-force Seth/Ganesha.[163] This combat also seems to have entailed the submersion of Earth beneath the primeval waters so that it henceforth forms

---

[151]   See S. Bickel, op.cit., pp.182ff.

[152]   See R.T. Rundle Clark, Myth and Symbol, p.171.

[153]   See below p.96.

[154]   See J.G. Griffiths, Conflict, p.175.

[155]   See E.A.E. Reymond, Mythical Origin, pp.56ff.

[156]   Ibid., p.64.

[157]   For a detailed account of the various stages of the formation of Earth and of the deities presiding over these see E.A.E. Reymond, op.cit., Chs.2-11.

[158]   Ibid., p.130.

[159]   Ibid., p.96.

[160]   The Island of the Two Flames is also to be found in the Hermopolitan theology (see K. Sethe, op.cit., p.49). From the Edfu records we discover that the two "flames" are the source of the two blazing eyes of Atum/Brahman (see E.A.E. Reymond, op.cit., p.83).

[161]   Ibid., p.68.

[162]   Ibid., p.107.

[163]   See below p.65.

the Underworld.[164] This may be the reason why the place called "the Beginning of the Earth" was at the same time a burial place for Osiris.[165]

In the Heliopolitan theology, the island of Earth is represented rather as a mound that emerged from the primeval waters.[166] However, in the Edfu myth about "the Island of the Egg", it is revealed that the creation of the mound is a secondary creative act.[167] It is said to have been created by the deities called "shebtiw".[168] The Edfu records also refer to several "pāy" lands which emerge after the initial mound.[169] These may correspond to the the islands or continents encircling the central one in the Indic and Iranian cosmologies.[170] There are also allusions to secondary "pāy" lands, which may represent other heavenly bodies in the universe, though the defeat of the snake is necessary before the gods can occupy these lands.[171]

In CT 80 Geb is called the "lotus" on which Atum could find a seat.[172] The Edfu texts also confirm that the lotus serves as the throne of the solar god.[173] The Edfu description of the original island is also very close to the Hermopolitan since both call it the "island of the two flames".[174] The Edfu texts also associate the "island of the two flames" with the creation of light.[175] The solar force, is indeed said to be born thrice, first from Heaven, then from Earth and finally from the Waters.[176] The Egyptian Geb/Tatenen (Earth) is thus depicted, especially in *The Book of the Earth*, in the depths of the Abyss receiving the incipient sun before it is ejected from the waters of Nun.[177]

---

[164] *Ibid.*, p.127.

[165] *Ibid.*, p.117; cf. *BD* Spell 175, which refers to the disappearance of Earth under the waters after its first creation.

[166] *Ibid.*, p.59.

[167] *Ibid.*, p.93.

[168] *Ibid.*, p.139.

[169] *Ibid.*, pp.151ff.

[170] See above p.45, below p.122.

[171] *Ibid.*, pp.194-6.

[172] See J.P. Allen, *op.cit.*, p.22.

[173] See E.A.E. Reymond, *op.cit.*, p.84.

[174] See K. Sethe, *op.cit.*, p.49; E.A.E. Reymond, *op.cit.*, p.70. Like the Purānic division of the lotus into seven islands; the Edfu records too mention several "pᶜy" lands which arise after the central island (iw) around it (see E.A.E. Reymond, *op.cit.*, p.171).

[175] See E.A.E. Reymond, *op.cit.*, p.68.

[176] Cf. p.156f below.

[177] See E. Hornung, *op.cit.*, p.102.

Brahman

The other product of the second cosmic egg which develops in the womb of the supreme deity[178] is the perfect Light of the divine Mind, Brahman.[179] The Intellectual Light (Brahman) of the universe represents also the Self-Consciousness of the deity. In the Purānas, Purusha [i.e. as Brahman] is indeed called the mirror of divine self-consciousness, the coming to consciousness of the supreme Self (*BP* VI,5,17).[180]

The emergence of the light of the universe,[181] which is called Protogonos in the Orphic theogonies, occurs, according to the *BP*, in the first manvantara of the second kalpa, since Protogonos' Indic counterpart, Priyavrata, as we have seen, is said to be the son of the very first Manu, Swāyambhuva Manu, who is the same as the Purusha.

The divine Light or Consciousness of Brahman shines atop the lotus-form of Earth. In the Egyptian Ramesside theology, the tremendous brilliance which emerges on the separation of Earth and Heaven is considered the "face" of the supreme deity, called, Atum, or, more precisely, Re (Aton), the full-fledged (noonday) sun.[182] The term Atum ("the perfected") refers particularly to the perfected sun-disk at sunset, but it signifies more than the sun itself, being as it is the light of the universe. That Atum is not merely the sun is made clear by the fact that he is adored in the Edfu Temple as the "majestic God who constantly shines with his two eyes [i.e. the sun and moon]",[183] which he acquires later, after the formation of the universe. Like the Orphic Phanes or Protogonos, Atum

---

[178] See above p.39.

[179] See above p.38.

[180] This is also the real significance of the obtuse biblical rendering of the same idea in *Genesis* I:27 as God creating "man" in "his own image". Adam, meaning "man" in Hebrew, is linguistically the same as Purusha. The god who creates Adam is El and not Jahve, for, according to the Phoenician mythology ascribed by Philo of Byblos to Sankhuniathon, the Phoenician counterpart of Chronos was El, son of Ouranos and Ge (see Philo of Byblos, *op.cit.*, p.49; cf. H.G. Güterbock, "Hittite Mythology" in S. Kramer, *Mythologies*, p.160). This El is the same senior god whom the Hebrews too once worshipped in their originally polytheistic pantheon before they transferred their sole allegiance to his son, Jahve, under the tutelage of Abraham. Since El is Chronos, the "man" that he creates is the anthropomorphic Brahman/Phanes (see p.42 above).

[181] The emergence of the first solar light in the universe is calculated by modern astrophysicists at around 100,000,000 years after the "Big Bang" (see below p.54), which is during the first Manvantara.

[182] cf. *RV* X,7,3, where Sūrya is addressed in the same manner: "I honour as the face of lofty Agni in heaven the bright and holy light of Sūrya."

[183] K. Mysliwiec, *Studien*, II:191

is also adored, especially in the New Kingdom and after, as the "boy in the heavens",[184] showing that Atum is the same as the manifest Heavenly Light, An, Brahman. Amun too is addressed, also in the Berlin Papyrus 3055, 20,6/7, as "the divine boy from Hermopolis". This juvenile Amun is, more accurately, the "face" (Atum) of the supreme deity, the solar energy which manifests itself as Horus/Phanes/Brahman.

That Atum is ultimately the same as Amun/Ātman, as well, is made clear by the fact that Atum is also called, much like Amun, "the God whose name is hidden"[185] and Soul.[186] It is interesting to note that Shamash too, in Babylon, sometimes bears the name "Amna",[187] which may be related to Amun. In the Heliopolitan cosmogony, Atum is, like the Hermopolitan Amun/Shu, and the Indic Brahman/Prajāpati,[188] worshipped as the creator of the entire universe since it is he who creates seed itself.[189] (Re, the other solar form, is also adored as "the lord of Maat [Tefnut]"[190] just as Shu/Amun is.) Also, just as Amun, Atum himself is said to be the one whose "primordial liquid" created the egg.[191]

Atum emerges from a lotus [Earth/the material universe of Geb] in the watery abyss, Nun. In the Edfu texts (III,186,4) we have a striking reference to the birth of the divine light from the lotus, "This august god who came into being in the Great Pool and was led forth from Nun within the lotus".[192] Brahman too rises from the lotus which grows from the navel of Vishnu, the supreme lord, in the Purānas. In STG no.69 III, there is a reference to the "living fire that came forth from Nun, who makes light for the heavenly people [the gods]".[193]

In Heliopolis, the principal sons of Geb (Chronos) and Nut are called Horus the Elder and Osiris. These are the twin aspects of the primal deity as the solar light, the former (Suwalliyat/Tasmisu/Shamash) being the

---

[184]   *Ibid.*, p.147.

[185]   Pap. Greenfield, in K. Mysliwiec, *op.cit.*, p.194.

[186]   *Ibid*, p.201. It is clearly a lack of cosmological insight which prompted the peremptory substitution of Amun with Aton in the reign of Akhenaton (see S. Quirke, *Cult*, pp.167-9).

[187]   See A. Deimel, *Pantheon*, p.252. In Sippar, the city of the sun-god, too, we find the divine name "amnanu"; see H. Zimmern, "Religion und Sprache", p.487.

[188]   See above p.37.

[189]   CT 306 IV 60e-f; see S. Bickel, *op.cit.*, p.38; cf. p.63 below.

[190]   Pap. Boulaq 17 (see A. Barucq and F. Daumas, *op.cit.*, p.193).

[191]   CT 648 VI 270m-n (S. Bickel, *op.cit.*, p.234). This identifies him with the Amun-Shu/Enlil stage of the cosmic evolution.

[192]   See E.A.E. Reymond, *op.cit.*, p.82.

[193]   See J. Assmann, *op.cit.*, p.104.

first pure light, and the latter the moribund. Horus the Elder is generally understood as a sky-god, and his name has been understood to mean "face" (of the supreme deity) or "heaven".[194] It is more likely that the name is related to Iranian Hvare and Skt. Svarya /Sūrya ("the shining one", "the golden"), which denote the solar force. This is corroborated by the fact that the name Horus is sometimes coupled with the sign for "gold", which can also be read as "of the city of Ombos" (whose chief god was Seth, who represents his stormy aspect). After the 12th Dynasty, the customary interpretation of the name was as "the golden Horus".[195]

The description of Re in the Suty-Hor hymn is also evocative of the Sumerian An's divine virtue as the light of the universe:[196] "The brilliance of heaven is like your brilliance,/ Your colour shines more brilliantly than its skin".[197] Horus may thus be understood as the aethereal brilliance of Re.

Horus the Elder is the consort and son of Hathor.[198] Hathor's consort is particularly Horus of Edfu.[199] Hathor is derived from Nut (Heaven, who is the actual "mother" of Horus the Elder) and is said to be "the Great who lives in the seed in her name of Nut [the sky]" (Theb. T.283b,5).[200] This indicates that Nut is the same substance which turns into Hathor at the stage of the emergence of the divine Light, Atum. In fact, Hathor herself is a goddess of the "sky" and both Nut the sky-goddess and Hathor are represented as a cow, though she symbolises the heavenly part of the cosmic egg, whereas Hathor represents the primordial matter of our universe.[201]

Hathor is characterised as golden, "the gold of the gods",[202] since the Cosmic Egg from which the Light emerges is a "golden egg" and she is the consort of the brilliant Horus the Elder. After the descent of the divine light into the underworld, Hathor becomes the mother of the sun, Horus

---

[194] See S. Mercer, op.cit., pp.96f.

[195] Ibid., pp.77f.

[196] See below p.53.

[197] See J. Assmann, op.cit., p.95.

[198] See S. Mercer, op.cit., p.89. The Vedic and Purānic Vishnu too is considered to be at once the consort and son of Aditi (see below p.76).

[199] See E. Drioton, Texte dramatique, p.59, where it is made clear that her son is Horus the Elder.

[200] The "seed" is that which first flows out from Amun (the Soul) and is the basis of the cosmic egg which is constituted of heaven (Nut) and earth (Geb) (see K. Sethe, op.cit., p.118). It is possible that Hathor is related to the Vedic Aditi even linguistically, and its common interpretation as 'the house of Horus' a later imposed Egyptian one.

[201] See M.E. Lefebure, Tombeau I, 1886, IV, XVff.; cf. C.J. Bleeker, Hathor, p.48.

[202] See A. Barucq, op.cit., pp. 445ff.

the Younger. Indeed Hathor's name could also mean "house of Horus".[203]

Exactly like Brahman in the Purānas, and Atum, Horus the Elder too is represented at Dendera as a child (or a serpent) resting on a lotus that rises above the water.[204] Horus the Elder is also called "the youth who emerges from the phallus"[205] which must be a reference to the phallic hill which emerges from the Cosmic Egg. Horus' first appearance from the waters of Nun is indeed "on the high ground",[206] or the primeval hill representing the phallic force of Shu which holds the heavens and earth apart.[207] Like Osiris, Horus represents a later manifestation of the primal creator god Osiris/Enki infused with the life-force of Shu/Vayu/Enlil.[208]

At first, Horus the Elder is called "the Sightless", since the sun is formed in the firmament after the sacrifice of Osiris.[209] Later, he is called 'the two-eyed',[210] when the mature (Aton) and dying (Atum) phases of the sun of our system serve as his right and left eyes.[211] Sometimes his two eyes are represented by the sun and moon, the "lesser" and the "greater" lights.[212] Though Horus the Elder is considered a brother of Osiris, the two are, in fact, one god. For, Osiris too is called the sky in a lament for Osiris, where Seth is said to have "felled the sky to the ground".[213] We shall see that Osiris is a son of Geb/Enki/Kumarbi/Kronos, who is overcome by Seth/Teshup/Zeus, another son of the same parent.

Horus the Younger is, as we shall see, a rejuvenated form of Horus the Elder-Osiris, after the felling of the sky by Seth. However, he is often addressed in close association with Horus the Elder, since they are both forms of Shu:

> His magnificent image is the 'form of the god of the horizon' [Horus the Younger]
> ...

[203] See J.G. Griffiths, *op.cit.*, p.13.

[204] See C.J. Bleeker, *Hathor*, p.63.

[205] See A. Barucq and F. Daumas, *op.cit.* p.137.

[206] CT 335 (=*Book of the Dead*), 17, in J.P. Allen, *op.cit.*, p.32.

[207] See K. Sethe, *op.cit.*, p.79.

[208] In an inscription on the walls of the temple at Ombos, he is identified with Shu; see E.AW. Budge, *op.cit.*, I, 468.

[209] Pap. Bremner-Rhind (see R.T. Rundle Clark, *op.cit.*, p.92).

[210] Pap. Bremner-Rhind, 34 (see J.P. Allen, *op.cit.*, p.28).

[211] Cf. p.53 below.

[212] See p.61 below.

[213] Pap. Bremner-Rhind, 5,7,8 (see H. Te Velde, *Seth*, p.85).

Lord of the two divine eyes [Horus the Elder]
In front of whom are the sun and the moon,
His right eye and his left eye are Aten [the mature sun] and Atem [the setting sun].[214]

In the Hurrian poem of Ullikummi, Teshup is constantly seen in the company of his "pure brother" Tashmishu, the Hurrian form of Suwalliyat, the Hittite-Hurrian Sūrya.[215] Tashmishu and his stormy brother, Teshup, are the two gods of Heaven that are the Hittite counterparts of Horus the Elder/Osiris and Seth. Tashmishu (Horus the Elder), Saushga/Ishtar (Isis), and Teshup (Seth) are represented as going in search of the stone Ullikummi,[216] which is symbolic of the phallus of An castrated by their parent Kumarbi/Chronos.[217] The vital power of the phallus is that of Enlil, the wind-god, whose Emesal name 'Mullil' gives the divine phallus its name Ullikummi (Mullil of Kummiya).[218]

In the Sumerian cosmogony, An, the light of the heavens, is clearly the great light of the universe. Just as Mitra and Varuna are considered as forms of Agni,[219] so too, in an Assyrian exegetical text, An is identified with Girra, the fire-god.[220] In the Akkadian Akitu ritual too, the 'star' An is called "furious Gibil".[221] In the Late Babylonian period, the quality of An is described, in a temple hymn (A.O. 6494 and B.R.M. IV:8), as a "fearsome radiance" which may be identifiable with Mitra/Xvarenah of the contemporary Persians.[222]

Tammuz too is identifiable with the Osirian aspect of An since he is said to be destroyed by a "flood" and forced into the underworld.[223] Tammuz, who is normally one of the gatekeepers of heaven, thus bears the same solar force as Anu.[224]

---

[214] See A. Barucq and F. Daumas, op.cit., p.167.

[215] See H.G. Güterbock, "The god Suwaliyat", p.12.

[216] See H.G. Güterbock, "Hittite Mythology", p.168.

[217] See p.42 above.

[218] Kummiya was the city of Teshup.

[219] See below p.121.

[220] See above p.42n.

[221] See F. Thureau-Dangin, Rituels, p.138f.

[222] H. Wohlstein, Sky-god, p.123.

[223] See below p.98.

[224] See O 175, l.9 (RA XVI, p.145) (see H. Wohlstein, op.cit., p.100).

In Assyria, Anu is called Essarhadon, "The First-born",[225] and this is the same as Protogonos, or Phanes, the first light of the cosmos.

In the Orphic theogonies, the tremendous light of the ideal universe which is born of the cosmic egg and is adored as the lord of the universe is called Protogonos,[226] or Phanes. He is, according to the Hieronyman theogony, at first visible only to Night and only after the two mate do Earth and Heaven emerge as manifest entities.[227] In the pseudo-Lucianic *Amores,* Eros, who is the same as the Orphic Phanes, is apostrophised in the following manner:

> thou from obscure and disordered formlessness gavest form to everything. So from the whole world thou didst remove, as it were, a universal shroud of death, the Chaos which lay about it, and banished it to the furthest recesses of Tartarus.[228]

This initial appearance of the light is also attested by modern cosmological research. The current astrophysical investigations posit the first appearance of solar light at around 100 million years after the "big bang".[229] This primal light results from the coalescence of hydrogen gas clouds around the densest regions of dark matter which produces a nascent fireball about 200 times larger than our sun. This light is at first occluded by the hydrogen fog which still surrounds it, though it succeeds in burning it away through its intense radiation.[230] What modern scientists cannot know is that this dazzling effulgence born of the golden egg is also the Intellect, or Consciousness, of the cosmos.

Like Phanes, the Thracian god Dionysus is also represented as a golden child.[231] Dionysus is indeed considered to be a son of Zeus Aitherios and Semele. If we refer to Cicero's enumeration of the different Zeus' in *De Natura Deorum,*[232] we may consider Zeus Aitherios as the

---

[225]   See H. Wohlstein, *op.cit.,* p.160.

[226]   Cf. below p.67n.

[227]   See M.L. West, *Orphic Poems,* p.208f.

[228]   *Ibid.,* p.255.

[229]   The "big bang" theory posits a primeval "fireball" which encompassed the entire universe in a state of utmost concentration before it exploded into the myriads of continuously "expanding" galaxies that constitute our universe. This fireball corresponds to the golden Cosmic Egg of the ancient mythologies.

[230]   See T. Folger, *op.cit.,* p.42.

[231]   Diodorus quotes an Orphic hymn to Helios in which Phanes and Dionysus are identified (see M.L. West, *Orphic Poems,* p.206).

[232]   See Cicero, *De Natura Deorum,* III,21.

"first" Zeus and identical to Chronos. This Zeus marries Rhea and engenders Demeter.[233] Then he consorts with his daughter Demeter (*Theogony* 1.912) to produce Persephone. Zeus Aitherios also consorts with Semele to produce Dionysus (1.940), whom we have identified as the divine light, Horus the Elder/Brahman/An. Dionysus, according to Nonnos, is the "second Zeus".[234] The name Dionysus is perhaps derived from the name of the Thracian sky-god Dios, corresponding to the primal sky-god Zas[235] (who is the counterpart of Dyaus, the heavenly form of the cosmic man). And his name, when broken up as Dios Nysos, could mean 'God the son'.[236] Dionysus is also commonly called "ʽο παῖς", the son.

Dionysus is another representative of the Osirian aspect of the solar cosmology especially in his dramatic dismemberment and resurrection. Dionysus' destruction corresponds to the felling of Horus the Elder-Osiris, who is forced to descend into the underworld before he is resurrected.[237] Phanes, as we shall see, is swallowed by Zeus Adados/Teshup/Seth. It is not surprising that Herodotus (II, 156) identifies Dionysus with Osiris. Plutarch (*De Iside et Isiride*, 364d) too expressly identifies Osiris with Dionysus. In a late Hellenistic Orphic hymn to Helios (fr.237), Dionysus is called the one who "first came to light, and was named Dionyus/ because he whirls (dyneitai) through infinite Olympus".[238] This reminds us again of Priyavrata/ Protogonos.

In the Indic cosmogony, the principal product of the Cosmic Egg is the perfect Light and Intellect of the deity called Brahman, who, like Atum, is said, in the Purānas, to be situated above the lotus Earth growing from the navel of the Lord.[239] In the *BP* XII,9,21, as well as in the *PP* I,39,103 Brahman (An/Mitra) appears as a radiant child atop a fig-

---

[233] See "Hymn to Demeter", 460ff.

[234] See Nonnos, *Dion.*, 10,298. The third Zeus mentioned in Cicero, the Cretan Zeus, is the same as Dionysus (Osiris), since he is said to be the son of Chronos. Our sun (Helios), however, is the son of Hyperion (1.371) who is a Titan "brother" of Chronos (and consort of Theia). Helios is the same name as Suwalliyat/Sūrya (bearing in mind that Greek always substitutes 'h' for Sanskritic 's').

[235] See A.B. Cook, *op.cit.*, II, 277ff. Zeus, as we have seen, is a stormy solar deity, just as Zas his forebear is the primal Heaven/Dyaus (see above p.42). In Hesiod, Zeus as the son of the Titan Cronus, is the counterpart of Ganesha, son of Shiva, while his "uncle", the Titan Hyperion, father of Helios, Eos and Selene, approximates more to the figure of Brahman.

[236] See A.B. Cook, *ibid.*, II, 288.

[237] See p.67 below.

[238] See M.L. West, *Orphic Poems*, p.253.

[239] See above p.44.

tree.[240] The infant shape which the Lord assumes in these Purānas is said to be "the self of all", that is, of the universe, since he is but the manifest consciousness and brilliance of the Purusha. Thus the first fully conscious form of the ideal Macrocosmos, Purusha, in our cosmos is as the divine Light, Brahman. This marks the beginning of the first Yuga, Krita Yuga, of the second kalpa, Padmakalpa. It is Brahma who divides this lotus (*BP* III,10,8) into three worlds (heaven, earth and its mid-region) to serve as the region in which the souls transmigrate for the enjoyment of the fruits of their action (karma).

The emergence of the light of the universe, which is called Protogonos in the Orphic theogonies, occurs in the first manvantara of the second kalpa, since Protogonos' Indic counterpart, Priyavrata, is said to be the son of the very first Manu, Swāyambhuva Manu (*BP* V,1), [241] who is but a form of Brahman. In the *BrdP* I,ii,9, as well as in the *BP* III,12,49ff, after the creation of the seven sages, Brahma divides himself into male and female, Manu and Satarupa, and the two join together sexually. From this very first sexual union is born Priyavrata (Protogonos, Phanes) and his siblings. Priyavrata, like Protogonos/Mitra, divides Earth into seven "islands" by riding around Mt. Meru in his chariot (*BP* V,16,5-7).[242] Priyavrata is clearly the original of the Orphic Protogonos.

Brahman/Mitra as the Lord of Creation is called Prajāpati, who is thus said to be produced within the golden cosmic womb, "Hiranyagarbha" (*RV* II,35,13).[243] In *KYV* VII,1,4, Prajāpati is used as a name of the primal Mitra/Vishnu, since he is said to have mated with his "mother" Aditi and thus created the world of the gods and the Ādityas. In *AV* XIX,53,8, Prajāpati, like Brahman, is called the son of Kāla (Chronos/ Shiva/Agni), since it is Shiva's castration of Varuna/Dyaus which produces the Cosmic Egg. In *AV* X,8,15-16, Brahman is described as the substratum of the entire circuit of the sun:

---

240 See S. Shastri, *The Flood Legend*, p.39; p.62.

241 The emergence of the first solar light in the universe is calculated by modern astrophysicists at around 100,000,000 years after the "Big Bang", which is during the first manvantara.

242 According to the *BP*, the Padma Kalpa lasts 4,380,000,000 years and we are half way through it in the seventh Manvantara. Our planet earth is calculated by geologists to be around 4,500,000,000 years old, which suggests that its age according to the Purānic history of the cosmos, is to be calculated from the recovery of Earth by the Boar-form of Vāyu during the Night of the Supreme Lord at the end of the first Brahma Kalpa.

243 Cf. *RV* X, 121.

A mighty Being in creation's centre: to him the rulers of the realms bring tribute.
That, whence the sun arises, that wither he goes to take his rest,
That verily I hold supreme: naught in the world surpasses it.

According to the *Manusmriti*,[244] when the Lord manifests himself as Brahman (also as a macroanthropos) from the egg, he creates the gods, the sacred sacrificial rites, the Vedas, the various qualities, and the castes. At this point, He divides his cosmic Self into male and female and creates the material phenomena of the universe.[245] In order to create beings, he first produces ten great Sages, as well as the seven Manus, the gods, and then the lower forms of being.[246] We note here the priority of the Sages and of the Manus in the order of the creation.

According to *SB* VI,1,2,9-10, the third phase of creation consists of Prajāpati's production of divine beings using only speech and mind. The result of this is the various deities associated with the four cosmic realms: the Vāsus (associated with the earth and Agni), Vāyu and the Rudras (associated with the mid-region), Āditya (the sun of our system) and the Ādityas (associated with the heavens) and Chandramas (the moon) and the Vishvadevas (associated with the quarters). The gods of the universe are all produced in the basic element of Aditi. Aditi produces Vāk, the Word, which is the original creative agent, as the *Tāndya Brāhmana* makes clear: "Prajāpati emitted the Word and it pervaded this whole [universe]. It rose upwards as a continuous stream of water". In *RV* X,125, Vāk declares that

5. I, verily, myself announce and utter the word that Gods and men alike shall welcome.
...
7. ... my home is in the waters, in the ocean.
Thence I extend o'er all existing creatures, and touch even yonder heaven with my forehead.
8. I breathe a strong breath like the wind and tempest, the while I hold together all existence.

---

[244] This major law-book of the Hindus was probably composed between the 2nd c. B.C. and the 2nd c. A.D.

[245] See *Manusmriti*, I,i,32.

[246] It is important to note that the sages precede the Manu's, since they are all intellectual ("mind-born") creations of the supreme deity (cf. p.38 above).

Vāk is sometimes identifed with Aditi as well as with Virāj, and later even with Saraswati, the consort of Brahman/Prajāpati. Aditi and Virāj represent the primal cosmic waters, as well as the later Earth, and are represented as a Cow. Aditi is also considered as a daughter of Daksha, one of the seven sages created intellectually by Brahma.[247] "In her Prajāpati [Dyaus as god of generation] made effort. He produced the gods, Vāsus, Rudras, and Ādityas [sons of Aditi]" (*KYV* VII,1,4).[248] In *RV* X,121, too,

---

[247] See p.129n.

[248] In *BAU*, IX,2,ff. the eight Vasus are called "fire, earth, air, the sky, the sun, the heavens, the moon, the stars", the eleven Rudras are called "the ten breaths along with the mind" and the twelve Ādityas are called the "twelve months of the year", keeping in mind that the "year" is the same as the "universe", for the Ādityas are indeed the suns of different universes (see below).

According to *RV* X,72,8 there are eight Ādityas, of which one, Mārtanda, died soon after birth. They are, according to the commentator Sāyana: Mitra, Varuna, Dhatar, Aryaman, Amsha, Bhaga, Vivasvān, Āditya. The names of the first and last two Ādityas confirm that they are indeed all solar phenomena, and *RV* IX,114,2 decares: "Seven regions have their several suns ... seven are the Āditya deities". Vivasvān is virtually the same as Āditya, the sun of our system. Mārtanda may be identified with Varuna. The reference to Mārtanda's death may be related to the killing of Osiris which causes the sun to first descend to the underworld and be regenerated there, an incident cryptically referred to also in *RV* X,72,9: [Aditi] brought Mārtanda thitherward to spring to life and die again."

As Bergaigne has shown, Mārtanda, the sun, and Indra are differentiated from the other Ādityas, whom Aditi grants the status of "ancient gods" (see A. Bergaigne, *La Religion Védique*, III,107). This suggests that the other Ādityas, who are the suns of other systems, may be older than our sun.

Aryaman is understood as the god of friendship and sexual harmony, Bhaga is the dispenser of fortune, Amsha is the distribution of fortune, and Dhatar represents the ordainer of the universe.

Sometimes the number of the Ādityas is given as six, with six female consorts so that the total number is enlarged to twelve. In *BP* VI,6,39 the Ādityas are twelve in number and all male, called Vivaswān, Aryama (Vedic Aryaman), Pusha (Pushan), Tvashta (Tvashtr), Savita (Savitr), Bhaga, Dhata, Vidhata, Varuna, Mitra, Sakra, Urukrama (Vāmana). In *BrdP* I,ii,24,33, the twelve suns are named Indra, Dhātr, Bhaga, Pūsan, Mitra, Varuna, Aryaman, Amshu, Vivasvān, Tvashtr, Savitr and Vishnu. (In *RV* X,181,1 Daksha, who is also considered one of the seven sages, is addressed simultaneously with Savitr and Vishnu).

In Greece, the Ādityas, who are called Titans, include, in Hesiod, six male deities, Okeanus, Coeus, Crius, Hyperion, Iapetus, Cronos, and six goddesses Theia, Themis, Rheia, Tethys, Mnemosyne, and Phoebe. Of these we may recognise Cronos, Okeanus, and Hyperion as being identical to Shiva/Indra, Varuna (*AV* I,33,2) and Mitra. Hyperion's children include Eos, Helios and Selene, that is, dawn, and the "twins", the sun and the moon. In the *RV* too (VI,49,2), the sun and the moon are called Indra/Rudra's two "daughters", showing the solar (Mitra/Hyperion) quality of Indra in Vedic literature (cf. also p.89 below). The Titans are combated and vanquished by Zeus (GaneshaTeshup/ Seth). This defeat may correspond to that of the Asuras by the gods (also led by Indra) as well as to the killing of Osiris by Seth.

In the Avesta and the *Bundahishn*, the Ādityas, except Mithra and Airyaman, are

Prajāpati as primal creator is said to be the generator of the gods (Devas), the Vasus, the Rudras, as well as the Ādityas and all the worlds.

The Zoroastrian reform of the Vedic religion may have been a moralistic variant of the Vedic with a strong dualistic emphasis on the opposition between the divine Ahura Mazda and the satanic Ahriman (Vedic Angra Mainyu), since the latter is considered as the destroyer of the pure light of Ahura Mazda and the formation of the material universe.[249] That the Zoroastrian reform considered the latter itself to be evil is clear from the Manichaen development of this doctrine which maintained that "the bodily material creation is of the Evil Spirit – all the bodily creation is of the Evil Spirit".[250]

The Avestan Gathas associated with Zoroaster are a collection of sacrificial hymns but the cosmology of the ancient Iranians is revealed more clearly in the Pahlavi *Bundahishn*. Ahura Mazda and Ahriman are both present at the beginning of the creation, the former in the region of the Light (the Vedic Heaven) and the latter in the abysmal Darkness (Earth) between which two regions extends the Void or the Ether (the Mid-region). Ahura Mazda is characterised by "Endless Light" and "Infinite Time". He is thus the same as the Indic Brahman, the first light of Heaven. The Iranian Ahriman must, consequently, represent Earth.

In Ch.XXVI,127 the essence of Ohrmazd is said to be "warm and humid, shining and fragrant wherein ethereality is forthwith manifest". In 3-4, the light of Ohrmazd is described as being of three types, the "unseizable light [khwarrah] created by Ohrmazd, the light of Iran, and the light of the ruling Kays. The unseizable light Khvarrah is that of the Atharvans, "for sagacity is always with them" and Ohrmazd is Himself Atharvan. Khvarrah is perhaps related to the Brahman power,[251] since the Atharvans are the Indo-Iranian brahman priests and the *Atharva Veda* in India is typically associated with the brahman priest.[252] In *GB* I,1,4, too, Prajāpati, who is identical to Brahman, is identified with Atharvan, the founder of a semi-divine family of mythical priests.[253]

Ahura Mazda first creates the Yazads or "good progress, that spirit whereby He can make good His own material body when he may

---

absent. See p.121.

[249] Zoroastrianism is the origin of the Jewish dualistic theology as well.

[250] *Škend Gumānīg Wizār* 16,8ff (see B. Lincoln, *Death, War and Sacrifice*, p.180).

[251] See below p.196.

[252] See below p.253.

[253] See J. Gonda, *Prajapati's Rise to Higher Rank*, p.89.

contemplate the creation of the creatures, for He had lordship through the creation of the creatures" (I,35). The Yazads seem to be a later form of the energies that the supreme Soul activates in manifesting Itself in the Purānic literature. Then, thinking that "there will be no progress of the creatures except by Time", Ahura Mazda is said to have created out of His Infinite Time Time, the Lord of Duration (I,36-7). The Lord of Duration is the same as the Wind (I,53), the counterpart of the Indic Vāyu who, as we shall see, is the same as Kāla.

The first creations of Ahura Mazda (*Bundahishn*,I,44ff.) are in the form of astral bodies constituted of fire:

> Out of his own Self, out of the essence of Light, Ohrmazd created forth the astral body of His own creatures in the astral form of luminous and white Fire ... He created forth the astral body of the good Wind ... Out of the Essence of Lights, Ohrmazd produced Truthful Utterance ... the "Athro" astral form ... out of the "Athro" astral form arose Ahunwar, the Spirit of the "Yatha ahu vairyo" ... from Ahunwar arose the spiritual Year.[254]

In Ch.XXVIII of the *Bundahishn*, the entire universe is compared to a man, an analogy derived from the Indo-European Macroanthropos, Purusha. The skin of the world is said to be the sky, the flesh the earth, the skeleton the mountains, the veins the rivers, the blood the water in the sea, the stomach the ocean, the hair the plants, the bodily essences the metals, the innate wisdom human beings, the wisdom derived through hearing the animals, the heat fire, the implements of hands and feet the seven planets and the twelve constellations, the belly the cloud and the fire Vasishta,[255] inhalation and exhalation of the breath the wind, the liver the ocean Frakhvkart, the spleen the direction of the north, the heart the Aredvisur, the crown of the head and the brain the unapproachable lights, the head the abode of harmony, the two eyes the moon and the sun, the teeth the stars, the two ears the two windows of the abode of harmony, the two nostrils the two bellows of the abode of harmony, the mouth the gate leading to the abode of harmony, the fundament the wicked existence underneath the earth, the soul Ohrmazd, the intelligence, intellect, feeling, thinking, knowing and explication the six Beneficent Immortals (Amesha Spentas). Just as the seat of Ohrmazd is in the unapproachable lights, his access is to the abode of harmony and his energy reaches everywhere, so

---

[254] The Year is an Indo-European synonym for the universe (see below p.217).

[255] For the significance of the sage Vasishta in Indian mythology, see below p.138.

too the seat of the soul is in the pith of the head, its home is in the heart and its energy reaches throughout the body (5).

Owing to the intimate correspondence between the macrocosm and the microcosm, life, intelligence and others of this class belong to Ohrmazd, flesh belongs to Vohuman, the veins and fat to Ardwahisht, the bony frame to Shahrewar, the pith to Spandarmad, the blood to Hordad and the hair to Amurdad (22).

Ahura Mazda and Ahriman fight with each other for dominion over the cosmos and agree to divide a limit of twelve thousand years between themselves, so that the first age, lasting for three thousand years, will be ruled by Ahura Mazda, the next three thousand years by both Ahura Mazda and Ahriman and the final age will see the total victory of Ahura Mazda over Ahriman (Ch.I, 26-8, 42).[256]

As for the material universe, Ohrmazd formed first the Sky, second the Water, third the Earth, fourth the Tree, fifth the Beneficent Animal, sixth Man, [and the seventh in the order of material creations is, again, Ohrmazd himself]. In the *Bundahishn*, Ch.Ia, 4, we learn that Man is followed by the Fire Khvarag ... then he created the Ether in the astral form of a man of fifteen years. From the mention of "the Tree" we may infer that this is a paradigm of the entire animate universe which emerges in the Mid-region of the stars.[257]

The Egyptian counterpart of Purusha is Ptah, who is, in texts from the New Kingdom (Pap. Berlin 3048), described as a macroanthropos dwelling in the sky. Ptah is represented as spanning heaven and earth:

Your feet are on the earth, your head [in] the distant heaven,
...
You raise the work that you have accomplished
By leaning on yourself with your own strength
By raising yourself by virtue of the solidity of your arms.
...
It is your strength which raises the waters towards the distant heaven
The saliva which is in your mouth is the cloud of rain
The breath of your nose is the hurricane
And the water which you spread is on the mountains
The right eye of Ptah is the sun and his left the moon.[258]

---

[256] The Vedic ages, Krita, Treta, Dvāpara and Kali too last for a total of 12,000 divine years (*Manusmriti*, I,69ff.), which equal 4,320,000 human, or solar, years.

[257] See below pp.79ff.

[258] See A. Barucq and F. Daumas, *Hymnes et Prières*, p.396.

Ptah is said to have Horus the Elder (Brahman) as his "heart" [i.e. Intellect] and Thoth as his "tongue" [i.e. Mind]. Ptah is thus the "heart and tongue" of Atum "planning and governing everything he wishes".[259] The heart of Ptah is that element of the cosmic man which shines as the Light of the Cosmos (Atum/Brahman), while the tongue will form the vital moon (Thoth). The moon, as we shall see, is the repository of the seed of all animal life (represented by the slaughtered Bull in the Avesta) while the sun preserves the seed of the slaughtered first Man, Gayomaretan.

The Shabaka text reveals the final identity of Ptah with Horus the Elder/Atum/Brahman, since the latter is but the "face" (with its two luminous eyes) of the supreme deity [Amun/Ātman] whose body (constituted of the gods) is called Ptah (Prajāpati). Ptah is equally identified with the ithyphallic Amun of Luxor in a Saitic sepulchral text on the coffin of Princess Ankhnesneferibre,[260] since he is the same as Amun, whose "body" he represents.

In the Heliopolitan Tura hymn, we get a description of an anthropomorphic deity as the first animate form of the universe:

> He came forth as self-created
> All his limbs speaking to him
> He formed himself before heaven and earth came into being
> The earth being in the primeval waters in the midst of the "weary flood".[261]

In this verse, the "limbs" stand for the gods. In the "Memphite Theology" of the Shabaka stone, the gods are said to enter "every kind of wood, every kind of mineral, every kind of frit, everything that grows all over [Ptah]".[262] In CT 75 the primal god is said to contain in himself the totality of gods, their million "ka"s, or spirits.[263]

Amun is represented as speaking to his limbs, the gods, in the process of creating them. In the hymn to Amun from the 19th century,[264] Amun as Ptah is said to be "the venerable howler", an epithet also given to Rudra-

---

[259]   Memphite Theology, 9 (Shabaka stone) in J.P. Allen, *Genesis in Egypt*, p.43.

[260]   See M.S.-Holmberg, *op.cit.*, p.103.

[261]   See J. Assmann, *Re und Amun*, p.161.

[262]   See J.P. Allen, *op.cit.*, p.44.

[263]   *Ibid.*, pp.15ff.

[264]   See A. Barucq and F. Daumas, *op.cit.*, p.234.

Shiva in the Indic literature,[265] and this "howling" is related to Ptah's utterance of the divine words which create the gods:

> He made his cry resonate, he the venerable howler
> On coming to the earth which he had created when he was alone
> He articulated the [creative] words in the midst of silence
> ...
> He began to howl when the earth was silent
> His bellowing resonated when there was no one else but he
> What he had engendered he caused to live".[266]

In CT 312 IV 74g-75f, the gods are born as "spirits of light" from the "root of the eye" of Atum and constitute his "flesh".[267]

Ptah is also the dispenser of the ka's (characters) and the ba's (souls) of the gods as well as of men during the creation.[268] The ba's can be assigned to Osiris (or Thoth, the 'tongue', and corporealising agent of Ptah) and the ka's to Horus (the 'mind', and photogenetic agent of Ptah), respectively. Though Ptah may have originally been considered a son of Atum, in the Shabaka Ptah text, Ptah is rightly extolled above Atum. The seed and the hands of Atum used in the creative act (usually identified with Shu and Tefnut) are considered the "teeth and lips" of the mouth of Ptah.[269] The "mouth" of the supreme deity represents the power of annunciation: "I am Annunciation in (the Sole Lord's) mouth and Perception in his belly".[270] We notice therefore that this is a pristine, intellectual stage of creation, with the "Desire" of the creator manifest as intellection and intuition. The gods are indeed frequently adored as having been created of the mouth of Amun (that is, through his creative word, Hu).[271]

The Cosmic Egg is formed by Amun himself,[272] but Ptah (Amun's "body") is the name particularly of the materialising agent or the efficient

---

[265]   See *ShP* 12,30.

[266]   See A. Barucq and F. Daumas, *op.cit.*, p.222; cf. J.P. Allen, *op.cit.*, p.51.

[267]   See S. Bickel, *La cosmogonie egyptienne*, p.119.

[268]   This aspect of Ptah is represented by Heka (see S. Bickel, *op.cit.*, p.152ff.), who corresponds to the Vedic Brahmanaspati (see below p.70).

[269]   See M.S.-Holmberg, *op.cit.*, p.122.

[270]   CT 647, in J.P. Allen, *op.cit.*, p.39. Annunciation and Perception are deified as Hu and Sia.

[271]   See S. Bickel, *op.cit.*, p.140.

[272]   "[Amun] Who formed his own egg" (J. Assmann, *op.cit.*, p.138).

force of Amun.[273] In the relatively late Ramesside theogony of Memphis, Ptah is considered to be the demiurgic creator of the Cosmic Egg.[274] Ptah is also revered as the moulder of all living beings,[275] no doubt by virtue of his "tongue", Thoth/Tvoreshtar/Tvashtr, who represents the formative aspect of the supreme deity.

---

[273] See the Suty-Hor hymn (in J. Assmann, *op.cit.*, p,94f.):
"You [Amun-Re] are a Ptah, you cast your body from gold,
One who gives birth,
But is not born".

[274] Ptah is represented as fashioning the Cosmic Egg on a potter's wheel (see E.O. James, *Tree of Life*, p.132; cf. S. Marakhanova, "A Version", p.279).

[275] The Ptah priests are called "supreme leaders of handicrafts" (M.S.-Holmberg, *op.cit.*, p.50).

II.

THE SECOND SACRIFICE: BRAHMAN

T he perfect light of the cosmos that marks the beginning of the second kalpa called Padmakalpa does not last indefinitely as it did in the Brahmakalpa but is destroyed and forced to descend into the underworld whence it emerges later as the sun of our system. Interestingly, modern astronomers too speculate that even the first gigantic fireball, as the source of all the suns of the incipient universe (Mid-region), collapsed after about 3 million years (as supernovas still tend to do) and thereby created the seeds for all the future stars and solar systems of the universe.[276]

The mythological form of the destruction of the first light is to be found in the story of Zeus' swallowing of Phanes in the Orphic cosmogonies. This, as we shall see, is perhaps a euphemism for Zeus's swallowing of Phanes' phallus itself.[277] In the Egyptian mouth-opening rituals too, we note that the moribund Osiris is depicted as being revived with the "thigh" of Seth (the Egyptian counterpart of Zeus), which is clearly a euphemism for the sexual organ of Horus the Elder which he must, like Zeus, have swallowed.[278] In the Indic literature, Ganesha, like his counterparts Zeus/Teshup/Seth, is said, in the *ShP*, to have attacked Brahma – just as his father Shiva/Kāla attacked the primal Heaven of the Purusha. Ganesha is also depicted with a "pot-belly" which contains the

---

[276] See T. Folger, *op.cit.*, p.45.

[277] See below p.67.

[278] Cf. the *Book of Job*, 40:17 where the reference to the tail and thigh of Behemoth are clearly to his penis and testicles (see J.E. Hartley, *The Book of Job*, p.525). Horus is said to have "castrated" Seth as well in 'The Contendings of Horus and Seth' (see below p.68.)

entire universe, since he, like Zeus, must have swallowed the phallus of Brahman after attacking him.[279]

The stormy aspect of Kāla/Chronos/Kumarbi, who causes the castration of the Ideal Man and his subsequent impregnation resulting in the Cosmic Egg, thus persists in the turbulent nature of his offspring. This assault forces the light into the underworld. However, the storm-god also encourages the resurgence of the solar energy in the form of the incipient sun of our system.

In the Hurrian epic of the Kinsghip in Heaven, one of the products of the castrated Anu's seed formed in the belly of Kumarbi is Teshup, the Weather-god,[280] along with the other gods of the Mid-region who include Tashmishu (Suwalliyat, the sun-god), and Marduk. These are the gods who correspond to Seth, Horus the Elder, and Horus the Younger in the Heliopolitan cosmogony. Teshup interestingly is not merely a son of Kumarbi (Enki), but also of An, since it is the latter's seed that is preserved in Kumarbi when Kumarbi bites off An's genitals.[281] Teshup's mother is said to have been Earth (Text Ib9 of the epic) since Earth is the consort of Heaven, who is castrated by Kumarbi.[282] Tashmishu[283] who is called Teshup's "pure brother", may be the Hurrian counterpart of the Hittite Suwalliyat (Sūrya).[284] Teshup is indeed regularly coupled with his "pure brother" Suwalliyat, just as the storm-god Adad is with the solar Shamash.

Just as Seth is represented in Egypt as dragging Osiris down, and Zeus swallows Phanes, or his genitals, their Hurrian counterpart uses a sickle (much like that used by Kumarbi to castrate An) to sever the phallus of Heaven, Ullikummi, from off the shoulders of the giant Uppeluri (symbolising the Cosmic Egg) who bears Heaven and Earth. Since Uppeluri represents the Cosmic Egg, the severing of the "stone" Ullikummi from it clearly denotes Teshup's seizure of the phallus of An

---

[279]   See S.L. Nagar, op.cit., p.115.

[280]   Teshup is a later Hurrian form of the earlier Hattian deity adored in the form of a bull, Taru, Taurit (see KG, p.134f.).

[281]   Kumarbi is himself a chthonic deity. and androgynous, since he gives birth to Teshup and his siblings. Plutarch too (De Iside et Osiride, Ch.12) considers Chronos to be identical to Geb (though Geb is clearly masculine and his consort, Nut, feminine).

[282]   See H.G. Güterbock, Kumarbi, p.87.

[283]   The Hurrian form hides the Akkadian name of the sun-god 'Shamash' within it.

[284]   See H.G. Güterbock, "The God Suwalliyat reconsidered", 1-18. Güterbock considers these names to be indicative of Ninurta and he is right insofar as Ninurta is ultimately the same as his father Enki/Osiris-Horus the Elder, though he is properly the solar seed of his father.

from it. It is significant in this context to note that the commentator of the Orphic Derveni theogony explains that Zeus indeed swallowed "the sexual organ" (aidion).[285] In other versions of the Orphic theogony, Phanes is said to be devoured by Zeus,[286] thereby absorbing the original universe into himself, but we may assume that it is the phallus of Phanes that is thus consumed. From this Orphic evidence we may assume that the Hurrian Teshup too finally swallows this phallus so that the universal life that it contains moves into his own body.[287]

As Seth is given the dominion of heaven in Egypt,[288] so too Teshup's rightful domain as the storm-god is heaven. That Teshup is the equivalent of the Egyptian Seth is borne out by the cuneiform treaty of alliance between Hattusilis and Rameses II, where Shamash, the sun-god, and Teshup are mentioned in the same way as Shamash and Adad, the storm-god, are in Assyria.[289] (The "vizier" [brother] of Teshup is said to be Ninurta, who must then be identical to Suwalliyat/Tashmishu.)[290] We see therefore that the sun-god and weather-god are two aspects of the same deity and co-operate in the formation of the sun of our system. Thus the two are often considered as dual deities, as for instance, Shamash-Adad.

The Egyptian counterpart of Teshup, Seth, is a son of Geb, and the stormy brother of Osiris. An Egyptian text declares that Seth felled Osiris the sky.[291] This felling of the heavenly light is necessary for the emergence of the solar force in the mid-region, since it involves, crucially, the consumption of the heavenly phallus and its transference into the underworld. Thus, although Osiris is murdered by his "brother" Seth, he is later resurrected in the underworld as his son, Horus the Younger, the sun-god of the horizon.

The birth of the sun is related to the tragic passion which Osiris undergoes whereby the light of Heaven is transformed into the principal light of our solar system. Osiris may have been killed by Seth in the form

---

[285] See M.L. West, *Orphic Poems*, p.85. It is not surprising therefore that Protogonos is called both Phanes and Priapus in the Orphic Hymn VI (*ibid.*, p.252).

[286] See M.L. West, *op.cit.*, p88f.

[287] Cf. the similar case of Ganesha above p.65f

[288] See below p.93.

[289] S. Langdon and A.H. Gardiner, "The treaty of alliance between Hattusili, king of the Hittites, and the pharaoh Rameses II of Egypt", *JEA* 6 (1920), 187.

[290] See above p.53.

[291] See above p.52.

of a bull,[292] which is also the form of Teshup/Taru.[293] Osiris' resurrection is, as we shall see,[294] effected ritually in a mouth-opening ritual which requires the heart and the foreleg of a bull (representing Seth),[295] for the foreleg represents Seth's genitals. Seth is, however, merely the *alter ego* of Osiris.[296] That is why the mutilation of Re is also represented as a self-castration of Re in Egypt.[297] Seth, the stormy aspect of Osiris himself, is a god associated with intoxication, and especially the inebriating force of beer: "He confuses the heart to conquer the heart of the enemy".[298] Seth is occasionally also identified with Apop, the serpent that he combats,[299] since the latter represents the gaseous wind which surrounds Earth. Like them, too, Seth is clearly a phallic god, since the moon, Thoth, who is engendered by the homosexual union of Seth and Horus the Younger, itself needs the stimulation of Seth's phallus to become infused with light and sight.[300]

It is true also that Seth plagues the incipient sun, Horus the Younger, who is engaged in several battles with Seth according to 'The Contendings of Horus and Set'. These conflicts include the violation of Horus the Younger by Seth, the castration of Seth by Horus,[301] the decapitation of Isis by Horus for the sympathy shown by her to Seth, and the cutting off

---

[292]   See H. te Velde, *op.cit.*, p.86.

[293]   See below p.71.

[294]   See above p.65.

[295]   H. te Velde (*op.cit.*, p.89) thinks that the foreleg is Seth's, since, in "other texts", the foreleg of Seth is to be "strictly guarded by Isis and the sons of Horus". It is possible that the foreleg has a phallic significance as well since Zeus is supposed to have swallowed the phallus of Heaven (see above p.67). Seth is also represented in the mouth-opening ritual by his metal 'mshtyw', which is mentioned in the chant accompanying the ritual to open Osiris' mouth (*ibid.*, p.88).

[296]   That Seth is but Osiris' *alter ego* was brilliantly suggested by H. Te Velde, *op.cit.*, p.95.

[297]   See M.S. Holmberg, *op.cit.*, p.44.

[298]   Pap. Leiden I 348, rt.13,4; cf., H. Te Velde, *op.cit.*, p.7. The intoxication of Seth is surely related to that of Indra, the soma-drinker, and Dionysus the wine-drinker (see below pp.81,82,184.). According to a Leiden papyrus, his name represents the intoxicating power of beer. As the god of fermented liquor, Seth is clearly a "Bacchic" god. According to Plutarch, the name of Seth means "the overpowering" (see H. Te Velde, *op.cit.*, p.3ff.).

[299]   See H. Te Velde, *op.cit.*, p.104. Plutarch also considers Seth as the equivalent of Typhon (see *De Iside et Osiride*, 367).

[300]   See H. Te Velde, *op.cit.*, p.49f.

[301]   See PT 1463e: "Before the sexual strength of Seth was made impotent" (cf. te Velde, *op.cit.*, pp.57ff. It is not necessary that this line in itself indicate castration, but Horus' stealing of Seth's seed (CT IV,237b) is transformed in the cult to indicate actual castration.

of Horus' hands by Isis.[302] The occurrence of self-mutilation in the rites of
the Syriac god Attis too is related to the castration of Seth but is perhaps
also related to the earlier fate of the sky-god, since Attis is said to have
been castrated by Cybele or Rhea, who is the consort of Chronos.[303]

However, these internecine conflicts are finally resolved, and Seth and
Horus unite in the rule of Heaven and Earth, or the two lands of Egypt,
Upper and Lower.[304] Thus, although Seth is often considered a hostile
god since he kills Osiris, in a text in the Papyrus Jumilhac, Seth (also
called Bata) is depicted as an Apis bull carrying the coffin of Osiris on his
back.[305] The "arm" of Seth is a weapon with which he vanquishes Apop,[306]
to secure the passage of the sun-barque. It is important to note also that it
is Seth who is given rule over Heaven since Osiris/Horus has already been
dragged down from Heaven to the realm of Earth[307] whereas Seth remains
as a god of thunder and storm in the region above it, corresponding to the
Hurrian "weather-god", Teshup and Zeus Adados.

The precise counterpart of the Egyptian and Near Eastern storm-god
in India is Skanda's enigmatic "brother" Ganesha.[308] It is interesting that, in
the Mesopotamian 'An=Anum' list, Shamash the sun-god and his stormy
counterpart dIM are represented as d.Sulaat and d.Ha.ni.is respectively.[309]
The latter may well be the same deity as Ganesha in the Indic religion.
Ganesha is identified in the *RV* and the *AB* with Brahmanaspati, the

---

[302] *BD* Ch.113; see S. Mercer, *op.cit.*, p.74.

[303] See Lucian, *De Dea Syria, The Syrian Goddess*, tr. H.W. Attridge and R.A. Oden, Missoula, MT; Scholars Press, 1976, p.23; cf. p.10 above.

[304] The demonisation of Seth did not begin until the early 18th dynasty, as a reaction to the hateful domination of Egypt by the Hyksos, who worshipped a god identified with Seth (see Te Velde, *op.cit.*, pp.61, 68, 121, 141). According to Plutarch, *De Iside et Osiride*, 30, Seth is also said to have escaped on his ass, during one of his battles, to a place of safety and to have begotten two sons, Hierosolymus and Judaeus. The legend clearly associates Seth with the Hebrew god Yahwe and mocks the Jewish account of "the flight of Moses out of Egypt, and of the settlement of the Jews about Hierusalem and Judaea" (See Budge, *op.cit.*, II.254). The identity of Yahwe to the storm-gods under consideration is highlighted by the "wrathful" nature frequently attributed to him in the OT (cf. A.R.W. Green, *Storm-God*, 2003, Ch.IV).

[305] *Ibid.*, p.97.

[306] *Ibid.*, p.87.

[307] See H. te Velde, *op.cit.*, p.61.

[308] Just as Seth is coeval with Osiris as well as with Horus the Younger, his Indic counterpart Ganesha is equally so with Shiva and Skanda, since the latter is but the solar aspect of his "father".

[309] Tablet III, No.269ff; see R. Litke, *Reconstruction*, p.145.

power of light.[310] We may remember that it is Seth's phallus that infuses the light into the eye of Horus and, as Hornung perceptively suggested, it is possible that Seth is indeed identical to Heka, the Egyptian god who represents the magical source of light,[311] just as Ganesha is identifiable with Brahmanaspati.

Like Seth, Ganesha was apparently considered originally as a malevolent deity called Vināyaka who caused obstacles to men and inflicted barrenness and delirium on them.[312] The cruel aspect of the Sethian cults is reflected in some of the Ganesha cults in India too, which are given to worshipping an obscene image of the god in the course of drunken and sexually promiscuous revels.[313] Further, Ganesha obstructs the sacrificial devotions of the gods (*BrP*) and hinders men from worshipping Soma (*SP*).[314] In the *BrvP*, Ganesha is visited at birth by Sani (Saturn/Chronos, who is the same as Shiva himself),[315] whose maleficious gaze causes Pārvatī's son to lose his head, which is then replaced by Vishnu with the head of an elephant,[316] the form in which he is worshipped today in India. In the *ShP* and the *SP*, it is Shiva himself who beheads his son and then, on Pārvatī's pleading, finds an elephantine replacement for it.[317]

Indra is closely related to Shiva and is an "assistant" of Angra Mainyu (Shiva) in the Avesta. Indra is particularly the tremendous force of solar energy who is characterised especially by his weapon, vajra, which allows the solar energy to emerge as the light of the universe. Thus he is closely related to Shiva's son Ganesha/Seth, who aids the formation of the sun in the underworld. At the same time, Indra is also related to Skanda/Muruga/Marduk and therefore to Enlil's son, Ninurta or Inurta.[318] The latter, however, is indeed the same as his stormy brother since he too –

---

[310] *RV* II,23,1; X,112,9; *AB* IV,4; I,21 (see S.L. Nagar, *Cult*, p.44).

[311] See E. Hornung, *Das Amduat*, I, 81, cf. II, 98; also H. Te Velde, *op.cit.*, p.177.

[312] See the Mānavagrihyasutra and the Vājapayagrihyasutra (in S.L. Nagar, *op.cit.*, p.45).

[313] See 'Ganesa' in *Hindu World*, Vol.1, p.378.

[314] *Ibid.*, pp.16, 49, 52.

[315] See above p.43.

[316] *Ibid.*, p.12f.

[317] *Ibid.*, pp.8f.

[318] This variant spelling is attested in AKF II 12[8]. Among the Kassites, Ninurta is given as one of two Akkadian glosses to the name "Marattaš", which may stand for the leader of the Maruts (see fn. above). Indra is called "marutvat", accompanied by Maruts, in RV I,100,1 (cf. RV III,4,6; III,47,1; III,50,1). Dumezil has suggested that the other gloss, Gi-dar, is also probably a corruption of Indar (see G. Dumezil, *Dieux cassites*, p.27; cf. A. Deimel, *Pantheon*, "Nin-ib", p.210). It is possible also that it is to be read as Mitra (see below p.73n). At any rate, we note that Indra is identified with the solar son of Shiva, Skanda/Ninurta.

like his "brother" Teshup (Seth/Zeus) – is described as fighting the dragon and facilitating the development of the sun.

The birth of Indra, the chief of the gods, resembles that of Seth, who is said to have emerged "sideways from his mother".[319] At RV IV,18,1-2 Indra is said to have issued sideways from his mother Aditi and, on his birth, his mother hid him (IV,18,5). Although this awkward manner of his birth associates Indra with Seth, as well as with Zeus, Seth represents Ganesha, the son of Shiva, rather than Indra himself. Once again we note a fusion of the force represented by Indra/Shiva with Shiva's violent son, Ganesha, who himself is inextricably related to his solar brother Skanda. Indra, who is closely associated with Shiva, is indeed split into the two forces (or "sons") which constitute the solar energy, Skanda and his storm-force Ganesha.

Indra represents the seminal solar force of Shiva which will form the sun. Indra's vital and heroic quality – that of Zeus/Teshup/Ganesha – is emphasised by his frequent epithet of divine 'Bull'.[320] The Bull is also a typical epithet of Teshup of the Hittites, who is a counterpart of Seth/Zeus Adados.[321] Similarly, in Sumer, the term "Bull of Heaven" is used of Girra (Agni), and it also serves as an appellation of Enlil, (CT 24,5,41 and CT 24,41), as well as of Adad (CT XV, 3f.), that is, of the stormy wind-like stages of solar evolution which, finally, are of greater importance in the formation of the sun than the purely luminous element represented by the pure brother of Adad/Seth/Teshup/Ganesha.

Since Indra is associated with Angra Mainyu/Manyu, the opponent of the perfect Light of Ahura Mazda, the Zoroastrians excoriate Indra as an evil 'deva', particularly in the Vendidad. The hostility towards Indra among the Iranians is matched by the later hostility towards Seth among the Egyptians.[322] One further reason for the animosity of the Zoroastrian reformers towards the devas and their leader may have been the fact that Indra, the leader of the gods, as the drinker of Soma may have also

---

[319] See Plutarch, De Iside et Osiride, Ch.12; cf. H. Te Velde, op.cit., p.27.

[320] The adoration of deities in the form of a bull may be traced back to Anatolia, where bovine altars are found in the ruins of Çatal Huyuk from the 7th millennium B.C. The founders of this most ancient culture may have been proto-Hurrians/Dravidians since the Subartu (=Hurrian) culture was widespread in the Near East from very early times (see A. Ungnad, Subartu, p.114) and the transmission of the bull-cult to Sumer may have been via Elam, where the temples, like the present-day South Indian ones, bore bull's horns on their tower (see W. Hinz, Lost World, p.56).

[321] See G. Wilhelm, Hurrians, p.70.

[322] See H. te Velde, op.cit., pp.61, 68, 121, 141.

been worshipped as an orgiastic deity.[323] This may have intensified the Zoroastrian ostracism of his cult.[324]

In Greece, Zeus is the storm-force which swallows Phanes, or his phallus. He thus forces the life and light of Ouranos down into Earth before it can rise up to the sky as the sun. In Homer, Zeus is recognizable as a storm-god, and, according to Diogenes of Apollonia, the Homeric Zeus is the "apotheosis of air [Vāyu]".[325] Zeus is also identified by Herodotus with Teshup's Syrian counterpart, Adad, as Zeus Adados.[326] The fact that Phanes is swallowed by Zeus [Adados] renders more easy the identification of the divine pairs, Phanes and Zeus, Horus the Elder-Osiris and Seth, Tashmisu-Suwalliyat and Teshup, Ninurta and Adad, Skanda and Ganesha, for it is due to the absorption of the vital power of Heaven by the storm-god that the cosmic light is reborn in our system as the sun.

In the Underworld: Varuna-Aditi

In the Egyptian CT, 'Book of the Two Ways', it appears that the course of the solar force of the Heavens is one that takes it into the Earth, that is, the "underworld". Rosetau, for instance, is described as being "at the boundary of the sky" and contains the corpse of Osiris "locked in darkness and surrounded by fire",[327] Osiris' corpse being in the depths of the netherworld.

Interestingly, the waters reached by the sun in the second hour of the *Amduat* are called Wernes, which is reminiscent of the Vedic Varuna.[328] The waters of Wernes are followed by those of Osiris in the third hour. In the fourth hour, however, the waters are replaced by the desert of Rosetau, or Sokar. In the sixth hour, that is, halfway through its passion, the sun of the underworld reaches the waters of Nun after leaving the desert

---

[323] In RV VIII,81, Indra is called, exactly like Shiva, "the dancer" and "the lover of carouse". Indra in the *MBh* is called the god of the seed who is symbolised by "Indra poles" similar to the Shivalingam (see W. O'Flaherty, *op.cit.*, p.85).

[324] S.A. Cook (*The Religion of Ancient Palestine*, p.70) points out a related example of aversion to the orgiastic Dionysiac religion evidenced in a Nabatean/Palmyrene inscription on a seal in the British Museum, where the sky-god or "god of heaven" is called the one "who does not drink wine" as well as the "good and rewarding god".

[325] See A.B. Cook, *Zeus*, I:351.

[326] By the end of the second century B.C., Zeus comes to be identified quite commonly with Adad as Zeus Adados (see A.B. Cook, *op.cit.*, I:549).

[327] *Ibid.*, p.11.

[328] See E. Hornung, *Ancient Egyptian*, p.34.

of Sokar and lies in the waters as the corpse of Osiris. These waters are clearly regenerative, as the Tenth Hour of the *Amduat* makes clear.[329] It is during the sixth hour that the corpse of Osiris is united with the spirit of Re. In *The Book of Caverns,* Osiris, who lies within the earth sphinx Aker at the centre of the underworld, becomes ithyphallic when the spirit of Re passes through the cavern. Since Osiris is but the underworld form of Horus the Elder/Brahman/Ouranos who has been castrated by his son, we see that the sixth hour in the underworld marks the return of his sexual potency. According to the Pyramid Texts, too, Osiris in the underworld is assimilated to Re, the solar force, at midnight.[330] Since it is Zeus/Teshup/Ganesha/Seth who preserves the divine phallus in himself we may also reasonably associate Re with Seth.[331]

In the Indic literature (*KB* 18,9) the sun is said to enter the waters and there become Varuna. This is not just a reference to the setting sun but to the birth of the sun itself in the underworld. Varuna in the underworld. is the same as the Heavenly light Brahman/Mitra that has been shattered by Angra Manyu. From the underworld the solar force rises to the realm of Soma (Mind/Moon/Nanna)[332] and then emerges as the rising sun, Sūrya/Horus the Younger/Shamash. Varuna's typical location in the west[333] corresponds to Osiris' typical appellation as the god of the setting sun and of the spirits of the west, or the "westerners". The western region ruled by Varuna is the entrance to the underworld, the realm of Osiris.

The close relationship between Indra/Shiva/Agni and Varuna (Osiris) is borne out by more than one passage in the Vedas. In *RV* IV, 42, Indra calls himself Varuna "I am King Varuna". However, Indra is not exactly the same as Varuna but a form of him since, in *RV* VII, 82,5 we read that "In peace and quiet Mitra waits on Varuna, the Other [Indra] awful, with the Maruts seeks renown".[334] In *RV* VI, 68, 2, Indra with the mace used against the dragon Vrtra and Mitra are described as companions with

---

[329]   *Ibid.*, pp.33ff.

[330]   See E. Hornung, *Conceptions,* pp.93-6.

[331]   The Indic counterpart of Re is Agni (see p.100 below).

[332]   In the *BP* (V,22,8), the moon (Soma representing the nutritive and energetic force of the moon) is located above the sun ("in the north"), just as the twenty eight constellations are situated above the moon one above the other (V,22,11).

[333]   See *BP* VI,21,7, and below p.299.

[334]   According to the *BP* VI,18,10ff., the Maruts are the sons, not of Aditi, but of Diti, who, like Aditi, is one of the thirteen wives of Kashyapa. They are borne by Diti as Asuras in order to destroy Indra, chief of the devas. However, Indra succeeds in entering Diti's womb and cuts the foetus into seven parts, which multiply seven-fold to form the forty-nine Maruts, who are later converted into devas by Indra and led by him.

contrary characteristics: "One with his might and thunderbolt slays Vrtra; the other (Mitra) as a Sage stands near in troubles" Mitra is typically the "brāhmanical" god, since he is originally the same as Brahman. Indra, on the other hand, is the "kshatriya".

In the Avesta, Xvarenah is the force of the Lord of Earth. This is made clear by the fact that the Zamyad Yasht which is dedicated to the Lord of Earth is actually addressed to Xvarenah. Xvarenah is, in Zamyad Yast (XIX),18, said to belong to all the Amesha (immortal) Spentas (blessed spirits) "who are the makers and governors, the shapers and overseers, the keepers and preservers of these creations of Ahura Mazda". Yima (called the ruler of the universe, the "sevenfold earth" in the same Yasht,31),[335] for instance, succeeds for a while in retaining this xvarenah, but loses it once falsehood enters his mind, at which point the xwarenah flies out of him in the form of a falcon (wareghna), which happens also to be the seventh incarnation of Werethraghna (Bahram Yasht (XIV),19ff).[336] Yima, the ancestor of the present human race, is, we may remember, the counterpart of the seventh Manu of the Padmakalpa, Manu Vaivasvata, Manu of the Sun. So the falcon form of Werethraghna is related to the seventh Manu of our cosmic age. However, Yima's rulership over Earth suggests that he is ultimately the same as the First Man and identifiable with Ptah-Tatenen.[337]

In its falcon form Xvarenah first flies to Mithra (35), then to Thraetaona, and finally to Keresaspa,[338] son of Thraetaona. Mithra is equivalent to Horus the Younger. Thraetaona[339] is said to battle the monster Asi Dahaka[340] (Zamyad Yasht XIX,37; Fargard XX) for the possession of this precious substance. In Zamyad Yasht VIII,45,52, Atar combats the same serpent for the Xvarenah, so Thraetona must be closely related to Atar. In Zamyad Yasht XIX,51ff, Atar succeeds in restoring the

---

[335] The xvarenah is said to belong particularly to "the Aryan countries" (Yasht XIX,56).

[336] Of the ten incarnations of Werethraghna, the first is as Vāyu (the Wind), then as a bull, a horse, a camel, a boar, a youth, a falcon, a ram, a goat and, finally, a man. Since the falcon is a typical symbol of the sun of ours system, it is possible that each incarnation corresponds to an Indian "manavantara". However, the ten incarnations cannot be easily made to correspond to the fourteen manavantaras. Also, these incarnations do not correspond exactly to the ten of Vishnu in the Purānas. Further, in *BP* II,7, Vishnu is given more than ten incarnations.

[337] See below p.77. Tatenen is the later, universal form of the cosmic Ptah. So the seventh Manu too is a form of the first. That is why the name Ymir is used for the first Manu, the macroanthropos, in the Germanic Edda (see below p.220).

[338] Keresaspa may be the Iranian original of the Sanskrit Kashyapa (see below p.129).

[339] It is not certain if Thraetona is related to the Traitona of *RV* I,158,5.

[340] Asi Dahaka is the same as the Sumerian Asakku (see below p.110).

Xvarenah to the Vouru-Kasha sea (the Abyss). Atar is the same as Seth/ Teshup/Ganesha, and, as we have seen, also identifiable with Heka/ Brahmanaspati.[341] In the Avesta, Atar is called a son of the primal god Ahura Mazda (Yasna 62,7).[342] Atar may also be identified with the deity called "Apām Napāt" (child of the waters) who is also equivalent to Agni, particularly as the incipient sun. Atar is thus the stormy-force (Ganesha/ Seth) in the underworld that helps in the formation of the sun of our system.[343] Thraetona is also called Āthwya[344] and may thus be the same as Trita Āptya, who is a form of Agni[345] that helps Indra in his fight against the monstrous Vishvarupa for the release of the solar force (SB I,ii,3,1- 2).[346] For Thrita too is referred to in Yasna IX,10 as smiting the serpent Dahaka, which equates Dahaka with Vishvarūpā.

When Thraetona's son Keresaspa takes possession of the xvarenah, he similarly does battle with the serpent as well as with "the golden-heeled Gandareva that was rushing with open jaws, eager to destroy the living world of the good principle" (Yasht XIX,41).[347] When it finally reaches the Vouru-kasha sea,[348] where is no doubt situated the cosmic tree representing the new universe, it is guarded by Apām Napāt (Agni as the child of the waters), who bestows it then to the material world, along with "the waters" and the "mighty Wind" and the "frawashis [souls][349] of the faithfull" (Tir Yasht (VIII), 34).[350]

---

[341] See above p.70.

[342] See below p.254.

[343] Since Brahmanaspati is also identical with Seth/Ganesha, it is not surprising that he is called "Atharvan" in AV IV,1,6.

[344] See A.K. Lahiri, op.cit., p.188.

[345] The three Āptya forms are Ekata ("the first"), Dvita ("the second"), and Trita ("the third") (SB I,ii,3,1).

[346] In RV X,8,8 Trita Āptya is said to have killed the three-headed son of Tvashtr, while in RV X,8,9, Indra too is credited with this deed. However, Trita Āptya is, in SB I,ii,3,2, characterised as a brāhmanical force (just as Mitra is; see below p.121) in contrast to Indra, the kshatriya. In SB IV,i,4,4, kshatram (sovereignty) is attributed to Varuna, who is equivalent to Indra. In SB IX,iii,4,18, however, Brahmanaspati symbolises the priesthood, while Indra represents the nobility. We note again the familial partnership between the Vedic Indra and Atar/Brahmanaspati/Ganesha, a partnership that the Zoroastrians who decry Indra are obviously unaware of.

[347] Gandharvas are heavenly singers in the Vedas and it is interesting to note them too included as enemies of the fire-god in the Avesta.

[348] In the Sumerian and Indic literature Enki and Varuna are especially connected to the Tree of Life in the Abyss (see below p.80).

[349] The Iranian term "frawashi" is related to the Sanskrit "urwashi" meaning a female spirit.

[350] We see here that Agni/Atar takes the place of Indra as purveyor of fire to our universe.

The Lordship of the Abyss in the Iranian religion is thus represented by the fire-god in the extreme fiery form of Xvarenah. In Mihr Yasht (X),127 Xvarenah is represented as going before Werethraghna (Vishnu),[351] who himself precedes Mithra – who heralds the sun, Hvare. Werethraghna himself is preceded by Atar, who, we have just seen, is identifiable with Seth/Brahmanaspati. In Mihr Yasht (X),70, we find Werethraghna/ Vishnu, as Mithra's herald in the form of a boar (the original form of the wind Vāyu through which Vishnu first extracts Earth from the Abyss). That Vāyu is a form of Werethraghna/Vishnu futher confirms the solar quality of Vāyu/Enlil as the second incarnation (birth) of Agni. In Mihr Yasht X,13, too, the sun Hvare follows Mithra. Thus we see that the order of the solar formation, Xvarenah (Agni), Werethraghna (Vāyu), Mithra (Āditya) is the same in the Avesta as in the Vedas. This order is, besides, a repetition in the underworld of the cosmic sequence which produced the Heavenly Light of Brahman.

In the Vedas, the watery consort of the solar force in the underworld, Varuna, is Aditi. One of the typical forms of Aditi as goddess of Earth is as a Cow (Prishnī).[352] The consort of Aditi, Varuna, is sometimes called Vishnu since it is Varuna that develops into Vishnu, the solar force that eventually rises as the sun of our system.[353] Vishnu is not only a son of Aditi but also her consort, that is, both Horus the Younger and Horus the Elder/Osiris. In *KYV* VII,5,14, Aditi is described as Vishnu's consort. Sesha, the serpent on which Vishnu sleeps, is the Māyā or illusory power of Shiva himself. We note that the sleep of the solar force in the underworld is a repetition of the original sleep of the Ātman in the cosmic waters. It may also be remarked that the serpentine form of Osiris around the underworld resembles that of the wind-serpent (Shu/Chronos) around the original Cosmic Egg.[354]

We have seen that Indra is indistinguishable from Shiva, who is the first form of Agni according to the Purānas (see p.42n).

[351] That Werethraghna corresponds to Vishnu/Varuna is made clear by the fact that in the Werethraghna Yasht (14), 2, Vāyu is the first incarnation of Werethraghna (see above p.74), Vāyu being the form that the deity assumes to operate on the waters (see above p.39).

[352] Prshni, the consort of Rudra, who is called the Cow in *RV* VI,66,1, is identifiable with Aditi (see Sāyana's commentary to *RV* II,34).

[353] See *KYV* VII,5,14.

[354] See Epiphanius' account of Epicurus' cosmology, in M.L. West, *Orphic Poems*, p.202.

The Rising Earth

We have seen that, in *The Book of Caverns,* the dead Osiris at the centre of the underworld becomes ithyphallic when the spirit of Re passes through the cavern. This represents the reviving light of the universe, as well as of the soul (Ātman), which is now in the process of being regenerated as the sun after the purging of the passionate element represented by Osiris' *alter ego* Seth. Osiris as the solar force of the universe thus begins to rise from Earth, which is represented by a primeval mound, Tatenen (who is identical to Osiris' father, Geb), and surrounded by the serpent Nehaher, who is but another form of himself.[355]Since Earth constitutes the "trunk" of the Tree of Life that is based in the Abyss and whose branches represent the Mid-region between the Earth and Heaven (where the sun is located), it is the lowest part of the universe, whose highest realm is ruled by the sun. Tatenen is identified also with Geb in the "Book of Gates" (scene 51), and with Osiris,[356] since the universe that rises from the underworld is indeed the restored phallic force of Osiris. In the "Book of Earth", the identification of Tatenen and Geb with Osiris is glossed with the explanation that, while Geb is the name of the God of Earth itself, Tatenen is that of the god as hidden in the serpent,[357] that is, as the nascent universe.

The god who rules Earth itself is also called Ptah-Tatenen.[358] Tatenen is an aspect of Ptah as the "rising universe".[359] Tatenen is also the creator of gods and men.[360] In a hymn to Amun, the supreme god is described as having first assumed the form of the Hermopolitan Ogdoad and then that of Tatenen in order to bring forth the primeval gods.[361] In a Theban hymn from the time of Rameses II (Pap. Leyden I, 350), Amun is said to have transformed himself into Ptah-Tatenen "in order to give birth to the Primordial gods".[362]

---

[355]   See R.T. Rundle Clark, *op.cit.,*pp.169ff.

[356]   See J. Assmann, *op.cit.,* p.146 (cf. H.A. Schloegl, *Der Gott Tatenen,* p.35).

[357]   Tatenen, like Geb, is closely associated with the snake which guards the solar force within its coils in the underworld (cf. E. Hornung, *op.cit.,* p.100; H.A. Schloegl, *op.cit.,* p.96). Tatenen is an aspect of Osiris, lord of the underworld, and helps bring forth the sun, Horus the Younger (see H.A. Schloegl, *op.cit.,* pp.84ff., p.117).

[358]   See E.A.E. Reymond, *op.cit.,* p.63.

[359]   Cf. H.A. Schloegl, *op.cit.,* p.71.

[360]   See W. Helck, *Urkundenen,* 284 (cf. H.A. Schloegl, *op.cit.,* p.39).

[361]   See J. Assmann, *Ägyptische Hymnen,* p.315 (cf. H.A. Schloegl, *ibid.,* pp.75ff.).

[362]   See M.S. Holmberg, *op.cit.,* p.168.

The Djed column, which is a symbol of Geb, is also a most ancient symbol of Osiris himself,[363] since Osiris and Seth are but two aspects (sons) of Geb. The pillar is considered as the "backbone" of Osiris.[364] R. Cook has suggested that the Djed has the form precisely of the sacrum, the lowest joint of the backbone, which is the seat of sexuality wherein the serpent Kundalini (of the Indian Yogic system)[365] resides.[366] And the aim of yogic discipline as well as of the cosmic evolution is to purify the passions in order to allow the spiritual light to emerge as the light of the universe.

The universe is considered as having emerged from a "navel", which is the "sanctuary" within the original Abyss. In Mesopotamia, Eridu[367] may have been considered the earthly manifestation of the navel of the universe in much the same way that, much later, Jerusalem was considered the sacred sanctuary of Israel,[368] and Madurai of the Indic Dravidian lands.[369] In the Sumerian myth of "Enki's Journey to Nippur", too, Enki is represented as raising the "city" from the Abyss as a mountain above the waters,[370] which is clearly symbolic of the first emergence of the universe. The sanctuary, the 'navel' of the macroanthropos, is, as we shall see,[371] associated with a high mountain that cannot be touched by the deluge and thus survives it. The ancient temple structures of India, Sumer and Egypt embodied the navel and the primeval hill in their shrine and tower respectively. The mountain and navel also represent the phallic deity Shiva and his consort Parvathi (representing the cosmic vulva), together constituting the entire emergent universe. In the RV, the navel whence the universe arises is called the place of the "sacrifice", and the womb of

---

[363]   See E.O. James, op.cit., p.38. Osiris is, like Enki/Ninurta/Varuna, the Lord of Earth.

[364]   See LÄ I:1100ff.

[365]   See below pp.314ff

[366]   See R. Cook, Tree of Life, p.14. As V.G. Rele, op.cit., p.104, suggests, Kundalini is probably the same as the Vedic Vrtra.

[367]   The original form of Eridu may have been Uru-du, meaning "good(=holy) city".

[368]   See A. Wensinck, op.cit., p.15. Mt. Sion especially was considered the centre of the navel by the Hebrews. Some Moslem theologians transferred this centre to Mecca, though others continued to consider Jerusalem as the source of the creation, especially the Holy Rock, under which arises all the "sweet water" of the world (ibid., p.33). The concept of "sweet" waters is clearly derived from the Enki/Varuna theology of Eridu (see below p.279).

[369]   See D. Shulman, Tamil Flood Myths, pp.311ff.

[370]   See S. Kramer, Sumerian Mythology, 61ff.; E.O. James, op.cit., p.139.

[371]   See below p.137.

Rta [Maat].[372] The Vedic sacrificial altar is also considered as the womb of the entire universe (Earth) which is ritually created and sustained by the Vedic priests.[373]

In the *AV* X,7,[374] the phallic power of Purusha is addressed as Skambha, the Pillar or Fulcrum of life, that on which "Prajāpati set up and firmly established all the worlds/ The universe which Prajāpati created, wearing all the forms, the highest, midmost, lowest". The head of Skambha is formed by Agni Vaishvānara, the Angirasas constitute his eye, and Yātus his corporeal parts. In Skambha are contained all the "thirty three deities" who are disposed as "his limbs". Skambha is also identified with Indra and Brahman, whose "base is Earth, stomach Air, head the Heavens", eyes the sun and moon, mouth Agni, two life-breaths the Wind, his sense-organs the regions. He is finally identified with "the Reed of Gold that stands amid the flood". The flood and the reed we shall encounter and study a little later.[375]

Ashvattha – the Tree of Life

The reviving potency of Osiris in the sixth hour of the *Amduat* betokens the rise of the universal life contained in the phallus of Heaven (Horus the Elder-Osiris) into the Mid-Region of our universe between Heaven and Earth. We know also that the divine phallus was absorbed by Zeus/Teshup/Seth so that the entire universe moved into his "stomach". This suggests once again that Seth is indeed the life-force of Osiris. The rising phallic force of this deity is often represented as a "tree" of life.

The universal tree has its roots in the Abyss while its trunk represents Earth and branches the Mid-region. Atop its branches, in Heaven, will emerge the full-fledged sun. In the Indic sacred literature, the 'ashvattha' fig-tree is considered to be inverted, so that its roots grow upwards and its branches spread downwards.[376] That the tree is an analogue of the phallus is made clear by the reference in *LP* 17ff. to the phallus too as an endless column of fire which fills the universe, and at the top of which is Brahma in the solar form of a swan (hamsa) and at the base of which is Vishnu in

---

[372] See *RV* II,3,7; *RV* IX,72,7; *RV* IX,82,3; *RV* IX, 86,8.

[373] See below p.297.

[374] See below pp.339ff.

[375] See below p.136.

[376] *Katha Upanishad*, VI,1.

the form of a boar.[377] The sun-god (Sūrya/Āditya) is a later manifestation within our universe of the original light of the universe, Brahman, which appeared above the "lotus" Earth.

In India, as in Sumer, the tree of life spans the entire universe comprising the three regions of earth, the mid-region, and the heavens, which are dominated respectively by the three forms that the solar energy assumes in our universe as well as in the primal cosmos – Agni, Vāyu, Āditya. Agni is, in *KYV* V,5,1, called "the lowest of deities", while Vishnu (i.e. as Āditya) is the highest. In the *Maitrāyana Upanishad* VI,4, the tree (called metonymously "Brahman") is called "three-footed", and from the evidence of the Germanic Edda we may consider these feet or roots as not restricted to heaven but as equally embracing Heaven, Earth and the Mid-Region.[378]

Just as the Sumerian Enki does, so too Varuna, in *RV* I,24,7, "sustaineth erect the Tree's stem in the baseless region [the Abyss, apsu]", for Varuna is the Lord of the Abyss. The roots of the tree arise from deep within the Abyss, while the trunk represents Earth. The branches of the Tree of Life represent the Mid-region of the manifest universe and the sun which arises from atop them rules this region as well. The passage from the *Maitrāyana Upanishad* mentioned above further makes clear that the "branches", which represent the Mid-region of the manifest universe, contain "space, wind, fire, water, earth and the like". The summit of the tree, that is, the highest point of its branches, represents Heaven, the domain of the gods. The highest of the three heavens serves as the seat of the gods (*AV* V,4,3,4). There the Ādityas enjoy their nectar of immortality,[379] while Yama (*RV* X,135,1) is ruler of the lowest heaven. According to *AV* V,4,3, the original location of Soma, which infuses the entire Tree, is in the highest heavens.

In the *MBh*, the infant Vishnu is found *under* an "ashvattha" tree during the flood, which may be a depiction of the sun of the underworld since the roots of the tree are in the Abyss.[380] The use of Vishnu as the

---

[377]   The representation of Vishnu as a boar corresponds to Vāyu as the life of the universe (see above p.38). The boar form of Verethreghna also heralds Mithra in the Avesta, Mihir Yasht XVIII (see below p.346).

[378]   Moslem literature too retains the image of a downward tending cosmic tree which reaches to the lowest heaven. A similar tree growing from the lowest depths of Hell, however, grows upwards (See A.J. Wensinck, "Tree and Bird", pp.33,35).

[379]   The first of the Ādityas, Mitra-Varuna, are the lords of rta, or the me's, of the universe, the waters in which they were born being the seat of these me's.

[380]   Within the human microcosm, Rele identifies Vishnu with the spinal cord itself (see V.G. Rele, *op.cit.*, pp.71-3).

deity at the base of the phallus [tree] in the *LP* is related to the evolution of the solar force from the moribund Varuna. In the Avesta, interestingly, Vishnu (Werethraghna) is represented as a boar, which is the form associated with Vāyu.[381] In fact, the Tree is the locus of the second universal form of Agni arisen from Earth[382] and one displaying the power of Vāyu, the Wind-god.[383]

The tree of life holds Heaven and Earth together and is also identified with Indra,[384] who, as we have seen, was also identified with the Ideal Man, Purusha.[385] Indra is called "the Bull" who has drunk the powerful Soma:

6. This Bull's most gracious far-extended favour existed first of all in full abundance.
By his support they [the Ādityas] are maintained in common who in the Asura's mansions dwell together.
7. What was the tree, what wood,[386] in sooth, produced it, from which they fashioned forth the Earth and Heaven?
These Twain [earth and heaven] stand fast and wax not old for ever:
...
... He is the Bull, the Heaven's and Earth's supporter.

In *AV* IV,11,2 Indra is called the "draft ox" who sustains the earth and heaven.

In *RV* III,31, Indra develops into a universal tree as a result of his consumption of soma and this soma-inspired growth holds Earth and Heaven together:

11. For [Indra] the Cow [Aditi], noble and far-extending, poured pleasant juices, bringing oil and sweetness.
12. They [the kine] made a mansion for their Father [their protector, Indra], deftly provided him a great and glorious dwelling/ With firm support parted and stayed the Parents [Heaven and Earth], and sitting, fixed him there erected, mighty.

---

[381] See above p.38.

[382] See below Ch.III.

[383] Cf. the association of Wotan with the Yggdrasil tree below p.115.

[384] Indra is the mystical name of Indha, which, according to *SB* VI,i,1,2, means "the blower", a name that relates Indra to Vāyu.

[385] See above p.38.

[386] This particular curiosity with regard to the "wood" of the tree is clearly addressed to the erect phallus as well.

13. What time the ample chalice [of soma] had impelled him, swift waxing, vast, to pierce the earth and heaven.

and *RV* II,15:

High heaven unsupported in space he stablished: he filled the two worlds [earth and heaven] and the air's Mid-region.
Earth he upheld, and gave it wide expansion. These things did Indra in the Soma's rapture.

Indra is always closely associated with the "Soma" or seminal fluid of the universe and he is called the "lord of the seed".[387] Indra is said to have imbibed the sap of life, Soma (seed), in the dwelling of Tvashtr, who is an aspect of Dyaus. Soma is described in *RV* III,48,2-3 as that milk which Indra's mother, Aditi, "poured for thee [Indra] in thy mighty Father's dwelling./ Desiring food he came unto his Mother, and on her breast beheld the pungent Soma."[388] At *RV* III,I,7, the infant "Agni" is said to be nourished by the "milch-kine" (solar rays) which are present in the seven cosmic rivers which issue out of the mountain when Indra destroys the serpent Vrtra. The "cows" (the water of Aditi) are said to be impregnated by the "bull". At *RV* I,84,15 the "milch-kine" are said to have recognized their lord as Tvashtr's Bull in the mansion of the moon, the moon being the heavenly body in which the Soma will be finally stored.[389]

Indra's intoxication with Soma is also the source of the Dionysiac and Bacchic wine-rituals. Soma thus represents the creative potency of fire which is responsible for the formation of our universe and its light but must nevertheless be controlled in order to allow the sun to emerge as the ruler of the universe. In this context, it may be noted that, in the Brāhmanas, the moon (*SB* I,vi,4,18) as well as Soma (*SB* III,iv,3,13) is called Vrtra,[390] the serpent, which we shall see is also infused with Soma and Agni. The moon, which is always associated with Soma, is indeed considered to be a form of Agni as Kāma (Desire).

---

[387]   *MBh* I, 57, 1-27.

[388]   That soma is ultimately the same as (Ger.) Samen/seed, which infuses Indra as the "Tree" of Life, is clear from this reference to Indra consuming soma at his mother's breast, since, according to the *Bundahishn* Ch.XVI,5, the woman's milk is produced by the male seed just as blood is produced by the female.

[389]   See below p.91.

[390]   See A.K. Lahiri, *Vedic Vrtra*, pp.181,183.

It has been suggested, also, that, in the human microcosmos, the Tree may be manifest as the central nervous system.[391] Since the base of the spinal cord is the seat of unconscious, as well as of sexual, activity, it is indeed the task of spiritual man in the yogic system to rise to supraconsciousness by mastering the "serpent".[392] The tree which sustains the microcosmos as well as the macrocosmos is, indeed, filled with the seed of desire which, when it succeeds in producing the clear light of consciousness (Brahman) in enlightened man, at once prompts the destruction of the tree itself as an illusion.[393]

In Mesopotamia, the solar deities Tammuz and Dionysus and Ninurta are all admired as a Tree of Life, which is indeed symbolic of the entire universe at the head of which appears the sun. Shamash and Tammuz, representing the sun of heaven and the sun of earth, are indeed represented as the guardians of the Tree of Life.[394] In the Sumerian poem, "Enki and the World-Order", the roots of the cosmic tree are generated by Enki in the Abyss. Enki is called (l.3) the son of Enlil (Shu) and of An (Horus the Elder), though he is the same as both. Enki is said to have planted the "me tree" or the tree of life in the Abzu. This tree, called a "kishkanu" (Sumerian "gishkin") tree in an Akkadian hymn to the "tree of Eridu", extends from the depths of the apsu, where Enki dwells, to the heights of heaven, and represents at the same time the pathway of Enki to mankind.[395] In the 'Epic of Gilgamesh' (IX,164ff) too, the hero finds a tree of "cornelian"and "lapis lazuli" at the eastern end of Earth, from whence the sun, Shamash, ascends to the heavens.[396] The protective shade of the tree is said to spread over the entire universe. At l.69 of "Enki and the World-Order" Enki is called the "great light who rises over the great below", as well as the "great lord of Sumer".[397]

---

[391] For an understanding of the tree within the human microcosm as the structure of the entire nervous system itself see V.G. Rele, *op.cit.*, pp.26f. The two hemispheres of the brain are considered by Rele as symbolic of the two heavens, while the base of the spinal cord represents Earth.

[392] See below p.105.

[393] This characteristic Indo-European spirituality is recovered in the West in the philosophy of Arthur Schopenhauer (especially in his masterwork, *Die Welt als Wille und Vorstellung*, 1819).

[394] See S. Langdon, *Tammuz and Ishtar*, p.31.

[395] See 'The Poem of Erra', I,150; cf. M. Rutten, "Les Religions Asianiques", p. 98f.

[396] See A.J. Wensinck, "Tree and Bird", p.3. In *Daniel* 4:10-17, Nebuchadnezzar describes a dream of a similar cosmic tree, and so too does Ezekiel in *Ezekiel* 31:3 (cf. A.J. Wensinck, *ibid.*, pp.25f.).

[397] Sumer itself is most probably the name of the "primordial hill" of the central island

That Ninurta is only a continuation of Enki is made clear by the reference to Enki's 'makurru' boat (l.107), the sun-barque which is featured prominently as Ninurta's own in *Lugal e*. In fact, Enki is said to have received the "lofty sun-disk" in Eridu (l.121) showing that as ruler of the underworld he is identical to the "dead" Osiris who is transformed into Horus the Younger. Since Ninurta is a counterpart of Marduk, it is not surprising that Marduk is also called "Ea" in *EE*, VII,120. However, as we shall see, Marduk is particularly the force of the incipient sun in the underworld.

Ninurta is also admired as the axis of the universe or tree of life. That the tree of life is a symbol of Enlil's warrior son, or "strong arm",[398] Ninurta, is made clear in the epic *Lugal e* (l.189), where Ninurta is called "the cedar which grows in the Abzu" (l.189)[399] as well as "the great Meš tree" (l.310).[400] Ninurta is also called the "date-palm" in the An=Anum god-list, Tablet I, ^dLugal.giš.gišimmar ($ŠA_6$).[401] The mešu tree is like the kishkanu tree since, in the Irra myth,[402] its roots are said to be in the Ocean and its top touches the heavens. The mešu tree is called the "flesh of the gods" (*Poem of Erra*, I,150), since, as we have seen, its trunk represents 'earth', the material substance of the universe.[403]

We have noted that Indra is infused with the powerful seminal force of Soma, It is not surprising that Ninurta, like Shiva's son, Skanda, represents the seed of Enlil.[404] Ninurta is, like his father Enlil, also said to be a great "mountain" [i.e. phallus] which extends from earth to heaven. According to KAR 142,I,22ff, Ninurta's seminal force appears in seven forms as dIB (Urash),[405] Nin-urta, Za-ba-ba,[406] Na-bi-um, Ne-iri-gal, Sa-

---

of Earth, through which the solar force of the universe emerges since Sumer is called "the great mountain, the land of the universe" in l.192. Sumeru ('Holy Meru') is also a name of Mt. Meru in *BrdP* I,ii,15,42. The names of the other lands around Sumer – Ur, Meluhha, Dilmun, Elam-Marhasi, and Martu - which Enki blesses in the poem of "Enki and the World-Order" may have similar cosmological significances.

[398] See J. Van Dijk, *Lugal ud*, p.29. The strong arm of Ninurta is itself personified as Adad/Sarur (see below p.118).

[399] *Ibid.*, p.75.

[400] *Ibid.*, p.90.

[401] See R. Litke, *op.cit.*, p.46.

[402] See E. Ebeling, KARI, 168, Rs.I, l.28ff.

[403] See above p.80.

[404] So in the myth "*Lugal-e*" (see T. Jacobsen, *Treasures*, p.131).

[405] Urash refers to Enki as Lord of Earth, or the underworld, where Varuna/Osiris lies before his development as the sun.

[406] This is also an appellation of Marduk (See K. Tallquist, *Akkadische Götterepitheta*, p.364).

kud and Pa-bil-sag.[407] The Dilmunite[408] name of Nabium/Nabû, d.En-
sa6-ag, in the myth of "Enki and Ninhursag", also contains a reference to
the date-palm, just as the date-palm branch engraved on the left side of a
Rimum inscription also hints at this metaphorical name of Nabû.[409] Nabû
is particularly the force within the moon (Soma).

According to the Iranian *Greater Bundahishn*, Ch.XIV, the First Man,
Gayomard gave birth autoerotically to the twins Mashye and Mashyane,
who grew up "in the semblance of a tree, whose fruit was the ten races
of mankind" (10). We have seen that the Tree of Life represents the life
of the universe in the Mid-Region between Earth and Heaven. Gayomard
is the same as Brahman/Prajāpati/Horus the Elder, who is struck down
by Ganesha/Zeus/Seth and forced into the underworld. These twins of
Gayomard are said to have offered the first sacrifice (21): "They dropped
three handfuls of meat into the fire and said, "This is the share of the Fire",
and they tossed a portion of the rest to the sky, and said, "This is the share
of the Yazads".

In the Avesta (Rashn Yasht, XII,17), it is stated that, in the centre of
the Vouru-kasha Sea (the Abyss), stands "the tree of the eagle ... that is
called the tree of good remedies ... on which rest the seeds of all plants".[410]
At the base of the tree is a "lizard" created by Ahriman to destroy the tree.
However ten fish save the tree by continually swimming around it.[411]

As regards the "sun-bird" or "eagle" that appears also in the fire-altars
of the Vedic Indians,[412] we note, on the Indic Mitanni seals of the second
millennium B.C., that the winged disk representing the emergence of the
sun[413] is sometimes supported on a sacred pillar, while on other seals the
wings of the disk are transformed into the branches of a tree. The branches
of the Tree of Life, as we have seen, represent the Mid-Region between
heaven and earth, and the bird itself must represent the eagle of the

---

[407] See K. Tallquist, *op.cit.*, p. 421

[408] We have seen already that Dilmun itself signifies the spot at which the sun rises, and
is the paradise (the lower heavens) to which Ziusudra, the survivor of the cosmic flood
(Yima/Manu), is sent at the end of his life.

[409] See K. Al-Nashef, "The Deities of Dilmun", p.346.

[410] Yasna 42,4 also mentions a sacred [unicorn] beast which stands in the Vouru-kasha
sea; cf. *Bundahishn*, XIX, which refers to a three-legged ass with one horn, and the Indus
seals with their many representations of a beast resembling a unicorn bull.

[411] See *Bundahishn*, XVIII,2. These piscine forms reappear in the story of the fish which
saves Manu during the flood (see below p.104).

[412] See below p.230.

[413] The wings are those of a falcon, which, in Egyptian as well as Avestan religion,
represents a solar form of the divine energy.

Avesta. In Assyria, too, Ashur is frequently represented by a winged disk hovering over a tree.[414] In the biblical book of *Ezechiel* 31:3, for example, Assur, the Assyrian king, is described in the image of a cosmic "cedar of Lebanon".

In the poetic Edda, the name of the Yggdrasil ash-tree may be phonetically related to the Vedic Indra.[415] We may note the similarity of the description of this tree in "Voluspa" and "Grimnismal" to those in the Vedas, and in Mesopotamian and Egyptian cosmological literature:

> I know an ash-tree stands called Yggdrasill,
> a high tree, soaked with shining loam.[416]

and:

> Three roots there grow in three directions
> under the ash of Yggdrasil;
> Hel lives under one, under the second the frost-giants,
> the third humankind.

> Ratatosk is the squirrel's name who has to run
> upon the ash of Yggdrasil;
> the eagle's[417] word he must bring from above
> and tell to Nidhogg below.[418]

---

[414] See E.O. James, *op.cit.*, pp.43,97. If Ashur as the divine power of the sun seems to resemble here the Babylonian Marduk ("the one within the sun"), that is due to the ultimate identity of Marduk and Ea (*EE* II,8), who, as we have seen, is but a form of Enlil (see above p.44).

[415] See below p.185n for the use of the suffix 'šiel' with Indic divine names among the Mitanni. The popular interpretation of Yggdrasil, however (see, for instance, R. Cook, *op.cit.*, p.23), is as "steed of Odin", from Ygg, one of the names of this god meaning "the terrible" (see 'Grimnismal', st.54). The tree is associated with the horse in the Odin myth as well as in shamanistic rituals which depict the "ride" or "ascent" of the shaman to heaven (see M. Eliade, *Shamanism,* p.270). Indeed, the Vedic term "ashvattha" for the fig-tree itself contains the word for horse "ashva" (see J. Miller, *op.cit.*, pp.249f.). The conflation of arboreal and equestrian symbolism is perhaps related to the original conception of the universe as a phallus and of the sun that illuminates it. In the royal horse-sacrifice of the Indo-Āryans, the horse is said to be produced from the "left eye" of Prajāpati (*SB* XIII,iii,1,1) so that the sacrifice of the horse is meant to restore this eye to its proper place. The eye is here clearly a symbol of the sun.

[416] Voluspa, 19, in *Poetic Edda*, p.6. The "shining loam" is the same as "soma", the life-giving sap of the cosmic tree.

[417] The eagle represents the sun (see. p.208 below).

[418] Grimnismal, 31-32, in *Poetic Edda*, p.56.

Like the Indian tree, the Yggdrasil also grows downwards, since one of its roots is said to be based in the heavens, where the gods (Aesir/Asuras) hold court. Under this root is the well of Urd.[419] In one region of heaven called Valaskjalf (the hall of the slain) is to be found the seat of Odin, called Hlidskjalf, whence he surveys the nine worlds covered by the tree [there being three heavens, as well as three mid-regions and earths].

The second root reaches the Ginnungagap (the Abyss), where the "frost ogres" dwell. Here is to be found an oracular spring guarded by the sage Mimir.[420] This region represents the waters from which the sun is finally born (just as it is born also from Heaven and from Earth). The third root ends in Hel, or Niflheim, which is Earth as well as the land of the dead, the underworld. At the base of this region dwells the serpent Nidhogg[421] in the well called Hvergelmir.

We may assume that between Niflheim and heaven is the realm of Ymir, which is the Mid-region of the material universe. In Indic literature, the lower heavens is ruled by Yama, who is also the king of the dead.[422] The "squirrel" which bears the "word" of the eagle in the branches of the cosmic ash to the serpent below must represent the jīva as described in the *Dhyānabindhu Upanishad* and the Kundalini-Yoga system.[423] That the Nordic tree represents the axis from which the sun is born is made clear in the verses that refer to "Arvak and Alsvid", two horses which "must pull wearily the sun from here".[424]

Soma

It is interesting to note that, in the *Skanda Purāna,* the fig tree (which symbolises the life of the emergent universe as the phallic Tree of Life) at the centre of the cosmic streams is said to be unshaken by the "doomsday

---

[419] "Gylfaginning" ("The Deluding of Gylfi") in *Prose Edda*, p.42f.

[420] A spring is found also at the base of the sacred oak of the Pelasgian Zeus at Dodona (cf. E.O. James, *op.cit.*, p.29). Mimir may be the Germanic version of Mummu in the Babylonian *Enuma Elish*.

[421] The name "Nidhogg" means "striker that destroys" (cf. *Prose Edda*, p.43). It is interesting to note that the serpent is said to be situated at the bottom of Niflheim rather than of the Abyss, as in the other mythologies.

[422] See below p.137n.

[423] See below p.317.

[424] 'Grimnismal', 37. The name of the shield of the sun, "Svalin", in 'Grimnismal', 38, may be derived from the same root ("svar") which gave Suwalliyat/Sūrya.

hurricane".[425] In the Nordic Edda too, the Yggdrasil which is destroyed at Ragnarök will inevitably revive the creation after this destruction since it contains within its trunk all the seeds of life.[426] This plenitude of life within the tree is also symbolised by the Moon, which bears the seeds of universal animal life, according to the *Bundahishn*.[427]

In Sumer, the moon is the first son of Enlil's and called Nanna/Nannar (the counterpart of the Indo-Iranian Soma/Haoma). The moon is the first son of Enlil to be raised to the upper world while Nergal remains in the underworld as a substitute for it. Nanna, as the great light, has priority over the rising sun, Utu (Shamash). Hence the moon is considered the elder or the great light in Sumer (Gishnugal), as well as in Egypt.[428] The moon is also referred to as Magur$_8$, referring to the "makurru" ship of Ninurta as he rises as the sun.[429] Since the barque is the barque of earth, we may assume that the life of Earth, i.e. of the entire material universe, is that which is concentrated in the moon. Thus, before the sun is free to rise into the Mid-region of our universe, the moon is established therein bearing within it the life of the universe. In all the cosmologies that we are studying, the moon bears the seeds of life. While the "moon" bears the seeds of universal life, the sun which is borne by it bears the seed only of man.

The form of Nanna's Akkadian counterpart, Sin, like that of Indra, is that of a bull. In Hurrian and Middle Assyrian ritual literature, Sin is typically associated with the impregnation of a cow,[430] which may represent the material substance of the earth. Like Soma, Sin is particularly associated with the sources of life, which he guards as a "herdsman" of "cows".[431] The myth of "Nannar's journey to Nippur", for instance, relates how Nannar milked his cows, poured their "milk" into churns and gave his father Enlil the best of his pure products.[432] One of the attributes of Enannatum, the high-priestess of Nannar is indeed "the bearer of the life-

---

[425] See S. Shastri, *op.cit.*, p.65.

[426] See "Voluspa"; cf. R. Cook, *The Tree of Life*, p.12.

[427] See below p.91.

[428] See below p.94.

[429] See K. Tallquist, *op.cit.*, p.443; cf. Maqlu III,123ff.; cf. p.84 above.

[430] See N. Veldhuis, *A Cow of Sin*, Groningen: Styx Publications, 1991; cf. V. Haas, *Geschichte*, p.316. The complaint of the cow in the Iranian Yasna 29 is also for a protector, whom she obtains in the form of Zarathustra/Ziusudra, the first man.

[431] The moon bears the seed of the murdered Bull of Heaven (representing all animal life), or Hoama, in the Avesta (Fargard XXI, 9). The seed of the waters, of the earth and of the plants, on the other hand, is stored in the stars (Fargard XXI, 13).

[432] See T. Jacobsen, *Treasures*, p.127.

giving egg",[433] since the high-priestess is considered to be the spouse of her god, who represents the generative potency inherent in the moon. Again, in a Sumerian 'ersemma' hymn to Nannar, we find the following verse emphasising the intoxicating quality of the life-force stored in the moon:

> When you, father Nanna, rise to the shining sanctuary,
> Father Nanna, when you travel on the high flood as on a ship,
> When you travel there, when you travel there, when you travel there,
> When you travel there, when you pour out the intoxicating drink, when you travel there,
> When you feast yourself lavishly on the intoxicant that has been poured out, ...

We may compare this to the Vedic hymn to Soma (also called Indhu) who represents the life-force or seed stored in the moon as well as the vital substance of the light:[434]

> These rapid Soma-streams have stirred themselves to motion like strong steeds,
> ....
> Immortal, cleansed, these drops, since first they flowed, have never wearied, fain
> To reach the regions and their paths.
> Advancing they have travelled o'er the ridges of the earth and heaven,
> And this the highest realm of all (*RV* IX, 22)

And

> Swift Soma drops have been effused in streams of meath, the gladdening drink,
> For sacred lore of every kin.
> Hither to newer resting-place the ancient Living Ones [Soma drops] are come.
> They made the Sun that he might shine. (23)[435]

---

[433] en-sal-nunuz-zi ᵈNannar (SAK 206 b2,1; see A. Deimel, *Pantheon*, p.236f).

[434] The association of Soma with the moon which is typical of Indo-Āryan mythology is thus also observable in the mythology of Nanna among the Sumerians.

[435] The conception of the moon-god as a cow-herd is carried over into the mythology of Krishna (who is considered one of the later incarnations of Vishnu), since Krishna is descended of the *lunar* Aila dynasty (see *BP* XIV,XXIV).

Just as Nannar is said to have milked his cows, Soma too is described as rich in cows that have been milked: "Down to the waters Soma, rich in kine, hath flowed with cows, with cows that have been milked" (*RV* IX,107,9) . Soma is the life-force of the universe and the Purānas equate it with the tears which are shed by the creating god. In the Purānas (*PP* V,12,1-13; *MP* XXIII,1-10) these tears are received by the sky to form Soma.

We may note, at this juncture, a popular legend which recounts the insemination of Pārvatī by Agni. When Shiva, her husband, sees her writhing in pain with the fiery seed of Agni (here the underworld god), he sheds tears, and from his tears is produced a "little man who used a torch and incense to smoke Agni out of the body of Pārvati".[436] In *MP* 23,1-10, Atri, one of the seven sages created by Brahman, sheds tears from which Soma is formed as a young boy.[437] The homunculus in the first account may thus represent the infant moon.[438] Shiva is also frequently represented with the moon arising from his head just as Thoth does from Seth's.[439] The moon contains the Soma with which Shiva/Indra/Seth himself is infused.

The animal life of the universe, as we have noted from the Iranian evidence, is stored in the moon. In *RV* IX,93,1, it is interesting to note that Soma is called the "child of Sūrya", since this may be related to the Egyptian doctrine of the moon's being formed of the seed of Horus the Younger through the stimulation of Seth. However, the Vedic passage does not clearly distinguish the sun of the underworld (Vishnu) from that of the heavens (Sūrya), nor the latter from its original form as the cosmic light, Brahman. According to *RV* IX,42,1, Soma is considered as the progenitor of the sun. This is no doubt due to its chronological priority to the sun. The moon itself is said to be formed by the infusion of Soma into the waters (*SB* IV,vi,7,12). Soma then engenders the sun in floods along with the other stars. Soma here is clearly identical to Indra/Ninurta filled with Soma. Indeed, in *RV* IX,5, Soma is hymned as the bull and the "self" of Indra himself.

---

[436] See A. Miles, *Land of the Lingam*, London, 1933, p.219f. (cf. W. O'Flaherty, *op.cit.*, p.107).

[437] Cf. *PP* V,12,1-13.

[438] Interestingly, in Egypt, mankind itself is formed from the tears of Re (CT 1130 VII 465a, CT 714 VI 344f-g; see S. Bickel, *op.cit.*, p.199). Re sheds tears when his eye (the sun) goes out from him. This must refer to its manifestation in our universe. In an Orphic hymn to Helios too, it is stated that "Thy tears are the race of suffering mortals" (see M.L. West, *Orphic Poems*, p.213).

[439] See W. O'Flaherty, *op.cit.*, p.50.

Exactly as in the Iranian sacred literature,[440] the pressing of Soma is considered as a sacrifice of the god Soma. Soma is identified with the primal Prajāpati himself in *SB* III,9,4,17, since, as we have seen, the latter's sacrifice is essentially a castration of his seed-filled phallus, and the seed of Prajāpati, Soma, is the life of the universe. Soma is commonly understood to be an intoxicant pressed from the soma plant and consumed by the Āryan priests during the ritual.[441] The Scythians, as we have noted, are indeed called "haomavarga Sakas", or soma-drinking Scythians,[442] and archaeological finds at the BMAC in Afghanistan include vessels stained with plant-juice. But the real significance of Soma in the Āryan literature is as the life-force of the macroanthropos. Indra's establishment of the solar force in the heavens is due to the potency derived from the Soma within him.

In the Iranian *Bundahishn*, the seed of the Bull (representing all animal life)[443] slaughtered by Angra Mainyu is purified and stored in the moon,[444] just as the seed of the slaughtered First Man (representing all human life) is stored in the sun.[445] The Bull is thus, in the *Greater Bundahishn*,[446] likened to the shining Moon just as, in Egypt, the seed of Horus reappears on Seth's forehead as the moon, Thoth. Similarly the First Man is likened to the shining sun (where his seed will be purified). In the Haoma-sacrifice, Hoama is represented anthropomorphically, for the pressing of the soma plant in this sacrifice is represented as a slaying of a primal god, Haoma or his anthropomorphic form Duroasha (or Frashmi), in order to extract his productive essence.[447] Duraosha is said to have been in existence even before Vivanghavant, the solar father of Yima (Manu Vaivasvata).[448] Yima is said to be the one who corrupted the Haoma rite

---

[440] See below.

[441] The Vedic sacrifice involving the extraction of soma is called "kratu", while that without it is a "yajna".

[442] So in the inscriptions of Darius I (see P.O. Skjaervo in G. Erdosy, *op.cit.*, p.157). Herodotus (VII,64) mentions that Saka was the name given by the Persians to the Scythians. The Behistun inscription (ca.522-486 B.C.) of Darius the Great refers to the Sakas in its Babylonian section as "Gimmirai" (Cimmerians), showing that they were closely related to the Celts in spite of the fact that the latter were western, centum Āryans.

[443] The seed of the dead Bull stored in the moon is the same as the life of the universe preserved after the "deluge" by the first man, Yima/Ziusudra/Manu.

[444] See *Bundahishn* X, 1-2; cf. *Fargard* XXI,9 and *Sirozah* I,12.

[445] *Bundahishn* XV.

[446] See RC. Zaehner, *op.cit.*, p.40.

[447] See E.O. James, *op.cit.*, p.26.

[448] Yasna IX,17,27; X, 21; XLIII,5.

by burning the sacred plant (Yasna XXXII,8). Haoma is declared to have been prepared for the corporeal world first by Vivanghavant (the sun) (Hom Yast IX, 3), and fourthly by Pourushaspa,[449] father of Zarathustra. Duraosha is sacrificed so that the vital force of Haoma may be expressed in the world. In the haoma-sacrifice, therefore, the pressing of the soma plant thus symbolises the extraction of the life-force of Haoma/Soma.

Haoma is considered by the Zoroastrians to be not only a source of immortality but also a destroyer of the Daevas (I,6). In the Vedas, Indra is the chief of the Devas, who, as we have seen, kills Vrtra. However, the moon and also Soma are themselves often identified with Vrtra,[450] the serpent killed by Indra, just as Seth and Apop are identified with each other in Egypt.[451] Indeed, Soma, symbolising the moon is said to be the "food" of the sun (also a form of Indra) (SB I,vi,4,18), since the sun "consumes" its soma. Vrtra as well as Soma represent the powerful seminal force which informs the universe. Though, it is clear that Soma is more particularly that thermal energy which, combating the frigid Panis, produces the sun.[452]

The moon god is no less important among the Egyptians than among the Mesopotamians and Indians and Iranians. Indeed it is in Egyptian mythology that we get the clearest account of the birth of the moon. Horus the Younger is said to have been violated by his "uncle" Seth, the storm-god, with the result that Horus is sexually excited and emits his seed. We have seen above that Scth, the stormy aspect of Osiris himself, is a god associated with intoxication, and especially the inebriating force of beer, which serves as the Egyptian counterpart of the soma.[453] Isis, however, contrives to collect the seed of Horus on lettuce which Seth, a lover of lettuce, subsequently eats. "Pregnant" with the seed of Horus, Seth then "gives birth", significantly from his forehead, to the golden disk of the moon, called Thoth.[454] Thoth is also identified with the moon-god Aah-Tehuti,[455] and he and Re, as the moon and the sun, are considered the two eyes of Horus (the Elder).

---

[449] It is not clear if Pourashaspa is the same as the Indic Purūravas who is said to have derived fire-worship from the Gandharvas (see below p.142).

[450] See A.K. Lahiri, op.cit., pp.172-87.

[451] See above p.68.

[452] See above p.107.

[453] See above p.68.

[454] See H. te Velde, op.cit., p.43f.

[455] E.A.W. Budge, op.cit. I, 412.

In some versions of the story of Horus and Seth,[456] Seth too, in seducing Horus, emits or "loses" his seed, an action which may have been interpreted as loss of sexual power or castration. The eye of Horus and the testicles of Seth are related to each other in a causal connection of light and life. In the town of Saka, Seth as a bull undergoes self-castration and, in the Pap. d'Orbiney, Seth (called Bata in Saka), castrates himself in order to avoid the sexual advances of his sister-in-law, and then goes into exile in foreign lands.[457] This story may also be related to similar legends of Shiva/Indra in the Indian Purānas[458] and of Attis in Syria.[459]

The phallic importance of Seth, however, is not diminished in this story of seduction and punishment since, even though the moon (Thoth) that is created from the union of Horus and Seth is called the "eye of Horus" (being formed of his seed), it is the "finger"[460] of Seth which is finally required to instil light in it.[461] The "finger" may have a phallic connotation and the force of light is intimately connected to that of life,[462] which Seth, like Indra, eminently embodies. Thus finally, after the separation by Re[463] of Horus and Seth locked in sexual union, the two gods are reconciled, as Horus the sun, representing the light of earth in the Mid-region,[464] and Seth, the stormy life-force embodied in the thunder of the higher region of heaven. In historical terms, Horus and Seth were united as the rulers of Lower and Upper Egypt.

Moreover, in Pap. Hearst XIV, 2-4, Isis brings the moon "to her son [Horus, the incipient sun] to purge his body [after his sexual initiation

---

[456] For instance, Pap. Jumilhac (see H. te Velde, *op.cit.*, p.41).

[457] See H. te Velde, *ibid.*

[458] See A. Daniélou, *Shiva and Dionysus*, p.62.

[459] Cf. the reference to Lucian, *De Dea Syria,* above p.22.

[460] The typical depiction of the young Horus (Harpocrates) with a finger in his mouth, generally considered an indication of his infant nature, may also be a suggestion of the phallic violation of Horus by Seth.

[461] PT 48 (see H. te Velde, *op.cit.*, p. 49).

[462] See H. te Velde, *op.cit.*, p.51. This cosmological event may also be an explanation of the Egyptian temple ritual of touching the mouth of the deity with the finger (see p.276 below).

[463] Pap. Boulaq 17; in the "Contendings of Horus and Seth", it is Thoth who separates his "parents" Horus and Seth (see H. te Velde, *op.cit.*, p.61).

[464] Though the sun is primarily situated in the Mid-region, it begins as a light of earth, that is, in the underworld.

by Seth]" in order to purify "the evil[465] which was in his body"[466] We have noted that, in the Avesta, the seed of the bull of heaven (Osiris) which is killed by Angra Mainyu (Seth) is concentrated and purified in the moon. We see that the moon is considered in Egypt too as a purificatory body and note once again a similarity between the Egyptian and Iranian theologies.

In the Theban cosmology, Khonsu is the moon-god, counterpart of Nanna. Khonsu is called the "great light",[467] just as, in Sumer too, the moon is called Gishnugal, the great light, since it is elder to the sun. Indeed, Khonsu is not merely the moon but also a twin of the solar force in the underworld, Horus the Younger.[468] In Hermopolis, Amun engenders the moon-god Khonsu through his union with Mut/Hathor. Mut is particularly a form of Hathor in the underworld, where the moon is born.[469] Amun's pneumatic virtue is similar to that of the Heliopolitan Shu/Enlil.

Khonsu, son of Amen-Ra and Hathor/Mut, like Enlil's "son" Nanna and the Vedic "moon" god Soma, is a repository of the vital power of generation. Thus Khonsu is a god of fertility who causes women to conceive, cattle to become fecund, and the germ to grow in the egg.[470]

Among the Hurrians and Hittites too, the Egyptian moon-god Khonsu was worshipped as Kusuh, and his identity with Nanna (Sin) is made clear by the fact that his consort is called Ningal.[471] In the Hittite religion, the moon-god of the waters (dEn.Zu u-i-te-e-ni),[472] is mentioned along with dUTU u-i-te-e-ni (the sun-god of the waters) (Kbo V 2 ii 13),[473] since both the sun and the moon are finally born of the waters surrounding the material matrix, Earth.[474]

---

[465] This may refer to the animal life in the universe which comes to be stored in the moon, since the Zoroastrians generally consider the material universe as a corruption of the Ahura Mazdean.

[466] See H. te Velde, *op.cit.*, p.48

[467] See K. Sethe, *op.cit.*, pp.31,114. In Sumer, too, the moon is called Gishnugal, the great light (since the moon is senior to the sun, Utu).

[468] We may remember that Sin and Nergal are called the "great twins" mashtabba-galgal in Sumer (see below p.95).

[469] See E.A.W. Budge, *op.cit.*, II:29.

[470] See E.A.W. Budge, *op.cit.*, II:35.

[471] See V. Haas, *Geschichte*, p.374.

[472] Kbo V 2 ii l.11. In another text (KUB VII 5 I i 24ff.), the author beseeches the moon-god and stars to bring the sun-god of Earth along with them.

[473] See E. Tenner, "Tages- und Nachtsonne", p.186. dUTU me.e (KUB V 6 i l.6. ii l.14) is also a term for the sun-god of the water (*ibid.*).

[474] See below p.108.

III.

THE THIRD SACRIFICE: ASHVATTHA

Agni – the Sun-God of Earth

The solar force that is contained in the seed of the divine phallus that is now erect and resembles the Tree of Life gradually begins to be developed in the underworld into the sun of our system. The developing sun, like the original cosmic Agni, assumes three forms, the first representing Agni, the second Vāyu, while the third is called Āditya. The first form of the sun, the sun of earth, is formed in the underworld only after the moon is first formed therein and elevated into the Mid-region of our universe. In Sumer, Nergal is the twin surrogate for the moon in the underworld while the latter is raised into the upper world by Enlil.[475] Thus we have frequent references to the sun and moon as the 'mashtabbagalgal', the great twins.[476] The moon is indeed termed the "great light", Gishnugal, since it appears before the sun of the heavens, which is called Gishnu .[477] Utu (Shamash), the heavenly sun, is formed after the moon. In an ancient manual on astronomy and astrology, as Hehn has pointed out, it is stated that "Shamash (the risen sun) and Nergal are

---

[475] See H. Behrens, *Enlil und Ninlil*, pp.220ff.

[476] "^{il}Sin u ^{il}Nergal" (A. Deimel, *Pantheon*, p.178); cf. H. Behrens, *op.cit.*; also the "Enlil and Ninlil" myth in E. Chiera, *Sumerian Epics*, 76,77; S.N. Kramer, *Sumerian Literary Texts,* 19; T. Jacobsen, *Treasures*, p.104. The "lesser twins" are formed by the son of Nanna, Ningublaga and Nanna's vizier Alammuš (see "Mondgott" in *RLA* VIII:365).

[477] See below p.122.

one".[478] This reminds us once again that the different names of the sun denote the various stages of the developing sun.

According to a Babylonian exegetical text, Kiurash (the god of earth) is the form of the sun when it sets. This is the same as Enki. Nergal is equally called the "King of the Setting Sun" in BL 196,[479] which suggests that he takes the part of Osiris in Egypt. Nergal is also called Enlilbanda, "Enlil the Younger" (SRT 12,19), just as Enki too is (CT 25, 33,18).[480] Enki is hymned as being both glorious in both the heavens and in the underworld,[481] just as Osiris/Ninurta/Marduk also are. Nergal is also called Lugalgalabzu, the great king of the Abyss, or Lugalaabba, king of the (underworld) ocean, thereby showing his ultimate identity with Enki/Osiris. However, we may note Nergal's identity with Horus the Younger as well, for, in the myth of Nergal and Ereshkigal (EA 357:44, ANSt.10, 120 iv 31', 124 v 40), Enki is termed his "father", just as Horus the Younger is considered the "son" of Osiris.

Nergal's close association with his father, Enlil/Vāyu, is apparent from the fact that fever is generally said to emerge from Ekur, the house of Enlil.[482] The malevolent character of the chthonic solar deities does not preclude their beneficent virtues, for Nergal as god of fever, plagues and death can also cure and revive dying men.[483] The name Nergal itself may be related to the Sanskrit 'Narak' meaning Hell or the Underworld.[484] Not surprisingly, Nergal and Nusku are both identified with Girra,[485] the god of fire. Nergal shares many qualities with the god of fire, Agni, especially since the latter is the first form of the solar force in the underworld.[486] In this context, the two names of Nergal, Meslamtea[487] and Lugalirra,

---

[478]   Sp.I 131 Rs.54 (see J. Hehn, op.cit., p.79).

[479]   See S.H. Langdon, *Babylonian Liturgies*, 196, vs.27 (cf. M.K. Schretter, *Alter Orient*, p.108).

[480]   See A. Livingstone, op.cit., p.46.

[481]   See L.W. King, *Babylonian Magic*, no.27.

[482]   CT 17:12,3;25:1,2;26:52.

[483]   See J. Hehn, op.cit., p.81.

[484]   See, for instance, the description of the 28 levels of Hell in *PP* V,32.

[485]   For Nergal see IV R 24, no.1, 12f. (J. Hehn, op.cit., p.80); for Nusku see the Maqlû series (Deimel, op.cit., p.195). Nusku is particularly the light of the night. Hence he is considered to be the son of the moon, Nanna (see S.A. Cook, op.cit., p.120; cf. *RLA* VIII:631).

[486]   See below pp.63ff (cf. F Hrozny, "Un dieu hittite Ak/Nis", 34-36). The Urartian counterpart of Agni is Haldi, a name that is possibly related to the Greek Hades, who represents the (sun-)god of the underworld, just as his brothers Poseidon and Zeus represent the sun-gods of the waters and the heavens..

[487]   T. Jacobsen (*Treasures*, p.17) interprets the name to mean "He who issues from the

may refer to the beneficial and baneful aspects of this deity, since they are represented in a Sumerian hymn as the "white raven" and the "black raven".[488] We may remember that the Germanic Wotan (Wata/Enlil) is also accompanied by two such ravens.[489]

Nergal is the same as Enlil's "son" Ninurta/Marduk/Muruga, who is the force of the sun in all regions.[490] According to KAR 142, I, 22ff, Ninurta appears in seven forms as dIB (Urash), Nin-urta, Za-ba-ba [Marduk], Na-bi-um [the force within the moon], Ne-iri-gal [the underworld sun], Sa-kud and Pa-bil-sag.[491] Nergal's identity with Ninurta is also made clear in the hymn to Ninurta where the god is addressed as one who "goes about in the night as Irra [i.e.Nergal]".[492]

Ninurta in Ekur,[493] who may be identified with Nergal, is, like Horus the Younger, called the one who "avenged his father" (VAT 9817 rev.20-5,1).[494] Nergal, who is also called "the avenger of his father", is himself the leader of the "rebellious" gods of the underworld, the Anunnaki.[495] Also, Nergal, is worshipped sometimes as a god of war who destroys all hostile forces including the great serpent.[496] Nergal is usually represented

---

thriving mesu tree". This tree may be equated with the phallic tree of life held in the Apsu by Enki/Varuna (see above p.83).

[488] In fact, Nergal has, according to some accounts (KAR 142 iii 27ff.), seven forms, which may even identifiable with the seven warriors that act as his armed force (Epic of Erra, 32-93). These may be the same as the seven Asakku demons engendered by Anu through earth (see below p.110n). It is interesting that Nergal's *alter ego*, Ninurta, too has seven forms. It may also be noted that the "seven gods" in Mesopotamia are called the "seven gods of Elam" (An=Anum VI 183), showing their eastern affiliations. These "seven gods" may be the same as the deities hymned in the Vedas as "sāmānya", meaning "all gods", since "seven", being a number of perfection, has the significance of "all" in Sumerian.

[489] See 'Grimnismal', 20. We may assume that the Germans got this mythology of Enlil and his children from the "Trojans", or Hittites.

[490] One of the names of dUTU is dMi-it-ra (CT 25.25.10) which, being an Emesal form, would have been the counterpart of Sumerian dGidra, which may be related to the name Gi-dar which Dumezil (see above p.47n) identified with Indra.

[491] K. Tallquist, *op.cit.*, p. 421. In the Gula hymn of Bullutsa-rabi, the goddess' husband is called successively Ninurta, Ningirsu, Ninazu, Zababa, Utulu and Lugalbanda (See J.V. Kinnier Wilson, *Rebel Lands*, p.85).

[492] See A. Falkenstein, *Sumerische und akkadische Hymnen*, p.60.

[493] Ekur, which means 'mountain-house', must refer to the earth of our universe which arises from the underworld.

[494] See A. Livingstone, *op.cit.*, p.125. For Nergal/Erra, see K.D. Macmillan, "Some Cuneiform Tablets, 642f., vs.5f (cf. M.K. Schretter, *op.cit.*, p.53).

[495] AGH 112, 2-4 (see J.V. Kinnier Wilson, *op.cit.*, p.38).

[496] As we have seen, Ninurta represents the entire range of Enlil's progeny, Nergal (Agni), Sin (Soma) and Utu (Sūrya), that is, all the forms of solar energy.

by a martial "sword-god", U-gur,[497] who may also have been deified independently as his vizier.[498]

It is interesting to note that Marduk, according to the fragmentary myth, "Marduk's Ordeal",[499] is said to have been banished to the underworld and tormented there. The crime for which he is so punished must be his violence against his father Anu., since In VAT 9947 obv., l.11[500] Marduk, who becomes identified with Enlil, is represented as cutting off Anu's neck. As the descent of the solar force is due to Seth/Teshup/ Zeus, we see that Marduk embodies both the solar and stormy aspects of Seth and Horus the Younger respectively.[501] Tammuz too was most likely represented as bound with an "evil" companion in the underworld, just as Marduk is in the fragment found in the company of a "criminal".[502] This evil companion perhaps represents the Sumerian counterpart of Seth/Teshup,[503] and embodies the passionate element, or alter ego, of the solar force that has to be overcome before it can emerge as the sun of the heavens. These episodes of the suffering solar force must be related also to the sacrifice of the tree that we shall study later.[504]

Among the Hittites, Telipinu, the son of the Hatti bull-god Taru/ Teshup and the sun-goddess of Arinna,[505] is the same as Nergal. It is possible that the Hittite Telipinu was also considered the sun-god of Earth.[506] We know that the Hittites also distinguished three forms of the

---

[497]   See K. Tallquist, op.cit., p.389. The warlike Scythians, according to Herodotus (Histories, IV,62), too worshipped Ares, god of war, in the form of a sword. Ares is the same as Herakles/Verethragna since Verethreghna is designated on the tomb of King Antiochos I as "Artagnes [=Verethreghna], Herakles, Ares" (see P. Kretschmer, op.cit., p.313).

[498]   Cf. W. Lambert, "Studies in Nergal", p.356; cf. An=Anum V, 52.

[499]   See A. Livingstone, op.cit., Ch.VI.

[500]   See A. Livingstone, op.cit., p.127.

[501]   In the Egyptian Osirian mythology, we know that Seth, who causes Osiris' similar descent, is but the stormy aspect of Osiris, the solar energy itself. The stormy aspect of Ninurta/Marduk is Adad. Just as Adad and Shamash are regularly evoked together in prayers, so also are Marduk and Shamash (C.A.H., pl.i, 226b) (see S. A. Cook, op.cit., p.42).

[502]   It is obvious that the passion of the Christ is based on Marduk's Ordeal since he too is accompanied in his crucifixion by a criminal, Barabbas.

[503]   See the ritual text in S. Langdon, Tammuz and Ishtar, p.35, where a morbid suppliant appeals to Tammuz to be freed of the "evil spy, the adversary" who is bound with him, so that he may live.

[504]   See below pp.113ff.

[505]   See V. Haas, op.cit., p.322, p.443.

[506]   The original form of Telipinu was "ta-a-li-i-pi-in-nu" (see E. Laroche, "Recherches", p.34). Since –pinu means 'son' in Hatti, we may assume that 'tali' is a corruption of "taru" and his name means Calf, just as that of Marduk (Amar-utuk, sun-calf; see W. Lambert,

sun, the sun-god of earth, the sun-god of the waters and the sun-god of the heavens.[507] There is also a reference in the Hittite Telipinu myth (KUB XVII 10 iv ll8ff)[508] to the "way of the sun-god of the earth" (taknaš ᵈUTU-us), which is contrasted to the "kingly path" (kas lugal) followed by the sun-god of heaven (1.12). The paths of the suns in Hittite religion may be related to the three steps taken by Vishnu through Heaven, the Mid-region and Earth, called paramapada (the supreme step), pitrayāna (the step of the *manes*),[509] and devayāna (the step of the gods).[510] If they are, then the kingly path of the Hittite sun-god of heaven must correspond to the paramapada, the way of the sun-god of earth to the devayāna, and the path of the sun-god of the waters to the pitrayāna.

It should be noted that, in Hittite, while the fire-god is commonly referred to as ᵈPahhur (from Sumerian pah-har),[511] there are some ritual texts which refer to ᵈAkni as well.[512] Agni, in these Hittite texts, seems to be an appellation of Fire in its destructive aspects and related to Nergal, who is also characterized by intense brightness.[513] What is especially interesting is that the ritual texts in KBo XI and KBo XIII seem to equate Agni with the sun-god,[514] which must here be the sun-god of the earth.[515]

"Studies in Marduk", *BSOAS*, 47, p.8) also does. The daughter of the sun-goddess of Arinna and Teshup is also called Tappinu (or Mezzulla) – who is coupled with Hulla (see V. Haas, *Geschichte*, pp.426ff.). It is possible that the daughter and the son of the sun-goddess of Earth and the weather-god represent the same early form of the sun.

[507] Cf. p.126 above.

[508] See E. Tenner, *op.cit.*, p.189.

[509] The manes are, in *Manusmriti* III,192ff, said to be the offspring of the Seven Sages and from them in turn sprang the gods and dānavas.

[510] See below p.120.

[511] The Sumerian meaning of "gatherer" identifies this fire-god with Horus the Younger, who is also called "one who gathereth together all seed" (E.A.W. Budge, *op.cit.*, I:341), which suggests the generative power of the fire and sun. "Pah-hur/pahhur is clearly the source of the Greek 'pur'=fire. The Sanskrit epithet of Sūrya (the sun), "pāvaka", meaning 'the purifier', may be related to it, since the sun purifies the seed of the slaughtered first Man in the Iranian cosmogony (see above p.91).

[512] This was first discovered by F. Hrozny, "Un dieu hittite Ak/Nis"; cf. J. Friedrich, "Agniš," *RLA* I:42; F. Sommer, "Review of H. Eheloff", p.688; H.Otten and M. Mayrhofer, "Der Gott Akni, p.545-52. The Sumerian word for fire, Girra, is probably also related to the Sanskrit 'agni', since the original form of 'agni', according to SB VI,i,1,xi is 'agri' (see U.C. Pandey, *Cosmogonic Legends*, p.32).

[513] See J.V. Kinnier Wilson, *op.cit.*, p.38. H. Otten and M. Mayrhofer (*op.cit.*, p.549) suggest that Agni was imported into Hattusa from the south-eastern part of Anatolia.

[514] See H. Otten and M. Mayrhofer, *op.cit.*, p.548.

[515] This close similarity of the Hittite religion to the Indic (represented in the ancient Near

In the Vedic literature, Agni is said to have been born in the womb of Earth (*SB* VII,4,1,8-9). In *SB* VI,7,4,3 the second birth is said to be one effected by the brāhman priests themselves since they represent Prajāpati (Brahman) and are the lords of Earth:[516]

'from us [the brāhman priests] the second time, the knower of beings,'—inasmuch as he, man-like, on that occasion generated him a second time;

Similarly, in *KYV* IV,2,2, the second birth of Agni as Brahman is described as equivalent to that which occurs in the kindling of the sacred fire by the brāhman priests:

From us secondly [was born] he who knoweth all[517]

In *KYV* IV,2,2, we get a glimpse of the form of Agni in the Earth:

Agni hath cried, like Dyaus thundering,
Licking the earth, devouring the plants;
Straightway on earth he shone aflame.

In *KYV* I,3,14, the solar fire Agni (Re/Girra) is said to be manifest in a trifold form as Agni-Vāyu-Āditya, Agni being the solar force in the underworld of Varuna, Vāyu the fiery life of our universe, and Āditya the sun of the heavens.

In Heliopolis, Re, the solar energy of the primal deity that manifests itself as the sun, is represented also as the consort of the waters. In the papyrus text entitled "The Book of Knowing the Evolutions of Re, and of Overthrowing Apepi" (Pap. 10,188, BM) dated around 312 B.C., in which Re announces his various manifestations, Re declares that he first existed alone in the material basis of Nun[518] and manifested himself in the form of Khepera (who is represented as a sun-bearing scarab beetle).[519] Re-

---

East by the Mitanni kingdom) suggests that the Hittites may be considered as part of the Indo-Iranian Āryan culture in spite of their centum language. The Kassites also seem to have been an Indo-Āryan people (see above p.70n).

[516]   See below p.198.

[517]   i.e. Agni Jātavedas (see below p.207).

[518]   In the 'Seventy Five Praises of Ra' which are inscribed on the walls of royal tombs of the XIXth and XXth dynasties at Thebes, Khepera, like Amun, is further called "the hidden support of Anpu" (see E.A.W. Budge, *op.cit.*, I:339ff).

[519]   See J.P. Allen, *op.cit.*, p.19f.

Atum-Khepera is said to have laid a foundation in Maat (here Nunet) and made the forms of life. The entire universe is said to be brought forth by Re through an act of masturbation, since, as we have seen, the moribund Osiris/Re is now ithyphallic:[520]

[Re] made the universe when he joined with his fist in pleasure.[521]

In another almost identical version of the same story, however, Re-Kephera is replaced as creator by Osiris, the Lord in, and of, the Waters.

The solar force in the underworld descried as "the developer" Kephera represents the reviving Osiris. It is interesting that, in PT 587, Pyr.1587a-d, Khepera is is also addressed as the primordial hill,[522] which is the appellation of Geb, the god of Earth,[523] from which the sun emerges. In the Fifth Hour of the *Amduat*, the hill is represented as a tumulus over the grave of Osiris (in the desert of Rosetau) from which the sun will emerge – in the Twelfth hour – in the form of a scarab.[524] In the Twelfth Hour of the *Amduat*, the scarab is indeed elevated into the daytime sky by Shu.

The Battle Against the Serpent

The rise of the solar force in the underworld into the Mid-region of our universe as the sun is indeed not possible until the serpent at the foot of the Tree, in the depths of the Ocean, is destroyed. This serpent, which represents the force of Earthly constraint, is destroyed not by the solar god himself, since he is at first moribund in the underworld (as Osiris) and then puerile, as the incipient sun (Horus the Younger), but rather by the storm-god (Seth, Teshup, Zeus) who was initially the adversary of his solar counterpart, Osiris. The vital force which fells the fiery sky or solar force and causes the latter to descend into the "underworld" is, thus, not an entirely inimical one since it is the same that will destroy the serpent, separate the earth from heaven in our universe and allow, first, the moon and, then, the sun to rise to the Mid-region of the stars.

---

[520]   See above p.73.

[521]   CT 321 IV 147d-e (see S. Bickel, *op.cit.*, p.73).

[522]   See S. Bickel, *op.cit.*, p.44.

[523]   See above p.27. The Sumerian Enlil is also called "the great mountain" ("kurgal"). Indeed, one of the Egyptian terms for the hill, q3, is similar to the Sumerian 'kur'.

[524]   See E. Hornung, *Ancient Egyptian Books*, p.37.

In the Egyptian text entitled "The Book of Knowing the Evolutions of Ra, and of Overthrowing Apepi" (Papyrus BM, no.10,188) dated around 312 B.C., the birth of the sun is described rather elaborately. Shu (rather than Osiris) and his consort, Tefnut, were enclosed for several aeons in the watery mass of Nun hiding within themselves the sun. After Shu and Tefnut were raised up from their original matrix by Kephera,[525] the sun was able to emerge as the eye of Nun. The sun, however, is not liberated without a battle waged against the monster of darkness, Apop, which obscures the waters of Nun. Apop may be subtly distinguished from another serpent which serves as a symbol of the primordial waters and of the supreme spirit which dwelt in them, that is, Amun himself.[526] This primeval serpent is sometimes simply called Amun.[527]

It is interesting to note that Osiris in the "underworld" is enfolded, as if in mummy bindings, by the serpent Nehaher ("the Fearful Face").[528] In the *Amduat* the eleventh hour marks the encirclement of the corpse of the dead Osiris (representing the solar light) in the coils of the serpent called "the World-Encircler".[529] Even though the latter is normally considered inimical to the solar light, the serpent preserves Osiris' corpse and is gradually cast off as Osiris revives and emerges in the twelfth hour as the light of the universe from the mound of Earth. Osiris (as Enki/Okeanos) too is identified with a serpent, as the following PT 1146 makes clear:

I am the outflow of the Primeval Flood,
He who emerged from the waters,
I am the "Provider of Attributes" serpent with its many coils ...[530]

The serpentine Ocean (Okeanos) coiled around Earth is thus a primordial form of the deity of the primordial waters (Osiris/Enki). Osiris is indeed sometimes represented as encircling the underworld.[531] Sito the serpent that surrounds the primeval Hill is also called "son of Earth", as Osiris also is.[532] The serpent first holds together the corpse of Osiris and then

---

[525] This account is important for stressing the importance of Shu (Enlil) and Tefnut in the formation of the sun.

[526] See R.T. Rundle Clark, *op.cit.*, p.53.

[527] PT 434 (see R.T. Rundle Clark, *op.cit.*, p.241).

[528] *Ibid.*, pp.167ff.

[529] See E. Hornung, *op.cit.*, p.41.

[530] *Ibid.*, p.50.

[531] See R.T. Rundle Clark, *op.cit.*, p.249.

[532] *Ibid.*, p.240.

accompanies the emergence of his son, the incipient sun, Horus the Younger.[533] Thus, when Osiris dies and descends into the underworld, his decaying corpse (represented as a mummy) is depicted in the *Book of Caverns* as being held together by Nehaher.[534] We will see also, further below, that this serpent of the Abyss is the one which serves as a rope between the boat [representing our universe] and the horn of the piscine form of the supreme deity that saves Manu during the flood in the *MP*.[535] This contrast between the two aspects of the serpent is highlighted in the last scene of the *Book of Caverns,* which depicts a serpent within a mound of earth that helps regenerate Osiris as Horus the Younger along with another serpent encircling the solar beetle (Khepry) that is cut into pieces.[536] In the *Amduat* too, while Apop is destroyed in the seventh hour, in the eleventh and twelfth hours the emergent sun itself appears within the bounds of the serpent called "World encircler".[537]

It may be noted, in passing, that the "hours" of the Egyptian books of the underworld certainly do not refer to our terrestrial hours[538] but, rather, to divine ones. We have seen that, according to the *BP*, a divine day is as long as a terrestrial year,[539] which is the period taken by the sun to revolve through the twelve constellations of the zodiac (*BP* III,11,13; V,22,5). It is possible that the sun's yearly revolution as well as its diurnal passage may have been considered in Egypt to be repeated rehearsals of the agony of its original creation. The original night in which the sun was formed, however, lasted around six Manvantaras (roughly 1,840,320,000 years),[540] since the Manu of our era, Manu Vaisvata, is the seventh.[541] And, as *BD*, 175, reminds us, at the end of time, the universe will revert to its primal state of chaos and the divinity will reassume the form of the serpent.

---

[533] See E. Hornung, *op.cit.*, pp.33ff; cf. R.T. Rundle Clark, *op.cit.*, pp.167ff.

[534] Cf. R.T.Rundle Clark, *ibid.*, p.169).

[535] See below p.141.

[536] See E. Hornung, *op.cit.*, p.90.

[537] *Ibid.*, pp.33ff.

[538] It is unfortunate that Egyptologists still refer to the "nightly" and "daily" journey of the sun, as if such a momentous event as the felling of the Heavenly Light (Horus-Osiris) and its transformation into the sun (Horus the Younger) could occur every evening.

[539] See above p.30n.

[540] Each Manvantara is made up of 71 Chaturyugas, each Chaturyuga being 4,320,000 solar years long.

[541] See below p.135.

In the tenth and eleventh hours of the *Book of Gates,* the solar odyssey is marked by the battle against the serpent Apop.[542] Apop itself is said to have originated from the spittle of Re's mother Neith in the primordial waters and taken the form of an enormous snake that revolted against Re. That Apop is, in his origin, related to Re is not surprising since we shall see that Vrtra too, like Agni, is born of Tvashtr. Vrtra is also infused with Agni.[543]

In fact, Apop is on occasion identified also with Seth, just as Ninurta[544] and Marduk are symbolised as dragons themselves. Ninurta in Sumer and Marduk in Babylon too assume the stormy aspect of the son of Chronos, even though they are the same as Enki/Osiris. Marduk and Shamash are invoked together in prayers (C.A.H., pl.i, 226b), exactly as Adad (Seth) and Shamash are. We have seen that Seth represents the passionate element just as the serpent does the lingering earthly aspect of the solar force. The serpent's obstruction of the emergence of the latter in the universe however can be combated only by the storm-god himself. Once again the contest is an internal one, just as the sacrifice of the Cosmic Man, as well as that of the First Man, was also a self-sacrifice. Seth overcomes Apop using his characteristic rage (nšn),[545] corresponding to the Indic 'manyu' and Iranian 'mainyu' which, as we have seen, are associated with Shiva/Indra.[546]

In the Heliopolitan myth of the sun too, Seth, though the murderer of Osiris, the divine Light, helps Horus the Younger fight Apop on the barque of Re in order to ensure Re's emergence as the solar light.[547] The barque itself represents the material universe, which bears the light of the universe, Re, and is called the "barque of the earth" in the *Book of the Gates.*[548]

The serpent at the base of the cosmic tree certainly represents the tāmasic force which is a persistence of the dull material aspect of the deity which brought about the first cosmic manifestations through its Māya, or power of illusion, which was also represented as the serpent Sesha on which the Ideal Man (Vishnu) reposed.[549] Indeed, in *BP* V,25,1,

---

[542] See E. Hornung, op.cit., p.64.

[543] See below p.106.

[544] BE XXIX 1, rev.iii, 9; see J.V.Kinnier Wilson, *op.cit.*, p.17.

[545] See H. te Velde, *op.cit.*, p.101.

[546] See above p.71.

[547] See H. te Velde, *op.cit.*, Ch.4.

[548] See E.T. Hornung, *Ancient Egyptian Books*, p.60.

[549] See above pp.30,76.

the serpent Sesha is described as being the tāmasic or Māya-associated aspect of the supreme lord which sustains this universe by the magical effect of sympathy. In the Eddas too, the Midgard serpent is represented as encircling the earth.[550]

In the Indian system of Kundalini Yoga, the Kundalini serpent (which is analogous to Vrtra)[551] is represented in the microcosm as the force of vitality as well as of sexuality coiled at the base of the spinal cord.[552] The aim of the yogic discipline is, as Cook puts it,

> to awaken this sleeping force and get it to climb the spinal tree, piercing the various spiritual centres (chakras) along its way, until finally it is released [like Brahman from atop the petals of the lotus in the Puranas or the sun from atop the sycamore in Egypt] from the Sahasra Chakra, the Thousand-petalled Lotus, at the top of the head. At this point the heavy material forces of the earth and the waters, ... take flight... The mythical eagle Garuda carries off Kundalini in its beak; heaven and earth, light and darkness, spirit and flesh are finally, ecstatically united.[553]

The sublimation of the serpentine force marks the rise of the soul, Ātman, to its original brilliance as the divine Consciousness, Brahman.

In the Vedas, Vrtra is a serpentine cosmic phenomenon represented as being located within a turbulent wind. Vrtra is a demon of resistance which prevents the "mountain" from ejecting its life-giving seed. In *KYV* II,5,2, Vrtra is said to be called Vrtra because "he enveloped these worlds".[554] In *TS* II,iv,12,2, Vrtra is said to have grown and enveloped the three worlds.[555] Indra is the hero chosen by the gods to defeat the dragon,

---

[550]   *The Prose Edda*, Ch.47; cf. "The Deluding of Gylfi".

[551]   See V.G. Rele, *op.cit.*, p.104.

[552]   See R. Cook. *op.cit.*, p.25. The fact that the serpent provides Adam and Eve with sexual awareness in Genesis reveals the ultimate reliance of the Hebrew Bible on proto-Indic sources, even though the spiritual significance of the story of the cosmic man is entirely ignored by the priestly redactors of the Bible.

[553]   See R. Cook, *ibid*. That this process is akin to a sexual orgasm is not surprising considering the significance of the phallus even in the macrocosmic creation. The "flood" which accompanies the emergence of the sun in our universe (see below pp.116ff) is thus naturally related to the waves of pleasure that suffuse one's mind in sexual ecstasy.

[554]   The etymology of the word, however, is more accurately preserved in the Avestan "Vrθra" meaning "resistance" (see A.K. Lahiri, *op.cit.*, p.73).

[555]   It is in order to combat this control of the three worlds by Vrtra that Vishnu expands through these worlds with his three gigantic steps (see below p.120) and thus allows Indra to hurl his thunderbolt against the monster (see A.K. Lahiri, *op.cit.*, p.195).

Vrtra, when all of the Ādityas, Vāsus, Rudras and gods were paralysed by the monster (*RV* 10,48,11). Indeed, Indra's freeing of the waters from the restriction imposed on them by the dragon Vrtra is associated with the creation of our heaven and earth, which are formed out of Vrtra's body (*RV* I,36,8).

Vrtra is considered as one of the Dānavas (the Asuras born of the female deity Dana, rather than of Aditi, whose sons are Ādityas), so that the Devas, or gods, opposed to Vrtra, represent the emanative solar impulse of the universe, while the Dānavas must represent the contrary restricting force. That Vrtra however hides Agni (Shiva) within itself is confirmed by *AV* III,21,1 where there is particular reference to the form of Agni within Vrtra along with those within the waters, man, stones, herbs, and forest trees. Besides, Agni is, like Vrtra, a creation of Tvashtr (RV I,95,2), since the latter is but the formative and fabricative aspect of Dyaus (Heaven). Similarly, in Egypt, Apop is also related to Re.[556]

In *BP* VI,9,18, Vrtra is said to cover the universe in darkness, which is not surprising considering that his father Tvashtr is the same as Tartarus, who, according to Hesiod (*Theogony*, 820-22), is the parent of Typhon.[557] And, as Plutarch noted of the Greek hydra, "Typhon is the element of the soul which is passionate, akin to the Titans, without reason, and brutish, and the element of the coporeal which is subject to death, disease and confusion".[558] In *RV* V,40,5, there is a reference to Indra's dispelling of the magical spell of the Asura "Svarbhānu" which surrounded the sun with darkness.[559] These passages thus seem to refer to the liberation of the solar energy from its original concealment in gaseous matter. Indra is thus associated with the discovery of the "lights" for the benefit of living creatures and men in particular (*RV* VIII,15,5). *RV* III,39,6 further states that Indra "took the light, discerning it from darkness". Indra is said to have discovered Agni (meaning here primarily Agni's Rudra form which rules the sun)[560] among the waters.

Vrtra is indeed an Asuric creation of Tvashtr (just as Typhon is a child of Tartarus) who developed this monster of resistance when Indra felled his first offspring, Vishvarūpa (*RV* II,11,19), who is represented as

---

[556]   See above p.104.

[557]   Cf. p.68n above.

[558]   Plutarch, *De Iside et Osiride*, p.197.

[559]   Indra is aided in his fight against Svarbhānu by Atri (*RV* V,40,8; cf. *RV* I,51,3), who is one of the seven sages, and who himself is helped by the Ashwins (*RV* VIII,62; *RV* X,143).

[560]   See above p.43n.

a "three-headed" monster.[561] Vishvarūpa is perhaps the counterpart of the Iranian Asi Dahaka[562] and the Sumerian Asakku,[563] though the latter resembles Vrtra as well. However, Indra is also considered the "protector" in the Vedas (*KYV* IV,6,2).[564] So his slaughter of the monstrous Vishvarūpa must have been conducted mainly to control the material substratum of animal life represented by it. The Manyu of Indra thus represents both the destructive and creative aspect of the emergent solar force.

Indra also succeeds in freeing the "cows" from the "vala", a rocky enclosure in which they are hidden by the evil Panis.[565] The "cows" in the vala myth (10.67,1-12) symbolise the radiant solar energy, since *RV* I,164,3 suggests that this is the secret name of the rays of the dawn.[566] In *RV* X, 108, 5, the "cows" are described as "flying around to the ends of the sky". The Panis themselves are described in *BP* V,24,30 as serpentine, Asuric creations of Diti and Danu and inhabit Rasātala, the sixth of the seven subterranean regions of the material universe bordering on the last, called Pātāla, below which lies the serpent Sesha. The Panis are thus related to Sesha/Vrtra and particularly associated with the primordial frigidity that obstructs the emergence of the solar rays in our system. "Vala", significantly, is the same term that is used in the Avesta ("vara") for the ark which bears Yima during the flood which accompanies the birth of the sun.[567] This ark, as we shall note later,[568] is representative of the life of our universe in the Mid-region. And we have seen that the barque of Re is also the "barque of earth".

It is apparent thus that the separation of primal Heaven from Earth by Kāla/Chronos is repeated in the underworld ("earth") by Indra in order to allow the rise of the solar energy from there into the Mid-region of the

---

[561] See *RV* I,161,6; cf. *KV* II,5,1; *BP* VI,9,11.

[562] See below p.109.

[563] See below p.110.

[564] Cf. *RV* III,31,12 (see above p.81).

[565] In the Vrtra myth (*RV* I,32,11) the waters confined by Vrtra are compared to the cows confined in the vala by the Panis. However, the Panis are here called 'Dasyus' and not 'Dānavas', as in *BP*.

[566] H.-P. Schmidt, *Brhaspati und Indra*, p.222.

[567] The Vedic vala myth is thus a cosmological archetype of the Flood story. The animals saved from the deluge in the later Sumerian and Indo-Iranian Flood stories, as well as in the account of Noah in the Hebrew Bible derived from them, are - unlike the elements of solar energy symbolically referred to in *RV* as "cows" - real animals, and therefore associated with the seeds of all animal life borne by the Vedic Cow [Earth], as well as by the Iranian Bull.

[568] See below p.138.

stars. In *RV* VII, 23,3, it is stated that "Indra when he had slain resistless foemen, forced with his might the two world-halves asunder". In *RV* VI,8, this act of separation of heaven from earth, normally attributed to Indra, is ascribed to Mitra (Horus), since Mitra is but the early form of Indra as the sun:[569] "Wonderful Mitra propped the heaven and earth apart, ... He made the two bowls [i.e. earth and heaven] part asunder like two skins".[570]

Vishnu is also credited with the accomplishment of this feat (*RV* VII,99,3), for we have seen that Indra and Vishnu bear the common epithet Vrtrahan/Weretraghna, in the Vedas and the Avesta. Vishnu represents the expansive and sustaining form of Agni much like Vāyu (Shu). In *RV* VII,99, Vishnu (like Marduk in *EE*, and Shu in the Heliopolitan cosmogony, who sustains the separated heaven and earth) is said to firmly support the two halves of the universe, heaven and earth, while he holds fast earth among the waters (Okeanos) which surround it by fixing it with "pegs". According to *SB* XI,viii,1, the "pegs" are "mountains" and "rivers": "He sets this [earth] firmly with the help of mountains and rivers". These mountains and rivers may not be terrestrial, since, as we have noted above, the source from which the material universe as well as its light arises is itself a mountain, while the rivers may be the seven streams flowing through the universe.[571] The universe is said to have been spread out through Vishnu's sacrificial fervour. It is thus spiritual intensity which apparently causes spatial expansion. But if we consider the phallic significance of Marduk's violation of Tiamat[572] as well as of the Soma sacrifices in India,[573] we may be justified in endowing the term "expansion" with the connotation of "penetration" and "fertilisation" as well.

In *RV* V,85, the separation of the heavens from the earth normally attributed to Indra is associated with Varuna, who is (like Indra and Shiva) said to have spread forth the earthly element "as a skin to spread in front of Surya" and "standing in the firmament hath meted the earth out with the sun as with a measure". In *KYV* I, 2, 14, Varuna is called the bull that "hath stablished the sky, the atmosphere/ Hath meted the breadth of the earth" (I, 2,8), for "All these are Varuna's ordinances".

---

[569] See below p.101.

[570] This recalls particularly the brutal image of Marduk's splitting of Apsu's consort, Tiamat (Aditi), into heaven and earth in (*EE* IV,137).

[571] See p.109 below.

[572] See below p.112.

[573] See below p.251.

The slaying of Vrtra not only forms heaven and earth out of the latter's body but also allows the elevation of the sun to the mid-region between them: "As you, Indra, killed Vrtra with power, you raised the sun in heaven to be seen" (RV I,51,4).[574] In the AV IV,10,5, the sun is said to be "born from the ocean, born from Vrtra".[575] According to RV X,121,7, it is Indra's deliverance of the waters from the grasp of Vrtra and their subsequent outflow which allow the waters to give birth to Agni (i.e. his third form as the sun). The waters, which are clearly related to seminal fluid, flow out as seven cosmic streams which are called "mothers" (RV II,12,3; X,17,10; VIII,96,1), who guard the birth of Shiva's solar son, Skanda (Muruga/ Marduk). The vital solar energy rises from the depths of the Abyss in this flood, since Indra/Soma is said in RV IX,42,1[576] to engender the sun in "floods" along with the other stars.[577] Thus the flood is the result of the splitting of the universe as well as the condition of the creation of its light. The final identification of Indra with the sun of the heavens is seen in several passages of the RV.[578] Indra is therefore the hero who facilitates the birth of our universe as well as releases the solar energy from the icy forces of resistance represented by the Panis and Vrtra.

In the Avesta, as in the Vedas, there are two monsters, Asi Dahaka and Apaosa. Thraetaona (Skt. Trita Āptya) is said to battle the monster Asi Dahaka for possession of the Xvarenah[579] (Zamyad Yasht XIX,37; Fargard XX). Asi Dahaka is referred to in the Vedas (RV VI,29,2;X,113,3) as Ahi and is perhaps the same (even etymologically) as the Sumerian Asakku. In Zamyad Yasht VIII,45,52, Atar[580] combats the same monstrous form. So Thraetaona must be closely related to Atar. Indeed, in Zamyad Yasht XIX,51ff., Atar succeeds in restoring the Xvarenah to the Vouru-Kasha sea (the Abyss).

Indra's destruction of Vrtra, the second "monster" created by Tvashtr, is celebrated with equal fervour by the Zoroastrians as an achievement not of Indra himself but, rather, of Verethraghna (Destroyer of Vrtra), who, as

---

[574] See A.K. Lahiri, op.cit., p.103.

[575] Cf. SB V,v,5,1-5.

[576] Soma is the potency imbibed by Indra (see above p.81).

[577] See RV II,19,3:

   "Indra, this mighty one, the dragon's slayer, sent forth the flood of waters to the ocean, He gave the sun his life, he found the cattle".

[578] See, for instance, RV VIII,6,24,30; I,83,5; III,39,7; VIII,69,2; X,55,3; X,111,7. The solar imagery associated with Indra is noticeable also in RV I,84,1, where his particular virtue (indriyam) is said to fill the deity as the sun's rays fill the darkness.

[579] See above p.74.

[580] See above p.75.

we have seen, corresponds to Indra's solar form, Vishnu. We may assume that Verethra is the "lizard" at the base of the Vouru-kasha sea, the Iranian equivalent of the Abyss. In the Tir Yasht devoted to the god Tisthrya, the release of the waters is due to the destruction of Apaosha (Yasht VIII,29) (a name which may be related to the Egyptian Apop)[581] as well as of the Pairikas (Yasht VIII, 40) (evil spirits that may correspond to the Panis of the Vedas). It is interesting to note that the waters when released are described as flowing into the Vouru-kasha sea (Yasht VIII,47).

In the Sumerian epic *Lugal e*, the outflow of waters resulting from Indra's defeat of Vrtra is reflected in Ninurta's causing a flood that accompanies the emergence of the sun. Like Indra and Adad, Ninurta is considered the "strong arm" of Enlil – who himself has a stormy character and both threatens the heavens and devastates the "lands that offer resistance".[582] However, Ninurta is also the solar force, and one of his seven forms is indeed Nergal, the sun of the underworld.[583] In the *Lugal e* epic, Ninurta is represented, much like Indra in the Vedas, as battling a monstrous creation (hidden in a mountain) of unseparated earth and heaven called Asakku (who may be a form of Antum, Earth itself),[584] which constrains, through its frigid force, the solar energy (the life-giving "waters") contained in the mountain.[585] The defeat of Asakku as well as of the Mountain which Asakku has dominated results in the separation of Heaven and Earth and a flood of cosmic waters which threatens to destroy all life in the cosmos.[586] Ninurta therefore constructs a dam out of the

---

[581]   The resemblance of Apaosha to the Egyptian Apop offers a further confirmation of the Iranian origins of the Heliopolitan religion (see above p.51).

[582]   See the hymn to Enlil, in A. Falkenstein, *Sumerische Götterlieder*, p.98 (cf. p.86n below for the term "resistance"). As Assmann has pointed out (*op.cit.*, pp.42,53), the resistance that is offered by Apop is both a physical withholding of light and life and a symbol of evil itself which has to be destroyed so that Maat (Rta), the divine order of the cosmos may be established; cf. the 19th Dynasty hymn to Amun where it is stated that each of "those who transgress [this] written order is a rebel against Re" (A. Barucq and F. Daumas, *op.cit.*, p.229).

[583]   See above p.97.

[584]   Cf. the liturgical commentary O175 where Asakku is equated with Antum (F. Thureau-Dangin, "An acte de donation", 144ff). Ninurta's destruction of Asakku then would be comparable to Marduk's destruction of Tiamat (see below p.112). This is confirmed also by the other correspondences between the Ninurta mythology and the Marduk (see W.G. Lambert, "Ninurta Mythology", 55-60; cf. also J. Day, *God's Conflict*).

[585]   In KAR 142 seven Asakku demons, sons of Anu – corresponding no doubt to the seven malevolent demons engendered by Anu from Earth (cf. p.97n above) – are said to be prisoners of Ninurta (see H. Wohlstein, *op.cit.*, p.158).

[586]   This cataclysm which precedes the emergence of our sun is similar but not identical to the destruction of the cosmos at the end of a cosmic age.

stony and metallic materials of the corpse of Asakku. This dam is called "hursag", or the foothills, and Ninmah, Enlil's wife and Ninurta's mother, is thus, at the end of the *Lugal e* myth, called Ninhursag, or Lady of the Foothills, which represent the earth of the material universe to which Ninurta has now directed the waters of the cosmic streams.

The mountain rising from the foothills passes from Earth to the Mid-region of the universe, and the seed of the "primordial hill", Ninurta himself,[587] will finally emerge atop it as the sun of the heavens. Indeed, in the epic, Ninurta, having accomplished his great deed, finally assumes his natural role as the sun by boarding a barque, a vehicle that will be familiar to us from the Egyptian solar theology:

The Hero had crushed the Mountain; when he moved in the steppes, he appeared as the [S]un (?),

....

Ninurta went joyously towards the "magur", his beloved boat,
The Lord set his foot on the Makarnunta'e (boat).[588]

The poem continues with Ninurta's disposition of the various elementary metals constituting the "hursag" according to their beneficent or baneful properties (*Lugal e*, ll.416ff.). From a similar reference to the metallic constitution of earth at the birth of Skanda (as the sun) in the *Mahābhārata*,[589] we may surmise that the destruction of Asakku is related to the formation of the universe as well as of the sun.

Ninurta's defeat of Asakku releases the life-giving seminal waters for the vivification and illumination of the universe.[590] Ninurta's mighty battle against the mountainous "regions of resistance"[591] is conducted with the aid of the mace fashioned for him by Ninildu that is identified with the stormy wind, Rihamun.[592] But since Ramman and Adad are identifiable

---

[587] Ninmah is said to have borne Ninurta in the Mountain itself (*Lugal e*, ll.390ff.).

[588] J. Van Dijk, *Lugal e*, p.137 (my English translation of van Dijk's French). The term 'utuaula'/ 'ut-tu gis-gal-a' used for Ninurta in *Lugal e* as well as in the Genouillac god-list (H. de Genouillac, "Grande liste", p.100) may refer either to the tempestuous storm which Ninurta sails over in his sun-barque or to his own stormy nature.

[589] See *Mbh*, Āranyakaparva, IX,43,14ff.

[590] See S. Kramer, "Review of A. Hendel", pp.70ff.

[591] See J.V.Kinnier Wilson, *op.cit.*, p.51.

[592] Similarly, Indra's thunderbolt, or Vajra (which, in *RV* III,30,17, is characterised as a "burning weapon"), is said to have been fashioned by Tvashtr, the creative aspect of Varuna (Enki)

with Seth, we see again that Ninurta, who is identical to Suwalliyat (Horus the Younger) and his stormy aspect are but the same deity. The storm-wind is necessary for the destruction of the serpentine force of resistance which itself is contained in a windy "mountain".

In the *EE* IV, the son of Enki,[593] Marduk, is the valiant warrior who defeats the watery dragon Tiamat, and her second consort, Kingu, in battle. Marduk, like Indra and Seth, is represented as a dragon-slayer,[594] since Tiamat has the monstrous dragon-form of the serpent at the bottom of the underworld of Earth.[595] Tiamat therefore is a counterpart of Vrtra, rather than of Vishvarūpā.

Both Asakku and Tiamat offer the same obstruction to the rise of the solar force. Indeed, Marduk himself is said, in *Šurpu* IV, 1-3, to have vanquished Asakku. Just as Ninurta in *Lugal-e* does, so also Marduk "fixes a bolt" and stations a watchman around the corpse of Tiamat so as "not to let her waters come forth".[596] It is interesting to note that Marduk combats Tiamat with a collection of winds which "disturb the inwards parts of Tiamat", as well as with the "thunderbolt, his mighty weapon" and his chariot "the storm". This is precisely similar to the use of Rihamun by Ninurta in his battle against Asakku.

In the *EE*, it is by dividing the corpse of Tiamat into two parts that the division of heaven and earth in our universe is effected. The Assyrian ritual text K 3476 rev. l.9 reveals the phallic role of Marduk in this aggression: "Marduk, who with his penis ... Tiamat".[597] The separation of heaven and earth resultant on the destruction of the serpent facilitates the rise of the sun to its position between them. After his control of the waters of Tiamat, Marduk is indeed able to construct the three heavens distributed among An, Enki and Enlil (*EE*, IV). Marduk's splitting open of Tiamat's body into two in the *EE* is also remarkably like the description, in the Tamil *Akam*, 59, ll.10-11, of Murugan's "vel" cutting "in two the side of Sura's [Asura's] body".[598]

---

[593]   See, for instance, Codex Hammurabi. I, 1-26.

[594]   The account of Marduk's battle with the dragon is preserved in CT XIII, pl.33f. Rm.282 (cf. *Enuma Elish*, pp.118ff.).

[595]   For the imagery of the fight between the eagle, representing the solar force, and the dragon, representing the primeval watery element, see A.J. Wensinck, "Tree and Bird", pp.46f.

[596]   Cf. *Proverbs* 8:29: "[God] gave the sea his decree that the waters should not pass his commandment"; and *Job* 26:10.

[597]   See A. Livingstone, *op.cit.*, p.123.

[598]   See K. Zvelebil, *Tamil Traditions*, p.80.

In the Germanic Eddas, the god who battles the serpent like Seth and Zeus is Thor, who is called "son of earth [Geb/Chronos]" in the Eddic "Lokasena", 58.

The Sacrifice of the Tree

The solar force, which has been forced into the underworld by the storm-force, has now to be gradually cleansed of its material elements. This purification which allows the sun to acquire its tremendous power in our universe is inextricably allied to the more general *contemptus mundi* and asceticism which underlie the theology of the solar religions, especially the Indic and the Dionysian-Orphic, as well as the Pythagorean-Platonic.[599]

We have seen that the Tree of Life may represent both the infrastructure of the material universe and the internal nervous structure and erotic energy of microcosmic man. The material universe being considered a result of the illusion of the divine Māya and incomparably inferior to the original Cosmic Light and Intellect, it is the duty of the yogi to detach himself from it by "cutting down" the Tree of Life. The Tree is itself thus represented as being cut down, or displaced, in some of the legends of the mythologies under consideration. Since the "tree" is an analogue for the divine phallus itself and its seminal power, Soma, the exhortation to cut it down in these mythic accounts is clearly one to asceticism as well. In the *SP* I,1,21,82-99, Kāma, who is Shiva's own erotic aspect and burnt down by Shiva in the form of a tree, is called the "evil at the root of all misery".[600] Here the contest is plainly between the ascetic Shiva and the erotic passion which engenders and sustains the illusion of the universe.

In the *MBh (Bhagavad Gita)*, too, Krishna counsels Arjuna to cut down the ashvattha tree since the tree represents the world of sense-experience, *samsara*.[601] The baneful aspect of the material manifestation of the cosmos is to be found in the Dravidian version of the *SP*, *Kantapurānam*. Here, the mango tree situated in the midst of the ocean is the second form taken by the demon Sūrapadman who himself is

---

[599] For the Orphic religion see W.K.C. Guthrie, *Orpheus and Greek Religion*, p.156f. It is interesting to note that according to Hecateus of Abdera Orpheus introduced the mysteries of Dionysus and Demeter into Greece which were modelled on those of Osiris and Isis in Egypt (see M.L. West, *Orphic Poems*, p.26). For the Pythagorean doctrines see J.A. Philip, *Pythagoras*, p.137f. We have also noticed the ritual castration in the cult of the Phrygian Attis (see above p.22).

[600] See W.D. O'Flaherty, *op.cit.*, p.159.

[601] See E.O. James, *op.cit.*, p.257.

concealed in a mountain (exactly as Asakku is in *Lugal-e*,[602] or Vrtra in the Vedas). The first form assumed by Sūrapadman is a monstrous multiform mockery of the Purusha characterised by a thousand arms and legs,[603] corresponding no doubt to the Vedic Vishvarūpā.[604] The son of Shiva born especially for the martial purpose of defeating the Asura Sūrapadman is Muruga, or Skanda, the counterpart of Marduk/Ninurta. Muruga destroys Sūrapadman's first form by revealing his own true, and eternal, form as the Purusha. Sūrapadman's second form, that of the "mango" tree, is also cloven into two by Muruga.

Just as Muruga in the Dravidian version of the myth is said to have cloven the "mango" tree,[605] Marduk too is said to have altered the position of the tree, in the *Poem of Erra*, I,148.[606] We note that Muruga/Marduk/Ninurta oppose the Tree though they themselves represent the Ideal form of it as the divine phallus.

The Sumerian kishkanu tree bears three inimical creatures in itself which have to be overcome before the light of the universe may be released. The Anzu bird nests in its upper branches (representing an obstacle to the emergence of the sun of heaven or its first inchoate form),[607] a serpent at its base (representing the dragon of resistance that the underworld sun has to combat), and a wind-demon, Lilith, in its trunk.[608] In the myth of the "huluppu" tree, Gilgamesh (Nergal) destroys all these creatures, the bird, the wind-demon and the serpent.[609]

We have seen that the serpent at the bottom of the Abyss from whence the tree emerges is identifiable with the Māyā of the supreme deity as well as – microcosmically – with the Kundalini serpent at the base of the spinal cord. The injunction to cut down the tree therefore signifies the severing of the illusion of Egoity which lies at the base of the axis of the universe through a mastery of the sexual force (Kāma, Desire) that is represented by the Kundalini serpent.

---

[602]   The lilith demon in the Sumerian tree of life may also be a counterpart of the same phenomenon.

[603]   See D. Handelman, "Myths of Murugan", p.143.

[604]   See above p.106f.

[605]   See D. Shulman, "Murukan", p.32.

[606]   See L. Cagni, *The Poem of Erra*, p.32.

[607]   In the *Epic of Anzu*, the bird is said to be a source of the waters which may bear the sun. However, the bird becomes traitrous to Enlil, and causes the waters to flood uncontrollably and steals the tablets of destinies from Enlil (*Epic of Anzu*, I). Thus it is killed by Ninurta, who then retrieves the tablets of destines from it.

[608]   We have seen that the trunk of the tree represents Earth (see above p.79).

[609]   See D. Wolkstein and S. Kramer, *Inanna*, p.9.

In Germanic mythology too the tree serves as the locus of the great self-sacrifice of the god Odin/Wotan/Wata to himself, which may be a repetition of the original killing of Ymir, the First Man:[610]

I know that I hung on a windy tree[611]
nine long nights,
wounded with a spear, dedicated to Odin,
myself to myself.[612]

It is as a result of this sacrifice – akin to the ordeals of Marduk and Tammuz and even the Christ[613] – that Odin achieves mastery of the magical runes, no doubt related to the esoteric sources of light, Heka, and the "brāhman" prayer. This episode is also similar to Shiva's burning of his erotic aspect Kāma in the form of a tree.[614] The reference to the "windy" tree reminds us of Wotan's own nature as wind-god (Enlil/Vāyu/Wata) as well as of the Purānic accounts of the deluge which accompanies the birth of the sun, where Manu/Mārkandeya/Shiva are, like Wotan, depicted as the only ones that achieve knowledge of the true nature of the universe.[615]

The Flood

We have already noted above that the battle against the serpent of restriction is accompanied by a "flood". In the SP, the flood is caused by Shiva (Enlil) and initiates a cosmic devastation. He splits "asunder these seven worlds[616] and breaks the [golden cosmic] egg higher than the highest". In the SP, Shiva is aided in his task of universal indundation by Indra, the martial aspect of Shiva/Enlil. We note from this, as from the

---

[610] See below p.220.

[611] We see that the description of the tree as being "windy" is connected to the lilith demon in the Sumerian mythology.

[612] 'Havamal', 138.

[613] See above p.98n.

[614] See above p.113. The sacrifice preceding the birth of the sun is certainly related to the passion of the Christ on the Cross. The identification of the Christ with Apollo that we witness in early Christian art, as for example in the pre-Constantinian necropolis under St. Peter's basilica, was possible because of the original solar significance of the Christ story (see, in this context, T. Harpur, *Pagan Christ*).

[615] See below p.139.

[616] That is, the seven "continents", or planets (see above p.45).

Egyptian account,[617] that there must have been a flood accompanying the birth of Brahman from the cosmic egg as well. Shiva is said to be "robed in Indra's thunder-bolts"[618] as he goes about his task of universal destruction.

Indra is, however, also considered to be the particular force which "gave being to the Sun, and Morning [Dawn], who leads the waters" (*RV* II,12,7). In *RV* IX,86,22, it is stated that the consumption of Soma, the "seed", or life-force, of Agni, by Indra results in the rise of the sun to its place in the universe: "Sinking into the throat of Indra with a roar, led by the men, thou madest Surya mount to heaven". Indra's establishment of the solar force in the heavens is thus due to the potency derived from his consumption of Soma. In *RV* IX,42,1, Soma, identified with Indra, engenders the sun in floods along with the other stars. These "floods" which accompany the birth of the sun are the same as the Deluge recounted in the mythological literature of Sumer, India and Israel. For the "ship" which saves Manu, that is, the seventh Manu, is the same as the universe itself bearing the seeds of all life within it.

In the Vedas, Indra's arm or "fist" is represented as a drum (*RV* VI,47,30-1). At V,20,3 the vehemence of the ritual war-drum is called "Indra-like". In ancient Mesopotamia, too, the hide of an ox was used to make the ritual war-drum, and the sound of the drum is said to represent the voice of god. More importantly, the drum is also identified by the Assyrian exegetes with "Indagara", a name which probably represents Adad/Ramman (CT 24,10,14), the storm-god, whose control of thunder-claps may account for the identification.[619] As we shall note below, Ramman (Adad) is the storm-force of Ninurta, in his battle against monstrous creations such as Asakku. The celebrated fight of Indra against Vrtra in the Vedas is conducted with a special weapon called "vajra" which is forged by Tvashtr and this weapon is indeed the same as the "storm-flood" of Adad.[620]

Just as Adad is an exceptionally stormy aspect of the primeval cosmic wind respresented by Enlil, in the Avesta, Ram represents the same aspect

---

[617]   See below p.119.

[618]   See S. Shastri, *op.cit.*, p.88. In the *VP* too, it is Indra who releases the doomsday clouds which destroys all the "cows". The latter are finally saved by Vishnu (*ibid.*, pp.43-6).

[619]   See A. Livingstone, *op.cit.*, pp.179,184. Nindagud, which is read 'Indagara', is identifiable with Adad (see A. Deimel, *op.cit.*, p.225). The phonetic resemblance of Indagara to Indra is indeed remarkable. It must be noted that Anu is also identified with the drum in BM 34035 (Livingstone, *op. cit.*, pp.173,184). For Adad, see A.R.W. Green, *Storm-God*, Ch.I. Cf. Thor, who is similarly called Donner, thunder, in southern Germany.

[620]   See below p.117f.

of Vāyu.[621] The Avestan 'Ram Yast', which is addressed to the same stormy deity as Adad/Ramman, is, significantly, about Vāyu, who represents the "breath" of the supreme deity and the second power in the solar triumvirate Agni-Vāyu-Āditya. Vāyu is Indra's close companion in the Vedas, and Ramman is thus a continuation and intensification of the force of Vāyu through which the sun is engendered.

In Babylon, the storm-god is attested as Rihamun (the howler).[622] And Adad, Ramman, Rihamun are typically called the "Bull of Heaven".[623] In the exegetical god list `Anu ša amēli', this god is described as representative of thunder, lightning, storm, etc., which evokes the peculiarly stormy nature of this cosmic god. Adad is called the stormy aspect of Marduk also in CT 24,50,10b,[624] Marduk being a form of Ninurta.[625]

The storm-force Seth, Adad is, not surprisingly, related to the birth of the sun.[626] The force which fells the sky is equally that which produces the flood which bears the sun aloft into our universe.[627] That the exact storm that Adad represents is identical to the flood which forms the sun is made clear in several sacred Sumerian texts, including the epic *Lugal e*. When Ninurta undertakes a mighty battle against certain mountainous "regions of resistance",[628] Enki calls to Nin-ildu, "the great carpenter [or

---

[621] The Ram Yasht is in fact a celebration of the god Vāyu. The Avesta (Yasht 14, Yasht 8) also uses the form Wata to denote the more corporeal form of the god of wind Vāyu (cf. *RV* X, 136,4 which refers to "the steed of Vāta, the friend of Vāyu"). The name Wata is also reflected in the Hittite divine name, Huwattassis, god of Wind (see E. Laroche, *Recherches*, p.69). The Germanic Wotan/Odin is etymologically related to Otem/Atem (breath) and mythologically to Vāta/Vāyu.

[622] From the Babylonian "ramamu" = to howl, scream (see H. Zimmern, "Religion und Sprache", p.445).

[623] See P. Jensen, "Adad-Mythus", *RLA*, I:26.

[624] "ilAdad=ilMarduk sa zu-un-nu".

[625] See above p.97. Ninurta (Lord of Earth) is indeed the name of the moribund solar force (Enki=Lord of Earth), while his Babylonian counterpart Marduk actually bears a name ("sun-calf") that is more suited to the incipient sun.

[626] In the Indian epic *Rāmāyana*, Rāma is the name of a princely scion of the *solar* dynasty of the Ikshvākus.

[627] See above p.69.

[628] See J.V.Kinnier Wilson, *op.cit.*, p.51. Kinnier Wilson's interpretation of this battle in geological, rather than cosmological, terms entirely unfortunate. The terms resistance and rebellion applied to the hostile forces which the gods combat are uniformly attested in the literature of Sumer, Egypt and India; cf., for example, the Egyptian references in AeHG no.30: "I beat the donkey. I punish the rebels/ I have destroyed Apophis in his attack"; and the hymn in the Medinet Habu sun-chapel: "... who drives off the rebel in his hour, and burns the enemies of Re" (Medinet Habu VI 421B). In the Vedas, the name of the serpent Vrtra itself suggests resistance (see A.K. Lahiri, *op.cit*, Ch.2).

demiurgus] of Anu",[629] who is the counterpart of Tvashtr, to fashion the mighty mace of Ninurta. Ninurta's "arm", or weapon, is itself represented as a separate deity called Sarur. The stormy nature of this mace is revealed in Gudea's Cylinder B, where the mace of Ningirsu [Ninurta as lord of the flood] is described as being the "fiery stormwind". This fiery storm wind is indeed deified as the storm god Ri-ha-mun or Adad. Adad is also called "the most powerful of the Weapons" of the "rebel lands", that is, of the Anunnaki, who are typically located in the underworld.[630]

That the stormwind is related to a cosmic flood is suggested also by the Sumerian term 'amaru' for weapon, which may be interpreted as "flood", as a hymn to Nergal makes clear:

> So strong was his Weapon, its upward rising was unopposable,
> In its aspect as a storm, it was the great Flood which none could oppose;[631]

From the reference to the floods which Soma engenders in *RV* IX,42,1 when liberating the sun,[632] also, we may identify this flood as being the cosmic storm in which the incipient sun is formed and borne aloft. Ramman is, again, called "bel abubi", lord of the deluge.[633]

It is important to note that, in the *Atrahasis* epic as well as in *Gilgamesh* (Tablet XI), it is the wind-god Enlil (Shiva) who causes the flood. In the Babylonian epic of Erra, Marduk, the counterpart of the solar force, Ninurta/Muruga,[634] takes the place of his father Enlil in causing the flood:

---

[629] Ninildu is an aspect of Enki's as the "fabricator" and equivalent to Nudimmud (see below p.131).

[630] See A. Falkenstein, "Sumerische religiöse Texte", *ZA* 55 (1962), p.36; cf. J.V. Kinnier Wilson, *op.cit.*, p.62.

[631] See Kinnier Wilson, *op.cit.*, p.53. Kinnier Wilson also suggests that the cause of the flood in *Atrahasis* may originally have been not the "noise" caused by man, but rather "the noise of the rebel gods, which will have disturbed [Enlil] – even as it disturbed Apsu in *EE* I,25ff." (*ibid.*, p.112). The rebel gods may be the Sumerian counterpart of the Iranian "daivas" and the Indic Asuras. In *BP* VIII,24,8, the reason for the flood at the end of the sixth Manvantara (which precedes the formation of the light in the seventh) is that the 'Asura' Hayagreeva (much like the Anzu bird) stole the Vedas from Brahman.

[632] See above p.109.

[633] H. Zimmern, *op.cit.*, p.448; p.555.

[634] For Marduk as one of the epithets of Ninurta, see K. Tallquist, *Akkadische Götterepitheta*, p.422. Ninurta is also called Madanu, one of the epithets of Marduk (*ibid.*).

I got angry long ago: I rose from my seat and contrived the deluge,
I rose from my seat, and the government of heaven and earth dissolved.
And the sky, lo! shook: the stations of the stars in the sky were altered, and I did not bring [them] back to their [former] positions.

....

The offspring of the living diminished, and I did not restore them
Until, like a farmer, I should take their seed in my hand.

....

I changed the place of the *mesu* tree and of the *elmesu* ...[635]

In his stormy nature, Marduk is very similar to Seth, Teshup, Zeus, who, as we shall see, are both the storm-force and the solar force at the same time.[636]

If we consider the Egyptian evidence next, we will note that, as Usener once pointed out,[637] the solar aspect of the flood is pointedly evident in the account of the sailing of Amun-Ra on the back of the cow, called Mehet Ouret ('Mh.t-wr.t', Great Flood) – a form of Hathor/Nut[638] – holding on to her "horns". We will encounter this bovine image of the goddess of the primeval waters and of the dawn also in the Indic sacred literature.

The hymn to Amun-Ra in the Darius temple to this deity declares that the original seat of Amun-Ra was the high ground of Hermopolis Magna, where the "eight gods" of the Ogdoad were worshipped. Amun-Ra is said to have left this oasis and appeared in the moist, hidden egg along with the goddess Amente. Then he takes his place on the Great Flood. At that time, "there were no plants. They began when ... the water rose to the mountain".[639] We note that the "great flood" in Egypt comes after the formation of the egg from which the divine light emerges, and long ages indeed separate the moment of the appearance of the divine light of Brahman from the emergence of the sun.

In the *Book of the Heavenly Cow*, the eye of Re, which is equated with Hathor, is said to be the instrument of the punishment of degenerate

---

[635] Tr. L. Cagni, *The Poem of Erra*, p.32. For Muruga's similar destruction of the cosmic "mango" tree in the Tamil *Kantapurāṇam*, see above p.113.

[636] Marduk's solar role is highlighted by the fact that he is considered "the one inside Shamash" (VAT 8917 rev. l.5; see A. Livingstone, *op.cit.*, p.82f.).

[637] See H. Usener, *Die Sintfluthsagen*, p.260.

[638] See PT 829 d/e; cf. R.T. Rundle Clark, *op.cit.*, p.184.

[639] *Ibid.*

"mankind".[640] Re embarks on this course of punishment in conjunction with the lord of the Abyss, Nun. A part of "humanity" is destroyed by the flood, but the remainder are saved by the sun-god's decision to stop Hathor's work of devastation by causing her to become drunk on blood-red beer. The sun then rises to the heavens on the back of the celestial cow.[641] The reference to beer is noteworthy since, as we have noted above,[642] inebriation by beer is in fact characteristic of Seth, the counterpart of the Vedic Indra, who also raises the sun into the heavens infused with the force of Soma.

Vishnu

After the purification of the solar force from the underworld elements which long encumber it, the sun is finally free to rise to its present life-giving position in the heavens. The early form of the solar deity is called Vishnu,[643] who is the counterpart of the Egyptian Horus the Younger. Vishnu's major contribution to Indra's cosmic accomplishment is the three gigantic steps with which he traverses the three worlds [i.e. Heaven, Earth and the Mid-region][644] that have been covered by the serpent Vrtra. Vishnu thereby "establishes the spaces" (*AV* VII,25,1) and his encompassing the three worlds represents the pervasiveness of the solar energy in the expanded universe.[645] The three steps of Vishnu are called 'devayāna'[646] (the path of the gods), 'pitrayāna'[647] (the path of the fathers or manes), and 'paramapada' (the supreme step). The first of these, as we have seen, may correspond to the pathway of Enki (Lord of Earth) to mankind described in the Akkadian hymn discussed above.[648] *RV* I,154 describes the highest point in the manifest universe as the region of Vishnu (representing his 'paramapada'). Again, in *KYV* V,5,1, Vishnu is said to be the highest form of Agni (=Varuna).

---

[640]   By "mankind" is probably meant a manifestation of quasi-human life anterior to our own.

[641]   Cf. E. Hornung, *op.cit.*, p.149.

[642]   See above p.68n.

[643]   We shall encounter this name in the Sumerian god-list CT 25,25,8 (see below p.122).

[644]   See *RV* I,154-6; *AV* VII,26,1.

[645]   In *RV* I,154,4 Vishnu is said to uphold Earth, Heaven and the Mid-region; cf. *RV* VI,49,13.

[646]   *RV* I,72,7; 183,6; 184,6.

[647]   *RV* X,2,7.

[648]   See above p.83.

In *AV* XIII,3,13 the different forms of the sun of our system are described in a way that recalls the Egyptian solar gods:

> This Agni becomes Varuna in the evening; in the morning, rising he becomes Mitra; he, having become Savitar, goes through the atmosphere; he, having become Indra, burns through the midst of the sky.

Here Varuna is the counterpart of the Egyptian Osiris, Mitra of Harakhte, and Indra of Aton-Re.[649] Savitr is an advanced aspect of Mitra as the "inciter" who spurs the full development of Sūrya.[650] However, the terms "morning" and "evening" do not refer to terrestrial time but rather to solar. And the "sun" which is adored in several forms, as the rising sun, the risen, the mid-day sun and the setting sun, is not really the star itself, but rather the changing solar energies that characterise it in these several phases.

Like the Avestan Mithra, the Vedic god Mitra is the same as the earliest form of the sun. In *RV* V,3,1, Mitra and Varuna are said to be the quiescent and enflamed states of Agni: "Thou at thy birth art Varuna, O Agni; when thou art kindled thou becomest Mitra".[651] Mitra is, on one occasion (*RV* VIII,25,4,), called a Deva (god), whereas his counterpart, Varuna, is in the same passage called an Asura, since the latter rules the underworld. Varuna is the quiet setting sun whereas Mitra is the rising. In *MBh* IX,44,5, Mitra is accompanied by two companions, Suvrata (true to his vows) and Satyasamdha (true to his contracts).[652]

According to the Avestan Mihir Yasht, the sun arises from the Hara mountain (Mihr Yasht, X,13) preceded by Mithra (Harakhte). Mithra is a son of Ahura, and, like the Vedic Mitra, is a priestly (brāhmanical) god (89). At 127 Mithra is described as being accompanied by Atar "all in a blaze" and the "awful king Glory" [Xvarenah-Varuna]. Mithra, who heralds Hvare [Sūrya/Indra], is himself preceded by Werethraghna and Xvarenah (Varuna), who together represent the different stages of the sun noted above.

---

[649] See below pp.123ff.

[650] See below p.208, where the falcon associated with the Avestan Mithra and the Egyptian Harakhte is an attribute of Savitr.

[651] Cf. *RV* VII,88,2: "And now as I am come before his presence, I take the face of Varuna for Agni's".

[652] These two companions correspond to those of the Iranian Mithra, Sraosha and Rashnu (see below p.122).

Mithra is often adored in the form of a bull (86) and is said to be "the lord of wide pastures", which is clearly a reference to the wide-ranging extent of his course as a "bull". We recall that Horus the Younger and Vishnu are also often admired for their wide strides. Mithra is said to move through all the seven continents (karshvares) of Earth (16). He is created by Ahura Mazda "possessing the most xwarenah of the supernatural gods" (Zamyad Yasht, 35), and is represented as bestowing the xvarenah upon all the seven continents (Mihir Yasht, 16).

Mithra moves in a chariot driven by "four stallions" (124-5) and is represented as a god of war (35-43). The solar force is originally invested with this martial virtue since, as we have seen, it has to battle the demons of darkness in order to maintain its glory. Mithra is also supposed to have a "thousand eyes" (or "spies") (82) with which he observes and judges the actions of man. Mithra is accompanied in his circuits by Sraosha (Faith) and Rashnu (Justice) (41).[653]

Among the Hittites, the sun-god of the waters, ᵈUTU ME.E or ᵈUTU ú-it-e-e-ni,[654] corresponds to the rising form of the sun, Harakhte/Mithra. The daughter of the sun-goddess of Arinna, who is perhaps the same as the sun-god of the waters (since Arinna is clearly related to the Ocean, "Arunas"), is also called Mezzulla, who may be a female form of Mitra.

In Sumer, the sun is sometimes called ᵈGišnu (TCL 15, 10, 173; CT 25,25,8). We have seen that Gishnugal meaning "the greater light" is an appellation of the moon, Nanna (which also has a higher numerical value, 30, compared to the sun, 20). So we may assume that Gishnu is the name of the first form of the sun that emerges in the Mid-region of our universe after the moon. The rising sun is also called Babbar, which name is explained as such in CT XII,6b,6.[655] The sun is said to rise from a mountain in the east between two peaks.[656]

In Babylon, Marduk is the counterpart of Horus the Younger, the early sun, Harakhte, is suggested by the original form of Marduk's name Amarutuk, sun-calf.[657] Marduk, like the Sumerian Dumuzi, is normally considered as the son of Enki (Osiris). However, he is also the son of Enlil/Shu, since he is said to have been created by Nunamnir, that is, Enlil, in a

---

[653]   In Srosh Yasht, Sraosha is called "the incarnate Word". In Vedic literature, Sūrya's daughter is called Shraddhā (Faith), according to *SB* XII,vii,3,11.

[654]   The waters from which the sun is born are represented by the sun-goddess of Arinna and ME.E/arunaz (see E. Tenner, *op.cit.*, p.186).

[655]   See P.A. Schollmeyer, *op.cit.*, p.3.

[656]   Cylinder seal (British Museum no. 89,110) (see P.A. Schollmeyer, *op.cit.*, p.5).

[657]   W. Lambert, "Studies in Marduk", *BSOAS*, 47, p.8.

hymn to Marduk,[658] which reveals the ultimate identity of Enki and Enlil.

It is interesting that Enlil himself is sometimes considered the form of the rising sun, since we have observed that Enlil [Vāyu/Wotan] is the vital force of the entire manifest universe in the Mid-region between earth and heaven. According to a Babylonian exegetical text, Enlil is the form of Utu (the sun) when the latter rises, just as Kiurash (Enki, the lord of Earth) is his form when he sets.[659] Since the setting sun is the same as Osiris/Atum, the former may be equated with Harakhte. Indeed, Enlil is related also to An[660] due to the fact that the supreme deity is in fact an integral solar trinity of Enki-Enlil-An (corresponding to Agni-Vāyu-Āditya).

Muruga in Dravidian mythology is, like Marduk, associated with the rising sun. In the *Paripātal* (ca. 300-400 A.D.) he is described thus: "his body was of the colour of fire, his garment and garland red, the colour of the shaft of his 'vel' like coral, and his face like the rising sun". Hence he is called 'Ceyon', the red god.

In the Egyptian Middle and New Kingdoms, especially under Akhenaton, Shu is identified with the solar deity Re (equivalent to the noon-day sun Aton) itself, though he is, as we have seen from the Mesopotamian evidence, more closely associated with the morning sun, Horus the Younger.[661] Horus the Younger is characteristically the sun at the horizon (Re-Harakhte), and he is called a falcon "who traverses the two heavens" and the "lower celestial vault".[662] Indeed, Horus the Younger is represented as coursing through all three regions of the universe. He is (exactly as Vishnu also is) particularly characterised by his large strides: "in your name of 'The Runner'/ You traverse millions and hundreds of thousands of nomes (schenes)".[663] And the term šnw n Hr (the circuit of Horus) itself denotes the universe in Egyptian.[664]

---

[658] W.G. Lambert, "Three literary Prayers of the Babylonians", *AfO* 19 (1959-60), p.62; cf. Kinnier Wilson, *op.cit.*, p.63

[659] See Weidner, *AfO*, 19, 110 (cf. A. Livingstone, *op.cit.*, p.47).

[660] For identifications of An with Enlil, see H. Wohlstein, *op.cit.*, p.35.

[661] See K. Sethe, *op. cit.*, p.112f.

[662] See A. Barucq and F. Daumas, *op.cit.*, p.140.

[663] See A. Barucq and F. Daumas, *op.cit.* p.176; cf also p.50: "Horus arrives! The Runner with the Large Strides comes!" (Pyr. 852-56), and p.123. The term "schenes" (šnz) refers to a particular ancient Egyptian nome (see *LÄ* V:576).

[664] See S. Mercer, *op.cit.*, p.194.

Āditya

The final perfection of the universe that has emerged in the Mid-region between Earth and Heaven is the sun of the heavens. The source of this third birth of Agni is, in the Vedas, said to be the waters surrounding Earth. In *KYV* IV,2,2, it is stated that

> In the waters thirdly [was Agni born] the manly
>
> ....
>
> The Manly souled [Indra-Soma] kindleth thee in the ocean, in the waters,
> In the breast of the sky, O Agni, he who gazeth on men.
> Thee [Agni] standing in the third region,
> In the birthplace of holy order [Rta], the steers [Mitra-Varuna] inspirited.

The third region is the mid-Region of our universe and the form of Agni as the one "who gazeth on men" is that of the sun-god of the heavens called Āditya (son of Aditi) or Sūrya. At *RV* X,72,7, the sun is said to be born of the waters and located in the highest heaven, surrounded by the waters.[665] At *AV* IV,39,6, Sūrya is called the "calf of the cow Heaven", just as Horus the Younger is the son of Nut/Hathor.

The sun is fixed in our heavens by Indra (*RV* II,21,4). In *RV* IX,63,8 Indra is said to make the sun move by yoking ten coursers to it. In *RV* I,24,8, the path of the sun in the system is said to be ordained by Varuna, who is but a form of Agni/Shiva/Indra and the counterpart of Osiris. The sun is also set in motion (*RV* VII,86,1) and established in its course (*RV* VII, 87,1) by Varuna. At *RV* I, 1145,5 the sun of the Heavens, Sūrya, is said to be the manifest form of Varuna. When the sun sets, it is said to become one with Varuna (*KB* XVIII,9). This is the same as the identification of the setting sun with Osiris, "chief of the western [gods]" in Egypt. In *RV* VII,99,4 Sūrya (Āditya, the sun of heaven), Dawn (representing the sun of the mid-region, or Vāyu) and Agni (representing the sun of earth) are said to be the children of Vishnu.

Among the Iranians, the sun of the heavens is called Hvare, which is the Avestan form of Svar (the shining one), another name of Sūrya.[666] We may note incidentally that the xvarenah when flying out of Yima,

---

[665] See W. Kirfel, *Kosmographie*, p.14f.

[666] Cf. the Hittite form, Suwalliyat, above p.66.

once he has become sinful,[667] takes the form of a falcon, the typical form of the Egyptian Horus. Yima is himself representative of the seventh Manvantara, according to the evidence of BP VIII,13. The symbolic importance of the falcon is most evident in the Horus cult of Egypt and, since the name of Horus is itself probably derived from the Iranian Hvare, this is another indication that the people who developed the Horus cult in Egypt from Elam and Mesopotamia were probably closely allied to the Iranian Āryans.[668] The cult of Seth in the south, on the other hand, seems to bear a resemblance to the worship of Teshup among the Hurrians, of Ganesha among the Indians and of Zeus among the Greeks.

The common name for the sun-god in Sumer is Utu. Another name of Utu attested in Mesopotamia is Mitra-šúdú (CT XXV,25,10), which may mean the perfect sceptre-bearer,[669] or perhaps the perfected Mitra. We have seen that Mitra is, in the Avesta as in the Vedas, especially used for the rising sun, Harakhte. In the Sumerian myth of "Enki and Inanna: The Organisation of the universe", Mitra is called the "great herald of An",[670] where An is the same as Shamash the sun in its perfect form (Hvar/Svar/Sūrya), while Mitra is the earlier, rising sun of the horizon. Thus also Harakhte heralds the full-fledged Re/Aton.

Mitra is the one who acts as judge among the gods, since he oversees the universe. This may explain the reference to "sceptre-bearer" in the Sumerian "Mitra".[671] However, we note that An himself is described as a sceptre-bearer in A.O.6461,[672] showing once again that Mitra-šúdú is a reincarnation of the first cosmic light specifically as the full-fledged sun. The association of Phanes, the Orphic counterpart of the cosmic light Brahman, with the sceptre is also clear in the Rhapsodic theogony: "for it was Phanes who first fashioned the sceptre".[673] This suggests that the role of universal judge is equally that of the first cosmic light (Phanes/Horus the Elder) and of the light of our universe.

---

[667] See above p.74.

[668] See above p.51.

[669] See P.A. Schollmeyer, Sumerisch-babylonische Hymnen, p.12.

[670] See S. Kramer and J. Maier, Myths of Enki, p.53.

[671] See A. Ungnad, "Ahura-Mazdah", p.200. The Sanskritic derivation of Mitra from "mit" to unite (thus, "friend") is doubtful. It must be noted that the Iranian Mithra is also called Mihir (cf. Mihir Yasht), in which the "h" may be a characteristic Iranian substitution of an original "s" or "sh". If this be so, the name may be related to the Hittite adjective "mišriwant", which may mean either brilliant or perfect (see The Hittite Dictionary, III:27). On the other hand, the Hittite form of Mitra may have been Mezzulla (see p.90 above).

[672] See H. Wohlstein, op.cit., p.103.

[673] See M.L. West, Orphic Poems, p.231f.

Among the Akkadians the sun-god is called Shamash and Shamash's role as a judge is parallel to that of his "twin" Sin as "illuminator of the night".[674] In the An=Anum list, one of the sons of Shamash is called Kittum [Fidelity] (CT 24, 31, 82), who is identified with his vizier Niggina (CT 24, 31, 81). These two figures are in turn identifiable with Nigzida, who is one of Shamash's emissaries along with Nigsisa (Righteousness/ Justice) (CT 24, 31, 74-75).[675]

The Hurrian version of the Akkadian Shamash[676] is Shimige who, like the Hittite sun-god, is represented as riding on a bull. This may be a local adaptation of the familiar Iranian Mithraic iconography.

The god-lists in the Hittite treaties[677] begin with the heavenly form of the sun, dUTU SAME/ nepisas, the Sun-god of Heaven. This is the solar light which reigns in heaven after rising from the waters as the sun-god of the waters. Muwattalli's prayer in KUB VI 45 III, 13ff. addressed to the sun-god of the heavens runs: "you rise, sun-god of heaven, from the waters, and enter heaven".[678] The Hittite sun-god of heaven must be the counterpart of Re/Aton/Sūrya/Hvare.

The "mid-day" sun is the full splendour of Re himself as the solar disk Aton or Aten. In Pap. Chester Beatty 9, BM 19689, Atum is said to have mastered the heavens as Re, the sun. We have seen that the solar force, is indeed said to be born thrice, from Earth, from the Waters and from Heaven. Nut thus serves as the last generatrix of the solar force, as the sun. In the *Book of the Day*, the sun is depicted as being born from the vulva of Nut and travelling towards her head where it is swallowed by the mouth of the sky-goddess.[679]

The "setting" sun is called Atum or Atem, though Atum's name is often used to denote the primal light of the universe, for Horus the Elder and Osiris (who "sets" or goes into the underworld) are virtually identical.

---

[674]   See the hymn to Marduk, CT 24, 50, 47406, obv.3-10: "Sīn is Marduk, the illuminator of the night,/ Shamash is Marduk of justice" (T. Jacobsen, *op.cit.*, p.235).

[675]   Cf. H. Zimmern, *op.cit.*, p.368; cf. P.A. Schollmeyer, *op.cit.*, p.17. Nigsisa is also called Bunene (see 'Nigzida' in *RLA* IX:313). Among the Hittites, Mešaru (akk. Mišaru) and Bunene are the viziers of the sun-god (see V. Haas, *op.cit.*, p.380). So Mešaru/Mišaru must be the same as Nigzida/Niggina/Kittum.

[676]   The original form of the name was Shimesgi, which is, like Tasmisu, derived from the Akkadian Shamash (Sumerian 'Utu').

[677]   See D. Yoshida, *Untersuchungen*, pp.12-29.

[678]   See E. Tenner, *op.cit.*, p.186.

[679]   *Ibid.*, p.117.

Among the Greeks, Apollo, the son of Zeus and Leto, is the equivalent of the Indic Sūrya. However, in Hellenistic times,[680] Apollo was identified with Helios, the son of the Titans, Hyperion and Theia,[681] who is the solar force in its earlier form as represented by the Mesopotamian Marduk/ Ninurta. Helios is represented as driving a chariot drawn by solar steeds called "fire-darting steeds" by Pindar (*Olympian Odes* 7,71).[682] According to Hyginus' *Fabulae*, 183, the principal steeds are called Eous, Aethiops, Bronte and Sterope (following Eumelus of Corinth), or Eous, Pyrois, Aethon and Phlegon (following Ovid). Eos is said to be the one that "turns" the sky, Aethiops is a burning steed, while Bronte is equal to thunder and Sterope to lightning.

---

[680] See Pseudo-Eratosthenes, *Catasterismi*, 24.

[681] *Theogony*, 371.

[682] The Indic Sūrya too drives a chariot drawn by seven bay steeds (*RV* I,50,8).

IV

MANU VAIVASVATA

The Seven Sages

One important phenomenon marking the stages that mark the birth of the sun is that of the Seven Sages. The sages are said to accompany the seventh Manu in the *MBh* version, but from the *GP* I,87 we learn that each Manu is accompanied by seven sages. The seven sages that accompanied the first Manu Svāyambhuva were called Marichi, Atri, Angira, Pulastya, Pulaha, Kratu and Vasishta. The seven sages that accompany Manu Vaivasvata are called Atri, Vasishta, Jamadagni, Kashyapa, Gautama, Bharadvāja and Vishvāmitra.[683] In *BrdP* I and *BP* VI, the sages are considered the "intellectual progeny" of Brahma who antedate the Ādityas, the twelve suns of the manifest universe. In

---

[683] In the *BrdP* I,i,5,70 there are nine sages, Bhrgu, Angiras, Marīci, Pulastya, Pulaha, Kratu, Daksha, Atri, and Vasishta. In *BrdP* I,ii,32,96-7 Manu is included after Kratu to make a total of ten sages. In *BrdP* II,iii,1,21 there are eight sages, Bhrgu, Angiras, Marīci, Pulastya, Pulaha, Kratu, Atri and Vasishta. In *BrdP* II,iii,1,7f. there are seven, whose names are given at II,iii,1,50 as Bhrgu, Angiras, Marīci, Atri, Pulastya, Pulaha, and Vasishta. In *Manusmriti* III,195ff. too there are seven, though Viraj takes the place of Pulaha. These are clearly the sages of the first manvantara.

In *BrdP* I,ii,38,26-33 there is a more specific reference to the incarnations of the seven sages in the present manvantara. The names of these are Vishvāmitra [who was originally a kshatriya and not a brāhman], Jamadagni [who is a descendant of Bhrgu], Bharadvāja [who is a descendant of Angiras], Saradvan, Atri, Vasuman, and Vatsara.

In the *Baudhāyana Shrauta Sūtra*, there are eight such sages, and they are Vishvāmitra, Jamadagni, Bharadvaja, Gautama, Atri, Vasishta, Kashyapa and Agastya. Agastya is obviously a later addition as the sage who transmitted Vedic learning to the "Tamils", i.e. proto-Tamils or Sumerians.

We may note the relative frequency of seven as the number of the sages in the Purānas, the *Mahābhārata*, in Sumerian literature, as well as in Indian astronomy.

the *BrdP* III,iv,2,29, the sages of the family of Angirases[684] are said to be located in the Bhuvarloka, which is the Mid-region between Earth and Heaven. At *BrdP* III,iv,2,49ff., however, all the sages including Angiras are said to originally reside in Janarloka, the fifth world, which holds the seeds of mankind. The brāhmans, as we shall see, trace their ancestry back to these seven sages.[685]

If we turn to the Egyptian king-lists, we will note that, in common with the Sumerian king-list, they begin with the reign of the gods, proceed to the demi-gods and spirits of the dead, and then, finally, to the human dynasties. Unlike in the Sumerian king-list, however, there is no mention of a "deluge" after the reign of the gods. The Egyptian gods mentioned at the head of the Manetho list are Hephaistos (Ptah), Helios (Re), Kronos (Geb), Osiris, Typhon (Seth), and Oros (Horus the Younger). Hephaistos is said to have "discovered fire for the Egyptians", which equates him with the Vedic Prajāpati, whose son is Agni. Osiris and Typhon are the two aspects, solar and stormy, of the divine light, while Oros is clearly the nascent sun, Mitra.[686] We see that the sun is the last god in the Egyptian king-lists as it is also in the Sumerian. In both the Egyptian king-lists and the Sumerian, as well as in the Sumerian Deluge myth, the order of the first kings and cities follows the order of manifestation of the solar force in the underworld As Manu is the ruler at the time of the Deluge and, indeed, of the incipient universe (corresponding to Ziusudra,[687] the son of the divine Ubar-tutu(k) of Shuruppak),[688] so the first "human" king – from Thinis, near Abydos, sacred to Osiris – in the Egyptian list is recorded under the name of Menes, which may be a cognate of Manu.[689] Menes corresponds to Manu, the ancestor of mankind and ruler, originally, not of Egypt, or Sumer, or India, but indeed of the entire material universe.

But it is most probable that there was a tradition of seven antediluvian kings who preceded the establishment of monarchy after the "deluge". The Palermo Stone, for instance, contains the names of nine kings of Lower Egypt (which represents Earth), while the Cairo fragment which may have formed part of the former contains a list of "kings" who clearly

---

[684] The Angiras family is most closely connected with the Soma sacrifices of the Vedic period (see J. Gonda, *Religionen*, I, p.108).

[685] See below p.197.

[686] For the different phases of the sun according to the Indic mythology, see above p.121.

[687] See W.G. Lambert and A.R. Millard, *Atrahasis*, p.19.

[688] See T. Jacobsen, *Sumerian King-List*, p.75.

[689] The Germans too considered Mannus as the ancestor of the race (Tacitus, *Germania*, 2).

precede the kings of the Palermo dynastic list.[690] Of these kings seven bear the double crown of Upper and Lower Egypt.[691] Since these "kings" – also of Thinis – precede Menes (who represents Manu Vaivasvata), we may reasonably surmise that these "kings" represented as ruling Upper and Lower Egypt, or Heaven and Earth are indeed the same as the Manu's who preceded the seventh Manu Vaivasvata.

The fact that the solar significance of the flood is most directly apparent in Egypt highlights the Egyptians' exclusive concentration on the solar aspect of the original religion. The Sumerians seem not to have left behind a cosmogonical version of the flood in Mesopotamia but only a popular transformation of it into a human deluge story. In the original Sumerian version of the Deluge, which may have served as the basis for the Babylonian *Atrahasis* flood story, we note again that the five antediluvian cities are directly ruled by gods:

> The first of those cities, Eridu, he gave to the leader Nudimmud,[692]
> The second, Badtibira, he gave to the 'nugig',
> The third, Larag, he gave to Pabilsag [Ninurta],
> The fourth, Sippar, he gave to the hero Utu,
> The fifth, Suruppak, he gave to Sud [Ziusudra?].[693]

Enki, the lord of the underworld, is followed by Dumuzi/Marduk/Ninurta, the solar energy, and the list ends with the sun, Utu and his "son", Ziusudra.[694] It may be noted that an Early Dynastic fragment from around 2500 B.C. replaces Ziusudra with UR.AŠ (Earth)[695] reminding us that the process of the manifestation of the solar force that finds itself in the underworld is similar to that which signalled the rise of the primal light of An, who also, in the "An-Anum" list, is preceded by Urash.IB. The UR.AŠ in the ED fragment may be an abbreviation of Ninurash,[696] who is

---

[690] Breasted thought that the Cairo fragments must also have originally contained a set of kings of Upper Egypt who followed those of Lower Egypt (see S. Mercer, *ibid.*). If this were indeed the case, it is likely that the most ancient dynasties were founded in Lower Egypt.

[691] See S. Mercer, *op.cit*, p.16. The set of seven "kings" of a united Upper and Lower Egypt is followed by the kings of Lower Egypt (in the Palermo Stone)

[692] Nudimmud is an aspect of Enki as the "fabricator".

[693] W. Lambert and A.R. Millard, *Atrahasis*, p.141.

[694] Yima, the survivor of the flood in the Iranian literature, is also called the son of the sun, Vivanghavant (see below p.137).

[695] See *Atrahasis*, p.19.

[696] It could also mean Enki, Lord of Earth, since Ninurta, like Marduk, is a development from him.

synonymous with Ninurta. Then, even Manu/Ziusudra may represent a form of the powerful Ninurta, who, as we shall see, is responsible for the transmission of the divine life and light to the universe.

In the antediluvian section of the Sumerian king-list, too, we find that the first mentioned cities are all representative of the various manifestations of the developing solar force in the underworld. The first mentioned is Eridu, the seat of Enki, the primeval deity of the Abyss who rules the underworld after the attack on An by his stormy aspect, Enlil in an Assyrian festival calendar.[697] Bad-tibirra, the second antediluvian city, was sacred to Dumuzi, the "son of the abyss", and Larak, the third, was the centre of a Pabilsag (Ninurta) cult.[698] The kings of Bad-tibirra and Larak are elsewhere identified with Dumuzi,[699] who is himself a form of the solar god, An. Thus En-men-lu-Anna, En-me-lu-Anna – who precede Dumuzi himself – in Bad-tibirra are said to be the same as Dumuzi in A.O. 4346.1-2 and CT 24, 9. The first king of Larak, En-sipa(d)-zi(d)-Anna is equally identified with Dumuzi (CT 24.9).[700] Ninurta, the god of Larak as Pabilsag, is thus identical to Dumuzi, the solar force. Sippar, the fourth antediluvian city, was the centre of Utu (sun) worship, and finally, Shuruppak was the home of Ziusudra, who is the same as the seventh Manu, Manu Vaivasvata, or Manu of the sun.

In the tablet W 20030,[701] we learn that each of the antediluvian kings (or, rather, gods) is accompanied by an extraordinary being called "apkallu" and, since this tablet lists only seven such kings, there are seven "apkallu" in all.[702] The apkallu are the sages who arise from the Abyss to reveal science, art and civilisation to incipient mankind.[703] The names of

---

[697] VAT 9947.

[698] *RLA* VI:495 (cf. F.R. Kraus, "Nippur und Isin", 78-80). Pabilsag may have originally been spelled Pabilhursag (see Poebel, *Historical and Grammatical Texts*, pl.i, p.51; cf. S. Smith, *op.cit.*, p.24).

[699] See W. Lambert and A.R. Millard, *Atrahasis*, p.26f.; cf. H. Zimmern, "Religion und Sprache" II:530ff.

[700] See W. Lambert and A.R. Millard, *ibid.* It should be noted that Dumuzi is listed also in the postdiluvian section as a king of Kuara (near Eridu) in the Uruk dynasty, after Enmerkar and Lugalbanda. It is possible that this is an unidentified king deified as Dumuzi.

[701] See J. van Dijk, "Die Inschriftenfunde", p.44ff.

[702] For the apkallu see E. Reiner, "The Etiological Myth", 1-11.

[703] The apkallu are indeed the prototypes of the patriarchs before Noah in the Hebrew Bible (see H. Zimmern, "Biblische und babylonische Urgeschichte", pp.26ff.). The apkallu are complemented in the postdiluvian section of this list by the "ummannu", or the scholars who aided the several postdiluvian kings in their respective reigns. In Indian astronomy, the "seven sages" are transformed into the Pleiades.

these apkallu are u-an [Adapa], u-an-du-ga, en-me-du-ga, en-me-galam-ma, en-me-bulug-ga, an-en-lil-da and u-tu-abzu,[704] and their respective appearances are in the reigns of "a-a-lu", "a-la-al-gar lugal", "am-me-lu-an-na lugal", "am-me-gal-an-na lugal", "e[n-m]e-usumgal-an-na lugal", "dumu-zi sipa lugal", and "en-me-dur-an-ki lugal".[705] From WB 1923,444 and W 20030,7, it is apparent that these kings ruled in Eridu (the seat of the god Enki, who is the same as Varuna-Osiris in the underworld), Bad-tibira (sacred to Dumuzi), Larak, and Zimbir (=Sippar, whose tutelary deity was the sun-god Utu) respectively, which establishes that the "apkallu" appeared during the development of the solar force in the underworld. The antediluvian "apkallu" of Sumer correspond to the Indic "seven sages". The first of these apkallu, U-An (identifiable with Adapa),[706] is characterised in Berossus' list by a piscine form, though the piscine Matsya incarnation of the supreme Lord in the Indian Purānas appears later, during the flood, with the seventh Manu, of the Treta Yuga.

In the biblical book of *Genesis* 5, there is a reference to the descendants of Adam, starting with Seth, and continuing with Enos, Ca-i'nan, Mahal'aleel, Jared, Enoch, Methu'selah, Lamech and Noah. Since the brāhmans are, in the the Ethiopian version of Pseudo-Callisthenes, said to be the sons of Seth,[707] and the brāhmans are descended from the seven sages, we may assume that the personages from Enos on are the Hebrew counterparts of the seven sages. Seth himself may be the same as the Egyptian Seth (Ganesha), who is the son of Horus the Elder/Brahman. Noah, however, is a Manu ("king" in the Sumerian and Egyptian terminology) rather than a sage.

In the Avesta, the six Amesha Spentas, the "well-doing ones", seem to correspond to the Seven Sages. Vohu-mano (good thought), Asha Vahista (excellent holiness, or the holy order of the universe corresponding to the Vedic rta), Kshathra Vairya (perfect sovereignty), Spenta Armaiti (divine piety, who reappears in the *RV* V,43,6 as "the great Aramati ... who knoweth Holy Law"), Harvatat (health) and Ameretat (immortality), all ruled by Ahura Mazda. The Amesha Spentas are, however, opposed by six evil counterparts [daevas] created by Angra Mainyu: Indra (or

---

[704] See J. van Dijk, *op.cit.*, p.44.

[705] *Ibid.* In WB 1923, 444, the names are "a-lu-lim" and "a-lal-gar" reigning in Eridu, "en-me-en-lu-an-na", "en-me-en-gal-an-na" and "dumu-zi sipa" in Bad-tibira, "sipa-zi-an-na" in Larak, and "en-me-en-dur-an-na" in Zimbir. In W 20030,7 the names are given as "a-a-lu", "a-la-al-gar", "am-me-lu-an-na", "am-me-gal-an-na", "enme-usumgal-an-na", "dumu-zi sipa" and "en-me-dur-an-ki" respectively (*ibid.*, p.46).

[706] *Ibid.*, p.48.

[707] See below p.146.

Andar), Akomano (evil thought), who opposes Vohu-mano; Sauru (Skt. Sarva),[708] who opposes Kshatra Vairya; Naunhaithya (Skt. Nāsatyas), who oppose Spenta Armaiti, Tarich and Zairich (*Bundahishn* XXVIII,7). The Iranian daivas, who are similar to the Anunnaki, seem to be a negative Earthly state inversely reflecting the Heavenly creation of Ahura Mazda. They represent a cosmic stage before the rise of the sun in our system. The Indic devas, however, are endowed with a more heroic quality since it is through their effort that the solar energy is liberated from the underworld. The Iranian daivas may have some relation to the Sumerian "seven gods" created by Anu out of Earth who serve as malevolent agents in the Myth of Erra.[709]

In the *Bundahishn* I,53, after the creation of the primal astral bodies, the Mazdean creation is said to continue with the the production of the "seven fundamental Beneficent Immortals", the Ameshaspends:

> of the material creations created in the spirit the first are six, He Himself as the seventh; for both spirit first and then matter are of Ohrmazd. He created forth Vohuman... then Ardwahisht, then Sahrewar, then Spendarmad, then Hordad and Amurdad [the seventh in the order of immortal beings is Ohrmazd himself]

These are derived directly from the Wind, which is the Lord of Duration. The Amesha Spentas also correspond psychologically to the faculties of the Ideal Man, Purusha, namely intelligence, intellect, feeling, thinking, knowing and explication.[710]

Of these beneficent Immortals, the first, Vohuman, represents the Good Progress of the creation and the Essence of Light (I,53). The second, Ardwahisht, represents the Law immutable and his material existence is Fire and its assistants are Atar, Srosh and Warharan (XXVI, 35ff). Atar is manifest as three essential fires, the Farnbag, the Gushnasp and the Burzin Mihr. Next to these are the other fires which sit in sanctuaries and which are enshrined to smite the druj [enemy], and for the protection of the creatures. Atar is therefore, originally, an ideal fire. In the material realm it becomes Khvarag. The Immortal Sahrewar represents Sovereignty and metal is his own material. He is assisted by Khwar, Mihr, Asman and Anagran. Khwar is the shining immortal, radiant, swift-horsed sun. The work of Mihr is to judge the world with truthfulness. "As one says, Mihr

---

[708] See above p.42n.

[709] See H. Wohlstein, *op.cit.*, pp.144f.

[710] See above p.60.

of the wide pasture lands, having a thousand ears and ten thousand eyes"
(70f). Asman is the spiritual sky which holds this sky and Anagran are the
spiritual unapproachable lights. Spendarmad represents the Nourishment
of the creatures and the earth is her material. The Immortal Hordad
represents the Year and water is her material. She is assisted by Tir, Wad
and Frawardin. The Immortal Amurdad is the chief of Trees and the tree
is her own material. She is assisted by Rashnu, Ashtadm and Zam Yazd,
the spirit of the earth.

The next creations are

eighth Truthful Utterance, ninth Srosh pertaining to holiness, tenth
Manthra Spenta, eleventh Neryosang, twelfth the Eminent Rad
Rathwo Berezato, thirteenth the just Rashnu, fourteenth Mihr of wide
pastures, fifteenth the good Ashiswang, sixteenth Parend, seventeenth
Sleep, eighteenth Vat, nineteenth Lawfulness, twentieth Peacefulness

The Immortal Parend is the light of fifty stars which was created with
Ashishwang for the use of the Beneficent Immortals. (121).

The Ship of Life

We have noted that the supreme Lord incarnates himself in various
forms (avatars) throughout the developing life of the cosmos in order
to elevate the creation spiritually. The incarnation of the Lord as a
Fish which transfers the first man of the universe, Shrāddhadeva (or
Vaivasvata) Manu, from his celestial origin to the earth occurs relatively
late since Shrāddhadeva Manu[711] is but the seventh Manu of our kalpa
(*BP* VIII,13,1), the Padmakalpa.[712] According to the *Sūrya Siddhanta,*

---

[711] The name Shrāddhadeva is possibly etymologically related to Zarath-ustra and Ziusudra.

[712] According to *VP* I,3,27f, however, the present kalpa is considered to be the Varāha
kalpa which follows the Brahma kalpa and the Padma kalpa and begins the second half
of the existence of Brahma. *VP* I,35ff also lists the major avatārs of the seven manvantaras
upto the present as Yajna, Ajita, Satya, Hari, Mānasa, Vaikuntha and Vāmana.

According to *BP* I,3, there are twenty-two avatārs, beginning with [Krita Yuga]
Chatursana (the four sons of Brahma), the boar Varāha, Nārada, Nara-Nārāyana, Kapila,
Dattatreya, Yajna, Rshabha, [Treta Yuga] the fish Matsya, the tortoise Kūrma, Dhanvantari,
Mohini, Narasimha, Vāmana, Parashurāma, Vyāsa, Rāma, [Dvāpara Yuga] Balarāma,
Krishna, [Kali Yuga] the Buddha, Kalki.

We note that Varāha is a principal incarnation of the Krita Yuga while Vāmana is one
of the incarnations of the Treta Yuga which witnessed the appearance of Manu Vaivasvata
himself. The list in *BP* above may therefore be of avatārs within our own, seventh

Ch.I, 22, Manu is said to have appeared in the 28th Chaturyuga of our [Padma] Kalpa.[713] And, in the *Mahābhārata*, Shantiparva, it is said that Manu manifested himself in the Treta Yuga. This seventh Manu, Manu Vaivasvata [of Vivasvant, the sun], is responsible for the transmission of the seeds of life to earth as well as for the mortality (Yama) of the forms that spring from these seeds.

The seeds of universal life are borne in a "ship" of life that is familiar from the biblical, Babylonian and Iranian flood stories. We have seen that the flood that accompanies the installation of the sun in our system is the flood that is recorded in the Sumerian king-list and in the Bible. In the Babylonian epic, *Atrahasis*, Enki particularly advises Atrahasis to "roof [the ark] over like the Apsu/ So that the sun shall not see inside it", which indicates that the vehicle which contains the seed of all animals is, like the shrine in Dravidian accounts, completely dark.

The curious passage in *Atrahasis*, III,20, where Ea speaks to the "reed wall" of Atrahasis' dwelling may be explained by the frequent Indian references to the lake of "reeds" in which the golden seed of Shiva is dropped after being infused with his fiery form, Agni.[714] In a Sumerian magical text, Urn.49, the holy reed is said to rise from the swamps of Engur=Abzu.[715] The "reed" thus is a symbol of the ship of Life as well as of the tree of life that we have already studied, since both contain the seeds

---

manvantara.

According to *VP* III,2,55ff, too, the divine incarnation as Kapila is dated to the Krita Yuga, Vyāsa to the Dvāpara Yuga and Kalki is predicted to be the last incarnation at the end of the present Kali Yuga.

In the *Garuda Purāna* I,87, we find another list of incarnations for all the fourteen manvantaras but this seems to differ from that found in *VP*. The first manifestation of the Lord is said to have occurred during the first manvantara, as Himself with a discus, the second in the second manvantara as an elephant, the third in the third as a fish (Matsya), the fourth in the fourth as a tortoise (Kūrma), the fifth in the fifth as a swan, the sixth in the sixth as a horse and the seventh in the seventh as a boar (Varāha). The Dwarf (Vāmana) incarnation, however, is said to occur (or perhaps reoccur) during the eighth manvantara, and the Padmanābha during the ninth, while the tenth manifestation of the Lord will be as Himself with a mace, the eleventh as Shrirūpa, the twelfth as a eunuch, the thirteenth as a peacock and the last, in the fourteenth manvantara, as Vyāsa [who will no doubt ensure the prevalence of perfect Vedic knowledge in the last manvantara of the kalpa].

[713]   See E. Burgess, *Translation of the Surya-Siddhanta*, 1860; cf. *VP*, I,3: "Twenty-eight times have the Vedas been arranged by the great Rishis in the Vaivasvata Manvantara in the Dvápara age, and consequently eight and twenty Vyásas have passed away; by whom, in their respective periods, the Veda has been divided into four."

[714]   See *RV* X, 51-3; *SB* 6, 3.1.31; *RV* X, 32.6; cf. W.D. O'Flaherty, *Asceticism and Eroticism*, 159, 285. The "golden" seed is obviously related to the golden Cosmic Egg, "hiranyagarbha" as well as to the sun which is produced from it.

[715]   See H. Steible, *Die altsumerischen Bau- und Weihinschriften*, I:110.

of the incipient universe as well as its light. Indeed, the boat of Ziusudra is also made of "reed".

A close analogue of the ship of life is indeed the shrine that is described in the Dravidian Indian accounts of the Deluge. David Shulman has pointed out that the creation stories in the Dravidian versions emphasise the importance of the shrine as the centre of the universe and seat of the renewed creation after the deluge.[716] Shiva interestingly names this shrine "the root of the universe", which is situated on a hill rather like the primordial hill from which the light of the cosmos arises in Egypt. The shrine therefore is the foundation of the universe itself. In the related Dravidian accounts of the deluge which engulfed the sacred city of Madurai, the latter city serves as an analogue of the shrine whence the universe emerges. In these stories, the flood is said to have been caused by Varuna [Enki] at the instigation of Indra.[717] The flood caused by Varuna, Lord of the Underworld, precedes the formation of the new sun. Shiva is the god who protects the city Madurai from the flood, no doubt that it may serve as the sacred foundation of our universe. The shrine atop the mountain is secure (as also is the sacred city of Madurai) from any destructive flood which may well up from the netherworld, Pātāla.[718] For the concept that the sanctuary is to be found atop a mountain at the navel or centre of the universe is to be found in Jewish (and later Muslim) theologians as well,[719] who no doubt derived it from Babylon. In Sumer, a fish with the head of a 'dara', or mountain goat, is symbolic of the shrine of Enki.[720]

In the Iranian Vendidad, we find that Yima the son of Vivanghavant (the sun)[721] is warned by Ahura Mazda of a "snow storm" which will

---

[716] See D. Shulman, op.cit., 27.

[717] See the *Tiruvilai* of Paranjoti, 12, 18, 19 (D. Shulman, op.cit., pp.311ff).

[718] The spire (gopurum/shikara) of the Hindu temple represents this mountain while the sanctum is dark and mysterious as the Apsu whence the universe and its light emerge. The waters of the Abyss are also symbolically remembered in the controlled water of the Dravidian temple tank, which has the same purifying and fertilising power as the "sweet waters" of Enki/Varuna.

[719] See A. Wensinck, *Ideas*, pp.15f, 19ff, 40.

[720] F. X. Steinmetzer, *Sachau Festschrift*, pp.62ff., quoted in A.J. Wensinck, "The Ocean", p.65. (For the reappearance of the fish during the Flood see below p.141). In Islamic literature too, we find that a "stormy wind with two heads ... wound itself like a serpent on the spot of the sacred house [sanctuary]" (see A. Wensinck, *ibid.*).

[721] In Iranian mythology the twins Yama and Yima represent death and life. Yima is called the first king and the founder of civilisation and his fabulous dwelling is in Airyanem Vaego, corresponding mythologically to the Indian Yamasadanam and etymologically to Āryāvarta, the name applied to the Indo-Gangetic Plain settled by the later Indo-Āryans.

turn into a flood on melting.[722] In the Avesta, as in the Purānas, Yima (Manu) is mentioned as seventh in the line deriving from the First Man, Gayomard.[723] In order to escape the cataclysm, Yima is asked to construct a "vara" [ark] which will bear the best examples of men, animals, and plants, and especially the "cows" which are on the mountains as well as in the valleys in "closed stalls".[724] Special reference is made to the fact that the "window which lets in the sunlight" be closed. That the Iranian version closely follows the Babylonian in this detail (which is perhaps found also in the original Sumerian though lost in its present fragmentary state) while ignoring the significance of the ark as the shrine of the universe suggests that the Āryan flood stories as well as the Mesopotamian are based on an older proto-Dravidian/Hurrian original.

At the end of the Vendidad account of the deluge, Ahura Mazda explains that "the lights which shone in the vara" were "natural and human lights. All eternal lights shine from above, all human lights shine below in the inside (of the vara). Along with them one sees the stars, moon and sun shining in space". It is clear that the "human lights" are the souls of terrestrial creatures within the universe arisen from Earth, while "space" is the entire Mid-region of the stars, and the realm of the eternal lights is Heaven. Thus we see that the dimensions of the ship of life are indeed universal.

Although the Vedas contain no specific reference to a flood *per se*, the veiled reference at *RV* VII,88,3-5 where the sage Vasishta (one of the "seven sages") declares that he embarked on a boat with the aid of Varuna and, riding over "ridges of waters" entered the latter's "lofty home" may be related to the deluge which precedes the emergence of the sun.[725] Vasishta in the *Tandya Mahābrāhmana* 15,5,24,[726] is said to be the first sage who received the knowledge of the sacrifice from Indra and is therefore the priest of the generations of Bharata.

Yima is to be distinguished from Gayomaretan (Purusha), who is the First Man, who is killed by Angra Mainyu and whose seed is purified in the sun so that human life might arise on earth (see above p.91). However, Gayomaretan too is considered to be the founder of the Āryan race, or the chosen mankind (Farvardin Yast, 24). This suggests that Yima is but a reincarnation of Gayomaretan.

[722] The "snow storm" is a reference to the icy state of the incipient universe that prevents the manifestation of the solar energy (see above p.109).

[723] See above p.143.

[724] See H. Usener, *op.cit.*, p.208ff.

[725] See S. Shastri, *op.cit.*, p.viii.

[726] Cf. *TS* III,5,2.

In the *SP*, the sage Mārkandeya – who substitutes for Manu – appeals to the Lord for a refuge in the boundless ocean, "the ocean of mundane existence", the Lord points out to him the holy heavenly river Narmada (a form of Parvathi, Shiva's consort), along the banks of which Mārkandeya as well as the other sages practise penance. Narmada also represents the flood which bears the sun. Narmada assumes for this solar birth the form of a cow with golden horns, a shape we have encountered in the representation of the flood Mehet Ouret, or Hathor, as the bearer of Horus, the sun, between her horns.[727] At the same time, Narmada represents Earth, the material universe, itself. This is in consonance with her role as the consort of Shiva, who is the counterpart of Geb/Chronos/Time.[728] The transformation of the elemental universal matter of Earth into a Cow that yields nourishment to the various forms of life in the manifest universe is indeed related in the *BP* IV,17ff.[729]

Mārkandeya is saved from the cataclysm by seeking refuge in Narmada's "flanks", for this cow's milk is said to be "ambrosial", just as Aditi's is since it contains the divine "soma" [seed]. The result of Mārkandeya's imbibing of Narmada's milk is that "Divine vital energy" … "streamed through [him]" so that Mārkandeya "was able to breast the raging sea". There is, as we have seen, an intimate connection between Hathor and the Tree of Life, which springs up from the waters of the Abyss, just as there is between Aditi and Indra in the Vedas, and Narmada is a form of Aditi as well as Parvathi. Both Hathor and Aditi represent the basis of universal creation after the periodic destruction of the cosmos, and the Tree of Life is, as we shall see, the form of the material universe itself which arises from the Abyss through the divine seed represented by Indra/Ninurta/Marduk. We see now that Mārkandeya is indeed a form of the sun-god himself, and that is the reason why Manu, whom he replaces, is equally one, as his name Vaivasvata suggests.[730] Both Manu and Mārkandeya are solar forces directed to our universe and mankind and are thus considered ancestors of the race. As he is dragged along by the cow, whose "tail" he holds, for thousands of ages, Mārkandeya catches a glimpse of the Purusha "asleep"[731] in the cosmic ocean.

---

[727] See above p.119.

[728] See above p.43.

[729] Cf. above p.39.

[730] We have noted that the Sumerian Ziusudra too is equated with Urash (Lord of Earth), who represents the solar force Ninurta (see above p.97).

[731] Or moribund, in Osirian mythological terms.

In Egypt, we note that the Hymn in the temple of the Great Oasis declares that the sun "appeared on the back of the Earth".[732] In the Egyptian *Book of the Gates,* the solar journey is undertaken in a barque which is called the "barque of the Earth".[733] Earth, we have seen, represents the "trunk" of the Tree of Life and is the source of the gods, whose "flesh" it constitutes. In both the *Book of the Gates* and in the *Amduat,* the solar journey through Earth is undertaken within the coils of the World Encircler, the gigantic serpent representing Time.[734]

Manu Vaivasvata

The fortunes of the first man, Manu,[735] during the deluge are recounted in detail in the Vedic *SB.* In *SB* I,viii,1, Manu is considered the son of Vivasvant [the sun].[736] Though Manu is differentiated in *RV* from Yama, who is considered to be another son of Vivasvant,[737] Yama bears the same epithet of "Shrāddhadeva"[738] (lord of Faith) which Manu also does in *BP* VIII,24. So it is likely that we are dealing with an *alter ego,* especially since the flood hero of the Avesta, Yima, has a twin called Yama.[739] Manu's "half-brother" (or *alter ego*), Yama is indeed ruler of the lower heavens, according to *RV* I,35,6, and the sun and moon themselves are located in the mid-region between Heaven and Earth.

---

[732] *Ibid.,* p.80.

[733] See E.T. Hornung, op.cit., p.60.

[734] *Ibid.* In the *Enigmatic Book of the Underworld,* the *ouroboros* serpents represent the birth and end of time (*ibid.,* p.78). In the Nordic Eddas, the Midgard serpent is called the "encircler of Earth" ('Voluspa', 60). Since the "magur" boat in Sumer is identified with the moon, we see why Vrtra (the serpent corresponding to the Egyptian "world-encircler") is identified with the moon (see above p.82)

[735] We have seen above (p.19n) that Mannus was considered to be the first man also by the ancient Germans.

[736] In *KYV* VI,5,6, Vivasvant is called an Āditya whose offspring are men and the one born after the first four Ādityas. In the *SB* III,1,3,3 Vivasvant is identified with Mārtānda, the eighth Āditya, who is at first unformed but later moulded into a man who generates the creatures of Earth. In the Avestan Hom Yast IX, Vivanghavant is called quite simply the "first of men".

[737] In *RV* X, 10ff, Vivasvant engenders Yama, as well as Yama's twin sister and wife, Yami, by mating with a daughter of Tvashtr.

[738] See *HW* II:615.

[739] Cf. p.137n above.

BP VIII,13 declares that this Manu begins the seventh 'manvantara', our own. Since each manvantara has a duration of around 317,000,000 years (*BP* III,11,24), life on earth must have begun more than 1,902,000,000 years after the inception of the second cosmic age. Manu is warned of the deluge by a fish (representing Prajāpati in his piscine incarnation). In the *MBh*, the divine identity of the fish is revealed to be that of Prajāpati/Brahman (the name of the supreme god in his luminous, creative aspect), since the fish declares to the "seven sages" – who, unlike in the *SB* version of the story, accompany Manu in the ship – "I am Brahma, lord of progeny [Prajāpati] ... I in the form of a fish have delivered you from this peril".[740] The fish goes on to state that Manu should create all creatures including "gods, asuras, and men and all the worlds and what moves and what does not move [i.e. animal and vegetable life]."

Manu saves himself in a ship which is tied to the "horn" of the fish[741] and is borne by the latter to the heights of "the northern mountain", which, not being specified as a Himalayan one, may well be an Armenian one.[742] It is important to note that Manu is the divine ancestor of the race that is to inhabit the earth. In the *SB*, Manu is described as offering a sacrifice after the flood recedes, and from this sacrifice arises, first, a "daughter" Idā [a variant of Ilā],[743] from whom is derived the human race. In the sacrificial rituals Idā is the name of the portion of the sacrificial victim that is distributed to the sacrificer and the officiating priests.[744]

In the *SP,* Idā is called the "potency of Shankara [Shiva]",[745] that is, a reincarnation of his consort Parvathi herself, and is identified with Narmada "who destroys sin and delivers (mankind) from transmigration". Narmada is, as we have seen, the power of the Flood itself which has borne aloft the incipient sun and the life of the newly formed universe.[746]

---

[740] *MBh* II,187,2ff. (tr. S. Shastri, *op.cit.*, p.9); cf. H. Usener, *op.cit.*, p.28ff.

[741] See *SB* I,viii,1,5. It is hard to determine what the "horn" of the fish might be, unless it were a sword-fish. On the other hand, we may recall the image of Re emerging as the sun by holding on to the horns of the Cow Mehet-Ouret. The Indic imagery may be a transformation of the Egyptian. This is reinforced by the fact that Manu's daughter, Ida, who in *SB* I,viii,1,11-12 is said to characterise "cattle", is, in *TS* I,7,1 and II,6,7, represented as a cow produced by Mitra-Varuna. We see above that Idā is the same as Narmada.

[742] See below p.145.

[743] Ilā and Idā are interchangeable in the *BP* (Ilā: IX,16,22) and other Purānas (Idā: *BrdP* III,60,11, *VP* 85,7) In *SP* (Vaishnava Kānda), it is a name of Narmada, the mighty river (and consort) of Shiva (see S. Shastri, *op.cit,* p.72).

[744] See M. Biardeau, *op.cit.*, p.17.

[745] See S. Shastri, *op.cit.*, p.72.

[746] Cf. S. Shastri, *op.cit.*, p.81.

Though Idā is the "potency" of Shiva, Manu himself is a form of the Āditya Vivasvan.[747]

Ida is another form of Ila, and Ila, according to Purānic legend, is supposed to have married Chandra, the Moon, (or sometimes Budh [Intellect], the father of the Moon, or sometimes even Manu himself, her father). Ila is the originator of the Lunar dynasty of kshatriyas, while Manu's son, Ikshvāku continues the Solar line of his father.[748] According to *Rāmāyana*, Uttarakanda, 100, Ila was the son of the Manu Kardama, and king of Bāhlika (Bactria).[749] Purūravas, a grandson of Chandra and Ila, acquired the sacred fires of the Āryans from the Gandharvas (Gandharva being a term for heaven as well as for a particular tribe).[750] Purūravas is said to have lived at the end of the Treta Yuga, at the end of which age too there was another flood when the earth was submerged under the waters. However, with the assistance of the sage Agastya the earth was recovered from the depths and life revived on it.[751] Of the Ikshāvku line, Rāma, the famous son of Dasharatha, is said to have been born at the beginning of the Treta Yuga (*Rāmāyana*, Uttara Kanda, 44).

According to the *Bhavishya Purāna*, Pratisarga Parva I, the following Dvāpara Yuga was marked by the establishment of three kingdoms, at Pratishthana (this being related to the dynasty of Purūravas himself), Mathura (associated with Krishna, the lunar/Aila deity)[752] and Marudesh (ruled by Shmshrupal[753] of the Mlecchas,[754] and comprising Iran, Iraq and

---

[747]   According to the *Vishnu Purāna* and the *Rāmāyana*, Brahma is said to have formed 10 Prajāpatis, of whom one Marichi sired Kashyapa, the father of the Ādityas, including the Sun, Vivasvan, whose son, in turn, is Manu Vaivasvata.

[748]   For the Īkshvakus and Ailas, see further below p.204f. Interestingly, Ida is one of the principal nadis of the body in the yogic system (see below p.211) and is considered a lunar channel, whereas Pingala is the corresponding solar channel. These two nadis seem to be microcosmic counterparts of the lunar and solar dynastic lines of Ida and Īkshvāku respectively. The central nadi is called Sushumna and this must correspond to Manu (man) himself.

[749]   Cf. S.B. Chaudhuri, *Ethnic Settlements in Ancient India*, p.110.

[750]   For the fire-worshipping Gandharvas, see below p.188.

[751]   The mention of Agastya in connection with the recovery of the earth from the waters is interesting since it is he who is supposed to have conveyed the Vedic wisdom to the Tamils (or proto-Tamils of Sumer) – see below p.153.

[752]   See above p.89n.

[753]   Shamash is the Akkadian word for the sun.

[754]   In the *Manusmriti*, 'mleccha' is a general term for non-Āryan (see below p.191). The *Mbh* uses the term to include various Indo-European tribes (see below p.192n). However, here it seems to refer particularly to the mostly Semitic Assyrians and Babylonians. The *Bhavishya Purāna* too associates the mlecchas with the Semites.

Arabia). Marudesh clearly denotes the Hamitic cultures of Mesopotamia and Egypt which must have started at the end of the Dvāpara age since their peak, in the late fourth millennium B.C., coincides with the start of the Kali Yuga, which is traditionally supposed to have begun around 3100 B.C.[755] The Dvāpara age is supposed to have lasted for 864,000 years, though there is, as yet, little evidence of the existence of enlightened mankind on earth until the end of the Dvāpara age. The Gandharvas and Purūravas represent the Āryan tradition marked by fire-worship, whereas the Hamitic is marked by temple worship and idolatry. As we shall see below, the scriptural records of the Indians suggest that the temple worshipping cultures are indeed younger than the Āryan.

According to the *Bundahishn*, Ch.31, the First Man, Gayomard was followed by several generations beginning with Mashye and continuing with Siyamak, Fravak, Hooshang, Yanghad, Vivangha [the sun], and Yima [Jamshed]. We note that Yima [=Manu Vaivasvata] is the seventh in the genealogical line from Gayomard, so we may assume that Mashye and the others before him represent earlier Manu's. According to Firdausi's *Shāhnāmeh*, it was Hushang who discovered fire and established the Sadeh Feast in its honour. The *Vendidad* too refers to Jamshed (Yima), son of Vivanghat [Brahman], as the survivor of the Flood. According to the *Greater Bundahishn* Ch.33, Yima marked the end of the "first millennium" of the creation.

The second millennium was marked at its commencement by the reign of Azi Dahak [Skt. Ahi Dahāka], who was another descendant of Fravak, and who, according to the *Bundahishn*, "cut up" Yima along with Spitur. The end of the millennium was marked by the eventual defeat of the dynasty of this evil ruler by Faridoon [Thraetaona, Skt. Trita Āptya].

The third millennium was begun by Faridoon, whose great grandson (*Bundahishn* 31,9) was Manuschihar, whose descendant at the end of the millennium was King Vishtasp.

The fourth millennium was marked by the establishment of the doctrines of Zarathushtra in Eranvej. Zarathushtra, the son of Pourushasp, is also descended from the line of Manuschihar.

According to the *Greater Bundahishn*, Fravak and his sister Fravaken gave birth to nine races which live in the "six regions", or planets, that surround the central "continent" [planet] of Earth, Xvaniratha (which perhaps corresponds to the Shakadweepa of the *Mbh*),[756] and six other races that inhabit Xvaniratha itself. The six regions which are inhabited

---

[755] See below p.177.

[756] See below p.181.

by the first progeny of Fravak and Fravaken, are named in Ch.XXIX,2 as Arezahi, Sawahi, Fradadhafhsu, Widadhafshu, Wourubareshti and Wourujareshti. The latter two are considered as being ruled by hostile devas (XXVIII,21). The six races that inhabit Xvaniratha include Taz and Tazak (in Dast-I Taziyan), Hooshang and Guzak (who give rise to the Iranians), and another couple that give rise to the Mazendarans.[757] The spiritual ruler of the whole of Xvaniratha is said to be Zarathushtra, son of Pourushaspa, son of Spitama. Xvaniratha itself is divided into several regions such as Kangdez [in the east], Sikistan [far in the direction of the north], the plain of the Tajis, the plain of Peshyansi [in Kavulustan], the river Naevatak, Eranwej [on the side of Atarpatakan], the enclosure which Jamshed [Yima] prepared [in the middle of Pars], and Kashmir [in Hindustan] (XXIX,5-15). The "Tree opposed to harm" is said to be in Eranwej.

We may note here that, in Mesopotamia, Sumer is most probably the name of the "primordial hill" of the central island of Earth, through which the solar force of the universe emerges since Sumer is called "the great mountain, the land of the universe" in l.192 of "Enki and the World-Order". Sumeru ('Holy Meru') is indeed a name of Mt. Meru in *BrdP* I,ii,15,42.[758] The names of the other lands around Sumer – Ur, Meluhha, Dilmun, Elam-Marhasi, and Martu – which Enki blesses in the poem may be named after the other original mountain formations of Earth. We note that the Sumerians and the Indo-Aryans have the same name, Meluhha/Mleccha, for a tribe that was probably Semitic in origin.[759] This is perhaps evidence that the Vedic lore was the creation of proto-Dravidians from the north of Mesopotamia who originated the Vedic knowledge later manifested among the Indo-Āryans as well as among the proto-Tamils of Sumer.[760]

Since it is most likely that the Noachidian race was indeed a proto-Dravidian one, it is probable that the yogic wisdom is derived from it. *BP* VIII,14,3 informs us that the role of a "Manu", who in *BP* VIII,24,13 is, as we have seen, called King of Dravida, is to maintain the cosmic order at the time of the creation of the universe. So we may assume that Dravida and its king Satyavrata represent the first fully enlightened mankind. We shall see also that the brāhmans were considered the "sons of Seth", the son of Adam. Since Noah is a descendant of Seth and Noah is the same

---

[757] Cf. the Māzanians who were identified as "daevas" see below p.187.

[758] See above p.84n.

[759] See above p.142n.

[760] See below p.266.

as Manu, who is a Dravidian "king" in *BP*, we have here a confirmation of the proto-Dravidian origin of the religion later represented by the brāhmans. F.E. Pargiter maintained that Brāhmanism itself was not originally Āryan but adopted into Indo-Āryan religion from Dravidian.[761] However, Pargiter did not consider the possibility that both Āryan and later Dravidian may have been derived from a proto-Dravidian/Hurrian spiritual culture.

Although the Vedic tradition places Manu Vaivasvata in the very distant Treta Yuga, it is possible to detect the historical development of the earliest Noachidian race of proto-Dravidians – or proto-Semites according to the biblical Table of Nations – by following the accounts of the flood in the related scriptural traditions of antiquity. In the Indian account of the Flood in the *BP*, the boat of Manu comes to rest upon an unnamed "northern" mountain (VIII, 24). In the *MP* we see the same Manu practising penance on a mountain simply called (in the Sanskrit text of the *MP*) Malaya, which is a Dravidian term meaning mountain. In the Babylonian history of Berossos, the boat of Xisouthros (corresponding to the Sumerian Ziusudra, the Babylonian Atrahasis[762] and Utnapishtim of the *Gilgamesh* epic[763]) lands in Armenia. According to Nikolaos of Damascus, a contemporary of Augustus,[764] the Armenian mountain on which the boat landed is the Baris mountain, which may be the same as Mt. Ararat (north of Lake Van) mentioned in the biblical Flood story of *Genesis* 8:3. According to Berossus, the Babylonians moved to different parts of Babylonia from Armenia.[765]

Since some of the earliest centres of historic, literate culture are those of the Canaanites, Hatti, Elamites, Sumerians, and Egyptians, it is possible that Mt. Ararat was the central region from whence the proto-Dravidians travelled to Palestine, Anatolia, Mesopotamia and Egypt. In one version of the Sumerian king-list, Ziusudra, the survivor of the Deluge, is also said

---

[761] See F.E. Pargiter, *Ancient Indian Historical Tradition*, Ch.26.

[762] H. Usener suggested that the right form of this name may have been Hasis-Atra, which seems likely as the Babylonian version of the Sumerian Ziusudra (see H. Usener, *Sintfluthsagen*).

[763] In the Gilgamesh epic (XI,204), Utnapishtim is said to be beyond the Ocean in the region whence "the rivers flow forth". We may surmise that Utnapishtim, like Manu, must be resident in the region of the Moon, the lower heavens.

[764] Nikolaos is reported in Josephus' *Jewish Antiquities*, I,93.

[765] See Berossus in W. Lambert and A.R. Millard, *Atrahasis*, p.136. Berossus, like all authors of terrestrial Flood stories, believes that the antediluvian history is also set on earth, in his case, in Babylonia.

to have lived in Shuruppak,[766] the last of the antediluvian cities, situated north of Uruk. In the Sumerian Gilgamesh epic, the mountain atop which the boat comes to rest is called Mt. Nimush (or Nisir), which may be in the Zagros.[767] If so, the region around this particular mountain may have been the home of the originators of the Gilgamesh story. It is noteworthy that the *BP* too begins its long narratives at the hermitage of the "Suta" in the forest of Naimish (*BP* I,1,4), which may indeed be the same as the mountain mentioned in the Gilgamesh epic.

In the Ethiopian version of Pseudo-Callisthenes, which incorporates information culled from the anonymous *History of the Blessed Men Who Lived in the Days of Jeremiah the Prophet*, the brāhmans are called the sons of Adam's son, Seth,[768] and Noah was considered a transmitter of the wisdom of Seth.[769] Since Adam is indeed the Cosmic Man and not a human, we may assume that the brāhmans referred to here are associated with the preservation of the Divine Consciousness of Brahman which arises from the Cosmic Egg and is later conveyed to humanity by the seventh Manu/Noah. Although the brāhmans formed the highest caste among the Indo-Āryans, in the Indian *BP* VIII,24, the survivor of the "flood", Manu (the counterpart of Noah) is himself called Satyavrata, King of Dravida. In the *MP* too, Manu is described as practising austerities (tapas) on Mt. Malaya, which is commonly identified with a mountain in South India,[770] though it may have originally been the name of a mountain outside India associated with the proto-Dravidians. As for Seth, Josephus declares that Seth

---

[766] W-B 62, where Ubar-Tutu(k) the king of Shuruppak is mentioned as the father of SU-KUR-LAM (representing Shuruppak itself), whose son is said to be Zi-u-sud-ra (see T. Jacobsen, *Sumerian King-List*, pp.75f.). Shuruppak is situated just south of Nippur.

[767] The name of the mountain is sometimes read as Nisir. It is probable that Nimush is the original version of the name in the face of the evidence of the *BP* (cf. M.L. West, *East Face*, p.492); cf. Ashurnasirpal, *Annals* II:34 (see Streck, *ZA*, XV, 272-5). M.G. Kovacs has suggested that it might be the same as Pir Omar Gudrun in southern Kurdistan (see M.G. Kovacs (tr.), *The Epic of Gilgamesh*, p.113).

[768] See E.A.W. Budge, *The Alexander Book*, pp.74ff. The identification of the brāhmans with Seth may be glossed with the reference in the *BrdP* I,i,1,8ff. to the fact that the Purānas (or the original Purāna which was later divided into the several extant Purānas) were transmitted by the sage Vasishta (one of the seven sages) to other divine sages Parāsara, Jātukarnya, and Vyāsa (also called Dvaipāyana) and the last then transmitted this divine learning to the mortals Jaimini, Sumantu, Vaisampāyana, Pailava, and, finally, Lomaharshana, the *Sūta*. However, a Sūta is not a Brāhman but the son of a kshatriya father and a Brāhman mother (see, for instance, *Gautama Dharmasūtra*, 4,15).

[769] See A. Annus, *Standard Babylonian Epic*, p.xxix.

[770] See D. Shulman, "The Tamil Flood Myths", p.296.

strove after virtue and, being himself excellent, left descendants who imitated the same virtues. All of these, being virtuous, lived in happiness in the same land without civil strife, with nothing unpleasant coming upon them until after their death. And they discovered the science with regard to the heavenly bodies and their orderly arrangement.[771]

Josephus identifies the land of Seth as located around "Seiris", which is also the land of Noah, who is said to have preserved the wisdom of Seth. In the Christian *Opus Imperfectum in Matthaeum* of Pseudo-Chrysostom, the books of Seth were supposed to have been hidden by Noah in the land of Šir, and the so-called "cave of treasures" in which they were hidden is identifiable with Mt. Ararat.[772] In *Genesis* 14:6, the Horites, or Hurrians, are particularly identified with Mt. Seir, and we note a close identification of the proto-Hurrians with the proto-Dravidians of *BP*, according to which Manu is King of Dravida. The brāhmans who are considered to be the "sons of Seth" must have originally constituted the priesthood of the proto-Hurrian/proto-Dravidian population,[773] though it is true that the Āryan, and particularly Indo-Āryan, line deriving from this original population seem to have retained the brāhmanical tradition best of all.[774]

As regards the proto-Dravidian folk, we may remember Lahovary's pioneering research into the Mediterranean race, which he identified with the Dravidian, as being the original inhabitants of the ancient Near East "in its largest meaning", that is, including "Anatolia, Syria, Palestine, Caucasia, Persia, Mesopotamia with its extensions towards India, as well as Arabia and the African regions facing Arabia, i.e. from the Nile valley to the high tablelands of East Africa".[775] Lahovary goes on to remark that

It was from this world of Anterior Asia, where the foundations of civilization had been already laid, that the bearers of the neolithic

---

[771] See Josephus, *Jewish Antiquities*, I:70-1. Mount Seiris may be a corruption of the name of Anzu's mountain Sarsar in the *Epic of Anzu* where Ninurta regains the tablet of destinies after battling Anzu (see A. Annus, *op.cit.*, p.xxviiiff.).

[772] See G.G. Stroumsa, *Another Seed*, p.117.

[773] The term "Hurrian" (derived from Suwalliyat/Suwariyat/Sūrya; see below p.151) however may not be equated with "Āryan" since both Iranian and Indian have distinct terms for the sun (sūrya, hvare) and for the community of Aryans (ārya, eira), respectively. Hurrian certainly includes a strong Dravidic element in it (see G.W. Brown, "The possibility of a connection", 273-305).

[774] See below p.196ff.

[775] See N. Lahovary, tr. K.A. Nilakantan, *Dravidian Origins*, p.2.

and chalcolithic civilizations of the Near East spread, by successive migrations, in general of relatively small groups over a period of more than three thousand years, first towards North-East Africa, and later, during the fourth, third and second millennium, towards Europe.[776]

The physical appearance of this race is described by Lahovary thus:

> From the Nile and Anatolia to western India and perhaps further still to the Ganges valley you had the same brownish white, long-headed population with a long, straight and narrow face, a narrow nose, and a pronounced chin, slim limbs, of gracile and small build ... In pre-dynastic Egypt and in a great part of India we meet with still another variety of this type, perhaps a little more primitive, the so-called Eurafrican or proto-Mediterranean type.

However, he takes care to add that

> It should also be mentioned that during the Upper Paleolithic and Mesolithic periods up to the late Neolithic, the Negroid element, formed probably in West Africa, is ... completely absent from North and East Africa, which were inhabited only by peoples who differed from the 'Mediterranean' type mostly only by their taller structure.[777]

It is possible that one of the earliest regions to be settled by the Noachidian peoples from neighbouring Armenia was Anatolia.[778] This is suggested by the great antiquity of the Neolithic archaeological finds at Çatal Hüyük in (ca. 7th millennium B.C.). The civilisation of Syro-Palestine may be even as old as that of Anatolia since settlements in Jordan are traceable from the late 7th millennium B.C. and in Byblos from the 6th.[779]

The early neolithic/chalcolithic sites of Yarim Tepe II (7th millennium B.C.) give some evidence of fire rituals in connection with funerary practices.[780] The chalcolithic sites (ca. 5000 B.C.) of Northern

---

[776] Lahovary particularly points to the legend of Cadmus the Phoenician bringing the arts of metallurgy and writing to Greece.

[777] N. Lahovary, *op.cit.*, p.7.

[778] Though the urban Neolithic achievements at Çatal Hüyük seem to be older than those in Armenia, there is evidence of similar development at the border of ancient Armenia in Jarmo (see D. Lang, *Armenia*, p.61).

[779] See G.W. Ahlstrom, *Ancient Palestine*; J. Cauvin, *Religions néolithiques*,1972; S.A. Cook, *op.cit* ; for Jericho, see K.M. Kenyon, *Digging up Jericho*.

[780] See P. Charvat, *Mesopotamia*, p.90.

Mesopotamia also provide similar evidence[781] and these may point to the presences of early Vedic peoples, proto-Semitic and proto-Āryan. These sites must then be ascribed to the end of the Dvāpara Yuga, which, according to the *Tārapradīpa*, witnessed the transition to the Tantric temple-worshipping tradition as well.[782] The earliest sites of Mesopotamian culture are to be found in the north, in Tel el Halaf, dating back to around 5000 B.C.[783] The powerful influence of the Halafian culture is attested in the imitations of its pottery in southern Armenia[784] as well as in northeastern Syria.[785] One major distinction of the northern culture is the aesthetically more advanced state of the pottery of the Tel al Halaf region in the north, which is contemporaneous with Ubaid I in the delta. The Ubaid I pottery, dating from even before 5000 B.C., on the other hand, is characterised by a much lower level of craftsmanship and artistry.[786] The Tel el Halaf pottery is marked by bucranium designs[787] which associate it with the seventh millennium shrines of Çatal Hüyük in eastern Anatolia,[788] which may have been established by the earliest proto-Dravidians or Hurrians.

Recently, Oates has shown that, in spite of their qualitative differences, there are generic similarities also between the Samarra and the Ubaid pottery.[789] And Charvat has revealed that the fundamental social and religious forms of later Mesopotamian culture, including that of Uruk, are evident already in embryonic form in the early chalcolithic sites of northern Mesopotamia.[790] Crematory practices associated with fire-rituals are noticed here[791] and Tell Arpachiyah (TT6) also gives the first evidence of the use of the white-red-black colour triad which persists from chalcolithic times to Uruk[792] and is representative of three of the

---

[781] See below.

[782] See below p.271.

[783] See J. Finegan, *Archaeological History*, p.7.

[784] See D. Lang, *op. cit.*, p.63.

[785] See G.W. Ahlström, *op. cit.*, p.107.

[786] See J. Finegan, *op.cit.*, p.9.

[787] *Ibid.*, p.7.

[788] For Çatal Hüyük, see J. Mellaart, *Çatal Hüyük*; also H. Nissen, *Early History*, p.35f.

[789] See J. Oates, "Ur and Eridu", p.42, where she suggests a common ancestry for both Samarra and early Eridu.

[790] See P. Charvat, *op.cit.*, pp.92,96.

[791] *Ibid.*, pp.45,90.

[792] *Ibid.*, p.92. In Greek antiquity, black may have denoted prime matter, red matter and white spirit (*ibid.*, p.93). This corresponds to the three basic energies in Indian philosophy,

four castes – the brāhman, kshatriya, and shudra – amongst the Indo-Āryans.[793] So we may assume that the proto-Dravidians including proto-Akkadians and proto-Āryans were present in the north as well as in Elam and Eridu. Since Armenia is the most likely place from which the cultures of both Çatal Hüyük and Tel el Halaf may have originated, it is probable that we are dealing, in the case of the sixth- and fifth millennium pottery of the north as well as the south, with the proto-Dravidian or Noachidian race.

In Mesopotamia, the earliest archaeological finds after the Halafian ones are those from Susa. Susa I dates from the sixth to the fifth millennium B.C. [Berossus' history mentions as the first king after the flood Euekhoios,[794] whose name may be a veiled Greek reference to Susa or a man (=king) of Susa (Greek "eu" corresponding to Sanskrit "su"), since it does not seem to correspond to the fragmentary name of the first king of Kish in the Sumerian king-list (Ga...ur)]. The earlier settlements in the Elamite highlands than in the neighbouring river-valleys may be due to the fact that it was not originally possible to cultivate land in the swampy plains of Mesopotamia.[795] Speiser considered Susa I to be related to similar cultures scattered across the whole of Mesopotamia and Persia, as well as in Armenia, Baluchistan, and a little later in Eridu.[796] He, along with Frankfort, conjectured that the source of this culture may have been in Armenia itself, especially since the farthest northern site to yield pottery of the Susa I type is Mt. Ararat.[797] So it is possible that we have in Elam, as in earliest Anatolia and Palestine, the same Noachidian proto-Dravidian people. As for the biblical account of the earliest Elamites, we have noted that it considers Elam as a son of Shem. This suggests that the proto-Akkadian Semites formed a major constituent of the proto-

---

Tamas, Rajas, Sattva (see above p.16). In Egypt, Osiris is frequently represented with black skin, indicating perhaps his lordship of Earth and of the dead (see R.H. Wilkinson, *Symbol and Magic*, p.109).The association of the three Indian castes with these colours is clearly due to the predominance of the sattvic, rājasic, and tāmasic elements, respectively, in them.

[793]   See, for instance, *BrdP* I,ii,15,18ff. The Vaisya caste is normally represented by the colour yellow. The absence of yellow in the pottery of this period suggests that the original "caste"-system of the Hurrians was a tripartite one comprised of priests, warriors and agriculturists (these are the same as the three "castes" mentioned in the Iranian Farvardin Yasht XIII,88).

[794]   Reported by Alexander Polyhistor (see G.P. Verbrugghe and J.M. Wickersham, *Berossus and Manetho*, p.51).

[795]   See H. Nissen, *op. cit.*, pp.55ff.

[796]   See E. Speiser, *Mesopotamian Origins*, p.63f.

[797]   *Ibid.*, pp.65ff. Speiser placed the "original center" of the First Aenolithic culture "somewhere between Anatolia and the Caspian" (p.66).

Dravidian/Hurrian population in Elam. Though, these proto-Akkadians may well have been just proto-Dravidians speaking the Akkadian dialect of the "eldest son" of Noah, Shem. The resemblances to Sanskritic vocabulary in Akkadian must derive from the common proto-Dravidian source which produced both Akkadian and, later, Sanskrit.

Of the early Ubaid culture of southern Mesopotamia, Eridu, which dates from the sixth millennium B.C., shows marked Elamite affinities. In fact, as Frankfort pointed out, in Elam "the stage corresponding with al-Ubaid" was found "overlying that called 'Susa I'".[798] According to Speiser, the original name of Ku'ara (near Eridu) in the first dynasty of Uruk[799] – HA.A[ki] – may be of Subarian, or proto-Hurrian origin.[800] The very term "subari" or, more precisely, "suwari",[801] is clearly related to Suvalliyat (Suvariya)/Sūrya, which is also the Hititte/Indic name of the sun-god. Hurri then would be the Iranian pronunciation of the same name, as the Iranian name of the sun-god, "Hvare", suggests. The Subarians were traditionally identified as a northern highland people, though they may have moved south to Elam as well.[802] The presence of the Hurrians in southern Mesopotamia is attested from the Old Babylonian period since magical ritual tablets of this epoch contain Hurrian language texts.[803] The wide-ranging extent of the Ubaid culture is evident from the fact that even the most northern city of Nineveh was continuously occupied from the fifth millennium.[804]

Of the three linguistic branches associated with the sons of Noah, the earliest literary evidence is indeed mostly of the Semitic proto-Akkadian. Many of the words of the earliest Uruk tablets that were designated as "proto-Euphratean" by B. Landsberger are most probably of proto-Akkadian origin, as G. Rubio has recently pointed out.[805] It is interesting

---

[798] H. Frankfort, *Archaeology*, p.19.

[799] See T. Jacobsen, *Sumerian King-List*, p.89. It may also be related to the original Akkadian A.a for Ea.

[800] See E. Speiser, *Mesopotamian Origins*, p.38f.

[801] *Ibid.*, p.39n; cf. the letter of Rîb-Aeldi, Prince of Byblos which refers to the land of Suru, which may be synonymous with Subartu (see A. Ungnad, *op.cit.*, p.50).

[802] According to Landsberger, the pre-Sumerian "Proto-Euphratians" of the south are to be distinguished from the pre-Semitic "Proto-Tigridians" of the north (see B. Landsberger, "Beginnings of Civilization" in *Three Essays*).

[803] See G. Wilhelm, *Grundzüge*, p.97.

[804] See G. Leick, *Mesopotamia*, p.222. Similarly Nippur, south of Babylon, was inhabited from the fifth millennium (*ibid.*, p.143) and Sippar, farther north, is mentioned in early cosmogonical texts, as one of the oldest cities in the land, much like Eridu (*ibid.*, p.172).

[805] See G. Rubio, "On the alleged 'Pre-Sumerian Substratum'", p.5.

to note, also, that, of twenty-two monarchs constituting the first dynasty of Kish (in the north), the names of twelve are Semitic, while six are Sumerian and four are of uncertain provenance.[806] This suggests that the proto-Akkadian Semites were widespread throughout the region,[807] even though the first two kings of Kish (as also the last two) bear clearly Sumerian names.[808] Some scholars have even gone so far as to note that there are "few indications of the Sumerian language in the archaic tablets from Uruk and Jemdet Nasr; especially distressing is the dearth of recognizable Sumerian personal names".[809] Indeed, none of the oldest city names such as Urim, Uruk, Larsa, Adab, Lagas, and Zimbir is Sumerian but belong to what Landsberger called a "Proto-Euphratian" substrate,[810] which may be related to the proto-Akkadians. Langdon, however, noted that most of the Semitic names were concentrated in the north, "none of the southern pre-Sargonic dynasties, Erech, Ur and Adab, show Semitic names, whereas the northern dynasties Kish, Maer and Akshak have a mixed nomenclature", and this suggests the "entrance of the Semites into the northern area at Kish and Maer at a very early period".[811] The Semitic Akkadian culture of northern Mesopotamia must have been related also to that of Elam, which is described in *Genesis* 10:20 as a "son" of Shem.

The "proto-Euphratean" relics from the Ubaid culture have, interestingly, been described by Landsberger as indicative of a predominantly agricultural society, which mingled with a more 'professional' Sumerian stratum that included scribes, physicians, and judges.[812] Thus the indigenous Mesopotamians, proto-Dravidian and proto-Akkadian may have been less gifted in the direction of urban culture, which was due more to the dynastic Sumerians.

As regards the linguistic question of agglutination and inflection in relation to inflected Akkadian and agglutinative Sumerian, we may remember Lahovary's suggestion that "proto-Semitic ... represents a later and more evolved layer of the neolithic languages of the Near East of which the first were probably polysynthetic languages of the Sumero-Asianic, Basco-Dravidian and Caucasian type".[813] However, the fact that

---

[806] See G. Roux, *Ancient Iraq*, p.102.

[807] See Poebel, *ZA* 39, p.149,n.2.

[808] See S. Langdon, *Excavations*, p.57.

[809] J.S. Cooper, "Sumerian and Semitic Writing", p.61.

[810] See B. Landsberger, *op.cit.*, p.9.

[811] See S. Langdon, *op.cit.*, p.58.

[812] See B. Landsberger, *op.cit.*, p.11f.

[813] See N. Lahovary, *op.cit.*, p.11.

the dynastic Sumerians spoke a language that was still agglutinative though chronologically later than the proto-Akkadians may only reflect an isolation of its speakers at a time when the Semitic and Japhetic branches of the race were developing their respective languages in a more inflected manner.

That Akkadian is an older language than Sumerian is suggested by the fact that the Akkadian vocabulary is closer to that of modern Dravidian than Sumerian itself, as the lexical lists presented recently by Muttarayan suggest.[814] This is in consonance with the traditional reverence for the sage Akkathiya (Skt. Agastya) among the Tamils, who consider the latter to be the one who imparted Vedic learning to them.[815] The fact that the Tamils consider Akkathiya as their tutor suggests also that the Tamils (and the Sumerians) are not identical to the original proto-Dravidians/Hurrians of Elam/Akkad. However, Tamil curiously retains some archaic forms of the proto-Dravidic language compared to Akkadian, for the Tamil word "vitu", for house, is clearly more original than Akkadian "bitu", Tamil "panu" than Akkadian "ban", and Tamil "ālu" than the Akkadian umlaut variant "awilu". The greater general deviation of Sumerian from modern Dravidian than that of Akkadian indicates also the relative lateness of Sumerian compared to Akkadian. The Sumerian voiced transformation of the voiceless sibilant in the Akkadian "apsu" as "abzu" confirms the greater antiquity of Akkadian. Again, the fact that the Sumerian word for water itself, "a", drops the final consonant of the Sanskritic (or proto-Dravidian) "ap", even though this final consonant reappears euphonically in the term "abzu", shows that the Sumerian of the Uruk period is a late variant of the original proto-Dravidian language of the Elamites and the Ubaid folk. It seems clear also that Akkadian, on the other hand, is a very senior branch of proto-Dravidian.

It is not surprising that the earliest Akkadians were closely associated with Hurrian tribes as well, with whom they seem to have shared a common historical tradition. A Hurrian magical ritual text mentions historical figures of the northern kingdom of Akkad such as Sargon and Naram-Suen along with a certain "Autalumna of Elam", showing that both Akkad and Elam were considered as parts of an integral Hurrian-Akkadian domain.[816] We have here another indication of the great antiquity of the Semitic Akkadian family. The apparently Sanskritic words that Akkadian contains are no doubt derived from Hurrian/proto-

---

[814] See K.L. Muttarayan, "Sumer", p.42.

[815] See below pp.266ff.

[816] See A. Ungnad, *Subartu*, p.101.

Dravidian originals.[817] The Akkadian word for the Abyss, "apsu", is related
to the "Sanskritic" word for water, "ap". The Akkadian term "sibittu" for
seven is also remarkably similar to the Hurrian "šitta" and the Indo-
Āryan "sapta".[818] Similarly, the Sanskrit term "hiranya" for "gold" is clearly
related to the Akkadian "hurasu", though the source of them both may
have been the Hurrian "hiyarruhe". The Akkadian word "atmanu" for
"sanctum" (*Gilgamesh* V,249, *Anzu* I,56) is also clearly cognate with the
Sanskritic "ātman", meaning soul, and is related as well to the Egyptian
Amun (imin), who is called the "inner support" of the entire universe.[819]
The Akkadian "atmanu" is the source also of the Sumero-Akkadian
term "temmenu"/"temen" for a foundation-stone, particularly that of a
temple.[820] The fact that the word "ātman" is no longer generally used for
the sanctum or its deity in India itself suggests also that the Indic peoples
were in Elam and Mesopotamia long before they migrated to India.

---

[817] D. Frayne ("Indo-Europeans") has suggested that many words in the earliest
Mesopotamian texts may have been loans from "Proto-Indo-European". But, apart from
the fact that PIE itself is only a hypothetical reconstruction, Frayne seems to think that the
Hurrian culture of Halafian Subartu – which he posits as the source of this language – itself
may have been a "proto-Indo-European" one. However, we must bear in mind that proto-
Indo-European is not the same as "Āryan", as most scholars who use the term PIE seem
to think, but the generic name of a linguistic prototype from which Semitic, Āryan and
Hamitic were derived (cf. *Genesis* 11:1 where the sons of Noah are described as speaking
the same language originally).

[818] See E.A. Speiser, *Introduction to Hurrian*, p.82. For the close relationship between the
Hurrians and Indo-Āryans see further below p.185.

[819] See A. Annus, *op. cit.*, p.xi.

[820] See *AW* III:1346. This term is carried over into Greek as "τέμενος".

V.

YOGA

The extraordinary cosmological and philosophical insights that inform the religions of the ancient world could only have been developed through yogic meditation, and this is confirmed by the *BrdP* I,i,3,8, as well. We note also that, in the *MBh*, XIII (Anushāsana Parva) 14,[821] Shiva himself is constantly addressed as the "soul of yoga" and the object of all yogic meditation. Similarly, his son, Skanda (Muruga, god of the Dravidians) is described as being endowed with yogic powers in *Mbh* IX (Shalya Parva), 44. The macrocosm and the microcosm in the most ancient religions are clearly understood in a yogic manner. For instance, the yogic notion of the Kundalini serpent and the awakening of this serpentine form to the light of Brahman lies at the basis of the Egyptian drama of Osiris in the underworld,[822] as well as of the concept of the universal tree of life which features in the cosmologies of all the ancient Indo-European cultures.[823]

The term "yoga" means "yoking" and signifies the union of the individual soul to the supreme, which is brought about through several strict physiological and mental austerities. The aim of all Vedic enlightenment, whether it be through Āryan fire-worship or the later Tantra, is thus the attainment of the ultimate identity of the ātman with Brahman. According to *Manusmriti*, I,86, austerities were performed first in the Krita age:

---

[821] Cf. *MBh* VII (Drona Parva), 202, where Shiva is called Yoga and the Lord of Yoga (Yogeshvara).

[822] See above p.78

[823] See above pp.79ff.

In the Krita age the chief (virtue) is declared to be (performance of) austerities, in the Treta (divine) knowledge, in the Dvapara (the performance of) sacrifices, in the Kali liberality alone.

In the *MBh*, VII (Anushāsana Parva), 16, Tandi, a sage of the Krita Yuga is said to have "adored Shiva for 10,000 years with the aid of yogic meditation". The "divine knowledge" said to have prevailed in the following Treta Yuga may have been derived from the ascetic disciplines practised in the Krita Yuga. In the Treta Yuga, we have noted that Manu himself is described in the *MP* and *SB* as practising tapas, or austerities, on Mt. Malaya,[824] but also as sacrificing.[825] In the *Rāmāyana*, Uttara Kanda, Sec.87, only the brāhmans are said to have practised austerities in the Krita Yuga. In the following Treta Yuga, kshatriyas were born and, gaining equal spiritual dignity with the brāhmans, practised austerities alongside them, while the vaisyas and shūdras served them. Then in the Dvāpara Yuga vaisyas started to practise austerities as well, just as the shūdras too began practising austerities in the Kali Yuga.

However, some maintain that fire-worship began already in the Krita Yuga.[826] Shriram Sharma, for instance, has suggested that "yajnas" were performed intensively already in the Krita Yuga:

The yajnas were ... performed in the divine Krita Yuga,[827] by the rishis [i.e. the seven sages] and the demigods since the demigods themselves were manifest on earth.[828]

These "yajnas" of the Krita Yuga peformed by the seven sages and demigods may have been different from the human fire-sacrifices which appeared after Manu Vaivasvata.[829] Regarding the forms of worship of the sages and sacrifices, *RV* I,84,2, declares that Indra attended eulogies sung by Rishis and yajnas conducted by humans. Shriram Sharma[830] points out that "In comparison to what man attains via yajnas, great Rishis attain much more via sankalpa/ strength of resolve and eulogy to God (*YV*

---

[824] See above p.145.

[825] See above p.141.

[826] See below p.177.

[827] According to the *Tārapradīpa*, Ch.1, too, the Satya (Krita) age was marked by Vedic knowledge, Vaidika Upasana.

[828] Shriram Sharma, *Scientific Basis of Yajnas*, Ch.20.

[829] See above p.105 and Chs.VIII-X below.

[830] S. Sharma, *op.cit*, Ch.20

17,28)." However, he suggests that "this power of eulogy was attained by the Rishis via fire worship (*AV* IV,23,5)".[831] The Atharvavedic reference he gives represents Indra as being aided by Agni in his battle against the sources of resistance (Panis) which obstruct the rise of the solar force into our system. It is possible that both yoga and fire-worship may have originally developed from a focus on the thawing power of fire required to release the solar force in macrocosm as well as microcosm. In the latter, it is manifest as the "heat" of yogic austerities or "tapas". Fire-worship, on the other hand, is a more external dramatic recreation of the macrocosmic solar force[832] than yoga, which seeks to realise the solar force within the human microcosm.

That yoga was the original means whereby the knowledge of the macrocosm was obtained is suggested by the extraordinary description of the different forms of primal light that is to be found in the yoga-based *Mandalabrāhmana Upanishad*, II:[833]

[antarlakshya] is the source of the five elements, has the lustre of many (streaks of) lightning, and has four seats having (or rising from) 'That' (Brahman). In its midst, there arises the manifestation of tattva. It is very hidden and unmanifested. It can be known (only) by one who has got into the boat of jñāna. It is the object of both bahir and antar (external and internal) lakshyas. In its midst is absorbed the whole world. It is the vast partless universe beyond Nāda, Bindu and Kara. Above it (*viz.*, the sphere of agni) is the sphere of the sun; in its midst is the sphere of the nectary moon; in its midst is the sphere of the partless Brahma-tejas (or the spiritual effulgence of Brahman). It has the brightness of Śukla (white light) like the ray of lightning. It alone has the characteristic of Śāmbhavī. In seeing this, there are three kinds of drshti (sight), *viz.*, amā (the new moon), pratipat (the first day of lunar fortnight), and pūrnimā (the full moon). The sight of amā is the one (seen) with closed eyes. That with half opened eyes is pratipat; while that with fully opened eyes is pūrnimā. Of these, the practice of pūrnimā should be resorted to. Its lakshya (or aim) is the tip of the nose. Then is seen a deep darkness at the root of the palate. By practising thus, a jyotis (light) of the form of an endless sphere is

---

[831] *AV* IV,23,5: "With [Agni] as friend the Rishis gave their power new splendour, with whom they kept aloof the Asuras' devices".

[832] See below Chs.IX,X.

[833] The most substantial information regarding the original yogic system is perhaps that to be gleaned from the yoga-based Upanishads derived largely from the Krishna and Shukla Yajur Vedas (see K. N. Aiyar, *Thirty Minor Upanishads*).

seen. This alone is Brahman, the Sachchidānanda. When the mind is absorbed in bliss thus naturally produced, then does Śāmbhavī take place. She (Śāmbhavī) alone is called Khecharī. By practising it (*viz.*, the mudrā), a man obtains firmness of mind. Through it, he obtains firmness of vāyu. The following are the signs: first it is seen like a star; then a reflecting (or dazzling) diamond; then the sphere of full moon; then the sphere of the brightness of nine gems; then the sphere of the midday sun; then the sphere of the flame of agni (fire); all these are seen in order.

(Thus much for the light in pūrva or first stage.) Then there is the light in the western direction (in the uttara or second stage). Then the lustres of crystal, smoke, bindu, nāda, kalā, star, firefly, lamp, eye, gold, and nine gems, etc. are seen. This alone is the form of Pranava.

The state of enlightenment is itself described in this Upanishad as an identification with the supreme light (*ibid.*):

When the triputi[834] are thus dispelled, he becomes the kaivalya jyotis[835] without bhāva (existence) or abhāva (nonexistence), full and motionless, like the ocean without the tides or like the lamp without the wind.

The process of the creation of the macrocosm as well as of the emergence of the Purusha from the Supreme Soul is detailed in another yoga-based Upanishad, the *Paingala Upanishad*:

... at first, this (universe) was Sat [Being] only. It (Sat) is spoken of as Brahman which is ever free (from the trammels of matter), which is changeless, which is Truth, Wisdom, and Bliss, and which is full, permanent, and one only without a second. In It, was like a mirage in the desert, silver in mother-of-pearl, a person in the pillar, or colour, etc., in the crystals, mūlaprakṛti, having in equal proportions the gunas, red, white, and black, and being beyond the power of speech. That which is reflected in it is Sākshi-Chaitanya (lit., the witness-consciousness). It (mūlaprakṛti) undergoing again change becomes with the preponderance of Sattva (in it), Āvarana Śakti named Avyakṭa. That which is reflected in it (Avyakta) is Īśvara-Chaitanya. He (Īśvara) has Māyā under his control, is omniscient, the original cause of creation, preservation, and dissolution, and

---

[834] Modifications of the mind.

[835] The light of isolation [from the phenomenal world].

the seed of this universe. He causes the universe which was latent in Him, to manifest itself through the bonds of karma of all creatures like a painted canvas unfurled. Again through the extinction of their karmas, he makes it disappear. In Him alone is latent all the universe, wrapped up like a painted cloth. Then from the supreme (Āvarana) Śakti, dependent on (or appertaining to) Īśvara, arose, through the preponderance of Rajas, Vikshepa Śakti called Mahaṭ. That which is reflected in it is Hiranyagarbha-Chaiṭanya. Presiding (as He does) over Mahaṭ, He (Hiranyagarbha) has a body, both manifested and unmanifested. From Vikshepa Śakti, of Hiranyagarbha arose, through the preponderance of Tamas, the gross Śakṭi called ahankāra. That which is reflected in it is Virāt-Chaiṭanya. He (Virāt) presiding over it (ahankāra) and possessing a manifested body becomes Vishnu, the chief Purusha and protector of all gross bodies.

The emergence of the physical cosmos and the gods is then described:

From that Ātmā arose ākāś; from ākāś arose vāyu, from vāyu agni, from agni apas, and from apas prthivī. The five tanmātras (rudimentary properties) alone are the gunas (of the above five). That generating cause of the universe (Īśvara) wishing to create and having assumed tamo-guna, wanted to convert the elements which were subtle tanmātras into gross ones. In order to create the universe, he divided into two parts each of those divisible elements; and having divided each moiety into four parts, made a fivefold mixture, each element having moiety of its own original element and one-fourth of a moiety of each of the other elements, and thus evolved out of the fivefold classified gross elements, the many myriads of Brahmāndas (Brahma's egg or macrocosm), the fourteen worlds pertaining to each sphere, and the spherical gross bodies (microcosm) fit for the (respective) worlds. Having divided the Rajas-essence of the five elements into four parts, He out of three such parts created (the five) prānas having fivefold function. Again out of the (remaining) fourth part, He created karmendriyas (the organs of action). Having divided their Sattva-essence into four parts, He out of three such parts created the antahkarana (internal organ) having fivefold function. Out of the (remaining) fourth part of Sattva-essence, he created the jñānendriyas (organs of sense). Out of the collective totality of Sattva-essence, He created the devatās (deities) ruling over the organs of sense and actions. Those (devatās) He created, He located in the spheres (pertaining to them). They, through His orders, began to pervade the macrocosm. Through His orders, Virat associated with ahankāra created all the gross things. Through His orders, Hiranyagarbha protected the subtle things. Without Him, they that were located in their spheres were unable to move or to do anything.

As we have noted in the Purusha Sukta of the *Rigveda*, X, 90, the cosmic Purusha contains the entire manifest universe as well as its several gods:

13. The moon was engendered from [the Purusha's] mind, and from his eye the Sun had birth;
Indra and Agni from his mouth were born, and Vāyu from his breath.
14. From his navel came mid-air, the sky was fashioned from his head, Earth from his feet, and from his ear the regions. Thus they formed the worlds.

In *AV* XI,8, we glimpse the power of 'tapas' (fervour/heat) in the formation of the mind and the sense faculties in the macrocosm before the creation even of the gods:

3. Ten Gods before the Gods were born together in the ancient time. Whoso may know them face to face may now pronounce the mighty word.

4. Inbreath and outbreath, eye and ear, decay and freedom from decay,
Spiration upward and diffused, voice, mind have brought us wish and plan.

5. As yet the Seasons were unborn, and Dhātar and Prajāpati,
Both Asvins, Indra, Agni. Whom then did they worship as supreme?

6 Fervour and Action were the two, in depths of the great billowy sea;
Fervour sprang up from Action: this they served and worshipped as supreme.

7. He may account himself well versed in ancient time who knows by name.
The earth that was before this earth, which only wisest Sages know.
From whom did Indra spring? from whom sprang Soma? Whence was Agni born?

8. From whom did Tvashtar spring to life? and whence is Dhātar's origin?

9. Indra from Indra, Soma from Soma, Agni from Agni sprang
Tvashtar from Tvashtar was produced, Dhātar was Dhātar's
origin.

10. Those Gods who were of old, the Ten begotten earlier than the
Gods, What world do they inhabit since they gave the world unto
their sons?

The following lines proceed to describe the creation of the prototype of
man by a variety of gods:

11. When he had brought together hair, sinew and bone, marrow and
flesh.
And to the body added feet, then to what world did he depart?

12. Whence, from what region did he bring the hair, the sinews, and
the bones,
Marrow and limbs, and joints, and flesh? Who was the bringer,
and from whence?

13. Casters, those Gods were called who brought together all the
elements:
When they had fused the mortal man complete, they entered into
him.

14. The thighs, the knee-bones, and the feet, the head, the face, and
both the hands,
The ribs, the nipples, and the sides—what Rishi hath constructed
that?

15. Head, both the hands, and face, and tongue, and neck, and
intercoastal parts,
All this, investing it with skins, Mahi conjoined with bond and
tie.

16. What time the might body lay firmly compact with tie and bond,
Who gave its colour to the form, the hue wherewith it shines
today?

17. All Deities had lent their aid: of this a noble Dame took note, Tsā,
the Consort of Command. She gave its colour to the form.

18. When Tvashtar, Tvashtar's loftier Sire, had bored it out and
hollowed it.
Gods made the mortal their abode, and entered and possessed the
man.

Then man is imbued with his various characteristics and fortunes,

19. Sleep, specially, Sloth, Nirriti, and deities whose name is Sin,
    Baldness, old age, and hoary hairs within the body found their
    way.
20. Theft, evil-doing, and deceit, truth, sacrifice, exalted fame,
    Strength, princely power, and energy entered the body as a home

    ...

    ...

26. Inbreath and outbreath, ear and eye, decay and freedom from
    decay.
    Breath upward and diffused, voice, mind, these quickly with the
    body move,
27. All   earnest   wishes,   all   commands,   directions,   and
    admonishments.
    Reflections, all deliberate plans entered the body as a home.
28. They laid in the abhorrent frame those waters hidden, bright, and
    thick,
    Which in the bowels spring from blood, from mourning or from
    hasty toil.
29. Fuel they turned to bone, and then they set light waters in the
    frame.
    The molten butter they made seed: then the Gods entered into
    man.
30. All Waters, all the Deities. Virāj with Brahma at her side:
    Brahma into the body passed: Prajāpati is Lord thereof.
31. The Sun and Wind formed, separate, the eye and vital breath of
    man.
    His other person have the Gods bestowed on Agni as a gift.
32. Therefore whoever knoweth man regardeth him as Brahman's
    self:
    For all the Deities abide in him as cattle in their pen.
33. At his first death he goeth hence, asunder, in three separate parts.
    He goeth yonder with one part, with one he goeth yonder: here he
    sinketh downward with a third.
34. In the primeval waters cold the body is deposited.
25. In this there is the power of growth: from this is power of growth
    declared.

The *Paingala Upanishad* describes the manner in which the Supreme Soul
creates the bodies of human beings:[836]

---

[836] Cf. also *Sarvasāra Upanishad*, 6.

Īśvara having taken a small portion of the quintuplicated mahā-bhūtas, (the great elements), made in regular order the gross bodies, both collective and segregate. The skull, the skin, the intestines, bone, flesh, and nails are of the essence of prthivī. Blood, urine, saliva, sweat and others are of the essence of āpas. Hunger, thirst, heat, delusion, and copulation are of the essence of agni. Walking, lifting, breathing and others are of the essence of vāyu. Passion, anger, etc., are of the essence of ākāś. The collection of these having touch and the rest is this gross body that is brought about by karma, that is the seat of egoism in youth and other states and that is the abode of many sins. Then He created prānas out of the collective three parts of Rajas-essence of the fivefold divided elements. The modifications of prāna are prāna, apāna, vyāna, udāna, and samāna; nāga, karma, krkara, devadatta and dhanañjaya are the auxiliary prānas. (Of the first five), the heart, anus, navel, throat and the whole body are respectively the seats. Then He created the karmendriyas out of the fourth part of the Rajas-guna. Of 'Olds' and the rest the mouth, legs, hands, and the organs of secretion and excretion are the modifications. Talking, walking, lifting, excreting, and enjoying are their functions. Likewise out of the collective three parts of Sattva-essence, He created the antahkarana (internal organ). Antahkarana, manas, buddhi, chitta, and ahankāra are the modifications. Sankalpa (thought), certitude, memory, egoism, and anusandhāna (inquiry) are their functions. Throat, face, navel, heart, and the middle of the brow are their seats. Out of the (remaining) fourth part of Sattva-essence, He created the jñānendriyas (organs of sense). Ear, skin, eyes, tongue, and nose are the modifications. Sound, touch, form, taste, and odour are their functions. Dik (the quarters), Vāyu, Arka (the sun), Varuna, Aśvini Devas, Indra, Upendra, Mrtyu (the God of death), Prajāpati, the Moon, Vishnu the four-faced Brahma and Śambhu (Śiva) are the presiding deities of the organs. There are the five kośas (sheaths), *viz.*, annamaya, prānamaya, manomaya, vijñānamaya, and ānandamaya. Annamaya sheath is that which is created and developed out of the essence of food, and is absorbed into the earth which is of the form of food. It alone is the gross body. The prānas with the karmendriyas (organs of action) is the prānamaya sheath. Manas with the jñānendriyas (organs of sense) is the manomaya sheath. Buddhi with the jñānendriyas is the vijñānamaya sheath. These three sheaths constitute the lingaśarīra (or the subtle body). (That which tends to[837])

---

[837] i.e. corrects.

the ajñāna (ignorance) of the Reality (of Ātmā) is the ānandamaya sheath. This is the kārana body. Moreover the five organs of sense, the five organs of action, the five prānas and others, the five ākāś and other elements, the four internal organs, avidyā, passion, karma, and Lamas—all these constitute this town (of body).

The constitution of the human body is recounted in the following manner in the *Garbha Upanishad* [derived from *KYV*]:

1. Why is the body called Panchātmakam? Because it is constituted of the five forces of nature- earth, water, fire, air and ether [sky][838]
3. Why is the body said to have six shelters? Because it can sense and distinguish the six forms of taste, sweet, sour, salty, bitter, etc.
    ...
    Why is the body said to be of seven compounds? When a man possesses and enjoys material objects ... six types of taste [rasam] are brought in. Out of such taste is created the blood, from the blood the tissue, from the tissue fat, from the fat the nerves, from the nerves the bones, from the bones the flesh, and from the flesh the reproductive fluids.

The *Yogatattva Upanishad* specifies the parts of the human body governed by the cosmic deities:

83b: There are five elements: Prithvi, Apas, Agni, Vāyu and Ākāsha.
84-87a: To the body of the five elements, there is the fivefold Dharana. From the feet to the knees is said to be the region of Prithvi
87b. The region of Apas is said to extend from the knees to the anus.
91. From the anus to the heart is said to be the region of Agni.
94b: From the heart to the middle of the eyebrows is said to be the region of Vāyu.
97-98. From the centre of the eyebrows to the top of the head is said to be the region of Ākāsha.

In the *Paingala Upanishad* the final step of the creation is described as the infusion of life into the various microcosmic forms in it:

Then He wished to infuse chetana (life) into them. Having pierced the Brahmānda (Brahma's egg or macrocosm) and Brahmarandhras (the

---

[838] The mahābhūtis.

head-fontanelle)[839] in all the microcosmic heads, He entered within. Though they were (at first) inert, they were then able to perform karmas like beings of intelligence.

The *Paingala Upanishad* further describes the jīva as being located in the middle of the eyebrows and pervading the entire body as its agent.

The *Brahmopanishad* describes the mode of operation of the jīva:

> As the spider throws out and draws into itself the threads, so the jīva goes and returns during the jāgrata and the svapna states ... Know that during jāgrata it (jīva) dwells in the eye, and during svapna in the throat; during sushupti, it is in the heart and during turya in the head.

The *Subala Upanishad* XI further describes the spiritual powers of the ātman within the heart:

> There is a mass of red flesh in the middle of the heart. In it, there is a lotus called dahara. It buds forth in many petals like a water-lily. In the middle of it is an ocean (samudra). In its midst is a koka (bird). In it there are four nādis.[840] They are ramā, aramā, Ichchhā and punarbhava. Of these, ramā leads a man of virtue to a happy world. Aramā leads one of sins into the world of sins. (Passing) through Ichchhā (nādi), one gets whatever he remembers. Through punarbhava, he splits open the sheaths; after splitting open the sheaths, he splits open the skull of the head; then he splits open prthivī; then āpas; then tejas; then vāyu; then ākāś. Then he splits open manas; then bhūtādi; then mahat; then avyakta; then akshara; then he splits open mrtyu and mrtyu becomes one with the supreme God. Beyond this, there is neither Sat nor asat, nor Sat-asat.

The process whereby the soul undergoes incarnation is described in *Katha Upanishad* V:

> I shall also tell you about the state of and whereabouts of the Jiva after death (when it has not learnt about the Brahman). Some of those who have born with bodies (the human beings), requiring other bodies reach the entry point again (the womb). Some others reach the state

---

[839] Chamber of Brahma.

[840] A nādi is a channel through which spiritual cognitive current flows. For the chakras see the *Sat Chakra Narupana* translated by John Woodroffe in *The Serpent Power*.

of plants (or other stationary objects). All these happen according to their actions, thoughts and knowledge.

The *Garbha Upanishad* identifies the precise moment when the jíva enters the embryo:

When there is a combination of the male and female reproductive fluids, the garbha is formed. That garbha is controlled by the Hridyam [heart]. The heart houses an ever-burning internal fire from which a biological fire is generated, which in turn gives birth to air. That air which runs throughout the body ultimately and dutifully traces back its route to the Hridyam.

On the uniting of the male and female reproductive fluids, after the lapse of one night, the embryo is in a mixed [semi-fluid] state. After seven nights, it takes the shape of a bubble formed out of water. At the end of a fortnight, it takes the shape of a solid lump. At the end of a month it gets solidified and hardened.

In 2 months, the head takes form. At the end of 3 months, the legs and foot are formed. And by the 4th month the wrist, stomach, hip, waist, etc. are formed. During the 5th month, the spine and the adjoining bones are formed. During the 6th month the mouth, nose, eyes, and the ears are formed.

In the 7th month life or the Jiva enters the body that has been shaped thus far. By the 8th month it attains full shape with all the other remaining parts. If the potency of the father is stronger than that of the mother, it becomes a male and vice-versa.

It is during the 9th month that all the sense organs and intellectual organs attain completion. During this time the Jiva is reminded of its previous birth and it realises its good and bad deeds committed during its previous births.

Thus thinks the Jiva:

"I have born and died again and again. All my near and dear for whom I performed various actions, whether good or bad, have enjoyed the benefits of my actions and have left me all alone. I am left behind all alone. Once I come out of this generative organ [the vagina], I am going to surrender myself to the destroyer of all sins and the provider of salvation – Mahesvara, Narayana. I am going to chant his name and other mantras to destroy all my sins carried from my earlier births.

Once I come out of this generative organ, I am going to practise Gnana Yoga strictly to destroy my sins and to release myself from the bondage of the actions of this world of matter. Once I come out of this generative organ I am going to contemplate the supreme divine Brahman."

These are the thoughts of the Jiva during the time it remains in the womb.

However when it reaches the generative organ and comes out of it with great difficulty to the earth, it is inflicted with the illusory force of Māya created by Vishnu and immediately forgets all its previous births and the deeds performed therein. Its memory is cleansed of all its history the very moment it first inhales the air on coming to the earth.

The Upanishad further describes the residence of the soul in the upper chakras of the body:

The juicy essences (of food) which arise out of digestion enter the womb which is suspended in the stomach of the mother and coming near the child's head nourishes the child's prāna through the sushumnā (on the head or pineal gland). Sushumnā is the Brahma-nādi. Prāna and others are found there. It (prāna) descends lower and lower as the time of birth approaches and settles in the heart when the child is born.

Since the aim of yoga is the realisation of the individual self as the Supreme Self or Purusha, it is important to realise the latter within the human microcosm, as the *Garbha Upanishad* goes on to explain:

Through yoga, it should be brought from the middle of the eyebrows to the end of sushumnā (*viz.*, the pineal gland), when he becomes the cognizer of the Real like the child in the womb. In the body of this nature, Ātmā is latent and deathless, and is the witness and Purusha. It lives in this body, being enveloped (by māyā). Prānī (or the jīva having prāna) has abhimāna (identification with the body) on account of avidyā. Ajñāna which surrounds it is the seed; the antahkarana (internal organ) is the sprout and the body is the tree.

The Vaishnavite *Katha Upanishad* II,4,12, internalises the Purusha in the following manner: 'The person (Purusha), of the size of a thumb, stands in the middle of the Self, as lord of the past and the future, and henceforward

fears no more'. At the same time, the macrocosmic Purusha is described
(III) thus:

> Beyond the sense organs are the objects of sense. Beyond them is the
> mind. Beyond it is the brain or intuition. Beyond that is the great soul
> (one of the aspects of the Atma).
>   Beyond that great soul is the unmanifest divine. Beyond that
> is the Purusha (the all knowing and all pervading Atma). There is
> nothing beyond the Purusha. That is the end. That is the supreme.

SB X,6,3,2 too understands the Purusha as the Self:

> Let him meditate on the Self, which is made up of intelligence, and
> endowed with a body of spirit, with a form of light, and with an
> etherial nature, which changes its shape at will, is swift as thought,
> of true resolve, and true purpose, which consists of all sweet odours
> and tastes, which holds sway over all the regions and pervades this
> whole universe, which is speechless and indifferent;even as a grain of
> rice, or a grain of barley, or a grain of millet, or the smallest granule
> of millet, so is this golden Purusha in the heart; even as a smokeless
> light, it is greater than the sky, greater than the ether, greater than the
> earth, greater than all existing things;—that self of the spirit (breath)
> is my self: on passing away from hence I shall obtain that self. Verily,
> whosoever has this trust, for him there is no uncertainty.

In the *Brahma Upanishad*, the macrocosmic Purusha is revealed to be
entirely concentrated within the human microcosm:

> 2. This being or Self is fully self-extended (into world-forms), he is
>   the indwelling controller of things and beings, he is the Bird, the
>   Crab, the Lotus, he is the Purusha, the Prana, the destroyer, the
>   cause and the effect, the Brahman, the Atman, he is the Devata
>   making everything known.
> 3. Now this Purusha has four seats, the navel, the heart, the throat
>   and the head. In these shines forth the Brahman with four
>   aspects: the state of wakefulness, of dream, of dreamless sleep,
>   and the fourth or transcendent state.
>   ...
> 21. The heart (i.e. the inner chamber of the heart) resembles the calyx
>   of a lotus, full of cavities and also with its face turned downwards.
>   Know that to be the great habitat of the whole universe.

22. Know the wakeful state to have for its centre the eyes; the dreaming state should be assigned to the throat; the state of dreamless sleep is in the heart; and the transcendent state is in the crown of the head.

The *Brahma Upanishad* gives a further description of the Purusha within the human being:

The Pursuha has four seats—navel, heart, neck, and head. There Brahman with the four feet specially shines. Those feet are jāgraṭa, svapna, sushupti, and turya. In jāgraṭa he is Brahmā, in svapna Vishnu, in sushupti Rudra, and in ṭurya the supreme Akshara [Vak, the Word]. He is Adiṭya, Vishnu, Īśvara, Purusha, prāna, jīva, agni, the resplendent. The Para-Brahman shines in the midst of these. He is without manas, ear, hands, feet, and light … In the Hrdayākāś (ākāś in the heart) is the Chidākāś. That is Brahman. It is extremely subtle. The Hrdayākāś can be known. This moves in it. In Brahman, everything is strung. Those who thus know the Lord know everything.

The heart is thus considered as a principal seat of the soul:

The heart is in the form of a closed lotus-flower, with its head hanging down; it has a hole in the top. Know it to be the great abode of All (*ibid.*).

In *BAU*, III,1,17, too the ātman, which is considered as being of the nature of Hiranyagarbha, and identical to the Purusha, is located in the heart. The *Subala Upanishad* IV gives a more detailed description of the constitution of the heart:

In the middle of the heart is a red fleshy mass in which is the dahara-lotus. Like the lotus, it opens into many (petals). There are ten openings in the heart. The (different kinds of) prānas are located there. Whenever he (Ātmā) is united with prāna, he sees cities with rivers and other variegated things; when united with vyāna, he sees Devas and Rshis; when united with apāna, he sees Yakshas, Rākshasas and Gandharvas; when united with udāna, he perceives the celestial world, Devas, Skanda (Kārtikeya or the six-faced [Muruga]), and Jayanta (Indra's son); when united with samāna, he sees the celestial world and the treasures (of Kubera); when united with rambhā (a nādi hereafter given out), he sees whatever is seen or not seen, heard or not heard, eaten or not eaten, asat or Sat and all else.

There are ten midis; in each of these are seventy-one. And these become 72,000 branch nādis. When Ātmā sleeps therein, it produces sound; but when Ātmā sleeps in the second kośa (or sheath) then it sees this world and the higher as also knows all the sounds. This is spoken of as samprasāda (deep sleep rest). Then prāna protects the body. The nādis are full of blood, of the colours green, blue, yellow, red, and white. Now this dahara-lotus has many petals like a lily. Like a hair divided into 1,000 parts, the nādis called hita are. The divine Ātmā sleeps in the ākāś of the heart, in the supreme kośa (or ānandamaya sheath); sleeping there, it has no desires, no dreams, no deva-worlds, no yajñas or sacrificer, no mother or father, no relative, no kinsman, no thief, or no Brahman-slayer. Its body is tejas (resplendent effulgence) and of the nature of nectar (or the immortal). It is as if in sport, a water-lotus. When he returns again to the waking state by the same way (he quitted or went in before to the heart), he is Samrāt ...

That which joins one place (or centre) with another is the nādis which bind them.

The *Mandalabrāhmana Upanishad* I describes the Purusha in the Sahasrāra in the brain:

Sahasrāra (*viz.*, the thousand-petalled lotus of the pineal gland) Jalajyotis is the antarlakshya. Some say the form of Purusha in the cave of buddhi beautiful in all its parts is antarlakshya. Some again say that the all-quiescent Nīlakantha accompanied by Umā (his wife) and having five mouths and latent in the midst of the sphere in the brain is antarlakshya. Whilst others say that the Purusha of the dimension of a thumb is antarlakshya. A few again say antarlakshya is the One Self made supreme through introvision in the state of a jīvanmukta. All the different statements above made pertain to Ātmā alone.

The Vaishvānara Vidya at the conclusion of Ch.V of the *Chāndogya Upanishad* points to the different forms of the divine Soul in the individual body as well as in the All (Vaishvānara):

Of that Vaisvânara Self the head is Sutegas (having good light), [841]the eye Visvarûpa (multiform),[842] the breath Prithagvartman (having various courses),[843] the trunk Bahula (full),[844] the bladder Rayi (wealth),[845] the feet the earth,[846] the chest the altar, the hairs the grass on the altar, the heart the Gârhapatya fire, the mind the Anvâhârya fire, the mouth the Âhavanîya fire.

The Vaishvānara however is the same as the Purusha within the human soul "as a span long and as identical with [oneself]" (V,18,1).

By contemplating the Yajna Purusha as the Supreme Soul, Ātman, we acquire the cosmic consciousness of Brahman. The bliss of the one who has realised the supreme Ātman is described in *Katha Upanishad,* V, thus:

Those wise men who perceive the Atman, which is the only Atman for all that is created and which is the Supreme Divine and which multiplies its single form into various, to be residing in themselves – only they are entitled to the limitless joy (arising out of such knowledge of the Self). Not the others.

Those wise men who perceive the Atman, which is the only stable thing in this transient world and which is the knowledge of the beings that possess knowledge and which, standing as one, grants the desires of all, to be residing in themselves – only they are entitled to the eternal peace (arising out of such knowledge of the Self). Not the others.

Although the pure ineffable supreme joy referred to as 'that' cannot be defined or explained about clearly, it is regarded as 'this' (that is clearly understandable and enjoyable here in this life) by the wise men. Is it self-shining or does it shine by reflecting the light of another? How will we understand that by our intellect?

The sun does not shine there; nor do the moon and the stars. Not even the lightning and certainly not this fire. All these shine only by depending on Him (the Atman) who is self-shining and self-illuminating. It is only because of His light that other things are seen and understood.

---

[841] i.e. heaven (V,12,1).

[842] i.e. the sun (V,13,1).

[843] i.e. air (V,14,1).

[844] i.e. ether (V,15,1).

[845] i.e. water (V,16,1).

[846] Prathishta (V,17,1).

The jīva or personal ego however is deluded by the illusory power of māya into thinking that it is identical to the body and it is this error that is sought to be corrected through yoga. The identification of the individual ātman with Brahman is, as we have seen, the same as the attainment of the abode of the Purusha/Vishnu, which is informed by Brahman,[847] and hence equal to Brahmaloka, from which one is not reborn. As Biardeau explains,

> il y a une hiérarchie de plans qui va des organes sensoriels au Purusa suprême, nommé ... Visnu ... L'atman est au-delà de l'ego limitateur et fait accéder à un stade où le Réel est non manifesté, l'atman lui-même se trouvant absorbé dans ce Réel informe avant d'accéder au Purusa Visnu, en qui il trouve la délivrance finale.[848]

We see therefore that the intense concentration on the Purusha in the macrocosmos and microcosm is what most probably served as the foundation of the most ancient religion of the Indo-Europeans. The fire rituals of the Āryans are, as we shall see, magical dramatisations of the cosmic workings of the solar force. These rituals serve to sustain the entire cosmos through an identification of the chief participants, that is, the sacrificer guided by the brahman priest, with the solar force. This identification is a result not of yogic psychosomatic exercices but of the high birth of the participants, originally kings and brāhmans. Yoga, on the other hand, allows any dedicated "adept" to attempt not only a higher brahmic consciousness but also a total liberation from the bonds of manifestation.

Yoga seems to have become popular in India especially from around the 9th to the 5th century B.C. judging from the numerous Sanskrit and Prakrit texts of this period which, according to Flood, stress the ideology of renunciation in which knowledge (jnāna) is given precedence over ritual action (karma) "and detachment from the material and social world is cultivated through ascetic practices (tapas), celibacy, poverty and methods of mental training (yoga)."[849] The doctrine of Jnāna Yoga[850] is enunciated in the 'Bhagavad Gita', Ch.II:[851]

---

[847] See above p.35.

[848] See M. Biardeau, op.cit., p.75.

[849] See G. Flood, An introduction to Hinduism, p.81.

[850] Cf. p.173 below.

[851] The 'Gita' advocates three types of yoga, karma yoga (which consists in the performance of action according to a sense of duty with a total disregard of the fruits of such action, 'Gita', III, 19), bhakti yoga (which enjoins a complete devotion to and absorption in the

When a man, O son of Prithâ! abandons all the desires of his heart, and is pleased in his self only and by his self, he is then called one of steady mind. He whose heart is not agitated in the midst of calamities, who has no longing for pleasures, and from whom (the feelings of) affection, fear and wrath have departed, is called a sage of steady mind. His mind is steady, who, being without attachments anywhere, feels no exultation and no aversion on encountering the various agreeable and disagreeable (things of this world). A man's mind is steady, when he withdraws his senses from (all) objects of sense, as the tortoise (withdraws) its limbs from all sides ... The man who ponders over objects of sense forms an attachment to them; from (that) attachment is produced desire; and from desire anger is produced; from anger results want of discrimination; from want of discrimination, confusion of the memory; from confusion of the memory, loss of reason; and in consequence of loss of reason he is utterly ruined. But the self-restrained man who moves among objects with senses under the control of his own self, and free from affection and aversion, obtains tranquillity ... The man who, casting off all desires, lives free from attachments, who is free from egoism, and from (the feeling that this or that is) mine, obtains tranquillity. This, O son of Prithâ! is the Brahmic state; attaining to this, one is never deluded; and remaining in it in (one's) last moments, one attains (brahma-nirvâna) the Brahmic bliss.

It is repeated in the treatise on ashtanga (eight-limbed) yoga, *Yoga Sūtras*, by Patanjali (2nd c. B.C.), where the state of yogic beatitude is understood as "the cessation of mental fluctuations". Patanjali's practical system, which is also called "Rāja Yoga",[852] consists of eight stages:

1. yama (ethical restraint)
2. niyama (discipline)
3. āsana (posture)
4. prānāyāma (breath-control)
5. pratyahāra (sense withdrawal)

---

deity, 'Gītā' IX, 34) and jnāna yoga.

[852] Besides rāja yoga, there are, according to the *Yogattatva Upanishad*, three kinds of yoga, mantrayoga, layayoga, and hathayoga. One of the major hathayoga methodologies was developed in the fifteenth century by Swāmi Swātmarāma. His system avoids the ethical yama and niyama of Patanjali but includes the awakening of the Kundalini. It aims at achieving a purification of the body and a resulting spiritual balance in its practitioners before the attainment of samadhi.

6. dhārana (concentration)
7. dhyāna (meditation)[853]
8. samādhi (absorbed concentration)

The goal is the achievement of a "supreme state" devoid of "mental fluctuations". Consciousness is absorbed in itself, and the self does not becomes "identified with" the Absolute, but, rather, is the Absolute itself, since there is nothing apart from it. The yogi aims to attain the supreme state: "That state in which the five sense organs[854] ... remain united with the mind, and where the intuition or the brain remains idle or blank without any thought is the ineffable, supreme state of bliss" (Katha Upanishad, VI).

The state of yogic enlightenment is the same as that of the Brahmaloka of the Purānas, since the soul is immobile in its absolute concentration. The Mandalabrāhmana Upanishad, II describes the state of enlightenment thus:

> He becomes a brahmavit (knower of Brahman) by cognising the end of the sleeping state, even while in the waking state. Though the (same) mind is absorbed in sushupti as also in samādhi, there is much difference between them. (In the former case) as the mind is absorbed in tamas, it does not become the means of salvation, (but) in samādhi as the modifications of tamas in him are rooted away, the mind raises itself to the nature of the Partless. All that is no other than Sākshi-Chaitanya (witness-consciousness or the Higher Self) into which the absorption of the whole universe takes place, inasmuch as the universe is but a delusion (or creation) of the mind and is therefore not different from it. Though the universe appears perhaps as outside of the mind, still it is unreal. He who knows Brahman and who is the sole enjoyer of brāhmic bliss which is eternal and has dawned once (for all in him)—that man becomes one with Brahman.

Once this concentration is relaxed, it is reborn just as the cosmos too is reborn from a disturbance of the perfect balance of the gunas in the supreme Ātman.[855] The ultimate aim of yoga thus is to prevent this

---

[853] According to the Yogattatva Upanishad, dhyana is described as the contemplation of Hari in the middle of the eyebrows.

[854] The action organs are referred to as karma-indriya and the sense organs are referred to as gnāna-indriya.

[855] See above p.32.

relaxation in order to achieve a "final liberation from the bonds of action and rebirth".[856] This is the liberation that is pithily described in *AV* X,44:

> Desireless, firm, immortal, self-existent, contented with the essence, lacking nothing,
> Free from fear of death is he who knoweth that Soul courageous, youthful, undecaying.

---

[856] M. Biardeau, *ibid*.

VI.

THE ĀRYANS

The fire-worshipping Vedic tradition is claimed by the Āryans to have prevailed from the first Krita Yuga, through the Treta Yuga and until the end of the Dvāpara Yuga, when the Āgamic, temple-worshipping, tradition of the Hamites superseded it in the ensuing Kali Yuga.[857] But we have seen that, according to the *Sūrya Siddhānta* and the *Mahābhārata*, Manu himself is supposed to have appeared only in the Treta Yuga of the 28th Chaturyuga of the second kalpa, the Padma Kalpa. The Vedic tradition that the brāhmans conserved, as well as the seven sages whom they derive their ancestry from, may however antedate the "flood" which accompanied the formation of the sun of our system and heralded the appearance of the seventh Manu, Manu Vaivasvat.

We have seen that the fire-sacrifices associated with the Āryans are ascribed by Manu to the Dvāpara age. However, the historical beginnings of this tradition among the Āryans are hard to trace, since the fire-worship associated with Vedic religion has not been discovered through archaeology before 2500 B.C. in Kalibangan,[858] that is, after the start of the Kali Yuga traditionally dated to around 3100 B.C. To observe the historical development of the Vedic Āryans themselves we must study the Āryan family, the so-called Japhetic sons of Noah, as a whole. Of the three sons of Noah, the eastern Japhetic group of Āryans, that is, the Iranians and Indians,[859] seem to have best preserved the oldest hieratic

---

[857] See below Ch.XII.

[858] See below p.187.

[859] The Scythians form an integral part of the Indo-Iranian group, but their spiritual tradition seems less developed (see below p.183f).

Vedic tradition as well the philosophical import of the ancient cosmology of the proto-Dravidians/Hurrians. This spiritual focus is evident in all of the Indic Vedic and Sanskritic literature, which was originally oral and not committed to writing until relatively recently.[860] As regards the origins of the Indo-Āryans, it may be noted that, in *Genesis* 9:2, the eldest son of Japheth[861] [the Āryan] is called Gamer, representing the Celtic Cimmerians, and he is followed by the Magog[862] (Magi) and the Madai (Medes), Javan (Greeks), Tubal (Iberians), Meschech (Cappadocians) and Tiras (Thracians). The sons of the eldest son, Gamer, include Ashkenaz (the Scythians), Riphath (uncertain) and Thokarmah (possibly the Tokharians). We see that the Celtic Cimmerians, Iranians, Indians and Greeks are roughly contemporaneous while the Scythians are a somewhat later branch of the Celtic.[863] The Cimmerians are described by Herodotus (IV,14) as having had their initial home "on the shores of the Black Sea". Diodorus Siculus (*Bibliotheca Historica* V,32) also states that the Celts living close to the Black Sea are scattered "as far as Scythia" and the northernmost of these Celtic tribes are the wildest and most powerful having apparently "wandered across and laid waste the whole of Asia, under the then name of Cimmerians". The Welsh (who are a southern Celtic people like the Bretons) call themselves, to this day, "Cymry".

The Celts, like the Germans, trace their origins, in their own legends, to Anatolia, whence they travelled to Iberia through Egypt. Archaeological evidence research suggests that they were early concentrated in Northern Germany and the Netherlands in the Urnfeld culture of 1200-700 B.C. But recent genetic researchers have suggested that the characteristic gene for "lactase persistence" found among the Celts originated near the Baltic Sea in the fifth millennium B.C. and may have spread from there to Iberia and Britain, which are also Celtic homelands.[864] So the Celts evidently travelled extensively over Europe but the biblical statements regarding

---

[860] For the early oral history of Sanskrit, see A.A. Macdonell, *History of Sanskrit Literature*, p.20f, and C.K. Raja, *Survey of Sanskrit Literature*, pp.11,168.

[861] Japheth is called Saptaputra ("having seven sons") in the *Bhavishya Purāna*, which incorporates several late interpolations relating to the early chapters of *Genesis*, as well as "predictions" about the foundation of Islam and its arrival into India. The Sanskritic name Saptaputra however seems an accurate one since Japheth, even according to the biblical record, has seven sons. The Biblical Noah and his descendants (including the family of Japheth) are designated in this purāna as "mlecchas" or non-Aryans who speak the mleccha language, which "is considered the lowest language because it bears the curse of the goddess Saraswati".

[862] Gog and Magog are, in *Ezekiel* 39:2 and elsewhere, representatives of the far North.

[863] See above p.91n.

[864] See B. Arredi, E. Poloni, C. Tyler-Smith, "The peopling of Europe".

the three sons of Noah coming to the plain of Shinar [Sumer] from the East suggests that the common original home of the Japhetites and of the Semites and the Hamites must have been more to the south, around Mt. Ararat and east of it, whence the Japhetites may have moved northwards as far as the Baltic.

A branch of the proto-Dravidian stock that seems to have spread through Celtic Europe as its priestly sect is the Druids.[865] The phonetic similarity of "Druid" to "Dravida" is obvious. In classical texts, the name of the Druids appears mostly in a plural form, as "druidai" (Gk.) or "druidae" or "druides" (Lt.).[866] In Irish, "drai" or "drui" is the singular form of a word meaning "wise man", of which "draod" or "druid" is the plural. The association of the Druids with the Greek word for "oak", first made by Pliny (*Historia Naturalis* XVI,95), is probably a later one due to the importance of tree-worship among the ancient Druids, as well as amongst most of the ancient Hamitic and Semitic peoples, since the sacred tree serves as a symbol of the divine phallus representing the life of the universe.

The Druids may have become the priests of the Cimmerian Celts when the latter moved into Europe, especially Gaul and Britain.[867] Among the Gauls, the Druids, along with the "equites", constituted the higher "castes". Piggott believed that the Druidic tradition may go back to at least the second millennium B.C. since it has much in common with the Indo-European language and ideology, especially Sanskritic and Hittite.[868] However, it is quite possible that the Druids were settled in Europe even earlier than the Āryans, perhaps as early as the third millennium B.C. The three-headed god attributable to the Druids in the Marne and the Côte d'Or is possibly related to the three- (or four-) headed god[869] of the Indus Valley of the third millennium B.C.[870] Hence it is not surprising that Clement of Alexandria believed that the Pythagorean and Greek philosophers derived their wisdom from the Gauls and other

---

[865] See S. Piggott, *The Druids*. J. Vendryes ("Les correspondances") counted the Celts and the Celtic priests "among the most conservative members of the Indo-Europeand family".

[866] See S. Piggott, *op.cit.*, p.89.

[867] The theory of the non-Celtic origin of the Druids is especially supported by the fact that, outside Britain and Gaul, there is no evidence of such priests in other Celtic territories such as the Danube, the Cisalpine and Transalpine Gaul. The Druidic type is perhaps most evident today among the Welsh, whose manner of English pronunciation is remarkably similar to that of the South Indians.

[868] See S. Piggott, *op.cit.*, p.74.

[869] The fourth head of the god is invisible since it is turned backwards.

[870] See, for instance, M. Jansen, *Die Indus-Zivilisation.*

barbarians,[871] by which he no doubt meant the Druidic priestly core of these tribes. Dio Chrysostom (1st c. A.D.) considered the Druids as being similar to the Persian Magi, Egyptian priests and Indian brāhmans.

Like Sanskrit, the Druidic language was an unwritten one, since, as Caesar reports, this guarded the secret wisdom of the Druids from the lay public.[872] It is particularly interesting that the only form of writing that has been associated with the Druids is the cryptic one called "ogam" or "ogham", terms that are related to Irish "oigheam" meaning "secret meaning". The symbolical poetic style of classical Dravidian literature is also called "agam" (meaning "interior") as distinguished from the plainer style called "puram" (meaning "exterior").

The religion of the Druids was clearly cosmological, as is attested in the commentaries of Caesar, who attributed to them much knowledge of the stars and their motion, and of the size of the world.[873] Ammianus Marcellinus declared that they investigated "problems of things secret and sublime".[874] Diodorus Siculus, following Posidonius, maintained that they held that "the souls of men are immortal, and that after a definite number of years they have a second life when the soul passes to another body",[875] which is also the doctrine of the most ancient Dravidians who formulated the tenets of Indian religion. The 1st century A.D. writer, Pomponius Mela declares in his *De situ orbis*, III,2,18-19 (basing his report on the lost Celtic ethnography of Posidonius) that

> [the Celts] have their own eloquence and their masters of wisdom, the Druids. These ones profess to know the size and form of heaven and earth, the motion of sky and stars, and what the gods desire. They instruct the noblest of their race in many things secretly and at length, twenty years, either in a cave or in remote woodlands ... that souls are eternal and there is another life among the Manes. Therefore they burn and bury with the dead that which is appropriate to living people ... and there were those who willingly threw themselves onto the funeral pyres of their relatives, as if expecting that they will live together thereafter.[876]

---

[871]   See S. Piggott, *op.cit.*, p.81.

[872]   See Caesar, *Gallic Wars*, VI,14.

[873]   *Ibid.*

[874]   See S. Piggott, *op.cit.*, p.101.

[875]   *Ibid.*, p.102.

[876]   See B. Lincoln, *Death, War and Sacrifice*, p.177.

It may be noted that there is no evidence of fire-worship among the Druids such as became characteristic of the Indo-Āryans and Iranians.[877] However the veneration of fire among the ancient Celts may be detected in the relative frequency of the appellation "Áed" (fire) among the legendary and early historical high-kings of Ireland.[878]

The Iranians may be recognized by their later hieratic name, Magi, in the "Magog" of the biblical record. The Iranians are represented in Herodotus as worshipping the "circle of heaven" (Ahura, from Ashur/Anshar=circle of heaven) as well as the heavenly bodies. The incantation that the priest utters during the animal sacrifice is supposed to evoke the creation of the heavenly bodies. This is in accord with the Vedic sacrifices, which mimic the creation of the universe. The Iranians discussed by Herodotus however did not build temples or worship statuary representations of their deities (I,131), and this emphasises their ancient affiliation with the Scythians, while the Mitanni- and the Hittite-Hurrians, however, were certainly not averse to such representations. Besides, the Iranian rituals are described by Herodotus as not involving fire, even though the later Zoroastrian religion – like the Indic – is indeed typified by its worship of fire, Atar. More recently Mary Boyce has pointed out that "no actual ruins of a fire temple have been identified from before the Parthian period".[879] This suggests once again that the Iranians, like their Mitanni kinsmen, must have come into contact in the south with the Pururuva Ailas [Elamites/Hurrians], who, as we shall see, derived their worship of fire from the Gandharvas who followed the settlers of the BMAC complex. Indeed the Iranians seem originally to have been nomadic peoples, as is attested by the imagery of the Old Avesta, wherein the cosmos is viewed as an enormous tent.[880]

As regards the Scythians, called Shakas in the Indic literature, Krishna's description of Shakadweepa in *Mbh*, Bhishma Parva, VI,11 is curiously the same as that of Jambudweepa in the Purānas so that Mt. Meru is its central mountain and Mt. Malaya its next highest, and so on. This suggests that the Indic Āryans may have originally lived in the north with the Shakas, or Scythians at the time of developing their cosmology and mythology. As for the historical evidence of the Scythians, ccording to Herodotus, the Scythians were located, in Darius' time, just north of

---

[877] See below pp.186ff.

[878] For instance, Áed Rúad (see the *Lebor Gabála Érenn*).

[879] See Mary Boyce, "On the Zoroastrian temple-cult", p.454.

[880] See P.O. Skjaervo, "The Avesta as source", p.168.

the Gandaridae (in the 15th satrapy),[881] and considered themselves as the "youngest of all nations" (Herodotus IV,3). That the Scythians depended for their limited cosmological understanding and religious practices on their Iranian kinsmen is plausible given the linguistic borrowings from Iranian noted among them. For instance, the word for hemp in most Central Asian cultures is derived from the Iranian "bhangha".[882] The predominance of the Iranian language in the regions inhabited by Cimmerians and Scythians, that is, from the Danube to the Dnieper, is evidenced also by the names of the Danube, Dnieper and Dniester, which employ the Avestan term "danu" for river.[883] Darius I (522-486 B.C.) himself refers to the Sakas as "unruly" and not devoted to Ahura Mazda.[884]

Herodotus' account of the religious customs of the Scythians (IV,59) indeed reveals their sharp focus on martial life, since they apparently did not set up altars or statues to any god except Ares, god of war. According to Herodotus (IV,18-19; 53ff), the most powerful of the Scythians were the "Royal Scythians".[885] The warlike aspect of the Scythians is revealed in the importance given to royal burials. These have been discovered mostly in the lower bends of the Dnieper, especially around Kamskoe Gorodišče. The king was indeed the cultural centre of Scythian society, but the importance of a caste system in it similar to that of the Iranians[886] is also evidenced in the myth of the first king, Skolo, who became the ruler by virtue of possessing the symbols of all the three orders of society, the warriors, priests, and agriculturalists and shepherds.[887] The royal hearth was the most sacred place in the Scythian domain and and solemn oaths were sworn there (Herodotus IV,68). This may be related to the veneration of the Royal Fire, the Ātash Bahram, among the Iranians.[888] When the king died, the royal funeral cortege travelled throughout the Scythian kingdom for forty days in order to receive the homage of the people, some of whom even mutilated themselves in partial self-sacrifice.

Other practices that link the Scythians to the Indo-Iranians is their

---

[881]   On the Gandharvas, see p.189f below.

[882]   See M. Eliade, *Shamanism*, p.400f.

[883]   The Russian Slavic word for god "bog" is also derived from Iranian "bhaga".

[884]   See W.W. Malandra, *Introduction to Ancient Iranian Religion*, p.24.

[885]   Herodotus also mentions that the northern Scythians were not nomadic but agricultural.

[886]   In the Farvardin Yasht XIII,88, for instance, Zarathustra is called "the first priest, the first warrior, the first agriculturist".

[887]   See B. Lincoln, *Death, War and Sacrifice*, p.189.

[888]   See below p.255.

custom of soma-drinking which accounts for their ancient designation as "hoamavarga", or "soma-drinking", Scythians.[889] However, Eliade's researches in Central Asian shamanism, which may be a vestige of ancient Scythian religious practice, point to a rather rudimentary practical application of the spiritual bases of the cosmological religion of the ancients in the shamanistic rituals.[890] The use of intoxicants for the acquisition of transcendental states is, according to Eliade, a relatively inferior path in comparison to the inner spiritual discipline advocated by yoga,[891] and the reduction of yogic knowledge to ecstatic flights among the shamans[892] is an indication of a certain degeneration of the wisdom of the ancient Near East in its transmission to the north. As Eliade pointed out,

> let us emphasize once again the structural difference that distinguishes classic Yoga from shamanism. Although the latter is not without certain techniques of concentration, ... its final goal is always ecstasy and the soul's ecstatic journey through the various cosmic regions, whereas Yoga pursues entasis, final concentration on the spirit and "escape" from the cosmos.[893]

The Indians, like the Iranians and Scythians, seem to have originally been a nomadic tribe. We may remember Megasthenes' report that

> The Indians were in old times nomadic, like those Scythians who did not till the soil, but roamed about in their wagons, as the seasons varied, from one part of Scythia to another, neither dwelling in towns nor worshipping in temples;[894] and that the Indians likewise had neither towns nor temples of the gods, but were so barbarous that they wore the skins of such wild animals as they could kill ... they subsisted also on such wild animals as they could catch, eating the flesh raw, – before, at least, the coming of Dionysus into India.

---

[889] So in the inscriptions of Darius I (see P.O. Skjaervo, in G. Erdosy, *op.cit*, p.157).

[890] Cf. M. Eliade's discussion of shamanism among the Scythians, *op.cit.*, pp.394ff.

[891] See M. Eliade, *op.cit.*, p.401.

[892] The term "shaman" may be related to the typical Indian bráhmanical patronymic "Sharman" (the corresponding patronymics for the kshatriyas, vaishyas and shudras being "Varman", "Gupta" and "Dāsa"; see *VP* III,10,9).

[893] *Ibid.*, p.417.

[894] The fact that the Scythians did not build temples or worship divine images is mentioned also by Herodotus, *Histories*, I,131.

Dionysus, however, when he came and had conquered the people, founded cities and gave laws to these cities, and introduced the use of wine among the Indians, as he had done among the Greeks, and taught them to sow the land, himself supplying seeds for the purpose ... It is also said that Dionysus first yoked oxen to the plough, and made many of the Indians husbandmen instead of nomads, and furnished them with the implements of agriculture; and that the Indians worship the other gods, and Dionysus himself in particular, with cymbals and drums, because he so taught them ... and that he instructed the Indians to let their hair grow long in honour of the god ....[895]

Since Dionysus is the same as the solar god An/Horus the Elder-Osiris,[896] and the earliest evidence of Muruga in India reveals a Dionysiac god, we may assume that the cultural contact being referred to by Megasthenes is that between the early Indo-Scythian settlers of India and Elamite Dravidians/Hurrians from the Zagros region.[897]

Literary evidence of the religion of the Indo-Āryans is manifest rather late, in the 16th century B.C., in the northern Mesopotamian kingdom of the Mitanni.[898] The original home of the Mitanni remains uncertain. The fact that the Scythians do not exhibit much sophistication in their religious rituals (Herodotus, IV,59) suggests that the Mitanni were not likely to have derived their cosmological insights from their Scythian kinsmen but from their earliest habitation amongst the Hurrians and Akkadians of northern Mesopotamia. It is possible that they may have arrived from the BMAC in Afghanistan (settled from 2200-1700 B.C.), where the evidence of fire-altars confirms the presence of Vedic Āryans.[899] That there was trade between Bactria and North Syria is also proved by the fact that from the 18th c. B.C. north Syrian seals show a typically Central Asian Bactrian camel such as is depicted in the BMAC seals.[900] However, there seems to be little evidence of fire-altars in the Mitanni

---

[895]   See Arrian, *Indica*, VII (in R.C. Majumdar, *Classical Accounts*, p.220f.).

[896]   See above p.54.

[897]   The theory that Āryan is pre-Harappan was put forward by A.D. Pusalkar, "Pre-Harappan, Harappan", pp.233ff.

[898]   The original cuneiform spelling of the kingdom used by Suttarna I (early 16th c. B.C.) was apparently "Ma-i-ta-ni" (see I. Gelb, *Hurrians and Subarians*, p.70).

[899]   This is the view of A. Parpola, "The Problem of the Aryans", p.369.

[900]   *Ibid.*, p.362.

region itself and it is equally possible that the Mitanni descended directly into Mesopotamia from the Caspian region rather than moving westwards from Afghanistan. The Mitanni themselves may be identifiable with the Medes, and, as Herodotus (VII,69) reveals, the Medes were once universally called Arians,[901] as well as perhaps with the proto-Iranians, since several Median words are traceable in Old Persian.[902] It is clear that the Mitanni culture informs both the Indo-Āryan and the Iranian.

The Mitanni exhibit an adherence to an Indo-Āryan, Vedic, and not Zoroastrian Avestan, form of religion along with the Hurrian. The Indo-Āryan culture, as we have seen, may have been a combination of that of the earliest Elamite and Mesopotamian Hurrians who adopted fire-rituals from the northern "Gandaridae" of the BMAC no earlier than the 23rd c. B.C. The first coherent list of Indic gods in the treaty of the Mitanni-Hurrian king Šattiwaza and the Hittite king Šuppililiumas I dating from the sixteenth century B.C. includes the names Mitra-Varuna, Indra, and Nāsatyas,[903] though Indra and Naonhaithya came to be considered as demons by the Zoroastrians. It is important to note that the Hurro-Akkadian version of the Lord of the Waters among the Mitanni is 'Uruwana' or 'Aruna'. In the Vedic *GB*, I,1,7, Varana[904] is indeed the secret form of the name Varuna,[905] and this repeats the penultimate vowel of both (Mitanni) "Uruwana" and (Gk.) "Ouranos". The form "Aruna" is perhaps related to the Hittite term for "ocean" "arunas",[906] which exhibits the vowel-shift of "a" to "u" that resulted in the Vedic Varuna. Further, the Sumerian name of the sun-god Utu may have been conserved in the Vedic Brāhmanas as the secret name of Sūrya, Ud.[907] The fact that some of the esoteric names of the Indo-Āryan deities, Agni (as Agri) and Sūrya (as

---

[901] That the name "Mede" may be related to the term Mitanni has been suggested by J. Charpentier, "The Date of Zoroaster"; B. Landsberger and T. Bauer, "Zu neueröffentlichen Geschichtsquellen"; E. Forrer, "Stratification des langues"; and F. Cornelius, "Erin-Manda".

[902] See P.O. Skjaervo, in G.Erdosy, *op.cit.*, p.159.

[903] The text (CTH 51 and 52 (see D. Yoshida, *op.cit.*, p.12; cf. V. Haas, *Geschichte*, p.543) reads "Dingir MešMitraššiel, Dingir MešUruwanaššiel, DIndar, Dingir MešNašattiyana", where the suffix "šiel" is uncertain.

[904] Following the example of Latin phonology, we may assume that the original Sanskrit of this region also favoured the "u" sound for the phoneme later transcribed with a "v".

[905] "being Varana, he is mystically called Varuna, because the gods love mysticism" (see U. Chouduri, *Indra and Varuna*, p.95).

[906] See G. Wilhelm, "Meer" in *RLA* VIII:3. Wilhelm suggests that this term is not of Indo-European origin [by which he no doubt means that which is properly called Āryan; see p.108n above], but, rather, Hattic.

[907] See *Taittriyopanishad Brāhmana*, I,45,4: "Yonder sun, that same is *ud*, fire is *gi* [cf. the Sumerian fire-god, Girra], the moon is *tham*".

Ud), are possibly of Sumerian origin suggests that the Sanskrit language itself may have been fully developed only after the establishment of the Sumerian Uruk culture.[908] The priesthood at Uruk too must have included a brāhmanical element that persisted from Ubaid times. It is possible also that the brāhmanical language behind Akkadian "apsu" and Sumerian "abzu" was ultimately proto-Dravidian, which was loaned into Āryan, Akkadian and Sumerian equally.

The presence of Indo-Āryan cultural elements in later Mesopotamia is attested by the occurrence of the divine names Mitra, Gishnu [Vishnu][909] and Sūrya [as 'Suliaat', from Hittite-Hurrian 'Suwaliyatta'][910] in the Sumerian god-list contained in CT 25, which, though dating from Assyrian times, around the seventh century B.C., must reflect a more ancient list of Sumerian deities translated into Akkadian. The description of the fire-god Girra as the "child of the Apsu" in an Akkadian hymn to the fire-god[911] also corresponds exactly to Agni's typical appellation "apām napāt", child of the waters.

It is to be noted that the Āryans designated the Dasyus or non-Āryans as Anagni, the fireless. The reference in *Manusmrithi* X:43-45 to "the Dravidas, the Kāmbojas, the Yavanas [Ionians], the Sakas [Scythians], etc." as kshatriya races which have sunk to the level of shūdras on account of their neglect of the sacred rites and the authority of the brāhmans suggests that Brāhmanism, though based on the spiritual insights of the proto-Dravidians, was formulated by the Indo-Āryans as an exclusively fire-worshipping cult. Although the Aryan religion was based on fire-rituals, there is as yet little archaeological evidence of fire-worship in the north.[912] However, from 2200-1700 B.C., there is clear evidence of typical Indo-Āryan settlement in the Bactro-Margiana Archaeological Complex (BMAC). The BMAC is not far north of Mundigak, where from 3000 B.C. we notice extensions of Elamite culture resembling that of the Indus Valley.[913] It is difficult to determine whether the Āryan

---

[908] See below pp.264ff.

[909] The lack of the "w" phoneme accounts for the translation of Vishnu into Gishnu in the Sumerian, "g" regularly substituting "w" in that language.

[910] See H.G. Güterbock, "The god Suwalliyat reconsidered".

[911] See M.-J. Seux, *Hymnes et Prières*, p.251.

[912] Recently, however, Anders Kaliff (*Fire, Water, Heaven and Earth*) has suggested that Bronze Age and early Iron Age cremation sites in Scandinavia from around 1800 B.C. to 400 A.D. point to the probable use of sacrificial fire and altars in rituals akin to the Vedic.

[913] Herodotus's description of the inhabitants of the various satrapies of Darius suggests that this region in Afghanistan may have been settled by Bactrians (Darius' 12th province) or Sattagydae, Gandaridae, Dadicae and Aparytae (7th province) (cf. J.P. Mallory and V. H.

settlements of BMAC represent a continuation of the early Elamite Hurrians of Mundigak or are new immigrants from the Andronovo culture associated with the Indo-Āryans (1800-900 B.C.).[914] The latter is indeed the more probable. The Andronovo culture is itself derived from the Hut Grave and Catacomb Grave culture of 2800-2000 B.C.[915] and the Sintashta culture of the southeast Urals (2300-1900 B.C.),[916] which is marked by chariot burials and may have been proto-Āryan rather than proto-Indo-Āryan. The fact that there is clear evidence of fire-worship in the BMAC and little evidence of it in Mundigak suggests that the former is derived from the Andronovo rather than from the Elamite colonies. Elaborate fire altars are evident in the ruins of the BMAC complex which correspond to the Āryan fire-sacrifices. The temples also contain rooms with "all the necessary apparatus for the preparation of drinks extracted from poppy, hemp and ephedra" that may have been used for the soma-rituals.[917] The BMAC may have thus been the centre of cultural contact between the proto-Dravidian/Hurrian peoples of Mundigak and the later Indo-Āryans. It is interesting to note too, in this context, that the Avesta (which is geographically centred in eastern Iran) mentions the Māzanian daevas as worshippers of the Indian gods. According to Burrow, Māzana is known in Iranian sources as the territory between the southern shore of the Caspian Sea and the Alburz mountains.[918] It may be related also to Margiana and the Indo-Āryan culture noted there.

It must be noted that there are indeed fire-altars even in the Harappan sites of Kalibangan, in Rajastan, and Lothal, in Gujarat, which may be dated to around 2500 B.C. So it remains a moot question whether the BMAC fire-altars were introduced from the north or the south, or whether they formed part of an extensive north-south Aryan cultural continuum. Indeed the Allchins surmise that there were probably also fire-altars in Harappa and Mohenjaro Daro though these have been missed in the mass-diggings conducted at these sites.[919]

Mair, *The Tarim Mummies*, p.45f.; p.262).

[914] Andronovo type pottery has been found in the early layers of Margiana (see A. Parpola, "The problem of the Aryans", p.363).

[915] The Hut Grave culture apparently separated into the Timber Grave (proto-Iranian) and Andronovo (proto-Āryan) cultures. The fourth millennium predecessor of the Hut Grave and Catacomb Grave cultures may have been the Yamnaya culture dating from 3500-2800 B.C. (*ibid.*, p.356).

[916] See J.P. Mallory and VH. Mair, *op. cit.*, pp.260f.

[917] *Ibid.*, p.262.

[918] See E.Bryant, *Quest*, p.130.

[919] See R. and B. Allchin, *The Rise of Civilization*, p.183. See also D. K. Chakrabarti, "The

In any case, it is clear that fire-worship was maintained particularly by the Āryan branch of the Indo-Europeans. For fire-worship is also observed among the Prussian-Lithuanian cult of szwenta (holy fire), as well as among the Greeks and Romans who maintained a cult of hestia or vesta.[920] Plutarch (*Numa*, II) informs us that "Numa is said to have built the temple of Vesta in circular form as protection for the inextinguishable fire, copying not the fire of the earth as being Vesta, but of the whole universe, as centre of which the Pythagoreans believe fire to be established, and this they call Hestia and the monad". The Scythians too worshipped a goddess called Tabit whose name is probably related to the Sanskrit tapti denoting heat.

On the other hand, we must remember Herodotus' statement that the Iranians did not worship fire originally.[921] In the Purānas, too, Purūravas, the early Aila [=Elamite?] king, is said to have obtained sacrificial fire from the "Gandharvas", who also taught him the constitution of the three sacred fires of the Āryans.[922] Purūravas is stated in the Puranas to be an Aila king of Pratishthana. The Ailas themselves are designated as Karddameyas which relates them to the river Karddama in Iran, particularly in the region of Balkh.[923] The kshatriya ruler of the lunar dynasty, Purūravas, is, according to the *Bhavishya Purāna*, Pratisarg 3, the son of Budh, the son of the Moon, Chandra,[924] who himself was the son of the sage Atri born of Brahma. The rise of both Chandra and Purūravas is dated to the Treta Yuga. Fire-worship was thus perhaps not universal among the earliest Āryan tribes. The fact that the Purūravas are said to have learnt the fire-rituals from the Gandharvas suggests that the early Hurrians of Elam and the earliest Iranians did not worship fire and learnt it from a more northerly wave of Āryans who must have, at a very early date, moved eastwards from their Armenian homeland. However, even the Gandharas are included among the Aila [=Elamite?] dynasties in the Purānas, which suggests that these Āryans too were a northern and eastern branch of proto-Hurrians identifiable with the Japhetites. The Japhetic tribes that moved northwards to the Pontic-Caspian steppes

archaeology of Hinduism", pp.44f.

[920] See M. Sharma, *Fire-worship*, p.19.

[921] See Herodotus, *Histories*, I,132.

[922] See F.E. Pargiter, *op.cit.*, p.309. In the *Mbh* I, 75, Purūravas is said to have brought the three kinds of sacrificial fire from the Gandharvas.

[923] See *Rāmāyana* VII,103,21ff.

[924] Budh was married to Ila, the daughter of Manu Vaivasvat or Shrāddhadeva.

created the Yamnaya culture there[925] which is considered the major source of the Āryan tribes.[926]

The Gandaridae are also mentioned by Herodotus (III,91) as one of the Indian tribes of the seventh satrapy of Darius I (550-486 B.C.) and can be located near the Bactrians of the 12th satrapy. The archaeological evidence of the early Gandharvas may be that found in the Gandhara Grave culture of the Swat settled from 1700-1400 B.C., which followed the BMAC. The occupants of the BMAC may have been related to the same family as the later Gandhara. Since the Gandhara culture also bears the first evidence of cremation rituals in South Asia, we may consider them to have indeed consolidated the Vedic customs of the Indo-Āryans. Cremation is evidenced also in the Andronovo culture.[927] At the same time, the neighbouring Bishkent culture, which is contemporaneous with the Gandhara and is related to the northern BMAC type, exhibits also a curious quasi-Scythian custom of inhumation involving the removal of the entrails and their replacement with clarified butter which may have persisted among the Vedic Indians, as is suggested by *SB* XII,v,2,5.[928]

The Purūravas who adopted fire-worship from the Gandharas may thus represent an Elamite branch of the proto-Āryan family, while the Gandaridae, who may have arrived from the south-east Caspian region (since the BMAC culture is apparently derived from the latter)[929] may be a typically Indo-Āryan, north-eastern branch of the same family.[930] That

---

[925]   W. Bernard suggested that the human remains from Period I of Gandhara bore resemblances to those of Bronze Age and early Iron Age crania of 2500 B.C. – A.D. 500 from the Caucasus and Volga region as well as from Tepe Hissar in Iran (see K.A.R. Kennedy, "Have Aryans been identified", p.49).

[926]   See A. Parpola, "The Problem of the Aryans", p.356. It is possible that Gandharva is related to Goidelic, the term used to designate the Irish, Scots and Manx forms of Celtic, but there is little evidence of a precise fire-worshipping identity either in the archaeology or in the mythological literature of the Irish except the occurrence of the appellation "Áed" (fire) in the royal names noted above (p.181n).

[927]   *Ibid.*, p.366. It is interesting to note, however, that the earliest Neolithic caves of Palestine in Gezer (7th millennium B.C.) already give evidence of a culture that practised cremation. Inhumation appears in these sites only much later in the fourth millennium B.C. (see S.A. Cook, *op. cit.*, p.74). This confirms the possibility that Palestine and Anatolia were first inhabited by proto-Dravidians/Hurrians before they were settled by the Armenoid peoples who practised inhumation. The early neolithic/chalcolithic levels of Yarim Tepe II (7th millennium B.C.), near Assyrian Nineveh, also reveal crematory practices (see P. Charvat, *op.cit.*, p.45). So we may assume that cremation was the earliest funereal mode of the entire Noachidian race.

[928]   See A. Parpola, *op.cit.*, p.365.

[929]   See J.P. Mallory and V.H. Mair, *op.cit.*, p.262.

[930]   It is possible that the Gandharas themselves were later considered as not belonging to

the Indic Vedic culture itself may have been developed after an original formulation at a proto-Indo-Iranian stage is suggested by the greater elaboration of the name of the god Tvoreshtar amongst the Iranians - representing the older religion of the proto-Āryans - compared to the Vedic Tvashtr.[931] Indeed many of the characteristic traits of the rituals of ancient India derive from an Indo-Iranian period as is attested by the similarity of the terms, yajna/yaja, soma/haoma,mantra/manθra, nama/nəmô. Even the term atharvan has only an Iranian etymology âθravâ.[932]

However, it should also be remembered that this fire-worship is employed in a religion which formed the basis of the solar religions of the Sumerians or Egyptians as well. In the Sumerian religion too, the chief solar god An is equated to Girra, the fire-god (in an Assyrian exegetical text)[933] and Re in Egypt is the same as the solar force, Agni. So that it is possible that the adoration of the solar force as divine fire may have been an integral part of the original proto-Dravidian religion that was shared by Semites, Japhetites and Hamites. But the actual fire-rituals may have been preserved more carefully by the Japhetic Indo-Āryan stock that had migrated at a very early date northwards to the Yamnaya and Andronovo cultures whence they moved southwards again later, in the second millennium B.C., towards northern Mesopotamia, Iran and India. The eastward movement of proto-Dravidians-Hurrians (Ailas as well as Ikshvākus) with Elamite forms of the Brahmanical religion may have encountered the more northerly fire-worshipping Gandaridae tribes to form the typically Indian branch of the Āryan family.

Pargiter has suggested that the Dravidian "brāhmanical" institution was also considerably transformed by the Āryans. While the original [proto-] Dravidian priesthood was characterised by the practice of yogic austerities (tapas) which gave them magical powers, the Āryan was preoccupied with the performance of sacrifices, especially revolving around the worship of fire.[934] The Indo-Āryan religion thus seems to have combined the ancient proto-Dravidian wisdom of the Elamite/Mesopotamian Hurrians with more northerly fire- and soma-rituals and horse-sacrifices. And the original proto-Dravidian or Noachidian

---

the Brāhmanical orthodoxy since, in *Mbh*, Shanti Parva, 12.65, they are classified along with the Yavanas (Greeks), Kiratas, Sakas, etc. as outsiders living within the dominion of the Indic Āryans.

[931] Cf. A. Jacob, "Cosmology and Ethics", p.96.

[932] See P. Kretschmer, *Kuhns Zeitschrift* 55, p.80; cf. J. Gonda, *Religionen Indiens*, I, p.107.

[933] RA 62-52,17-8 (see A. Livingstone, *op.cit.*, p.74); cf. K170+Rm520rev. (*ibid.*, p.30ff).

[934] See F.E. Pargiter, *op.cit.*, p.308f.

wisdom[935] is also best preserved in the cultivated [sanskrit=refined] and inflected language of the upper castes of the Indo-Āryans, though Sanskrit retains several Dravidian elements in it.

It is interesting in this context to note that Herodotus, *History of the Persian Wars*, III,102, refers to other Indians who "dwell northward of all the rest of the Indians" and describes them as following "the same mode of life as the Bactrians", which shows that the Indian Āryans were originally derived from the BMAC. However, the Indo-Āryans seem to have been long resident in India and to have come to consider it their home. For, in the *Manusmrithi*, Chapter II, the land of the Indo-Āryans is described in fully Indian geographical terms:

17. That land, created by the gods, which lies between the two divine rivers Sarasvati and Drishadvati, the sages call Brahmāvarta.

19. The plain of the Kurus, the country of the Matsyas, Panchālas and Sūrasenakas, these form the country of the Brahmarshis, which comes after Brahmāvarta. [The brāhmans are derived from the sages of this realm].[936]

Then comes the middle region, Madhyadesha:[937]

21. That country which lies between the Himavat and the Vindhya mountains to the east of Prayāg [which is in the west] and to the west of Vinashana (where the Sarasvati disappears) [which is in the east] is called Madhyadesha.

22. But the tract between those two mountains [Himavat and Vindhya] as far as the eastern and western oceans the wise call Āryāvarta.

23. That land where the black antelope naturally roams[938] one must know to be fit for the performance of sacrifices; the tract different from that is the country of the Mlecchas.

24. Let the twice-born men seek to dwell in those [lands]; but a Shūdra, distressed for subsistence may reside anwhere.

---

[935] That the biblical Noah, a descendant of Adam's son, Seth, represents the wisdom of Seth is evident from the Gnostic tradition (see G.G. Stroumsa, *op. cit.*, p.107). Josephus' *Jewish Antiquities*, I, 70-71 also makes clear the association of the line of Seth with cosmological learning (see A. Annus, *op.cit.*, p.xxvii).

[936] This realm corresponds macrocosmically to Heaven, Asgard.

[937] This corresponds macrocosmically to the Mid-Region, Midgard, Airyanem Vaego.

[938] India, which is the natural habitat of the black antelope.

According to *Vishnusmrithi*, LXXXIV,4, "Those countries are called barbarous (Mleccha) where the system of the four castes does not exist; the others are denoted Āryāvarta."

Some of the kshatriya tribes too are, according to *Manusmrithi* X, described as having sunk to a lower social level, that of shūdras, on account of their disregard of the brāhmanical rites:

43. In consequence of the omission of the sacred rites and of their not consulting Brāhmanas, the following tribes of Kshatriyas have gradually sunk in this world to the condition of Shūdras:

44. The Paundrakas,[939] the Kodas, the Dravidas,[940] the Kāmbojas [Persians],[941] the Yavanas [Ionians, Greeks], the Sākas [Scythians], the Pāradas, the Pahlavas [Parthians?],[942] the Kīnas, the Kirātas, the Daradas [Dardic tribes].

While the vaisyas represent the people in general,[943] engaged in agriculture and trade, the shūdras represent the artisans and servile caste of Indo-Āryan society.[944]

In *Manusmrithi* X,45 we learn that many so-called Dasyus were also sons of the sage Vishvāmithra.[945] Manu goes on to declare that "All those tribes in this world, which are excluded from the (community) of those born from the mouth, the arms, the thighs, and the feet (of Brahman) are called Dasyus, whether they speak the language of the Mlecchas

---

[939] Paundraka is the King of Karūsha in *BP* X,66,1, a pretender allied with the King of Kasi against Krishna. As regards the Paundrakas, *Aitareya Brāhmana* VII,18, states that "Andhras, Pundras [between Himavat and Hemakunt mountains], Shabaras, Pulindas, Mūtibas [are] older than Madhuchandas, whom Vishvāmitra favours of his 101 sons [who were kshatriyas]."

[940] *Mbh*, Ādi Parva, I,177 associates the Dravidas, along with the Sakas, Yavanas, Kiratas, etc., as Mleccha armies raised by the sage Vasishta.

[941] *Mbh*, Shānti Parva, (12.207) mentions the Yavanas, Kambojas, Gandharas, Kiratas and Barbaras as belonging to Uttarapatha (the northern part of Jambudveepa) and dating from the Treta Yuga. Kambujiyas is also the original form of the name of the Achaemenid Persian emperor, Cambyses, 6th c. B.C. In *Mbh*, Udyoga Parva, V,19, the Kambojas are allied to the Sākas and Kurus. The tribes from Uttarapatha may have been Indo-Iranian and Scythian.

[942] The Pāradas are associated in the Purānas with the Sākas, Yavanas, Pahlavas, Kambojas as the Pancha-gana (five hordes), kshatriya tribes that were divested of their high status by the Iksvhāku King Sagara of Kosala (*Mbh*, Vana Parva, Tirthayātra Parva, 106)..

[943] The term for 'all' in eastern Slavic is still 'visye'.

[944] Cf. 'Bhagavad Gita', XVIII.

[945] See below p.197.

(barbarians – non-Āryans, casteless) or that of the Āryans." It is not clear who the Dasyus are but they seem to have been considered as virtually non-human since they are not derived from the Purusha at all. It is possible that they are non-Indo-European aboriginals. They also seem to be as lowly placed in the caste hierarchy as the so-called 'untouchables' of later Hindu society.

VII.

THE BRĀHMANS

The typical characteristic of ancient Indo-Āryan culture is the eminence of the brāhmanical caste therein. The only other caste that approaches the brāhmanical in spiritual and social dignity is that of the kshatriya. For instance, the *Gautama Dharmashāstra*, VIII,1 states that "there are in the world two who uphold the proper way of life – the king and the Brahmin deeply learned in the Vedas. And on them depend the life of the fourfold human race and of internally conscious creatures that move about, fly, and crawl; as well as their increase, protection, non-intermixture, and adherence to the Law".[946] However, the brāhman is clearly above the kshatriya too. According to *RV*, X,90,12, Purusha Sūkta:

> The Brāhman was his mouth, of both his arms was the Rājanya made.
> His thighs became the Vaisya, from his feet the Shūdra was produced.

The term 'brahman' is derived from an obscure root, perhaps, but not certainly, 'brh- brmhati', which means 'to cause to grow up, strengthen', etc. It is more probably derived from an old form of the modern Dravidian 'peru' meaning 'to engender'.[947] As Gonda points out, the Sanskrit word is principally associated with the potency or principle from which all things are derived – as the ultimate basis of the world.[948] It is thus perhaps related also to the German 'gebären' and English 'to bear'.

---

[946] See P. Olivelle, *Dharmasūtras*, p.90.

[947] *DED*, art. 4422.

[948] See J. Gonda, *Notes on Brahman*, p.1.

Another possible cognate is the Hebrew "brh", the root that is used in the Bible solely in connection with god's act of creation.[949] This root is especially used to connote the formative process of creation, an operation that is encountered also in the pseudo-Lucianic *Amores*, where Eros (who is the same as Brahman and the Orphic Phanes) is apostrophised in the following manner: "thou from obscure and disordered formlessness gavest form to everything".[950]

A brāhman was originally a sort of superhuman by virtue of his magical powers. Indeed magical power, and not saintliness, is the original characteristic of the brāhman. As Charpentier suggested, the brāhmans are therefore "über Könige und Fürsten durch die ihnen beigeborene, schreckenerregende Macht weit überlegen und müssen überall mit Huldigung und Gehorsamkeit empfangen werden".[951] Indeed the significance of Brahman is that Brahman represents the original source of life in the universe, it is the life-principle of the gods themselves and equal to the soma of immortality (corresponding to the Greek mead). Hence Wackernagel equated Brahman with the soul (ātman) of man as well as of the universe.[952]

A brāhman is consequently one who has a knowledge of the structure of the universe and of the nature of the divine powers. According to the Ethiopic version of Pseudo-Callisthenes, the brāhmans declare to Alexander that they "are men poor and needy, and ... have neither possession nor wealth ... have no occupation of any kind except the worship of God" and that they indeed "have knowledge of everything which is in the world". To such an extent indeed that the prophet Elijah (speaking on behalf of the Israelite king Ahab) says to his own god, "they have slain Thy prophets, they have overthrown Thy altars. I, even I only, am left to make mention of Thee, and they are seeking my life to destroy it".[953] The *Vājrasūchi Upanishad* too insists that spiritual enlightenment is the truest characteristic of the brāhmans:

> Whoever he may be, he who has directly realised his Ātmā and who is
> directly cognizant, like the myrobalan in his palm, of his Ātma that is

---

[949]   Cf., in this context, N. Lahovary's comment (*op.cit.*, p.368f) that "phonetically as well as morphologically western Semitic (Hebrew, Canaanean, Aramaean) is found to be less different, in its most ancient texts, from Basque and Dravidian than the other Semitic languages, with the exception perhaps of Akkadian".

[950]   See M.L. West, *Orphic Poems*, p.255.

[951]   See J. Charpentier, *Brahman*, p.83f.

[952]   See J. Wackernagel, *Ueber den Ursprung*, p.30.

[953]   See E.A.W. Budge, *The Alexander Book*, p.75.

without a second, that is devoid of class and actions, that is free from the faults of the six stains and the six changes, that is of the nature of truth, knowledge, bliss, and eternity, that is without any change in itself, that is the substratum of all the kalpas, that exists penetrating all things that pervades everything within and without as ākāś, that is of nature of undivided bliss, that cannot be reasoned about and that is known only by direct cognition. He who by the reason of having obtained his wishes is devoid of the faults of thirst after worldly objects and passions, who is the possessor of the qualifications beginning with śama, who is free from emotion, malice, thirst after worldly objects, desire, delusion, etc., whose mind is untouched by pride, egoism, etc., who possesses all these qualities and means—he only is the brāhmana.

Considering the primordial, antediluvian origins of the brāhmans that we have noted in the Ethiopian version of Pseudo-Callisthenes,[954] it is not surprising that the brāhmans trace their ancestry back to the Seven Sages, Kashyapa, Atri, Bharadvaja, Gautama, Vishvāmitra, Jamadagni, and Vasishta. Of these, Vishvāmitra is said to have been born a kshatriya[955] and later become a brāhman.

The pre-eminence of the brāhman is clear from the *Manusmriti,*1:

93. As the Brahman sprang from (Brahman's) mouth, as he was the first-born, and as he possesses the Veda, he is by right the lord of this whole creation.

    ...

96. Of created beings the most excellent are said to be those which are animated; of animated those which subsist by intelligence; of the intelligent mankind; and of men the Brahmanas;

97. Of Brahmanas those learned (in the Veda); of the learned those who recognise (the necessity and the manner of performing the prescribed duties); of those who possess this knowledge those who perform them; of the performers those who know the Brahman.

98. The very birth of a Brahmana is an eternal incarnation of the sacred law for he is born to (fulfil) the sacred law, and becomes one with Brahman.

99. A Brahmana coming into existence is born as the highest on

---

[954] See above p.133.

[955] In the *Panchavimsha Brāhmana* Vishvāmitra is represented as King of Jahnus.

earth, the lord of all created beings, for the protection of the treasury of the law.

100. Whatever exists in the world is the property of the Brahmana; on account of the excellence of his origin the Brahmana is indeed entitled to all.

...

105. (A Brahmana who studies the laws of Manu and faifthfully fulfils his duties prescribed therein) sanctifies any company (which he may enter) ... and he alone deserves (to possess) this whole earth.

According to *Manusmrithi* XII,41-51, shūdras are produced by a predominance of Tamas, kshatriyas by that of Rajas and brāhmans by that of Sattva. However, it must be noted that it is the brāhmans who, like the divine Brahman-Prajāpati, represent the creative force of the universe that is maintained by the kshatriyas within their kingdoms. Heesterman, following his general tendency to consider the warrior class of the ancient Indo-Europeans the originally dominant caste, suggests that the brāhmans were not a priestly sect at first, since the sacrifices could have been performed by any rich sacrificer by himself (and were later performed in India by lower castes as well). However, it is clear that the elevated importance of the brāhmans arose from their unique creativity as masters of the magical sacrifices. In the opening ceremony of the Darshapūrnamāsa sacrifice, the brāhman priest declares: "I am the Lord of Earth, the lord of the world, the lord of the great creation ... Brhaspati is the Brahman of the gods, I am the Brahman of men".[956] It is interesting to note also that, during the sacrifice, the brāhmans, representing Prajāpati, are, fed the miniscule prāshitra portion of the sacrificial oblation which represents the sting of the arrow of Rudra with which he pierced Prajāpati (*SB* I,7,4,1-18; *TS* II,6,8,3-7).

Wackernagel attempted to demonstrate the similarity of the brāhman priesthood to the role of the 'pontifex maximus' in ancient Rome who was responsible for the supervision and management of the sacrifice and had authority in choosing and disciplining the other priests under him.[957] Wackernagel further pointed to the fact that the title pontifex (derived from pons, bridge) itself is related to the brāhman's role of building a bridge through the sacrifice between the earth and the heavens.[958] However, little can be stated with certainty regarding the original office of

---

[956]   See A. Hillebrandt, *Das altindische Neu- und Vollmondsopfer*, I, p.16.

[957]   See J. Wackernagel, *op.cit.*, p.32.

[958]   *Ibid.*, p.34.

a pontifex maximus that was designed by Numa during the foundation of Rome apart from the fact that such a personage served as an advisor to the king. After the overthrow of the monarchy, the pontifex's role may have been expanded to include the performance of certain rituals previously conducted by the king. It seems possible that the pontifex's role in ancient Rome normally combined religious and political duties. Hocart, on the other hand, related the brāhman priest to the kerux or herald of the ancient Greek state and of the Eleusinian mysteries since the latter was a leader of rituals.[959] But if this is so, the office is a dilution of the original brāhmanical one since the kerux's role gradually deteriorated to that of a public crier.

The *Bhavishya Purāna*, 133, points to three original types of sun-worshippers, sun-worshipping Magas, fire-worshipping Magas and sun-worshipping Bhojakas. The Magas are in general related to the Magi of Iran. The Shakaldwipa brāhmans of India, who call themselves Maga brāhmans, consider themselves as originating in Shaka Dweepa, rather than in Jambu Dweepa, where Bhāratavarsha (India) is situated.[960] According to the *Bhavishya Purāna*, the people of Shaka Dweepa were divided into four castes, Maga, Mashaka, Manasa and Madanga. Some of the Maga brāhmans married women of the Bhojavamsha[961] and thus started the Bhojaka clan. *Mbh*, Bhishma Parva, VI,11 refers to the first caste as Mrigas and considers them as brāhmans, and the others, Mashaka, Manasa and Madanga, as kshatriyas, vaisyas and shudras respectively.

By the 11ᵗʰ century A.D.,[962] the brāhmans in India were divided into two groups, the northern Pancha (five) Gauda brāhmans and the southern Pancha (five) Dravida brāhmans. The first include the Saraswat, Kanyakubja, Maithili, Gauda, and the Utkala. The latter are constituted of the Āndhra, Dravida (Tamil and Keralite), Karnātaka, Mahārāshtra and Gujarāti. The brāhmans, as we have seen, claim direct descendance from one of the Seven Sages and the descendants of each sage form a "gotra". A man from one gotra cannot marry a woman from the same gotra since they are considered to be brother and sister.

A brāhman's life is divided into four Āshrama's or stages of life, beginning with brahmachārya (studentship, between the ages of five and sixteen),[963] and followed by the grihasthya (householder stage,

---

[959] See A.M. Hocart, *Kings and Councillors*, pp.189f.

[960] See above p.45f.

[961] The Bhojavamsha are derived from King Bhoja (*Mbh*, Shānti Parva, 166).

[962] This division is mentioned in Kalhana's history of the kings of Kashmir, *Rājatarangini*.

[963] See *Manusmriti* II,36-40. The years of brahmachārya are different for kshatriyas and

lasting 25 years), vānaprasthya (forest-dweller stage, lasting 25 years)
and sannyāsa (hermit) stages. The last two are obviously not compulsory
since their progress is not evidenced in the twelve or sixteen sacraments,
or Samskāras, which mark the life of a brāhman.[964] The grihasthya is
governed by the rules prescribed in the Grhyasūtras. The vanaprastha
may be accompanied by his wife, but the sannyāsi is a solitary. In fact,
a sannyāsi abandons his household fire and, throwing the sacred thread
which is the mark of his brāhmanhood into the fire, adopts the garb of
a mendicant. It is interesting that, at the last fire-ritual he performs, he
symbolically breathes in the flames so as to internalise the fire.[965] A
sannyāsi renounces even sacrifice and the entire order of the manifest
world. Just as the married grhastha was the protagonist of the sacrificial
stage of the human drama, the celibate ascetic is now that of the final act.
Mānasa yoga is now practised as a mental sacrifice.

The entire life of a brāhman is marked by several sacraments or
Samskāras. The first of these is the Garbadhānam or the rite marking
conception. This is followed by by rituals performed in the third month
of pregnancy (Pumsavanam), and in the fourth month (Sīmantam). These
ceremonies are designed to remove the "sin" issuing from the parents.
On birth, a Jātakarmam is performed for the development of the child's
intellect with the administration of a small mixture of gold, ghee and
honey. According to the Grhyasūtras, the birth of the intellect occurs
immediately after the birth of the child. So the father "offers in sacrifice"
his own vital force into his baby breathing on the baby on his knees and
chanting "May Savitr give you wisdom".[966] Savitr is, as we have seen, is
the form of the sun before its full fluoresence as Sūrya/Indra.[967] Twelve
days after birth, the child's naming ceremony, called Nāmakaranam,
takes place. When the child is taken out of the house for the first time,
a Nishkrāmanam is performed. When it is six months old and eats solid
food for the first time, a few grains mixed with ghee are fed to the child
in the Annaprasanam ceremony. In his third or fifth year, a boy child has
his hair cut for the first time in the Chūdākarmam ceremony. Normally
the head is fully shaved except for a tuft of hair. The next samskāra,

---

vaisyas, beginning at the age of 11 in the case of the kshatriyas and at 12 in that of the
vaisyas.

[964] See, for instance, *Manusmriti*, II. See also the Grhya Sutras, most of which have been
translated by Oldenberg (1886,1892).

[965] See G. Flood, *Introduction to Hinduism*, p.91.

[966] See J. Gonda, *Religionen*, I, p.116.

[967] See above p.121.

Karnavedham marks the piercing of the ears, When the child is three or five years old, the samskāra called Vidyārambham (the beginning of education), when the phrase "Hari Sri Ganapataye Namah Avignamastu" is written with a piece of gold on the tongue of the child and the child is made to write the same sentence with its index finger on raw rice in a bell-metal vessel and recite it at the same time. When the child attains eight years, he undergoes the Upanayanam samskāra which marks a rebirth of the boy, hence the brāhman's designation as dvija, or twice-born. As in the sacrifices, the boy's guru makes an embryo of his pupil and dedicates him to Brahman as a brahmachārin.[968] At the initiation ceremony, the guru teaches the boy the Gāyatri or Sāvitri mantra from RV III,62,10: "May we receive this desirable light of the god Savitr which will give birth to our thoughts".[969] It is on this occasion that he starts to wear the sacred thread "Yajnopavitam" for the first time. The thread symbolises the umbilical cord that attaches the boy to the Vedas whence he is born during this "second birth".[970] The next sacrament, Praishartham, marks the learning of the Vedas and the Upanishads. When the boy attains his sixteenth year, he shaves his face for the first time in a ceremony called Keshāntam. For girls the corresponding ceremony is one to mark her first menstruation called Ritusuddhi. The end of a boy's formal education in the Vedas and his life as a brahmachārin is marked by the Samāvartanam. Marriage is celebrated in the samskāra of Vivāham and death is consecrated in the Antyeshti samskāra of the last rites.

The samskāras related to marriage and funeral ceremonies may be detected already in the RV X, 85 (which deals with the marriage of Sūrya and Soma) and RV X,14-18 respectively. During the marriage ceremony, the union of the bridegroom and bride are considered as similar to that of Heaven (Dyaus) and Earth (Prithvi).[971] The bridegroom and bride take seven steps representing the seven regions of the universe which Vishnu traverses with his three strides.[972] The nuptial fire is maintained constantly from hearth to hearth.

The funeral ceremonies are detailed in the Pitrmedha Sutras.[973] The

---

[968] Hocart (Kingship, p.202) conjectured that many of the brāhmanical rites including the initiation of young brāhmans and the matrimonial ceremonies may have been derived from those of the royal consecration (see below pp.233ff).

[969] See J. Gonda, op.cit., p.119.

[970] See A. Michaels, Hinduism Past and Present, pp.71ff.

[971] Cf. p.31n.

[972] See Hocart, Kingship, p.108; cf. above p.99.

[973] See C.G. Kashikar, Śrauta, Paitrmedhika and Pariśesa sūtras, 1964, pp. 460-501.

cremation represents the self-sacrifice of the sacrificer on the funeral pyre. If the dead man is a kshatriya, a bow is placed beside him on the pyre and then removed.[974] The pyre is lit by the three sacrificial fires, sometimes even the domestic fire is used for this purpose. The lighting of the pyre is accompanied by the chants "May his eye go to the sun, his soul to the air ... may the Maruts raise him", etc. After the cremation, those who assisted at it return home to undergo purificatory rites to avoid the evil consequences of contact with death. A child who dies before his upanayanam ceremony is buried not burnt, while a bachelor is incinerated with a special fire produced by the lighting of husks of grain in an earthen pot placed on a fire.[975] Ascetics who die are buried since they have already acquired immortality and do not need to be led to the other world by fire.[976]

Some days after a cremation, the bones are collected, purified and then placed in an urn in a deep pit.[977] To have a tumulus was a particular honour. The dead man's spirit was not considered to arise immediately to the realm of the ancestors but remains for a year as a ghost. The arrival of the spirit of a dead man in the realm of the ancestors is marked by a special ceremony called the sapindīkarana.[978] It seems that the Vedic Indians believed that men continued their afterlife in a corporeal form, as *RV* X,16,5, for instance, suggests.[979]

---

[974] See J. Gonda, *op.cit.*, pp.132ff.

[975] See M. Biardeau, *op.cit.*, p.38.

[976] See J. Gonda, *op.cit.*, p.134.

[977] See J. Gonda, *op.cit.*, p.135. Among the Zoroastrians the bones of an exposed corpse, representing the most material, and evil, part of the body, are thrown into the "tower of silence", where slaked lime decomposes them to powder (see A. Kaliff, *op. cit.*, pp.87ff).

[978] See *Manusmriti,* V,57ff.

[979] See J. Gonda, *op.cit.*, p.138.

VIII.

YAJNA I

The Brāhmanical Basis of Yajna

According to the *Manusmriti*,I,88, a brāhman has 6 duties: "Studying wisdom and teaching it to others, performing yajnas and directing others to do it, giving charity and encouraging others to give it."[980] The importance of sacrificing as the typical office of the brāhman is thus quite evident. Indeed, the Ideal macroanthropos, Purusha, is, in the *Manusmriti*, regarded as having first produced the brāhman through his mouth for the institution of the sacrifice:

> 94. For the Self-existent (Swayambhu), having performed austerities, produced [the brāhman] first from his own mouth, in order that the offerings might be conveyed to the gods and manes and that this universe might be preserved.

According to the *Brahma Purana* 116,54-57, Brahma himself is said to have offered a sacrifice after the universe emerged from the Purusha. His oblations in the gārhapatyāgni, dakshināgni and the āhavaniyāgni resulted in three forms of Purusha, white in the āhavaniya, black in the dakshināgni and yellow in the gārhaptya, the three colours

---

[980] Among the Zoroastrians too the function of the priest is said to be "to preserve the good religion, sacrifice, invocation of the good gods, to make observations regarding the law and justice and custom and social bonds as revealed in the pure Mazda worshipping religion and to make men know the goodness of virtue and to point out the path to heaven, the fearfulness of hell and the defense against hell" (*Mēnōg i Xrad*, 31; see B. Lincoln, *Myth, Cosmos and Society*, p.147).

emblematic of Indo-European societies.[981] Moreover, the entire sacrifice is a representation of Brahman himself. As the *Vasishta Dharmashāstra* declares,

> At this rite the altar is the body of the Brahmin occupying his seat, the sacrifice is his declaration of intent; the sacrificial animal is himself; the rope for tying is his intellect; the offertorial fire is the mouth of the Brahmin occupying his seat; [the south fire] is his navel; the householder's fire is the fire of his stomach; the Adhvaryu priest is his out-breath; the Hotr priest is his in-breath; the Brahman priest is his inter-breath; the Udgātr priest is his link-breath; and the sacrificial vessels are his sense organs.[982]

Although the Sanksrit root "yaj" means generally "to worship", it also has the more esoteric significance of a creative activity. Indeed the power of the brāhman priests who are delegated to conduct sacrifices is so extraordinarily great because their sacrifices imitate the original cosmic sacrifices of Purusha-Brahman that produced the light of the universe. This power is essentially a supernatural one. The significance of the Vedic priest as a sustainer of the cosmic order may be glimpsed also in the Hurrian sacrificial rites, as, for instance, in the address to Telipinu (corresponding to Agni[983]) in the following verse: "Behold, O Telipinu, I have sprinkled thy path with fine oil,/ Go now, Telipinu, on the path sprinkled with fine oil",[984] where the sacrificer initiates the activity of the god.[985]

The sacrifice is indeed a magical rite whose every gesture is imbued with miraculous power and the dangers of conducting a sacrifice imperfectly include death and destruction, personal as well as national. The brāhman priests create the desired results for the sacrificer, be these wealth or offspring or other benefits, through their various sacrificial rites, their chants and the metres employed in these chants.[986] As Shriram

---

[981]   See above p.150n; cf. below p.281

[982]   See P. Olivelle (tr.), *Dharmasūtras*, p.325.

[983]   See above p.98.

[984]   See V. Haas and G. Wilhelm, *Hurritische und luwische Riten*, p.9.

[985]   While in India the Brāhman priests are the sole initiates into the divine system of the cosmos, in the Hamitic culture of Egypt the pharaoh, as the representative or son of the sun (that is, as Horus the Younger), was invested with this divine knowledge, as well as with the concomitant responsibility of establishing divine justice on earth (see S. Quirke, *The Cult of Ra*, pp.17ff.).

[986]   See J. Wackernagel, *op.cit.*, p.29.

Sharma explains, the chanting of mantras produces "a sound vibration which awakens divine centres of the aspirant's body and in turn this attracts divine powers of the cosmos towards itself". Thus a bond is created between the performer of a yajna and the demigods (cosmic powers). The sacred significance of the brāhman in the sacrifice is further indicated by the belief that the brāhman priest who is satisfied with the offerings given to him is like a god satisfied with his.[987]

According to the Vedic tradition, the sacrificer himself must be a male of the three upper castes and a grhastha, that is, married, with a son to carry on his line.[988] He must also not be very old, or "with graying hair". The importance of this will be understood when we consider the identification of the sacrificer with the victim and the focus on the virility of the victim in the sacrifice. The sacrificer's wife participates in some of the rites of the sacrifices but plays an entirely dependent role therein. It is possible that the original sacrifices may have been public ceremonies[989] and the sacrificer typically a kshatriya, since it was the king's duty to sustain his kingdom.[990]

The Chief Deities of the Yajna

Although the brāhmanical rituals are numerous and complex, the basic focus is on the sustenance of Brahman, the divine Light and Consciousness that is forced into the underworld by the storm-force and is then resuscitated by the same storm-force to mount into our universe as the sun, Sūrya. Thus, for example, the principal deities in the Agnihotra ritual are Nārāyana (corresponding to the moribund Osiris) and Sūrya (corresponding to Horus the Younger). The priests use the ashes of the fire from the sunset ceremony in the lighting of the fire at the sunrise ceremony to symbolise the rebirth of the Nārāyana fire as the Sūrya fire. *AB* I,1,1, declares that Agni is the lowest of the gods, Vishnu the highest, between them are all the other deities, for Agni is the force that is transformed into Āditya, or the sun. And as Bodewitz comments on the Jyotishtoma ritual,

---

[987] See M. Biardeau, *op.cit.*, p.46.

[988] See J. Gonda, *op.cit.*, p.143.

[989] See below p.233.

[990] See M. Biardeau, *op.cit.*, p.28.

we may cautiously conclude that the Jyotistoma refers to the appearance out of darkness and the spread of cosmic light ... The sun's reaching heaven and the ascent to heaven of the sacrificer run parallel ... In a certain period at least the Jyotistoma was not just a Laud of Light, but rather a Laud for the obtainment of Light.[991]

The solar force is basically Agni itself, which, as we have seen, is the same force that is manifest as the sun. Agni, or the supreme fire, is an epithet of Shiva,[992] and is the characteristic form that he, the original divine Soul, or Ātman, assumes in the course of the cosmic manifestation. According to SB, the term 'agni' is said to be derived from 'agri', the first, or the leader.[993] According to RV III,29,11, the germinal form of this Agni is called "Tanūnapāt", as a new-born he is called "Narāshamsa", and "Mātarishvan" when he acquires form in his mother and "has become the rush of the wind [Vāyu] in his swift course". We have already noted the force of Vāyu as the fire that impregnates the waters to form Earth.[994] SB VI,7,4,3 thus recounts the first birth of Agni as Vāyu thus:

'From the sky [Heaven] Agni was first born;'—the sky, doubtless, is the breath, and from the breath he (Agni) was indeed first born,—

The second birth of Agni is from Earth:

'from us[995] the second time, the knower of beings,'—inasmuch as he, man-like, on that occasion generated him a second time;

The third generation of Agni by Prajāpati is from the waters that surround the universe and flow through the underworld where the solar force undergoes a passion. According to SB VI,7,4,3:

—'the third time in the waters,'—inasmuch as he there did generate him a third time from the waters;—he, the manly-minded, (kindling him) the imperishable ... the manly-minded, doubtless, is Pragâpati [Purusha]; and the imperishable, Agni;—'kindling him the mindful praises ... him,'—for he who kindles him generates him, mindful.

---

[991] See H.W. Bodewitz, Jyotistoma Ritual, p.108.

[992] See above p.31.

[993] The Yāska Nirukta 7,14 derives Agni from agra and ni and construes it as "the leader" [of the sacrifice].

[994] See above p.39.

[995] The brāhmans are indeed considered to be the lords of Earth (see above p.198).

This final material form of Agni in the universe is as the fire-ball of the sun (Āditya), though this too, as we have seen, begins from Varuna in the underworld as an Agni sun, then manifests itself in the universe as Vāyu and finally in the heavens as the sun of our system.[996] The final solar form of Agni is called Agni Vaishvānara described in *RV* VI,7,5-6 thus:

5. Agni Vaishvānara, no one hath ever resisted these thy mighty ordinances,
   When thou, arising from thy parents' bosom, foundest the light for day's appointed courses.
6. The summits of the heaven are traversed through and through by the Immortal's light, Vaishvānara's brilliancy.

Thus Agni-Vāyu-Āditya are the stages of the manifestation of Agni in our universe from the dormant Varuna in the underworld, as *RV* V,3,1ff. reveals:

1. Thou at thy birth art Varuna, O Agni; when thou art kindled thou becomest Mitra.
   In thee, O Son of Strength, all Gods are centred. Indra art thou to man who brings oblation.
2. Aryaman art thou as regardeth maidens mysterious, is thy name, O Self-sustainer.
   As a kind friend with streams of milk they balm thee what time thou makest wife and lord one-minded.
3. The Maruts deck their beauty for thy glory, yea, Rudra! for thy birth fair, brightly-coloured.
   That which was fixed as Vishnu's loftiest station—therewith the secret of the Cows thou guardest.

The *Brhaddevata* I,91ff, too describes the macrocosmic forms of Agni recognising three forms of Agni, the earthly one called Agni, the one in the mid-region called Jātavedas (Vāyu),[997] and the one in heaven Vaishvānara (Sūrya/Āditya). The corporeal form of Agni on earth is also called Pavamāna, or that which is in the process of being purified, its form in the mid-region Pāvaka (shining) and in heaven Shuci (effulgent). These three forms correspond to the fires in the gārhapatyāgni, dakshināgni and the āhavaniyāgni of the Vedic sacrifice.

---

[996] See above p.100; cf. S. Sharma, *op.cit.*, Ch.16.

[997] The central part of the sacred flame used in the Indic fire-rituals is itself called Jātaveda Agni (see also p.240 below).

AV III,21,[998] refers also to the different fires manifest in the universe, starting with that contained in stones, herbs, trees, cattle, birds, quadrupeds and bipeds, and moving to that in lightning and the heavens, that is, in the sun in its different phases as Mitra, Savitr, Indra, Varuna, as well as Brhaspati, the source of the light of Brahman. According to *SB* X,2,2,4, Prajāpati is identified with the first-born, well-winged "eagle" of Savitr. The eagle corresponds to the falcon which is symbolic of the first sun of the horizon, Harakhte, or Horus the Younger, the Egyptian counterpart of Mitra. Savitr himself is in *RV* 5,81,2ff called a "horse" who mingles with the rays of Sūrya, who represents the full-fledged sun-disk, Indra/Aton.

The twin horses of the sun, the Ashvins, are also of special importance in the Vedic sacrifices. RV IV,45, addressed to the Ashvins, makes clear the relation between the energy obtained from Soma and the rays of the sun:

1. Yonder goes up that light: your chariot is yoked that travels round upon the summit of this heaven.
    Within this car are stored three kindred shares of food, and a skin filled with meath is rustling as the fourth.
2. Forth come your viands rich with store of pleasant meath, and cars and horses at the flushing of the dawn,
    Stripping the covering from the surrounded gloom, and spreading through mid-air bright radiance like the Sun.
3. Drink of the meath with lips accustomed to the draught; harness for the meath's sake the chariot that ye love.
    Refresh the way ye go, refresh the paths with meath: hither, O Aśvins, bring the skin that holds the meath.
    …
5. Well knowing solemn rites and rich in meath, the fires sing to the morning Aśvins at the break of day,
    When with pure hands the prudent energetic priest hath with the stones pressed out the Soma rich in meath.
6. The rays advancing nigh, chasing with day the gloom, spread through the firmament bright radiance like the Sun;
    And the Sun harnessing his horses goeth forth: ye through your Godlike nature let his paths be known.

The fourth "skin" bearing mead that is referred to in the first verse is to the bliss that forms the essence of life, while the other three "shares of food"

---

[998] Like the Iranian *Vendidad*, see below p.255.

are more normal forms of physical and intellectual energy. The relation of the Ashvins to the full-fledged solar force, Indra, is evident also in the fact that the Rgvedic hymns to the Ashvins (for instance I,3 and IV,45) are immediately followed by those to Indra.

At the same time, the energy required for the revival of the solar force is provided by the seminal power of Soma. *SB* says that Agni is the same as Ātman, and Soma as Prāna. In a yajna, Agni is said to consume Soma as his food. Soma represents the male energy of a man, bull, or horse. It is clear that the sacrifices originally involved the offering of animals particularly chosen for their virile energy, such as a bull, horse or man. This is related to the vital importance of the phallus of the Purusha in the cosmic evolution and it is the brāhmans' duty to sustain the phallus-like universe and its light through their sacrificial rituals. The horse sacrifice (Ashwamedha yajna) so typical of the Indo-Aryans, for instance, must have originally included the veneration of the penis of the slaughtered stallion as is attested among the Nordic peoples in the *Volsa pattr.*[999] The horse, or its penis, represents the phallic axis of the universe (Tree of Life), at the head of which is the sun. And in the Indo-Āryan Soma rituals, the soma plant, which is itself a phallic Purusha symbol, is pressed with a phallic 'lingam' stone, since Soma represents the divine semen. In the *SB* XII,6,1, Soma is successively identified with thirty four deities beginning with Prajāpati and ending with the Brahman priest.[1000] The deity who is imbued with Soma is Indra.[1001] That is why the sun in its fullest development is identified with Indra.[1002] Indra is naturally the subject of a great number of Vedic hymns.

The Yogic Basis of Yajna

The fire-rituals of the brāhmans may have been an externalisation of the thermal disciplines of yoga since the *Rgveda* (X,154,2) itself mentions [yogic] tapas as that by which "one attains the light of the sun". Heesterman's conjecture that yogic asceticism was an "internalisation" of the Vedic sacrifices is thus somewhat inaccurate in its suggestion of the priority of sacrifice. Yoga recognises the essence of man as energy (Kundalini) and yajna too relates it to thermal energy or the vital fire

---

[999] This story is found in a chapter of *Óláfs saga helga.*

[1000] Cf. J. Gonda, *Soma's metamorphoses, passim.*

[1001] See above p.81.

[1002] See above p.121.

within man. But yajna is external and symbolic worship whereas yoga is internal and practical. As Flood points out, "the two most important elements within Hindu culture, sacrifice and renunciation ... are two sides of the same coin, the difference being that the householder is concerned with external sacrifice, whereas the renouncer has internalized the sacrifice".[1003] The identification of yogic meditation and fire-worship is evident also in the 'Bhagavat Gita', which stresses that yogic "tapas" and "karma" are both sources of sacrifice. Yogis offered their vital force to the cosmic Prāna, which is considered to be a spiritual Havan (offering). Or, as the 'Bhagavad Gita', 4,24, states, "The act of Havan is Brahman, Havi is Brahman. Havan is performed in the fire, which is Brahman. And it is Brahman who performs Havan". The self-control aimed at by yogic tapas is itself the source of a variety of possible sacrifices (*ibid*):

> Others offer up the senses, such as the sense of hearing and others, in the fires of restraint; others offer up the objects of sense, such as sound and so forth, into the fires of the senses. Some again offer up all the operations of the senses and the operations of the life-breaths into the fire of devotion by self-restraint, kindled by knowledge. Others perform the sacrifice of wealth, the sacrifice of penance, the sacrifice of concentration of mind, the sacrifice of Vedic study, and of knowledge, and others are ascetics of rigid vows. Some offer up the upward life-breath into the downward life-breath, and the downward life-breath into the upper life-breath, and stopping up the motions of the upward and downward life-breaths, devote themselves to the restraint of the life-breaths. Others, who (take) limited food, offer up the life-breaths into the life-breaths.

The Smārtasūtras consider the sacrifice of the self as the highest.[1004] According to the *Prāṇāgnihotra Upanishad* (derived from *KYV*), 17ff.,[1005]

> One should meditate on the Atman saying "I offer a sacrifice to Atman through fire" ... In order to set the sacrifice within the motion of the universe, one should make an offering to the interior of one's own body saying "Thus I set the sacrifice into motion".

[1003]   See G. Flood, *Introduction to Hinduism*, p.88.

[1004]   See Vaikhānasa smārtasūtra II,18 (cf. M. Biardeau, *op.cit.*, p.66).

[1005]   I follow here the French translation of M. Buttex based on the versions of A. G. Krishna Warrier and Paul Deussen.

The *Avyaktopanishad* treats dhyāna or spiritual meditation as a yajna and declares that one should offer one's self as an oblation into the fire in order to attain Brahman. As Shriram Sharma puts it,

> The supreme goal of a true yajna is to surrender one's entire being at the hallowed feet of almighty God. It involves offering (āhuti) one's mind, intellect, psyche, ego, 10 sense organs (5 of action and 5 of knowledge), 10 pranas, and ll our internal wealth to God. When we surrender all our internal possessions to God, like the wood fuel is surrendered to the fire, we become God himself just as the wood fuel merges into the fire.[1006]

According to the 'Gita', IV, knowledge (jnāna) itself is a supreme sort of sacrifice since "the fire of knowledge reduces all actions to ashes".

The metaphysical significance of the fire-rituals of the brāhmans is detailed in the Panchagni Vidya of the *Chāndogya Upanishad*, V,4ff, which identifies the five spiritual fires within the macrocosm (heaven, the atmosphere, and earth) and the macrocosm (man and woman). Panchagni rituals are conducted either in Uttarāyan (mid-January) or in Dakshināyan (mid-July). The former induces liberation of the soul. The latter signifies return to this life or rebirth. In the Yama-Nachiketa dialogue of the *Katha Upanishad*, too, five spiritual fires, Panchagni, are mentioned. These include the four fires lit by men and the sun. The *Prānāgnihotra Upanishad* similarly mentions five fires, four of which are within the human body:

19. The fire of the sun in the form of the solar disk whence millions of rays are diffused is found in the head correspondng to the Ekarshi fire.
The fire of vision is found ... in the mouth corresponding to the Ahavaniya fire.
The gastric fire which supports the digestive function is found ... in the heart, corresponding to the Dakshinagni.
Then there is the intestinal fire which cooks that which has been eaten, drunk, licked and masticated and is found towards the navel, corresponding to the Garhapatya fire.
20. Finally, there is the expiatory fire which is found under [the navel] and shares with it the three principal nadis (ida, pingala and sushumna) as its common spouses, and activates the process of

---

[1006] See S. Sharma, *op.cit.*, Ch.4.

procreation by means of the lunar light which circulates through them.

The five fires are indeed used as a stimulus to meditation since a person is required to meditate surrounded by the five fires. The Panchagni fires of the yajna are also used to clean the five internal fires such as passion, anger, greed, attachment and jealousy. Similarly, in yoga, Earth is represented by the Mooladhara chakra of the yogi and Heaven by the Sahasrara chakra[1007] and the Kundalini energy gets elevated to the Sahasrara chakra when it goes through the fire of Agni. This serves as a purification of the energy within.

The Panchagni-vidya includes not only knowledge of the fires within the body but also that of the different intensities within the flames of fire. According to the *Mundaka Upanishad* (I,2,4), Agni contains seven flames, Kālī (black), Karālī (terrific), Manogavā (swift as thought), Sulohitā (crimson), Sudhūmravarnā (purple), Sphulinginī (sparkling), and brilliant Visvarūpī (having all forms), which, like the sun-rays bear the sacrificer to the world of the gods. Agni is thus the link between Heaven and Earth. Within the body itself the ancients identify:

Durgarshatā = bodily strength
Jyoti = aura
Tāpa = body temperature
Pāka = digestive fire
Prakash = wisdom
Shauch = fire that destroys bodily dirt
Rāg = fire that possesses magnetic attraction
Laghu =fire that makes the body light
Taishnya = fire that raises the mental powers
Urdhwagaman = fire that joins the mental powers to the divine powers (demigods)

As Shriram Sharma points out,[1008] these ten qualities and functions of fire are related to the five prānas and five sub-prānas of the body.

The *Garbha Upanishad* mentions three forms of fire within the human body, koshta agni, darshana agni and gnāna agni, relating to digestion, sight, and knowledge. These are located in the stomach, face, and heart respectively and correspond to the three fires, gārhaptniyāgni, āhavaniyāgni and dakshināgni, in the fire-ritual:

[1007] The Manipura chakra is located in the middle – in the stomach. Aum chanting is done from the Manipurachakra.

[1008] *op.cit.*, Ch.9.

And of how many kinds is that agni? It has three bodies, three retas (seeds or progeny), three puras (cities), three dhātus, and three kinds of agni threefold. Of these three, Vaiśvānara is bodiless. And that agni becomes (or is subdivided into) Jñānāgni (wisdom-fire), Darśanāgni (eye-fire), and Koshthāgni (digestive fire). Of these Jñānāgni pertains to the mind; Darśanāgni pertains to the senses; and Koshthāgni pertains to dahara and daily cooks (or digests) equally whatever is eaten, drunk, licked, or sucked through prāna and apāna. Darśanāgni is (in) the eye itself and is the cause of vijñāna and enables one to see all objects of form. It has three seats, the (spiritual) eye itself being the (primary) seat, and the eyeballs being the accessory seats.

This Upanishad also describes the internalisation of the sacrifice within the human body in great detail:

Dakshināgni is in the heart, Gārhapatya is in the belly, and in the face is Āhavanīya. (In this sacrifice with the three agnis), the Purusha is himself the sacrificer; buddhi becomes his wife; santosha (contentment) becomes the dīkshā (vow) taken; the mind and the organs of the senses become the sacrificial vessels; the karmendriyas (organs of action) are the sacrificial instruments. In this sacrifice of the body, the several devas who become the rtvijas (sacrificial priests) perform their parts following the master of the sacrifice, (viz., the true individuality), wherever he goes. In this (sacrifice), the body is the sacrificial place, the skull of the head is the fire-pit, the hairs are the kuśa grass; the mouth is the antarvedi (raised platform in sacrifice); kāma (or passion) is the clarified butter; the period of life is the period of sacrifice; nāda (sound) produced in dahara (heart) is the sāmaveda (recited during the sacrifice); vaikharī is the yajus (or yajurveda hymns); parā, paśyanti, and madhyamā are the rks (or rgveda hymns); cruel words are the atharvas (atharvaveda hymns) and khilas (supplementary texts of each veda); true words are the vyāhrtis. Life, strength, and bile are the paśus (sacrificial creatures) and death is avabhrta (the bath which concludes the sacrifice). In this sacrifice, the (three) fires blaze up and then according to (the desires of) the worldly the devas bless him.[1009]

[1009] The *Prānāgnihotra Upanishad*, 22, gives a similar account of the yajna performed within the microcosm.

Indeed, according to the *Garbha Upanishad*, "There is none living who does not perform yajña (sacrifice). This body is (created) for yajña, and arises out of yajña and changes according to yajña."

The Solar Death, Rebirth and Liberation of the Sacrificer

Although the sacrifice has more mundane purposes such as the acquisition of offspring, cattle, health, wealth, and the brahmanic splendour,[1010] it also bestows "unseen" spiritual merit (punya) on the sacrificer. As Shriram Sharma points out, "The Yajna doer via Ahutis (offerings) gives subtle food to all world creatures and thus acquires punya or sacred merit".[1011] The final aim of the sacrifices, however, is to attain immortality by transfiguring the sacrificer into the solar force. The nectar of immortality that sacrificers seek for by toil and penance is indeed Soma (*SB* IX,5,1,8). The basic meaning of the Soma sacrifice is related to the idea of pressing, or killing the Purusha, as *SB* II,2,2,1 suggests: "in pressing out the king [Soma] they slay him". This may have a special phallic connotation as well since the soma juice is akin to the seminal power of Prajāpati which serves as the source of the sun that emerges as a result of the castration of the Purusha. Thus the sacrifice, though representing the death of the sacrificer, compensates the latter with his spiritual rebirth. This rebirth is essentially that of the solar force Agni that we have noted above.

According to the *Jaiminiya Upanishad Brāhmana* III,14,8, "As long as a man does not sacrifice, for that long he remains unborn. It is through the sacrifice that he is born". Thus the *Maitrāyani Samhita*, III,6,7, declares that man is indeed born three times, at birth, at the sacrifice and at death. Indeed *Manusmrithi* V also points out that even lower forms of life, such as plants, animals, trees, birds, which have been killed as sacrificial victims rise to a higher status when reborn. All sacrifice is, like the original sacrifice of the Purusha, a self-sacrifice followed by a spiritual rebirth wherein the sacrificer acquires the essential aspect of his existence, "uniform, undecaying and immortal" (*SB* X,1,4,1).

This rebirth is enacted during the sacrifice in the four-day purification ceremony called dīksha. *SB* III,1,1,8 reveals the importance of the consecration of the sacrificer in the dīksha ceremony whereby the sacrificer is rendered immortal: "He who is consecrated truly draws nigh to the gods and becomes one of the deities". The significance of sacrifice as a rebirth is evident in many of the texts related to it. *Taittirīya*

[1010]   See, for instance, *SB* II,3,3,15f; X,1,5,4, etc.

[1011]   S. Sharma, *op.cit.*, Ch.4.

Brāhmana declares that the fire taken from the hearth of the yajamāna and maintained for a year represents a year-long pregnancy of the new [solar] selves of the yajamāna and his wife. *AB*, I,3, declares that "the priests transform the one to whom they give the diksha into an embryo." The yajamāna and his wife should be dressed in clothes which correspond to the shell of an egg since they are going to be reborn.[1012] Though the sacrificer's wife participates in this ritual, it is principally the sacrificer himself who will be reborn as the sun. *AB* I,1,3, details the process whereby the sacrificer is turned into the embryonic form of Agni in the course of this ceremony:

> Agni whom they consecrate the priests make into an embryo again. With waters they sprinkle; the waters are seed; verily having made him possessed of seed they consecrate him. With fresh butter they anoint; to the gods appertains melted butter, to men fragrant ghee, slightly melted butter to the fathers, fresh butter to embryos. In that way they anoint with fresh butter … They anoint him completely; ointment is the brilliance in the eyes; verily thus having made him possessed of brilliance they consecrate him. With twenty one handfuls of darbha they purify him; verily thus purified and pure they consecrate him. They conduct him to the hut of the consecrated; the hut of the consecrated is the womb of the consecrated; verily thus they conduct him to his own womb; therefore (in and) from a firm womb he stands and moves; therefore (in and) from a firm womb embryos are placed and grow forth. Therefore the sun should not rise or set on the consecrated elsewhere than in the hut of the consecrated, nor should they call out to him. With a garment they cover him; the garment is the caul of the consecrated … Above that is the black antelope skin; the placenta is above the caul; verily thus they cover him with the placenta.[1013] He closes his hands; verily closing its hands the embryo lies within; with closed hands the child is born. In that he closes his hands, verily thus he clasps in his hands the sacrifice and all the deities …

Then the sacrificer is born anew:

[1012] See K.-H. Golzio, *Der Tempel*, p.113.

[1013] Cf. *SB* V,3,5,20ff, which refers to the three garments representing the two cauls, inner and outer, and the womb, of sovereignty.

Having loosened the black antelope skin, he descends to the final bath; therefore embryos are born freed from the placenta; with the garment he descends; therefore a child is born with a caul.[1014]

Interestingly, when the purificatory rite is completed, the dikshita is addressed as Brahman, even if he is not a brāhman. So too, in the climactic abhishekam of the rājasūya sacrifice, the king is addressed as "Brahman" by the four priests, which suggests that the sacrifice indeed imbues the sacrificer with the divine consciousness of Brahman.

The rebirth is consequently a means of acquiring an immortal life. It essentially entails the establishment of Agni within the inner self of the sacrificer. In the SB it is stated that in the beginning neither the gods nor their opponents, the asurās, were immortal since they lacked soul, ātman. Only Agni, the fire, was immortal. As Heesterman paraphrases it,

Fervently chanting and exerting themselves the gods finally beheld the rite of setting up the fire ... They then gained immortality by establishing the fire within themselves, and thereby obtained an ātman, the seat of immortality, as well. And so they overcame the asurās.[1015]

Further, according to the SB, "Once the fire has been ritually established in the inner self through the agnyādheya, it is the sacrificer's inalienable true identity, in short, his ātman." The internalisation of Agni within, and as, the individual soul, ātman, is made clear also by TS III,4,10,5 where, as Heesterman points out, we observe that "when the sacrificer symbolically has the fire mount the aranis by warming them over the glowing members of the dying fire, he makes it enter into himself ... When churning the fire to reinstall it, he churns it out of himself, exteriorizing, as it were, his own self, for he is himself the yoni, the womb of the fire... For the fire is one's atman".[1016] And SB II,2,2,17 declares that "as long as he lives the fire which is established in his inner self does not become extinct in him".

SB III,6,2,16 further reveals that "even in being born, man, by his own self, is born as a debt (owing) to death. And in that he sacrifices, thereby

---

[1014] As Hocart has shown, the rebirth of the king during the consecration in the Spanish royal rites is similar to that of the Brāhmanical sacrificial ritual since he is first decked in three robes (representing the embryonic cauls, as the Indian literature explains) and then divested of them before being attired in pure white vestments designed with special openings to admit of the anointing (see A.M. Hocart, *Kingship*, p.96).

[1015] See J.C. Heesterman, *Broken World*, p.215.

[1016] See J.C. Heesterman, *op.cit.*, p.101.

he redeems himself from death." The sacrificer thus has two bodies, one material and the other ritual/spiritual. Through the sacrifice he mounts to heaven to get a divine body and, on earth, he gives his material body to the gods. Thus his material body is sacrificed after purifications such as shaving the hair, cutting the nails, etc. (*TS* VI,1,1,2), although the sacrifice of his material body is, as we shall see, performed with a substitute victim. Though this victim was originally a man, it was later substituted with a horse or a bull, while, at the time of the composition of the *SB*, the most common substitute was the goat (*SB* VI,2,1,39).

The importance of Agni as an instrument of the rebirth of man in the heavenly realm is made clear in the *SB*, which declares that Agni entered into a compact with man saying: "I shall enter you; having given birth to me, you must maintain me. As you will give birth to me and maintain me, so I shall give birth to you in yonder world". Within the macrocosm, Agni serves to transfer the human soul to Heaven, as *SB* VIII,7,4,6 states: "The sacrifice in its entirety is a safe ship that leads to heaven". It allows the sacrificer to reach Brahmaloka through the northern path and not to be reborn. Indeed, according to *SB* XII,1,3,18,ff., in the last stages of the sacrifice,

> when the sacrificers worship the regions (dishāh) with a sacrifice, they become these deities, the regions. That means that they master the whole of the universe in respect to space. When they enter upon the chandomas, they worship these deities, the worlds, they become these worlds, that is the universe. When they enter upon the tenth day, they worship that deity, the Year, they become they Year. That means that they master the whole of the universe in respect to time. When they enter upon the mahavrata (day) they worship the deity Prajāpati; they become the deity Prajāpati ... That means that those who now experience intimate union with this god and "residence" in his sphere have reached this ultimate goal .. they establish themselves firmly in the world of heaven.[1017]

[1017] See J. Gonda, *Prajapati's Rise*, p.113f.

IX.

YAJNA II

The Original Sacrifices

The original sacrifice conducted by the ancient Āryans was perhaps a human sacrifice, Purushamedha, since it imitates the sacrifice of the Purusha whence all the other sacrifices arose. It is clearly related to the Purusha Sūkta of the *RV* X,90, where the head of the Purusha forms Heaven, his navel the Mid-region and feet Earth. Actual human sacrifice is indeed attested in a late Vedic text *Vadhula Anvakhyana*, 4.108.[1018] Although the ritual is now extinct, it is recorded as being a five-day sacrifice, of which the first day is an Agnishtoma, followed by an Ukthya, then an Atirâtra, then an Ukthya, and finally an Agnishtoma. The Purushamedha, which retains much of the liturgy of the Ashvamedha, with some additions, is said in the *Sānkhāyana Grhyasūtra* 16,10,1, to obtain all that the Ashvamedha does not. So it is likely that it is the original of the Ashvamedha.[1019] Indeed, *SB* VI,2,1,18 declares that man is the best victim, followed by the horse, bull, ram, and he-goat. The victim is specified as being either a brāhman or kshatriya (*Sānkhāyana Grhyasūtra* 16,10,9). In the *Vaitāna Sūtra* however, an enemy is allowed to replace them. There may, at some time in its later development, also have been many victims involved in this sacrifice (*SB* XIII,6,2,3ff) and these may have been symbolically chosen, as *SB* XIII,6,2,10 states: "for the priesthood a Brāhman is seized, for the nobility a Rājanya (kshatriya) is seized, for the Maruts a Vaisya, and for (religious) toil a Sūdra", though they are all, in the *SB*, said to have been set free soon after their selection.

[1018] See W. Caland, "Eine vierte Mitteilung", p.229.

[1019] *Ibid.*, p.173.

Although human sacrifice becomes symbolical by the time of the composition of the *SB*, which declares that a substitute is to be offered for the male sacrificial victim, the victim bound to the yupa and the sacrificer standing outside the ritual arena are identified with each other since the yupa is of the same height as the sacrificer and symbolises the sacrificer himself.[1020] The description of the Purushamedha in the *SB* XIII,6,1-2 also, as Tull points out, "homologizes the sacrificer's body with the material cosmos".[1021]

In the *Atharva Veda* (X,7) the phallic column referred to as skambha may be the same as the stambha, or sacrificial post. In *AV* X,7,41 and XVII,11,2 the skambha is called the "golden reed standing in the waves".[1022] At *RV* IV,58,5, the reed is said to be in the midst of the streams of ghee, and ghee is taken to represent the divine seminal power.[1023] The skambha therefore represents the emergent universe as a Tree of Life. That the Vedic human sacrifices involved phallic worship is clear from the numerous references to the Tree of Life and the *axis mundi* as synonyms of the Purusha and of Agni, as Snodgrass reveals:

> In the Vedic texts the symbolism of the "heaven-supporting pillar in the east" finds its classical expression in the person of Agni, the god of the sacrificial fire. He is the Pillar [RV IV,5,1) who separates the two worlds by propping them ... He is the World Tree with a thousand branches [RV VI,13,1;VIII,19,33; IX,5,10] who causes the sun to rise into the heavens [RV V,6,4;IV,3,11].[1024]

Human sacrifice is archaeologically evidenced in the early Bronze Age (fourth millennium B.C.) Luhansk site in the Ukraine which forms part of the Yamnaya culture associated with the Āryans.[1025] It is attested among the ancient Germanic peoples too. In the 'Vafprúðnismál' it is stated that "From Ymir's flesh the earth was made, and the mountains from his bones ..." In the 'Grímnísmal', Ymir's flesh forms Earth, his skull Heaven and his brows Midgard or the mid-region of the stars. As Lincoln has pointed out, similar passages may be found in Indic, Greek, Germanic, Celtic, Baltic

---

[1020] See H.W. Tull, *The Vedic origins*, p.46.

[1021] See H.W. Tull, *op.cit.*, p.55.

[1022] See J. Gonda, *Prajapati's rise,* p.95.

[1023] See below p.247.

[1024] See A. Snodgrass, *Symbolism*, p.170.

[1025] See above p.189.

and Slavic texts.[1026] It is interesting to note that Purusha is called Ymir among the Germans[1027] since Ymir is related to the Avestan Yima and the Sanskrit Yama, the last being symbolical of Death in Vedic literature, for this confirms self-sacrifice as the chief characteristic of the ideal cosmic Man. Human sacrifice is indeed discernible also among the Celts (in Caesar's writings), as well as among the Scythians, and Thracians.[1028]

Lincoln suggests that the sacrifice "as a ritual effectively repeats the cosmogony, shifting matter from a victim's body to the alloformic parts of the universe in order to sustain the latter against decay and ultimate collapse".[1029] This is based on the original Vedic understanding of the creation of the Purusha detailed in the *Aitareya Upanishad* I,4, where the Divine Self first creates the substance of heaven, the mid-region of the stars, and earth, and, only then, the Purusha, who is originally an amorphous mass. The Self, through yogic tapas, forms this mass into the cosmic man whose bodily parts are then disintegrated to yield the essential sense and intellectual facilities of man. Thus from the mouth of the Purusha emerges disembodied speech and from speech fire. From his nostrils emerges breath and from breath wind. From his eyes emerges vision and from the latter the sun. From his ears hearing and from hearing the quarters of the universe. From his skin emerges hair and from hair the plants and trees; from his heart the mind and from the mind the moon. From his navel the downward wind and from the latter death. From his penis emerges semen and from semen water. Then these energies such as fire, wind, the sun, etc. demand a receptacle for themselves to dwell in and so the Self brings the Purusha to them and fire, as speech, enters the mouth of the Purusha, and the remaining elements similarly. Thus, wind, as breath, enters his nostrils; the sun, as vision, his eyes; the four quarters, as hearing, the ears; the plants and trees, as hair, his skin; the moon, as the mind, his heart; death, as the downward wind, his navel; and water, as semen, his penis.

Death itself, as Lincoln points out, was regarded as a cosmogonic action, "a final sacrifice in which the material substance of the body was transformed into its macrocosmic alloforms, while birth was the

---

[1026] See B. Lincoln, *Death, War and Sacrifice*, p.168.

[1027] The Germans use the name of the survivor of the Flood, the seventh Manu, Vaivasvata, for the First Man, Purusha.

[1028] K. Rönnow, ("Zur Erklärung des Pravargya") has pointed to the signficant evidence of human sacrifice among the Germans, Celts, Scythians and Thracians and suggested that it must have been practised even by the Greeks and Indians, in spite of the dearth of such evidence among them (see B. Lincoln, *Myth, Cosmos and Society*, p.172).

[1029] *Ibid.*, p.170.

anthropogonic reversal of death in which cosmic matter was reassembled in bodily form".[1030] In the course of a sacrifice, the sacrificer's ritual death allows him to be reintegrated into the cosmic Purusha. As Tull has suggested, "just as the body of the primordial being was transformed into the cosmos, so too the individual becomes one together with the cosmos through his own ritual activity".[1031] In the course of an animal sacrifice, the parts of the animal are returned to the universe whence they emerged. Thus *AB* II,6, describes the dismemberment of an animal victim in the following manner:[1032] "Lay its feet down to the north. Cause its eye to go to the sun; send forth its breath to the wind; its life-force to the atmosphere; its ear to the cardinal points, its flesh to the earth". Similarly *SB* X,3,3,8 declares that, at death, a man "goes forth from this world. He enters the fire with this voice, the sun with his eye, the moon with his mind, the cardinal directions with his ear, the wind with his breath". Again, in the Iranian *Zad Spram*, 34,8-19, Ohrmazd says that the corporeal substance of the dead is received by five "collectors" – the earth, which absorbs the flesh and bone and sinews of men; water, which absorbs the blood; the plants, which absorb the hair; light, which absorbs fire; and wind, which absorbs the life-breath.[1033] It is clear from these sacrifices that human sacrifice (Purushamedha) and, later the horse-sacrifice (Ashvamedha) were considered as repetitions of the creation of the cosmos. However, as the consecration of the king, Rājasūya, as well as many of the lesser sacrifices that this was modified into, shows, the sacrifices were necessary for the creation of the solar light, and cosmic consciousness, of Brahman as well.[1034]

That the Indian brāhmanical rituals originally included human sacrifice is made clear also from the fact that the *SB*'s description of the Agnicayana rituals insists on real heads of five victims including a human, because, as it says, "only if the heads of living animals are united with their bodies (represented by the five layers of the fire-altar[1035] under which they were to be buried) do they become alive again". Karka, the commentator, also declares that "the bodies make the bricks firm",[1036] showing that the real reason for foundation sacrifices was to animate the bricks of the

---

[1030]   See B. Lincoln, *Death, War and Sacrifice*, p.172.

[1031]   See H.W. Tull, *Vedic Origins*, p.45.

[1032]   See B. Lincoln, *Myth, Cosmos and Society*, pp.50ff.

[1033]   *Ibid.*, p.122.

[1034]   See below pp.234ff.

[1035]   On the symbolism of the five layers of the fire-altar, see below p.228.

[1036]   See A. Parpola, "Human sacrifice", p.169.

building they were used for. As H.T. Bakker points out, "According to the Shrautasūtras of the *Black Yajur Veda*, the human head should be cut off of a kshatriya or a vaisya killed by an arrow or a lightning, after which it is to be covered with clay and set aside."[1037] However, the *Kātyāyana Shrautasūtra* (XVI,1,17) states that the victim, a vaisya or a rājanya, should be suffocated in a special secluded place, after which his head is to be taken, though it allows the option that a head of gold or clay may be used as a substitute.[1038] The bodies of the four animal victims are, further, thrown into the water from which the clay is taken to make the bricks,[1039] showing once again the intimate connection between the victims' heads and the strength of the bricks.

Human sacrifices are associated with the construction of buildings, perhaps religious ones in particular, in other Indo-European lands as well, since archaeologists have discovered sacrificial victims in building foundations in Rome as well as in Celtic regions. These foundation sacrifices are clearly related to the use of the heads of four animals and a man in the construction of the Vedic fire-altar (*SB* VII,5,2).[1040]

It is clear also that, according to the Vedic rules of sacrifice, the victims were chosen from special social categories. This specific choice of victims is related to the vital importance of caste distinctions in Vedic thought. The Purusha whose body is dismembered is not only an anthropomorphism of the supreme Soul but equally a crucial manifestation of the various social orders of humanity according to the predominance in the latter of the elements of sattva, rajas or tamas.[1041] Thus the head of the Purusha represents the hieratical intellectual caste of the brāhmans, his arms the warrior kshatriyas, his thighs the vaisyas and his feet the servile shudras.

However, later Brāhmanism considered human sacrifice as unclean since "the Vedic lists of 'unclean' animal victims (that are to be released)" correspond to "the Purānic lists of victims pleasing to the goddess [Durga]" and in both cases a human victim heads the list.[1042] Parpola

---

[1037] H.T. Bakker, "Human sacrifice", p.184.

[1038] *Ibid.* J.C. Heesterman (*Broken World*, p.207) suggests that the original form of human sacrifice may have been decapitation, rather than suffocation.

[1039] See H.T. Bakker, *op.cit.*, p.184.

[1040] *SB* VII,5,2,1: "The fire-pan being a womb, and the heads of the victims being animals, he thus establishes the animals in the womb". Later (*SB* VII,5,2,17), the head of the man (actually a mock-man) is placed on the milk with the verse: "'With milk anoint thou Âditya, the unborn child!' that unborn child, the man, is indeed the sun".

[1041] See above p.198.

[1042] See A. Parpola, *ibid.*, p.176.

conjectures that the human sacrifices were part of the religious tradition of the people called Dāsas whom he identifies with distant ancestors of the later Scythians or Sakas, who introduced headhunting and the skull cult to Afghanistan (Nuristan): "As the acculturated rulers of the BMAC culture, the Dāsas then took these gruesome cults to the Indus and the Ganges Valleys by the end of the third millennium B.C."[1043] These Dāsas then must be the same as the fire-worshipping 'Devas' of Margiana.[1044] Parpola continues to speculate that the Shakta tradition of India is "a direct continuation of the cultic practices involving human sacrifice that prevailed in South Asia before the coming of the Rgvedic Aryans." But this theory of an earlier wave of Āryans and later "Rigvedic" Āryans is hard to support since it would make the Vedas a type of secular literature that may undergo modifications under foreign influences such as that of the Dāsas.

In any case, the unquestionable significance of human sacrifice among the ancient Indo-Europeans is confirmed in its reappearance in the solar rituals of the Hamitic Egyptians. Procopius (6th c. A.D.), for instance, observes that certain Egyptian tribes called the Blemmyes were in the habit of sacrificing people to the sun before Justinian ended the temple cults of Philae.[1045] Like these late Hamitic examples of the solar focus of sacrifices, the Vedic rituals too reveal, in mimetic and poetic flashes, the spiritual signficance of Brahman and the sun as the primary effects of the cosmic sacrifice of the Purusha.

The horse-sacrifice or Ashvamedha is, much like the Purushamedha, a recreation of the sacrifice of Prajāpati. In fact, it may have been a substitute for the Purushamedha, and this is not surprising when we remember the veneration of the horse among the ancient Āryans. The Ashwamedha yajna came to be considered the most glorious of the sacrifices and was celebrated by a victorious king. It is a three-day Soma sacrifice[1046] and the preparatory ceremonies for it last one year. Its various rituals include an Agnicayana (building of the brick fire-altar), Pravargya, Sautrāmani, and, according to Baudrāyana, also the Chaturmāsyas.

On the first day the king and the four priests are present along with the king's four wives. In the evening, after the agnihotra, the king sleeps with his favorite wife, observing chastity so as not to lose his virile power.

[1043] *Ibid.*

[1044] See above p.187.

[1045] See H. Te Velde, "Human sacrifice", p.129.

[1046] The Ashvamedha is described in *SB* XIII,1-5. Cf also *KYV* Kanda V-VI. For a discussion of the sacrifice see J. Gonda, *Religionen*, pp.168ff.

On the second day the horse is brought in, a stallion that has drunk soma and is itself the offspring of two horses that have drunk soma. A dog, representing Indra's opponent Vrtra, is killed by a low-caste man. Then the horse is let loose, with hundred other castrated horses, to wander in the direction of the north-east, the direction of victory as well as the route to heaven (AB I,14) under the supervision of 400 young men, of whom hundred are princes. The latter should protect the horse's wandering and those princes who return with their mission successfully accomplished will in turn receive royal consecration. At the end of the eleventh month the horse is placed in an enclosure. At the same time there begins the building of the fire-altar with twelve days of dīksha, or initiation for the sacrificer. During twelve further upasad days the first gārhapatya fire is built, and then the mahāvedi. At this point the soma is purchased and installed on the throne as King Soma.

This is followed by three days of Soma sacrifices. On the first day an Agnishtoma is performed, on the second day a gilded chariot is brought in and the horse is attached to it along with three others. The sacrificing king mounts the chariot and goes to a pond. When he returns, the three principal wives of the king anoint the horse. The horse is then sacrificed. Around the horse are attached seventeen other victims, seventeen being the number sacred to Prajāpati, whom the horse represents. The horse is strangled and the first wife of the king sleeps with the dead horse briefly. Then follows a brahmodhya, or enigmatic theological dialogue between the priests.[1047] The "brahmodhya" between the priests in SB XIII,5,2 is particularly revealing:

12. The Hotri asks the Adhvaryu, 'Who is it that walketh singly?...' He replies to him, 'Sûrya (the sun) walketh singly...'
13. The Adhvaryu then asks the Hotri, 'Whose light is there equal to the sun?...' He replies to him, 'The Brahman is the light equal to the sun...'
14. The Brahman then asks the Udgâtri, 'I ask thee for the sake of knowledge, O friend of the gods [if thou hast applied thy mind thereto: hath Vishnu entered the whole world at those three places at which offering is made unto him?]' and he replies, 'I too am at those three places [at which he entered the whole world: daily do I, with the one body, go round the earth, the sky, and the back of yonder sky].'
    ...
20. The Udgâtri then asks the Brahman, 'Who knoweth the navel of

1047   On the significance of the brahmodhya see J. Gonda, Notes on Brahman, pp.57-61.

this world? [who heaven and earth and the air? who knoweth the birth-place of the great Sun? who knoweth the Moon, whence it was born?]' and he replies, 'I know the navel of this world, [I know heaven and earth and the air; I know the birth-place of the great Sun, and I know the Moon, whence it was born]'

21. The Sacrificer then asks the Adhvaryu, 'I ask thee about the farthest end of the earth, [I ask where is the navel of the world; I ask thee about the seed of the vigorous steed; I ask thee about the highest seat of speech];' and he replies, 'This altar-ground is the farthest end of the earth;[1048] [this sacrifice is the navel of the world; this Soma-juice is the seed of the vigorous].

We note, in the responses of the Udgātr and the Brahman priest in this catechism, the association of the former with the sun and the latter with Brahman.

The horse is dismembered and its entrails are offered into the fire and the flesh of the horse and of other sundry animal victims is cooked. The blood of the horse is offered as oblation. On the third day is performed an Atirātra comprising 24 musical stotras and 29 shāstras or solemn recitations. On the next day the king undergoes an avabhrtha or ritual bath. Then the four wives, or their attendants, are symbolically offered to the priests. The ceremonies conclude with a Sautrāmani, an oblation of fermented liquor, surā, as well as animals, to the Ashvins, Sarasvati and Indra to strengthen the sacrificer just as Indra had to be revived by surā when he performed the ashvamedha (*JB*, II,266).

The stallion represents the solar power of Indra and that is why the wife of the king undergoes a mock coupling with it (*SB* XIII,2,8). The horse encompasses the entire universe created by Prajāpati for, in dying, it reaches the three worlds of Agni, Vāyu and Āditya (*SB* XIII,2,7,13-15). It also leads the sacrificer to the heavenly world (*SB* XIII, 2,3,1). Yoked to the chariot, the horse particularly represents the sun: "the ruddy bay, doubtless, is yonder sun" (*SB* XIII,2,6), and the "eye" of Prajāpati, as *SB* XIII,3,1,1 declares:

Prajâpati's eye swelled; it fell out: thence the horse was produced; and inasmuch as it swelled (asvayat), that is the origin and nature of the horse (asva). By means of the Asvamedha the gods restored it to its place; and verily he who performs the Asvamedha makes Prajâpati complete, and he (himself) becomes complete; and this, indeed, is the atonement for everything, the remedy for everything.

[1048]   Cf. *Mahābhārata* III,114, 117-22, where the sacrificial altar is compared to the earth.

The horse's year-long course represents the solar year. The horse is offered to Varuna just as Prajāpati is, in *TS* II,3,12, said to offer a horse to Varuna to be freed of Varuna's fetter. Since this fetter, as we have seen, signifies the embryonic cover of incarnation,[1049] the horse sacrifice may be a means of passing beyond incarnation to immortality.

The Indian horse sacrifice is similar to the Roman Equus October ceremony[1050] and horse sacrifices are attested among the Iranians and Greeks as well. According to Xenophon (*Cyr* VIII,3) Persians offered the horse to the sun, and so too did the Armenians (*Anab*, IV,5), while Herodotus (I,216) reports the same of the Massagetes.[1051] Horse burials are found from Central Europe to England in the Middle Ages. Herodotus mentions the Scythian horse burials for kings. These are confirmed by the royal tombs of the Iron Age steppes – from the Ukraine to the Altai mountains. Horse burials are observed also in the Yamnaya and Catacomb cultures as well as in some sites of the Globular Amphora (ca. 3400-2800 BC), Corded Ware or Battle Axe culture (ca. 3200 BC/2900 BC to ca. 2300 BC/1800 BC) and Bell Beaker cultures (ca. 2800-1900 BC).

Indeed, the oldest appearance of horse bones and carved images of horses is around 4800-4400 BC in the Chalcolithic graves of the early Khvalynsk culture and the Samara culture in the middle Volga region of Russia. At S'yezzhe, a contemporary cemetery of the Samara culture, parts of two horses were placed above a group of human graves. The pair of horses here was represented by the head and hooves, probably originally attached to hides.[1052] Horse images carved from bone were placed in the above-ground ochre deposit at S'yezzhe and occurred at several other sites of the same period in the middle and lower Volga region. Together these archaeological clues suggest that horses had a symbolic importance in the Khvalynsk and Samara cultures that they had lacked earlier.

One of the most important of the rituals comprising the Ashvamedha is the Agnicayana, which recreates the birth of the universe in the form of Prajāpati as well as the birth of Agni as Agni-Vāyu-Āditya.[1053] The

---

[1049] Cf. p.234 below.

[1050] See J.P. Mallory and D.Q. Adams, *Encyclopedia of Indo-European Culture,* p.330. According to Festus (*De verb. sign.* 13), horses were offered by the Romans to the god of war (see P. Dumont, *L'Asvamedha*).

[1051] It is interesting also to note the evidence of the personal name Epomeduos among the Gauls (see J.P. Mallory and D.Q. Adams, *op.cit.*, p.278) since it is etymologically related to the Sanskritic "ashvamedha".

[1052] The same ritual—using the hide with the head and lower leg bones as a symbol for the whole animal—was used for many domesticated cattle and sheep sacrifices at Khvalynsk.

[1053] The Agnicayana rituals are described in *SB*, Books VI-X (cf. also *KYV* V-VI). They are

first rites of this ceremony are dedicated to the creation of Agni as the elemental solar fire of Agni. This is done through an initial sacrifice of five forms of animal life, starting with the human. These five victims also symbolise the five layers of the altar that is to be built in the course of this ceremony (SB VI,2,1,16). After the initial animal sacrifices, the fire-pan (ukha) is fashioned, which is considered to be the "ātman" of the fire-altar. It is four-sided to represent the four quarters of the universe. The first major step in this ceremony (SB VI,2,2,27) is the symbolic pouring of his seed by the sacrificer into the fire-pan representing a womb. As SB VI,2,2,22 declares "there is seed here in the sacrifice". SB X,4,1,1-2 explains that the pouring of the seed of the sacrificer into the fire-pan as into a womb is the same as the pouring of the seed of Prajāpati. SB X,1,1,4 further emphasises the importance of seed as the very aim of the Rk, Sāman and Yajus verses .

The "reed" that fastens the layers of the fire-altar is also said to be the natural womb of Agni (SB VI,3,1,26) and we may remember the significance of "reed" in the cosmological creation discussed above.[1054] A horse, an ass and a he-goat are brought forth, the first representing the kshatriya, the second the vaisyas and shudras, and the last the brāhman. The horse represents the tear which was formed at the creation, the ass the cry that accompanies it, the he-goat the juice that adheres to the shell of the Cosmic Egg, and the clay that is fetched alongside the shell itself (VI,3,1,28).

Agni is then looked for in the clay (SB VI,3,3) and dug up (SB VI,4,17) and then deposited on an antelope-skin representing earth (also called the "sacrifice") and a lotus-leaf representing the sky ("the womb"), for the first birth of Agni is indeed from the sky.[1055] Agni is poured as seed into the lotus-leaf (SB VI,4,3,6).

Then Agni is created for a second time from the earth, represented now by the fire-pan (SB VI,5,1,11-12), which is the "earthen womb for Agni" (SB VI,5,2,21). Milk is poured into it and Agni is generated as Vishnu (SB VI,6,6,2,16).

The sacrificer then fashions the "seed" of Agni in the form of a winged bird (SB VI,7,2,5). Next he takes the Vishnu strides which formed the universe (SB VI,7,2,10). The ashes of the fire in the fire-pan are then thrown into water (SB VI,8,2,2), since the last birth of Agni is from the waters.

Then follows the construction of the three hearths, the circular gārhapatya, representing earth and the world of men (SB VII,I,1) and

---

also detailed in the Shulba Sutras.

[1054] See above p.136.

[1055] See above p.40.

the square āhavanīya representing heaven and the world of the gods
(*SB* VII,2,2). The air of the Mid-region is represented by the āgnīdhrīya
fire (*SB* VII,1,2,12). During the building of the gārhapatya hearth, the
fire-pan is again impregnated with sand to conceive Agni a second time
(SB VII,1,1,41-42). In addition, a Nirriti hearth is built representing the
corruption and evil that have to be removed from the sacrifice (*SB* VII,2,1).
This is followed by the construction of the vedi, also representing earth,
and the mahāvedi, representing heaven (*SB* VII,3,1,27). The catvala (pit/
womb) represents the original site of the sun before it moved to the
heavens (*JB* I, 86,7).[1056] The area on which the fire-altar is to be constructed
is scattered with sand representing seed in order to fill Prajāpati with seed
(*SB* VII,3,1,42).

The construction of the fire-altar is begun a year after the ukha
is prepared (suggesting a year's gestation period). The process of
constructing the five layers of the fire-altar is described in *SB* VII,4,1-
VIII,5,1. A lotus leaf representing Earth is placed in the centre of the
altar site and on it a gold plate that the sacrificer has been wearing for
a year. On top of this plate, which represents the orb of the sun, a gold
man reresenting the Purusha within the sun (*SB* X,5,2,6) is placed facing
the east. The sacrificer sings over the gold man to transfer his virility
or semen into it (*SB* VII,4,1,24). *SB* X,4,1,6 equates the gold plate with
Indra symbolising kshatra (sovereignty) and the gold man with Agni
symbolising brahman (priesthood). The gold plate also represents Indra,
the kshatriya and the gold man Agni, the brāhman (*SB* X,4,1,5-6). The
identification of the yajamāna with the gold man stresses the identification
of the sacrificer with Agni as the Purusha.

Then the Purusha sāman is sung and the laying of the bricks is begun,
the first being the svayamātrrina ('the naturally pierced') placed on the
gold man to allow him to breathe. Within the first layer of the altar are
buried the fire-pan (representng a womb), a living tortoise and a mortar
and pestle (representing a penis in a womb). [1057] The tortoise, an avatār
of Vishnu, represents the form of the universe, comprising heaven
and earth.[1058] Thus the fire-pan and the lotus leaf are considered to be
"female"[1059] and the "womb" which the sacrificer impregnates in order to
generate Agni, the solar force, as Āditya.

[1056]   See H.W. Bodewitz, *The Jyotistoma Ritual*, p.146.

[1057]   *Ibid.*

[1058]   See M. Biardeau, *op.cit.*, p.18.

[1059]   See H.W. Tull, *op.cit.*, p.87f.

Next, after a square mortal (ulūkhulaka) made of udumbara wood is installed at the 'northern shoulder' of the fire-altar, the fire-pit (ukhā) is placed in the middle. The fire-pan that was used by the sacrificer for carrying around the fire for a year is buried in the first layer, and the heads of the five sacrificial victims are placed in it, the human head in the middle of the fire-pit, the head of a horse towards the west, of a bull towards the east, of a ram towards the south, and of a goat towards the north, while seven pieces of gold are laid in the seven orifices of the human head.[1060] The bricks of the altar are animated by vital breaths represented by certain bricks called "breath-holders" (prāna-bhrt).

The altar indeed represents the cosmic body of Agni as Purusha, and the brick-layers represent the various breaths of the Purusha. Thus *SB* I,3,2,1 declares:

> Now the sacrifice is the [Purusha]. The sacrifice is the [Purusha] for the reason that the [Purusha] spreads [1061] it; and that in being spread it is made of exactly the same extent as the [Purusha]: this is the reason why the sacrifice is the [Purusha].

Macrocosmically, Purusha's feet represent earth, legs intermediate space, waist the mid-region, chest intermediate space and head heaven.[1062] However, although vertically the altar represents the Purusha, horizontally, it represents the solar force in the form of a sun-bird with outstretched wings facing the east.[1063] According to the *Panchavimsha Brāhmana*, V,72,3,

> Its head is the eastern region, this is thousandfold through the metres; the one of its wings is yonder (world: the sky), this is thousandfold through the stars; its other wing is this (world: the earth), this is thousandfold through the plants and trees; its trunk is the intermediate region (the air), this is thousandfold through the birds; its tail is the western region, this is thousandfold through the fires and the rays (of the sun).

[1060]   See H.T. Bakker, "Human sacrifice", p.183.

[1061]   The term "spreads" used synonymously with "sacrifices" in the Vedic literature seems to be related to the erection of the phallus, which is iconically always represented in erect form and, in the construction of the fire-altar, as a sun-bird (cf. also p.85 above).

[1062]   H.J. Tull, *op. cit.*, p.93.

[1063]   Cf. the citation from the *Brahma Upanishad* (p.168 above) identifying the sun as a bird.

The fire-altar in the form of a sun-bird may fly to the heavens[1064] represents the phallic force of the Purusha that generates the sun.

The lowest level of the altar in which the image is embedded represents the Svarloka (Heaven), the third level the Bhuvarloka (the Mid-region of the stars), the fourth level Brahman and the immortal regions, and the fifth the Bhurloka (Earth). The first layer also represents the Soma sacrifice, the second the Rājasūya, the third the Vājapeya, the fourth the Ashvamedha, and the fifth the Agnisava (SB X,1,5,3).

After the completion of the five layers, the altar is sprinkled with gold-chips to confer a golden form to the body of the Purusha (SB X,1,4,9) as well immortality on Agni (SB VIII,7,4,7). Layers of soil are then scattered in between the brick-layers to represent the Purusha's marrow, bones, sinews, flesh, fat, blood and skin (SB X,1,4). A further significance of the seven layers filled with soil is offered in SB VIII,7,4,19-21, whereby the first layer of soil represents the legs and the downward flowing air, the second layer represents the parts of the body above the legs and below the waist, while the third layer represents the waist itself. The fourth layer is that part of the body that is above the waist and below the neck, the fifth layer is the neck, the sixth the head and the seventh the vital airs, which are also "the highest of all this universe" (SB VIII,7,4,21).

At SB VIII,7,4,12-18, the filling of the first layer is said to denote this world and represents the endowment of the earth with cattle, the filling of the second layer, denoting air, represents the filling of the air with birds, the filling of the third layer, denoting the sky, represents the filling of the sky with stars, the filling of the fourth layer, denoting sacrifice, represents the filling of the sacrifice with sacrificial gifts, the filling of the fifth layer, denoting the sacrificer, represents the filling of the sacrificer with progeny, the filling of the sixth layer, denoting the heavenly world, represents the filling of the heavenly world with gods, while the seventh layer denotes immortality, which is "the highest thing of all this universe" (SB VIII,7,4,18).

Then a hymn to propitiate the fierce form of Agni, Rudra is chanted (SB IX). This is followed by the chanting of sāman hymns representing the immortal vital airs (SB IX,1,2,32). The chanting of these hymns is said to make the priests who chant as well as the sacrificer "boneless and immortal" (SB IX,I,2,34). This is followed by the chanting of the Gāyatri hymn which makes the head immortal (SB IX,1,2,35). The right wing of the sun-bird which represents earth is made immortal by the chanting of the rathanthara hymn (SB IX,I,2,36), the left wing representing the

---

[1064] See A. Michaels, *Hinduism Past and Present*, p.249.

sky is made immortal by the chanting of the Brhat hymn (*SB* IX,1,2,37), the breath of the sun-bird is made immortal by the chanting of the Vāmadevya hymn (*SB* IX,1,2,38), the tail representing the moon is made immortal by the chanting of the Yagnyayagnīya hymn, and the heart representing the sun is made immortal by chanting hymns about Prajāpati and progeny (*SB* IX,1,2,40-42).

After the generation of Agni as the sun-bird Āditya, Agni is led to the fire-altar (*SB* IX,2) and installed there (*SB* IX,3). The aim of the Agnicayana ritual is for the flight of Āditya to the heavens The sacrificer too is thereby borne by the altar, or the sun-bird, to heaven.[1065] However, the sacrificer does return to the earth (represented by the gārhapatya hearth) after his journey to the otherworld. The purpose of the construction of the fire-altar, as Tull points out, is "to reunify man's material being with the essential aspect of existence and threby regain the original state of wholeness".[1066]

The Agnicayana ritual is considered one of the highest Vedic rituals and is devoted to the gods. It is also related to the final Vedic ritual, the funereal Shmashānacayana, which concerns the building of the tomb and includes sacrifices to the manes.[1067] As Tull points out, "The Śmaśānacayana was made to resemble the Agnicayana to ensure that the same otherworldly attainments experienced – albeit on a symbolic level – through the ritual building of the fire-altar are actually attained through this final riual".[1068] Thus *SB* XIII,8,1,17 declares:

> For an Agnichit [one who has built a fire-altar] one makes the tomb after the manner of the fire-altar; for when a sacrificer builds a fire-altar he thereby constructs for himself by sacrifice a (new) body for yonder world; but that sacrificial performance is not complete until the making of a tomb; and when he makes the tomb of the Agnichit after the manner of the fire-altar ... he completes the Agnichityâ.

The mound is normally square in shape (*SB* XIII,8,1,5) and signifies the four quarters of the universe, though among the "Easterners" the mound was circular signifying the visible universe.[1069] In the Shmashānacayana,

---

[1065] See H.W. Tull, *op.cit.*, p.95f. In *SB* X,2,1 the contraction and expansion of the wings of the sun-bird are depicted as being incorporated into the construction of the fire-altar.

[1066] See H.W. Tull, *op.cit.* p.101; cf. *SB* X,1,4,1.

[1067] See H.W. Tull, *Ibid*. The Shmashānacayana is described in *SB* XIII,8,1-4.

[1068] See H.W. Tull, *op.cit.*, p.112.

[1069] The circular tomb is the basis of the Buddhist stupa.

bricks are placed between the bones of the dead person in the form of a bird, exactly as Purusha is formed in the form of a bird in the Agnicayana ritual. However, the bird in the Shmashānacayana ceremony does not have wings or a tail.

The elaborate construction of the fire-altar in the Agnicayana ritual and of the tomb in the Shmashānacayana ritual may indeed be considered as forerunners of the temple constructions that marked the later Hamitic cultures, which we shall study below.[1070]

The other ancient Āryan sacrifice that is of crucial significance for the development of the rituals characteristic of later Hinduism is the Rājasūya, the elaborate ceremony in which a king is consecrated and divinised. This sacrifice indeed serves as the prototype not only of other Vedic household sacrifices that aim at the divinisation of the sacrificer but also of later Āgamic rituals that focus on the divinisation of the devotee as well as of the temple idol.[1071] The Rājasūya sacrifice,[1072] like the Ashvamedha, is certainly one of the most ancient, and public, of Vedic sacrifices. Hocart suggested that the Purushamedha itself may have been a prototype of the royal consecration since it involved a literal killing of a sacrificer and his rebirth as a divine ruler.[1073]

The exalted status of the king in ancient India is suggested by *Manusmriti* VII,5ff. which declares that the king is formed of particles of the eternal gods, Indra, Vāyu, Yama, the sun, Agni, Varuna, the moon and Kubera [god of wealth],[1074] and therefore "surpasses all created beings in lustre/ And like the sun he burns eyes and hearts, nor can anybody on earth even gaze on him." The king represents the entire state and, according to the dharma literature, is endowed with the responsibility of protecting the people, maintaining the social order by upholding the caste system, and administering justice. Indeed, as Hocart pointed out,[1075] the king not only represents Dharma but is, as an incarnation of the sun-god, even equal to it.

[1070] See Chs.XIII-XV below.

[1071] See below p.295f.

[1072] The Rājasuya is described in *SB* V (cf. also *KYV* I, 6). For a good description of it, see J. Gonda, *Religionen*, I, pp.163ff.

[1073] See A.M. Hocart, *Kingship*, p.202.

[1074] These gods are called the eight guardian deities of the world (*Manusmriti*, V,96).

[1075] See A.M. Hocart, *Kingship*, p.53.

At his consecration the king is divinised,[1076] and the rebirth which the king undergoes during the ceremony represents his rebirth as the solar force. During the rājasūya the king is also identified with King Soma, and, as soma is ritually killed in its pressing during a soma sacrifice, this identification points to a sacrificial death of the king from which he is reborn with a divine consciousness.[1077] The whole rite indeed marks the rebirth of the king as the cosmic Prajāpati/Brahman/Indra/Sūrya whose solar course is represented in the chariot drive section of the ritual.[1078] The king also represents the sattvic power of the Purusha as Vishnu. His power is essentially a charismatic one derived from the solar force and not from the actual social control of peoples and lands. That is why the office of the king is an immortal one passed on from father to son in the salutation "The king is dead, long live the king".[1079]

The consecration is preceded by one year of rites characterised by the chaturmāsyas (four-month sacrifices) or a dīksha of this duration and it is followed by another year of dīksha-like observances and a new inauguration. In the initial Vaishvadeva sacrifice the creatures are said to be brought forth, by the Varunapraghāsa sacrifice they are said to be freed from Varuna's "fetter", which is related to the embryonic cover, as TB II,5,6,1-3, makes clear, where a new born child is bathed to the following chant: "from kshetriya, from Nirrti, from wile, from Varuna's fetter I release thee".[1080] During the ishtis (sacrifices with burnt, vegetable, offerings) for Mitra and Brhaspati, the king representing the sun engenders himself, "performing by himself the cosmic process of ripening and birth".[1081] The sacrificer is presented with a bow representing vajra, the weapon used by the solar force Indra to slay Vrtra. The sacrificer then raises his arms standing on the throne as "a personificaton of the cosmic pillar resting on the navel of the earth (the throne) and reaching up to the sky".[1082] This is clearly a phallic gesture since the priests chant "Rise up, ye two arms, that we may live, besprinkle our pastures with ghee [i.e.

[1076] The Nepalese monarchy observes the custom of the divinisation of kings (see A. Michaels, *Hinduism Past and Present*, p.277).

[1077] Cf. p.257 below.

[1078] See J.C. Heesterman, *Royal Consecration*, p.149. The queen is during the royal consecration identified with Aditi, the Earth (SB VI,5,3,1; XIV,1,3,25).

[1079] See A. Michaels, *op.cit.*, p.280.

[1080] See J.C. Heesterman, *Ancient Indian Royal Consecration*, p.28.

[1081] *Ibid.*, p.51.

[1082] *Ibid*, p.101.

semen]."[1083] The king does not lower his arms until after the chariot race. Then the king mounts the dishāh (quarters) of space by making a step in each of the five directions [the four cardinal points plus the centre] and thereby attains the heavens. At one stage (SB V,4,2,6) the king also takes the three solar steps of Vishnu to indicate his lordship of the three worlds.

Then begins a chariot race whose circuit begins and ends at the same place, for the "sacrificer goes ... from the Ocean to heaven and back to the Ocean again, as does the sun, "since the wheel of the chariot is at first attached to the cāvāla representing the Ocean.[1084] This is followed by a raid on "1000 cows", representing the solar rays, which the king must acquire. In the invocation to the Navagvas "our (ancient) fathers" are said to have helped Indra in winning the 'cows' of the Panis". As Heesterman suggests, the invocation seeks to "win back the sun from the waters".[1085] Through the race and the raid the king sets in motion the vāja- or fertility powers through the cosmos.[1086]

The unction (abhisecanīya) rites mark the king's rebirth out of the sacrifice [of Prajāpati]. The sixteen or seventeen liquids used in the unction represent the primal 'sweet' waters of Varuna, from which the sun arose.[1087] Indeed the Rājasuya is also called Varunasava. For the prince becomes Varuna (Maitrāyani Samhita IV). Since the term 'rājasuya' means "generating royalty" it is probably derived from this particular unction ritual. Heesterman suggests that the king is first reborn as Soma, representing the creative power of Brahman, for brāhmanical power is in JB II,203 equated with a means of procreation (prajanam brahmā).[1088] However the true brāhmanical virtue is the rājasic one represented by Agni while Soma is rather the sattvic aspect of the supreme divinity.[1089] Soma is thus equated with Purusha and Vāyu is considered Soma's breath just as it is Purusha's.

The king's throne in the enthronement section (SB V,4,4,1ff) represents Varuna's watery seat and the womb of royalty. On the throne

---

[1083] Ibid.

[1084] Ibid., p.134.

[1085] Ibid. , p.187.

[1086] The chariot race resembles the course run by the Pharaoh in Egypt during the Sed festival, which was a royal jubilee normally marking thirty years of a pharaoh's reign (see W. Kaiser, "Die kleine Hebseddarstellung").

[1087] See above p.206.

[1088] J.C. Heesterman, op. cit., p.76.

[1089] Cf. KB 9,5: "Agni is the brahman power, Soma is the royal power"; also BAU I4,11: "the brahman is the womb of royalty".

the king is proclaimed a brāhman. It is interesting to note also that, after being hailed as a brāhman (i.e. as one endowed with brāhmanical consciousness) by the four priests, the king is identified with Savitr, Mitra, Indra and Varuna – which are, as we have seen, the four universal phases of the sun.[1090] The king is born in the centre of the universe as its lord. On birth, he is symbolically beaten with wooden sticks to remove the covers of the embryo and free him from death.

In the section devoted to a dicing game we are offered a ritual representation of the ordering of the universe, for, in AV IV,6,5, Varuna's ordering activity is likened to the throwing of the dice by the player, and the number of dice corresponds to the points of the compass plus the zenith. However, the king does not take part in the dicing game On the contrary it is the king's royalty that is to be won by the players.[1091] In the final bath, avabhrtha, the king is finally cleansed and regenerated.

In the Dashapeya sacrifice of the Rājasūya rituals, which is undertaken on the tenth day and is an Agnishtoma sacrifice (SB V,4,5), the aim is to make the king ascend to the heavens. This sacrifice includes a ceremony in which the sacrificer is joined by ten brāhmans (or sometimes by "thousand" participants) in drinking soma to suggest the permeation of the universe by the king's soma essence. The king makes his subjects and the universe partake of the vital liquids which have rolled off his body during the unction.

The concluding Sautrāmani sacrifice (SB V,4,8ff) is dedicated to the Ashvins who refilled Indra with Soma after he once happened to emit it all out. This sacrifice therefore highlights the importance of the conservation of the soma power of the king. In the additional "Truth-messenger" ishtis, homage is paid to the solar deities, Savitr, the Ashvins, (who carry the sun-maiden Sūrya in their chariot),[1092] and Pūshan, who is a son of the Ashvins. At this stage the king establishes satya, truth, in the cosmos.

After a year of sexual abstinence during which the king does not cut his hair an official hair-cutting ceremony takes place which may be related to the removal of the embryonic cover earlier on in the rituals, or a sign of renewed growth of the king's hair as well as of terrestrial vegetation.

The king is the typical yajamāna, patron of the sacrifice. As Heesterman has interestingly observed, some of the rites of the Rājasūya "not ony correspond to general śrauta rites but in point of fact seems to

---

[1090]   See above p.121. J.C. Heesterman, who points to this peculiarity in the rājasūya sacrifice (op.cit., p.160), does not see the solar significance of this episode.

[1091]   Ibid., p.156.

[1092]   See A.A. Macdonell, Vedic Mythology, p.50f.

have been the prototypes of these general rites ... the daśapeya probably represents a more original form of the Soma sacrifice as a rite of Somic communion bewteen the king, the people and the brahmins"[1093] Another aspect of this significant sacrifice that Heesterman points to is the "the intimate connection of royal and priestly power ... The brahman power has been seen to be the womb from which again and again the royal power comes forth. Between them the king and the purohita regulate the course of the universe".[1094]

The Sarvamedha is a ten-day sacrifice including different types of sacrifices such as the Purushamedha, Ashvamedha, Vājapeya and the Vishvajit and is aimed at the acquisition of supreme lordship. As *SB* XIII,7,1-2 declares:

At this (sacrifice) [the sacrificer] builds the greatest possible fire-altar, for this – to wit, the Sarvamedha – is supreme amongst all sacrificial performances: by means of the supreme (sacrifice) he thus causes him (the sacrificer) to attain supremacy.

Brahman Swāyambhuva is the model of the Sarvamedha since he is said to have meditated thus (*ibid.*):

Verily, there is no perpetuity in austerities; well, then, I will offer up mine own self in the creatures, and the creatures in mine own self.' And, accordingly, by offering up his own self in the creatures, and the creatures in his own self, he compassed the supremacy, the sovereignty, and the lordship over all creatures; and in like manner does the sacrificer, by thus offering all sacrificial essences in the Sarvamedha, compass all beings, and supremacy, sovereignty, and lordship.

[1093] See J.C. Heesterman, *op.cit.*, p.226.

[1094] *Ibid.*

X.

YAJNA III

Agni, the Sacred Fire

S|ince all the Āryan sacrifices are fire-rituals, we may study the significance of the sacred fire here briefly. Agni as the sacred fire is maintained at the home of a Hindu continuously from the stage of brahmachārya onwards. According to the *Vasishta Dharmasutra*, one who does not maintain his sacred fire becomes equal to a Shūdra. From the end of the brahmachārya to the stage of grihasthya, the Hindu sacrificer offers clarified butter and utters vyahrtis. After marriage, he offers clarified butter, as well as paddy or barley and utters the mantra "agnaye svāhā [Hail to Agni]" and "prajāpatye svāhā [Hail to Prajāpati]" in the evening and "sūryaye svāhā [Hail to the sun]" and "prajāpatye svāhā" in the morning. If the sacrificer cannot maintain a fire at any time in his adult life, it will be maintained by his wife, son, unmarried daughter, or disciple. A householder has to perform five daily mahāyajnas, one to living creatures and spirits (bhuta), one to men, one to the ancestors, one to the gods, and one to Brahman. Domestic or grhya fires as well shrauta fires are extinguished at the death of the master of a house, after having rendered their last service at his funeral. The cremation of his body is carried out with the fires that were preserved during his life.

The association of the sacred fire with the life-spirit of the sacrificer is evidenced equally in ancient Persia, where the sacred fires of the land were extinguished at the death of a ruler. In the Greek cities, a fire, hestia, was permanently maintained on the state hearth, in the prytaneion, just as in Rome the sacred fire was maintained in the Vesta temple. Apart from in the ashvamedha and rājasūya rituals, the more public and political dimension of the sacred fire seems to have become somewhat diminished in ancient Indian society. Heesterman conjectures that this may have been due to the nomadic origins of the Indian Āryan tribes, which were noted by Megasthenes as well,[1095] though this conflicts with what we know about the nomadic origins of the Iranians as well.[1096]

The vessel or place containing the sacred fire is called kunda. The Yajna kunda is the mouth of the Lord into which sacrificial offerings are poured in the morning and evening. The kunda has a different shape according to the caste of the person lighting the fire. For a brāhman it is square, for a kshatriya round and for a vaisya a half-circle or half-moon shape.[1097] Agni is indeed a god associated with the brāhmans, just as Indra is the god associated with the kshatriyās and Vishvadevas with the vaisyās.

The fire is said to be "churned' by means of fire-sticks (aranis), two pieces of wood from an ashvattha tree that has grown upon a sami tree without connexion with any other trees. The fire is also considered to descend through a process of attrition.[1098] The quasi-biological process of generating the fire is described in detail in *RV* III,29,1ff.:

1. Here is the gear for friction, here tinder made ready for the spark.
   Bring thou the Matron: we will rub Agni in ancient fashion forth.
2. In the two fire-sticks Jātavedas lieth, even as the well-set germ in pregnant women,
   Agni who day by day must be exalted by men who watch and worship with oblations.
3. Lay this with care on that which lies extended: straight hath she borne the Steer when made prolific.
   With his red pillar—radiant is his splendour—in our skilled task is born the Son of Ilā.[1099]
4. In Ilā's place we set thee down, upon the central point of earth,
   That, Agni Jātavedas, thou mayst bear our offerings to the Gods.
5. Rub into life, ye men, the Sage, the guileless, Immortal, very wise and fair to look on.

[1095] See above p.183.

[1096] See above p.181.

[1097] See M. Tachikawa and M. Kolhatkar, *Vedic Domestic Fire-Ritual*, pp.2ff.

[1098] See p.184 below; cf. J. Gonda, *Vedic Ritual*, p.164. M. Sharma (*op.cit.*, p.19) speculates that the swastika was perhaps a fire-drill that was later used to produce fire. Staal has suggested that the fire-drill may have a phallic significance since Agni is considered to be born of the fire-drill (F. Staal, *Agni* , pp.41ff.).

[1099] Purūravas, who is considered the founder of the fire-rituals, is a descendant of Ila (see above p.142).

10. O men, bring forth the most propitious Agni, first ensign of the sacrifice to eastward.

6. When with their arms they rub him straight he shineth forth like a strong courser, red in colour, in the wood.
Bright, checkless, as it were upon the Aśvins' path, he passeth by the stones and burneth up the grass.

7. Agni shines forth when born, observant, mighty, the bountiful, the Singer praised by sages;
Whom, as adorable and knowing all things, Gods set at solemn rites as offering-bearer.

In the passage above, Jātavedas Agni, the second form of the deity, corresponds to the phallic force of Indra which emerges as our universe. Hence the reference to its "red pillar" and its being positioned on "the central point of Earth".

In *RV* V, XI we get another glimpse of the birth of Agni as the sacrificial fire:

1. The watchful Guardian of the people hath been born, Agni, the very strong, for fresh prosperity.
With oil upon his face, with high heaven-touching flame, he shineth splendidly, pure, for the Bharatas.

2. Ensign of sacrifice, the earliest Household-Priest, the men have kindled Agni in his threefold seat,
With Indra and the Gods together on the grass let the wise Priest sit to complete the sacrifice.

3. Pure, unadorned, from thy two Mothers art thou born: thou camest from Vivasvān as a charming Sage.
With oil they strengthened thee, O Agni, worshipped God: thy banner was the smoke that mounted to the sky.

4. May Agni graciously come to our sacrifice. The men bear Agni here and there in every house.
He hath become an envoy, bearer of our gifts: electing Agni, men choose one exceeding wise.

5. For thee, O Agni, is this sweetest prayer of mine: dear to thy spirit be this product of my thought.
As great streams fill the river so our song of praise fill thee, and make thee yet more mighty in thy strength.

6. O Agni, the Angirases discovered thee what time thou layest hidden, fleeing back from wood to wood.

Thou by attrition art produced as conquering might, and men, O
Angiras, call thee the Son of Strength.

Agni is considered the "mouth of the gods" during the sacrifice since
it consumes the sacrificial offerings. As *RV* II,1,14 puts it: "In thee, O
Agni, with (thy) mouth all the guileless immortal gods eat the offering
which is offered to them. Through thee the mortals taste their drink".
Agni is thus the conveyor of the offerings to the gods (devatas). Indeed,
the gods are always invited to the Vedic sacrifice in order that they may
partake of the offerings directly. They are offered a comfortable seat on
kusha grass, lauded with hymns and given food and drink in the form of
oblations. This ceremonial order is, as we shall see, followed in mediaeval
temple worship, or archana, with its āvāhana, stotra, upachāra, etc.[1100] The
vivifying force of Agni, the sacred fire, is clearly stressed in *SB* II,2,2,8-
10, which declares that it is through the Agnyadheya, from the fire that is
led to them, that the gods receive a soul. This is in contrast to the normal
'asuric' fire that destroys objects. At the same time, Agni is also the
internal fire of the sacrificer and the officiating priests since it digests food
eaten at the end of the sacrifice, that is, the offerings remaining over from
that consumed by the gods.[1101]

There are two types of sacred fires, Grhya (domestic), or Aupāsana,
and Shrauta (from Shruti, the scriptures). The Aupāsana fire is lit at the
time of the groom's wedding in the ritual called Agnyādhana. The groom's
fire is taken from his father's. The Aupasana fire is divided into two,
one part of the fire being called grhyāgni or smārtāgni and is meant for
domestic sacrifices. The other is shrautāgni and is divided into three fires
(tretāgni): the Gārhapatya (circular in shape), Dakshināgni (semicircular)
and Āhavaniya (square). The square shape symbolises the four quarters
of the universe.[1102] Only the Aupāsana fire and the Gārhapatya fires are to
be kept burning continuously. The other two shrauta fires, Dakshināgni
and Āhavaniyagni, are extinguished after the performance of a shrauta
sacrifice.

The Gārhapatya fire is placed in the west, the Dakshināgni in the
south and the Āhavanīya in the east. The Gārhapatya represents Earth
(the realm of Agni), the Āhavanīya Heaven (the realm of Āditya) and the
Dakshināgni the Mid-region (the realm of Vāyu). The round Gārhapatya
fire is similar to the hearth of Vesta in Rome, while the square Āhavanīya

---

[1100] See below p.302.

[1101] See M. Biardeau, *op.cit.*, p.21.

[1102] This is true of the burial mounds too, which were typically square (see above p.232).

is like the public altars of Greece and Rome.[1103] The gārhapatya fire serves normally to cook offerings, the āhavanīya to receive them, and the dakshināgni to repel evil spirits.[1104]

At the centre of the three fires is the vedi covered with barhis where the gods will be seated and eat the offerings made to them. The vedi is not exactly the fire-altar itself, but is an elevated plot of ground strewn with darbha grass on which the sacrificial materials and implements are placed.[1105] For the soma sacrifices, a great vedi (mahāvedi) is erected in the north where the soma carts are placed.[1106]

The Conduct of the Sacrifices

Malamoud has identified the major stages involved in any sacrifice as 1. shraddhā, or confidence in the efficacy of the ritual, 2. dīksha, or consecration of the sacrificer, 3. yajna, or the sacrifice proper and 4. dakshina, or the honararium paid to the priest.[1107] The sacrificial offerings are consumed by the gods as well as by the brāhmans who thereby absorb the divine energy. Indeed, an important part of the sacrifice is the communal manducation of the Ida, which permits a communion with the ultimate master of the sacrifice who is Prajāpati.[1108]

The sacrifice starts with the brahmaudana cooked at the sacrificer's gārhapatya fire, which should be maintained for a year suggesting a year-long gestation.[1109] The sacrificer abstains from sex, meat-eating, etc, and chants from *TB* I,2,1,15: "from the human I go to the divine", "by lighting the fire I shall conquer the two spaces ... shall conquer death", etc. The importance of abstinence in the sacrifice is easily understood when one remembers the sexual sacrifice that precedes every birth of light in the cosmos, first the castration of the Purusha which produces the light of Brahman, then the castration of the latter which leads to the formation of the sun within the underworld, and finally the sacrifice of Wotan [Shiva] on the Tree of Life which is similar to a yogic tapas and produces the light of our solar system. The discipline of yoga too entails a

---

[1103] See J.C. Heesterman, *op.cit.*, p.125.

[1104] See J. Gonda, *Religionen*, I, p.141.

[1105] See J. Gonda, *Vedic Ritual*, p.174.

[1106] *Ibid.*, p.141.

[1107] See C. Malamoud, "Terminer le sacrifice".

[1108] See J. Gonda, *Religionen*, I, p.106.

[1109] See J. Gonda, *Religionen*, I, p.139. cf. above p.17.

concentrated direction of sexual energy towards the production of higher consciousness.

The sacrificer lights the fire of the new sacred fire which he wishes to establish by "impregnating" the sticks on the brahmaudanika fire, which is then extinguished. The rathantara sāman is chanted which speaks of Agni and the course of the sun. It is clear that what the fires represent is the birth and course of the solar light. The new fire is deposited in the gārhapatya fire. From the gārhapatya the sacrificer carries the fire to the place where the āhavanīya will be, preceded by a young horse signifying the sun. At the moment when the sun is half-risen the āhavanīya fire is established. This is the moment when Prajāpati created living creatures. The sacrificer is thereby assured of progeny himself (*TB* I,1,4,2). The last fire, the dakshināgni, is lit from the new fire, or from the gārhapatya, or even from the brahmaudana that has been conserved.

Milk offerings are made constantly to the three fires and the agnyupasthanam rite, which pays homage to the cow that has given the milk, is especially important (*SB* II,3,1,5: "The sun will not rise if one did not offer this sacrifice").

The Shrautasūtra Sacrifices

The sacrifices performed by householders in later Hinduism are described in the Grhya and Shrauta Sūtras. According to *SB* XI,5,6,1-3, the five daily sacrifices prescribed by the Grhyasūtras, the mahāyajnas, are those dedicated to the creatures, to men, to the manes, to the gods and to Brahman. The Grhyasutra rituals seem rather like simplified versions of the Shrautasutra ones, which are more elaborate sacrifices based on Shruti (the Vedas).

The Shrautasūtra sacrifices are divided into kamya-karma (optional) and nitya-karma (compulsory). Although there are 400 sacrifices described in the Vedas, only 21 are compulsory for every dvija, or twice-born, person. The 21 are divided into 3 groups of seven each:

a. 7 Pakayajna sacrifices – these are minor domestic (grhyakarma) sacrifices involving oblations of cooked food, rice, grain, sesame, milk, etc. These are also called Smartakarma, since they belong to the Smrtis. The *Āpastamba Sutra*[1110] lists the following seven pakayajnas:

[1110] The *Bodhayana Sutra* gives the seven Pakayajnas as Huta, Prahuta, Ahuta, Shulagava, Baliharana, Pratyavarohana and Ashtaka.

1. Aupāsana
2. Vaishvadeva
3. Parvana
4. Ashtaka[1111]
5. Masishraddha
6. Sarpabali
7. Ishānabali

b. Similarly, there are 7 Haviryajna sacrifices:

1. Ādhana
2. Agnihotra
3. Darshapūrnamāsa
4. Āgrayana
5. Chāturmāsya
6. Nirūdhapashubandha
7. Sautrāmani

While the Pakayajnas may be peformed by the householder along with his wife, the Haviryajnas require four brāhman priests, but the Udgatr who represents the Sāmaveda in the somayajnas is replaced in the Haviryajna by an Āgnīdhra. The importance of the brāhmans in the conduct of sacrifices is clear from the fact that only they may sacrifice on behalf of others and receive thanks offerings. Kshatriyas and vaisyas may only offer sacrifices but not receive these offerings since only the brāhman possesses a divine status.[1112] Of the Haviryajnas, the first, after the initial establishment of a shrauta fire in the Agniyādhana ceremony, is the Agnihotra. The Darshapūrnamāsa (darsha= new moon, purna= full moon), which is a half-monthly sacrifice conducted at the new- and full-moon,[1113] is the prakrti (archetype) of the Haviryajna.[1114] It is peformed on the first day (Prathama) of a lunar fortnight, when a Pakayajna and a Haviryajna are performed in the grhyāgni and shrautāgni fires respectively. The other Haviryajnas are called vikrti (developments). The first four Haviryajna sacrifices can be performed at home, the last three only in a yajashāla.

[1111] The Ashtaka is performed for the manes, or fathers.

[1112] See M. Biardeau, op.cit, p.27.

[1113] The Darshapūrnamāsa sacrifice is described in detail in SB I.

[1114] The *Krishna Yajur Veda*, which is the oldest text dealing with the rituals, describes only the Darshapūrnamāsa and the Sautrāmani among the Haviryajnas. The rest of the Veda deals with Somayajnas and the Agnicayana.

The Āgrayana (first-fruits) sacrifice is performed on the full moon of Ashvina. Chāturmāsya is peformed every four months, in Karttika it is called a Vaishvadeva sacrifice, in Phalguna a Varunapraghāsa and in Ashadha a Sākamedha.[1115]

The two last sacrifices in the list, however, are animal sacrifices, like the Somayajnas. In animal sacrifices there is a yupa stambha or sacrificial post. Animal oblations are meant to replenish the fire. As *SB* II,7,1,1 declares:

> As he is offering the oblations, the sacrificer's fires become decrepit, after them the sacrificer [himself] wears out [and] after the sacrificer [his] cattle and household; by offering the animal sacrifice he makes the fires new again, after the renewal of the fires the sacrificer [and] after the sacrificer [his] cattle and household [are renewed].

The *Panchavimsha Brāhmana* declares that "by meat offerings the gods conquered this world, by animal offerings the mid-region, by soma offerings that world, or the highest regions". In general, animal sacrifices are reserved for exceptional occasions such as marriage, sacrifices to the manes, etc.[1116] The Pashubandha sacrifice resembles the New Moon sacrifice though it has a special priest, the Maitrāvaruna, who carries a baton and invites the hotar to recite the yājyās.[1117] There is also an uttaravedi installed in the eastern part of the yajashāla. The animal is strangled by the officiating priest, while the assistants look away. In the Sautrāmani sacrifice, sura or liquor is offered to appease certain inferior deities.

In order to study the methodology of a typical Haviryajna we may consider the daily Agnihotra. This ritual is performed by a brāhman priest for his own benefit or for that of a sponsor, yajamāna. There may be one, three or five kundas for the Agnihotra. The agnihotri has to prepare the yajnashāla according to the measurements given in the Vedas. The yajna kunda and the vedi must be in the centre of the yajnashala.

The Agnihotra may be considered as the worship of Lord Nārāyana, Adi Nārāyana riding on the divine serpent and controlling the infinite cosmos by his will. The evening yajna is offered to Lord Agni Nārāyana and the morning yajna to Lord Sūrya Nārāyana. According to *SB* II,3,3-5,

---

[1115] See J. Gonda, *Religionen*, I, p.146.

[1116] *Ibid.*, p.125.

[1117] *Ibid.*, p.147.

when [the sun] sets, then he, as an embryo, enters that womb, the fire ... And when [the sacrificer] offers in the morning before sunrise, then he produces that [sun-child] and, having become a light, it rises shining. But assuredly, it would not rise, were he not to make that offering.

Two offerings of milk are into the fire, exactly at, slightly before, or after, sunset and sunrise. *Baudhāyana Sūtra* II,7:43.17 equates milk or ghee with the cow's seed just as rice grains are identified with the bull's seed. As we shall see, the female and male seed are used to mark the birth of Prajāpati. Vedic mantras are chanted that relate the fire and the sun to each other: in the evening, "agnir jyotir, jyotih sūryah svāhā", "sūryo jyotir, jyotir agnih svāhā" in the morning. This preserves the sun overnight, since the seed of light is "enclosed on both sides with the deity" (SB II,3,1,32) and the seed thus enclosed is brought forth again the next morning. This rite is followed by the worship of three or five sacred fires (agni-upasthana).

In the evening rite, the agnihotri performs Sandhyā Vandana, then, after a Sankalpa,[1118] wakes up the Lord with motherly care by uncovering the bhasma (ashes) from the sacred fire. Then a fresh fire is lit from cowdung cakes. Next Ahūtis (offerings) of samidh (pieces of small branches of wood from mango or pipal or palash tree most commonly), ghee, javtal are offered to Agni. Then the excellences of the Lord are sung in mantras of the Shānti Sūkta, Purusha Sūkta, Sūrya Sūkta from the *Yajurveda*. Flowers and tulsi are offered to the Lord. Then the Lord Nārāyana is meditated upon. There follows a waving of lights (ārti), mantra pushpānjali, circumambulation (pradakshina) and a pūja to Lord Mahāvishnu. Finally, the agnihotri makes the Lord sleep by covering the Agni with ashes. After the worship of Lord Nārāyana, Lord Mahādeva is worshipped.

Exactly at sunrise, the first mantra "Sūryaya svāhā" (hail to the sun) is uttered. When the word "svāhā" is uttered, one part of a small quantity of rice grains is poured into the fire. The mantra "Sūryaya idam, na mama" (this belongs to Sūrya not to me) is recited. While offering the other part of the rice grains into the fire, is chanted "Prajāpataye svāhā" and "Prajāpataye idam, na mama" (this belongs to Prajāpati, not to me). The so-called "tyāga (renunciation)" mantra, "Not to me, but to the deity", is symbolic of the self-abandonment that is enjoined on the sacrificer during the performance of the Vedic rituals.[1119] Every sacrificial oblation is indeed

---

[1118] See below p.302.

[1119] See J.C. Heesterman, *Broken world*, p.17; cf. M. Biardeau, *op.cit.*, p.19.

an abandonment of something that the sacrificer possesses approximatng to Prajāpati's primordial self-sacrifice as opposed to the Asura's arrogant offering of sacrifices to themselves which result in nought (*SB* XI,1,8). The agnihotri performs three yajnas daily, deva yajna (for the gods), pitra yajna (for the manes) and manushya yajna (for man). On the first day of Shukla Paksha and Krishna Paksha, the agnihotri gets his head shaved, his hair being offered as a mark of repentance and love for the Lord.

c. The highest category of shrauta sacrifices is that of the 7 Somayajnas consisting of

1. Agnishtoma, or Jyotishtoma
2. Atyagnishtoma
3. Uktya
4. Shodashi
5. Vājapeya
6. Atirātra
7. Aptoryāma

Soma, representing the life-force, constitutes the highest form of Vedic sacrifice. Most of the Soma sacrifices are dedicated to Indra, who, as we have seen, is imbued with the somic energy. The importance of Soma in Vedic culture has already been noted above. Soma is indeed the life-force of the universe and, according to Heesterman, in the shrauta rituals, the arrival of King Soma "at the śala, the sacrificial fire-hall, and then to the mahāvedi is akin to a conquering progress".[1120] The Agnishtoma is the prakrti of the somayajnas and is offered mostly at spring to maintain the current of universal life.[1121] The Vājapeya,[1122] preliminary to the Brhaspatisva, is conducted only by kshatriyas and brāhmans.[1123] In the course of this ritual, the kshatriya is identified with Indra and the brāhman with Brhaspati.[1124] It bears some similarity to the rājasūya since there is a chariot race conducted to obtain the vāja, the spiritual power or "food".[1125] It also involves the consumption of surā (alcohol) in addition to soma. The Atirātra is a soma sacrifice which entails a night-long vigil.

[1120] J.C. Heesterman, *op. cit.*, p.203.

[1121] See J. Gonda, *Religionen*, I, p.150.

[1122] The Vājapeya is described in *SB* V.

[1123] See A.B. Keith, *The Rigveda Brahmanas*, p.54.

[1124] *SB* V,3,1,2; V,1.

[1125] See J. Gonda, *op.cit.*, p.159.

In the soma sacrifices, the dominant feature is the singing of hymns, hence the Udgatr priest related to the Sāma Veda is required for the performance of these sacrifices. The four priests, Hotr, Adhvaryu, Udgātr and Brahman, related respectively to the Rigveda, the Yajurveda, the Sāmaveda, and the Atharvaveda, are assisted each by three others, to make a total of sixteen:

The Hotr, who invokes the deities, is assisted by a Prashastr (or Maitravaruna) (director) priest, a Grāvastut (in charge of the gravā, the stones for pressing the soma), and an Acchavaka priest.

The Adhvaryu, who is the chief officiant of the sacrifices, is assisted by a Pratiprasthātr, the Nestr, who normally leads forward the wife of the sacrificer, and the Unnetr.

The Udgātr, who is the leader of the Sāma Vedic chants, is assisted by the Prastotr, a Pratihartr and a Subrahmanya priest.

The Brahman priest, who supervises the entire proceedings, is assisted by a Potr (purifier), a Brahmanachhamsin, and an Āgnīdhra, who kindles the fire.

The four chief priests – hotr, adhvaryu, udgātr and brahman – have to be invited and brought to the fire from the four directions on chariots.[1126] This reveals the cosmic functions of the priests in the ritual creation of Brahman. Of all the priests, the most important is the brahman. In the AB V,34, it is stated that "The Brahman priest was, in the beginning, the sharer of half the sacred power along with the other priests, Hotr, Udgātr, Adhvaryu." According to Kaushītiki Brāhmana, VI,11: "There are two tracks of the sacrifice: one is performed with speech, the other with the mind; that which is performed with speech the other priests do, that which is [performed] with the mind, the Brahman does." Similarly, the BAU declares that the brahman priest wins with his mind alone an "unlimited world" whereas the other priests win by their efforts at the sacrifice only one or another world. Thus the brahman priest is clearly the most spiritually eminent of all.

The four major Vedic priests are also internalised within the Purusha in BAU III,1, 3-6: "speech is the Hotri" [Agni, Rik], "the breath is the Udgātri" [Vāyu, Sāma], "the eye is the Adhvaryu" [Āditya, Yajur], "mind [Manas] is the Brāhman" [Moon, Atharva]. Further, according to BAU, III, 1,3ff., the sacrificer too is spiritually elevated by the sacrifice: "The organ of speech [vāk] of the sacrificer is looked upon as Agni, ... the eye of the sacrificer as Āditya, ... the vital force (Prāna) of the sacrificer is looked upon as Vāyu, ... the mind of the sacrificer is Chandra ..."

[1126] See J.C. Heesterman, Broken World, p.205.

In the soma sacrifice, Agnishtoma, which is a Jyotishtoma, or laud of light, the declared aim is the attainment of Indraloka, the heaven of the gods. This is a more elaborate sacrifice lasting five or six days which can be performed only by a householder. However, the same focus on Agni (the fire) and Āditya (the sun) is to be noted here as in the Agnihotra. As *JB* I,240, declares:

> He (Agni) becomes established in yonder sun with twenty-one Trivrts [chants] and yonder sun in him with nine Twenty-onefolds. Thus the two become established in each other,[1127]

and I,241:

> yonder sun goes home (sets) towards this one here. This one here goes out towards (or visits) yonder one. ... These two deities are dwelling together. One obtains dwelling together with these two and they obtain dwelling together with him. They continuously remove all evil in these worlds.

On the first day, the Dīksha or "consecration" takes place. The Dīksha represents the death of the individual and his rebirth in a divine state. The sacrificer is shaved and, from that moment on, his food is restricted. He keeps his hands as much as possible in the form of a fist, indicating his status as an embryo. After the Dīksha the soma is purchased and is brought in like a king on his chariot. It is installed on a throne and addressed as Varuna.[1128] Then there may take place a special Pravargya ceremony to which the sacrificer's wife is not admitted. The Pravargya represents the sun (*SB* X,2,5,4) and is mainly addressed to the Ashvins, the twin solar horsemen or charioteers. It may be performed by an aspirant only after a long period of tapas which will contribute to "the strengthening of the sun".[1129] The rite involves a phallic Mahāvīra pot representing the sun. The gharma (hot milk) oblation poured into the pot symbolises the heating of the solar force so that it may achieve its full power.[1130]

This is followed by 'upasad' days which precede the soma pressings. On the second of these days, the mahāvedi is erected. The sacrifcer now opens his fist and unbuckles the belt which he received during the dīksha representing power (*SB* III,2,1,10). Then, on the 'great night,'

[1127]   See H.W. Bodewitz, *op.cit.*, p.134.

[1128]   For a good account of the Agnishtoma, see J. Gonda, *Religionen*, I, pp.152ff.

[1129]   See J. van Buitenen, *Pravargya*, p.41. The Pravargya is described in *SB* V.

[1130]   See *Ibid.*, p.31.

the instruments for the pressing are prepared. The soma is pressed and offered on the same day, in a series of three pressings, the Prāthasavana (Morning Pressing), Mādhyamdinasavana (Midday Pressing), and the Trtītyasavana (Third Pressing). The soma juice is poured into a receptacle filled with water and purified with a woollen filter. The brahman priests drink after the gods have been offered the juice. The gods addressed are the dual deities Indra-Vāyu, Mitra-Varuna, and the two Ashvins. The morning pressing refers to Indra's defeat of Vrtra and the midday pressing to his destruction of the "vala" which confines the solar energy.[1131] At the midday pressing the sacrificer symbolically distributes parts of his body to the priests, his voice to the hotar, his mind to the brahman, etc. After the evening pressing, the sacrificer and his wife undergo a final bath, the avabhrtha. They then adore the sun saying "By contemplating the radiant light, the god Sūrya, … we have moved from darkness to the radiant light" and add "we have drunk Soma, have become immortal, we have contemplated the light and found the gods" (TB III,2,5).

The seminal power symbolised by the soma is clear from the section of the sacrifice which adores King Soma in the following manner: "Swell, O Soma, may the male power join you from all sides".[1132] This power is also the source of immortality: "by swelling, O Soma, place your supreme glories in the heavens in order to become the liquor of immortality."[1133] The soma is prepared primarily for the consumption of Indra, since this is the power with which he conquers the serpent Vrtra: "[Having drunk this soma] may Indra massacre the Vrtras, conquer [their] race".[1134] At one stage are chanted the verses from RV VIII,17, 1-13:

4. Come unto us who bring the juice, come unto this our eulogy,
    Fair-visored! drink thou of the juice.
5. I pour it down within thee, so through all thy members let it spread:
    Take with thy tongue the pleasant drink.
6. Sweet to thy body let it be, delicious be the savoury juice:
    Sweet be the Soma to thine heart.
7. Like women, let this Soma-draught, invested with its robe, approach,

---

[1131] See Jamison and Witzel, p.39. In Iran, the demonic Apaosa is killed by Tistria at midday (Yt.8.26-8) and the dragon too at the same hour, by Keresaspa (Y 9.11).

[1132] See W. Caland and V. Henry, L'Agnistoma, p.44, cf. p.48.

[1133] Ibid., p.112.

[1134] Ibid., p.145.

O active Indra, close to thee.

8.   Indra, transported with the juice, vast in his bulk, strong in his neck
And stout arms, smites the Vṛtras down.

9.   O Indra, go thou forward, thou who rulest over all by might:
Thou Vrtra-slayer slay the fiends.

The solar significance of this act is clear from the fact that Indra represents the force that manifests itself in our universe as the sun. The priests too elevate themselves through the soma sacrifice. At one stage, for instance, the priests chant the Rigvedic verses *RV* VIII,48,3-4:

> We have drunk the soma, we have become immortal, we are allied to the light, we have found the gods, what can the demon do to us at the moment, what, immortal one, can the malice of a mortal do to us?

This is to be observed again in *TS* III,2,5, a-g:

> O drink, come, penetrate into me, for long life, the health of the body, the prosperity of wealth, splendour, the good prosperity ... for energy, the pious address, the prosperty of wealth, the good virility ... for male force, life and splendour.[1135]

[1135]   *Ibid.*, p.216.

XI.

YASNA

Scholars like Hillebrandt have pointed out that the Indic sacrifices are not local to India but derive from Indo-Iranian times. Hillebrandt has shown that many ritualistic details, for example, the formula "ye yajamahe" before the Yajya verses, are found also in Iran, and the cake offerings are used in the Darun ceremony of the Iranians as well as in the Purodasha ceremony of the Indians.[1136] Wackernagel has also observed that, while for the Indians the sacrifice is the vehicle of his wishes, wealth, long life and offspring, the Iranians however wish to acquire the aid of good spirits and the removal of bad ones.[1137] In fact, this latter feature is to be found in the *Atharva Veda,* which is replete with magical spells and charms, showing that this Veda is perhaps the oldest of all, hence its traditional association with the superb brahman priests, whereas the *Rgveda, Yajurveda* and *Samaveda* are associated with the Hotr, Adhvaryu and the Udgātr priests respectively.

Heesterman has suggested that the Iranians did not offer burnt oblations into their sacred fire and that consequently the fire was less used for consumption as for its own religious virtue as a cultic object that has to be maintained always in total purity.[1138] But we have seen that in the *Bundahishn* at least there is a clear account of burnt offerings involved in the first sacrifice undertaken by the progeny of the First Man, Gayomard.[1139] Thus the Zoroastrian reform seems to have reduced

---

[1136]   See A. Hillebrandt, *op. cit.,* p.viii.

[1137]   See J. Wackernagel, *op. cit.,* p.18.

[1138]   J.C. Heesterman, *Broken World,* p.87.

[1139]   See above p.85.

the original creative function of the fire-rituals by not offering animal, vegetal or even haoma oblations into it (the haoma is only carried round the fire and drunk by the priests).[1140] The prime importance of the purity of the fire among the Zoroastrians demonstrates once again the aversion that the dualistic Zoroastrians have to the creation itself. The complex internalisation of the fire in yogic practices, as well as in the sacrificial cult, and in the later temple worship shows that the Zoroastrians have an inadequate appreciation of the several transformations of Agni within the macrocosm and the microcosm. In this context we may also remember Heesterman's observation that the fire was more internalised among the Indians, who identified it with the self, or ātman, than among the Iranians, who tended rather to transcendentalise it.[1141]

Among the Zoroastrians, the sacred fire, Atar, is a symbol of Ahura Mazda himself and of the Truth. In Yasna 62, to the Fire, fire is addressed as "Ahura Mazda's son".[1142] The epithet for fire in the Gathas is "athro asha aojanho" (the true strong fire). Like the Vedic Agni, Atar in the Yasna (17,11) is also said to be the lord of all houses. In the Atash Niyayesh, the litany to Atar, we note that Atar is considered to be the sacred fire of the household:

8.   May you be provided with proper fuel! May you be provided with proper incense! May you be provided with proper nourishment! ... May you be maintained by one wise (in religion], O Fire, son of Ahura Mazda.

9.   In order to be burning in this house, in order to be ever burning in this house .... Even throughout the Long Time, until the mighty Renovation.[1143]

But the domestic hearth fire, called Ātash Dādgāh, is the lowest of the sacred fires, which is turned into a more significant cult fire by putting it in an appropriate place, i.e. a fire-temple. The fire room in the temple was itself constructed in the form of a dome recalling the dome of heaven.[1144] The Avesta indeed mentions three consecrated fires, a house-hold fire, a communal fire and a national. The Avesta (Yasna 62,5) values most of all

---

[1140]   J.C. Heesterman, op.cit., p.83.

[1141]   Ibid., p.6.

[1142]   Since the Vedic Agni is the son of Dyaus, we may presume that Ahura Mazda is the same as Dyaus.

[1143]   See The Nyaishes, tr. M.N. Dhalla.

[1144]   See J. Darmsteter, Zend Avesta, I, 152f;169).

the national fire, the Ātash Bahram, the fire of victory. This was the cult fire of the royal house of the Sassanians. The king himself is believed to be endowed with khvarena, the sacred victory-giving glory that is dispensed by Mithra.[1145] The consecration of the Atash Bahram is conducted with a collection of the sixteen fires mentioned in the *Vendidad*, Ch.8. The hymns used for its consecration are mostly directed to Srosh, the assistant of Mithra[1146] and the guardian of all that is pure and sacred in the world. The sacred fire of the second grade is called Ātash Adarān, meaning fire of [different] fires, i.e. taken from the embers of the hearth fires of the various castes, priests, warriors, farmers and artisans.

However, the manner in which the divine Fire is transformed into the sun is not so clearly understood by the Iranians as it is by the Indo-Āryans. This is probably because the Zoroastrian priests ignore the role of Indra in the formation of the sun and in general abhor him and the devas as being responsible for the destruction of the perfect light of Ahura Mazda. In the litany, Khwarshed Niyayesh, we note that the Sun, which is associated with the solar Mithra, is described as being threatened by the daevas:

11. When the Sun warms with its light ... there stand the spiritual Yazads, a hundred and a thousand. They gather this glory. They bestow this glory upon the earth made by Ahura ...
13. If indeed the Sun were not to rise, then the daevas would kill all things that are in the seven regions. Not at all would the spiritual Yazads find support and stability in the material world ...
16. We sacrifice to the immortal, radiant, swift-horsed Sun, with milk provided with Hoama, with the Barsom [grass], with skill of tongue, and with the spell, and with word, and with deeds, and with libations, and with rightly spoken words.

The Sun itself is not associated with Atar in any clear manner.

The *Vendidad*, Ch.8, however, mentions 16 fires ranging ranging from the household fire and lightning to the life of plants, the life of human beings, the energy of the universe, and upto to the fires Burzen Mihr, Adar Gushnasp, Farnbag, and finally Adar Shaidan. Of these, the fire Farnbag is the "athravan" (priest) of the fires, the fire Gushnasp the warrior, and the fire Birzin Mihr the husbandman. "They are the protectors of the world until the renovation of the universe" (17). Thus Farnbag has the ritualistic

---

[1145] Sol Invictus takes the place of the Avestan khvarena in the later Mithraic religion. All the Roman emperors after Commodus assumed this title.

[1146] Cf. Mihir Yasht XXV (see Appendix, p.348 below).

eminence of Agni as the brāhmanical god among the Indo-Āryans. He is assisted by two other fires, representing the warrior and the peasant, in his protection of the world.

In the *Greater Bundahishn* Ch.XVIII, mention is made of five fires, the Berezi-savang, Vohufryan, Urvazisht, Vazisht (one of the sages in the Indian tradition), and Spenisht. The Berezi-savang is "the fire which glitters before Ohrmazd the Lord". The fire Spenisht is that which is lit in the material world. The Vohufryan is "that which is in the bodies of men and animals", the Urvazisht is that which is in plants, and Vazisht that which is in clouds. Of Spenisht, the three principal fires are Farnbag, Gushnasp and Burzin Mihr. Descriptions of the various fires worshipped by the Zoroastrians is given also in the *Greater Bundahishn*, Ch. VIG, where the fire Vasisht is said to facilitate the production of rain, and the fires Farnbag, Gushpasp and Burzin Mihr the protection of the world and the preservation of the creatures. Other fires such as those within the plants, men and beneficent animals maintain and increase the life of these species.

The *Greater Bundahishn* I,a describes the process whereby Ahura Mazda manifests himself materially. First he draws forth, from his own Endless Light, Fire, and then Ether (the Sky) out of Fire, Water out of Ether, and Earth out of Water. Then he produces "the Tree" (which corresponds to our universe proper), followed by "the Beneficent Animal" (the Cow) and "the Holy Man" (Gayomaretan/the First Man). The Fire derived from the Endless Light is called Khvarag (4).[1147]

The other principal feature of the Zoroastrian fire-rituals is its use and glorification of the Hoama (Vedic Soma) plant in them. Soma in the Vedic religion is, as we have seen, related to the force of the moon. In the *Bundahishn*, the seed of the Bull (representing all animal life)[1148] slaughtered by Angra Mainyu is purified and stored in the moon,[1149] just as the seed of the slaughtered First Man (representing all human life) is stored in the sun.[1150] The Bull is thus, in the *Greater Bundahishn*,[1151] likened to the shining Moon just as, in Egypt, the seed of Horus reappears on Seth's forehead as the moon, Thoth. Similarly the First Man is likened to the shining sun (where his seed will be purified). In the Litany to the

---

[1147] See above p.61.

[1148] The seed of the dead Bull stored in the moon is the same as the life of the universe preserved after the "deluge" by the first man, Yima/Ziusudra/Manu.

[1149] See *Bundahishn* X, 1-2; cf. *Fargard* XXI,9 and *Sirozah* I,12.

[1150] *Bundahishn* XV.

[1151] See RC. Zaehner, *op.cit.*, p.40.

Moon, the moon is apostrophised as that which "has the seed of the Bull, of the sole-created Bull, of cattle of all species" (9).

Haoma is considered by the Zoroastrians to be not only a source of virtue and immortality but also a destroyer of the Daevas (I,6) and the Dragon (Yasna 9), which is clearly a reference to the Vedic serpent Vrtra. But Vrtra is, as we have seen, in the Vedic literature, indeed identified with the moon itself on account of its seminal force.[1152] And Vrtra is destroyed by Indra, the chief of the devas. So here again we have a battle of Indra with his own power resembling the self-sacrifice of the Purusha.

In the Iranian Haoma-sacrifice too, Hoama is represented anthropomorphically, for the pressing of the soma plant in this sacrifice is represented as a slaying of a primal god, Haoma or his anthropomorphic form Duroasha (or Frashmi), in order to extract his productive essence.[1153] Hoama and Duraosha are thus equated to Prajāpati, which identification is evidenced also in the Indic *SB* XII,6,1,1, which declares that "Prajapati is the sacrifice, is King Soma", whose body is constituted of the several deities worshipped in the sacrifice. Duroasha is said to have been in existence even before Vivanghavant, the solar father of Yima.[1154] Duraosha is sacrificed so that the vital force of Soma may be expressed in the world. In the haoma-sacrifice, the pressing of the soma plant thus symbolises the extraction of the life-force of Haoma/Soma. Haoma is said to have been prepared for the corporeal world first by Vivanghavant [the sun], father of Yima (Hom Yast IX, 3f), secondly by Athwya, thirdly by Thrita [Vedic Trita Aptya], and fourthly by Pourushaspa, father of Zarathustra.

Haoma is considered a purifying element, since, according to the *Greater Bundahishn*, 11c, Ahura Mazda promised the waters to "create one (i.e. Zoroaster) who will pour *haoma* into you and cleanse you again." According to *Zatspram* (19.2-3), Zoroaster frequently made offerings to the waters, and even received his revelation on a riverbank while preparing *parahaoma* (*Zatspram* 21.1).

The Haoma plant serves as the main ingredient for the *parahaoma*, the consecrated liquid that constitutes the offering (*zaothra*) in the Zoroastrian yasna.[1155] Two independent preparations of *parahaoma* are made for the offering, both made between sunrise and noon. The first *parahaoma* is prepared during the preliminary rites (prior to the *Yasna*

[1152] See above p.82.

[1153] See E.O. James, *op.cit.*, p.26.

[1154] Yasna IX,17,27; X, 21; XLIII,5.

[1155] For a detailed description of the yasna see F.M.P. Kotwal and J.W. Boyd, *A Persian Offering*.

service) in which the site of worship is consecrated. The second *parahaoma* preparation occurs during the middle third of the *Yasna* service. The recipes for the two *parahaoma* preparations, though not identical, are largely the same. In both cases, the ingredients include three small *haoma* twigs; consecrated water; twigs and leaves from a pomegranate tree. The second *parahaoma* also includes milk (in Iran from a cow, in India from a goat). The consecration of the water and *haoma* (accompanied by ritual laving) also occurs during the preliminary rites.

First pressing: In the first *parahaoma*, which is prepared immediately prior to the *Yasna* service (during the preliminary ritual that also sanctifies the site of worship), the leaves or small twigs from the pomegranate tree are cut into pieces, and together with the consecrated *haoma* twigs and a little consecrated water are repeatedly pounded and strained. The liquid is retained in a bowl, while the twig and leaf residue is placed next to the fire to dry.

Second pressing: The second *parahaoma* preparation occurs during the middle third of the *Yasna* service. The preparation is accompanied by the chanting of Yasna 22-34. It is prepared by the celebrant priest of the *Yasna* and is essentially the same as the first, but includes milk, and is accompanied by even more pounding and straining. This second *parahaoma* preparation begins with the recitation of *Yasna* 22, and continues until the beginning of *Yasna* 28. During the recitation of *Yasna* 25, the priest dedicates the mixture to "the waters", which mirrors the purpose of the *parahaoma* preparation. The mortar remains untouched during the recitation of *Yasna* 28-30. Finally, during the recitation of *Yasna* 31-34, the priest pounds the mixture a last time and then strains the liquid into the bowl that also contains the first *parahaoma*. The twig and leaf residue from the second *parahaoma* is also placed next to the fire to dry.

Offering: Yasna 62 marks the beginning of the final stage of the *Yasna* service. At the beginning of the recitation of that chapter, the priest who made the first *parahaoma* moves the (now dry) twig and leaf residue from next to the fire into the fire itself. Although this is done at a specific point during the recitation of the liturgy, the burning of the residue is not an offering to the fire, but the ritually proper way to dispose of combustible consecrated material. The service then concludes with the recitation of *Yasna* 72, immediately after which the priest carries the mortar with *parahaoma* to a well or stream. There, in three pourings, libations are made to the waters, accompanied by invocations to Aredvi [old Iran. *Harahvatī, Skt. Sarasvati] Sura Anahita (Yasna 65) who "purifies the seed of men, and wombs of women, and women's milk". The remaining *parahaoma* in the two bowls is given to persons attending the ceremony. Since the liquid, in its ritually pure state, is considered beneficial, participants may choose to drink a little of it, or provide some to infants or the dying. The remainder is poured away on the roots of fruit-bearing trees. We note that the haoma is not offered into the fire but rather into water, in order to fecundate the primeval waters of the cosmos (Yasna 68,1).

XII.

THE HAMITES

When we move from the early Āryan sacrifices to the later temple-based cultures of Egypt and Mesopotamia we are struck both by the continuity of some of the motifs of the sacrificial cult in the temple rituals and by the differences in emphases between the two forms of religious practice. The Hamitic cultures are certainly later than the proto-Dravidian and Āryan cultures and dated by the *Bhavishya Purāna* to the Dvāpara Yuga.[1156] The *Mahānirvana Āgama* and the *Tārapradīpa*, however, maintain that the temple-worship prescribed in the Āgamas is characteristic of the Kaliyuga. So it is possible that, despite the great antiquity of the Hamites, the flowering of their culture coincided with the Kali Yuga. Following the *Sūrya Siddhānta*'s calculations of the Yugas, and the fifth century B.C. astronomer, Aryabhatta's assertion that he was twenty-three years old when 3,600 years of the present Kaliyuga had elapsed, the beginning of the Kaliyuga may be dated around 3100 B.C., which coincides with the high Hamitic cultures of Sumer and Egypt.[1157] However, the oldest temple in Mesopotamia, in Eridu dates back to the sixth millennium B.C., which period may be considered as belonging to the transitional period at the end of the Dvapara Yuga when both Vedic and Hamitic Āgamic traditions flourished.

The oldest Egyptian civilisation, which we may characterise as Hamitic, following the Bible and Malalas, is attested in the pottery of the area around Badari and Wadi Hammamat. This pottery bears decorations

---

[1156] See above p.142.

[1157] This means that this culture is around two million years later than the appearance of the seventh Manu in the Treta Yuga.

that are different in material, colour and subjects from that of the later "Armenoid", so-called "New Race" which appears in Egypt around 3200 B.C. Petrie identified the group around Wadi Hammamat as "Punites", or the people who came from Punt and worshipped Min of Coptos.[1158] Wilkinson however has recently claimed that the petroglyphs from the Badarian period (5000-4000 B.C.) indeed suggest that the origin of Egyptian civilization is to be found in the Eastern Desert itself.[1159] Wilkinson maintains that the people who made the petroglyphs were indigenous Badarians since their boat drawings are earlier[1160] than those of the Mesopotamians, whom Winkler had considered as the source of his hypothetical group of "Eastern Invaders".[1161] However, even though the Badarians may have been long settled in Egypt, it is possible that the Badarians were not originally native to Egypt since the "rippling" evidenced in their ceramic decorations bears a resemblance to that of the Palestianians.[1162] This Badarian or "Punite" race may have been the Hamitic branch of the proto-Dravidian/Hurrian race which first settled Elam as well as Anatolia and Palestine.[1163]

The fact that the Badarians were followers of the most ancient religion is clear from the importance given to depictions of the boat as a funerary vehicle, for the motif of the solar barque persists in Egypt throughout its recorded history and points to the solar cosmology that informs all the most ancient cultures that we are studying. The bovine imagery found in Anatolia is also noticed in the Eastern Desert petroglyphs.[1164] Further, the red crown typical of Lower Egypt is already evident in the petroglyphs[1165] and a depiction of the ithyphallic Min points to the earliest worship of Amun.[1166] The culture of the later dynastic Egyptians probably involved a fusion of the original Badarian with the so-called "New Race".

G.E. Smith, in the case of pre-dynastic Egyptians of Naga-ed-der and Giza, and W.M.F. Petrie, in the case of the Naqada "New Race" graves,

---

[1158] See W.M.F. Petrie and J.E. Quibell, *Naqada and Ballas*, p.59ff.

[1159] See T. Wilkinson, *Genesis of the Pharaohst*.

[1160] The pottery of Naqada I (4000-3600 B.C.) too reveals the same boat drawings that are found in the Eastern desert (see T. Wilkinson, *op.cit.*, p.69f.)

[1161] See S. Mercer, *op.cit.*, pp.5ff.

[1162] See *OEAG* III:63.

[1163] See above pp.108ff. G. Steindorf suggested that the Badarians were Hamites (see G. Steindorf, *Aniba*, I, p.2).

[1164] See T. Wilkinson, *op.cit.*, pp.99f.

[1165] *Ibid.*, pp.80f.

[1166] *Ibid.*, p.191.

have shown that the original founders of Egyptian civilization are to be distinguished from an incoming "Armenoid" race. Smith noticed the difference between the indigenous dolicephalic variety and the alien brachycephalic type both at Naga-ed-der near Abydos and Giza in the Delta, that is, both in Upper and Lower Egypt.[1167] This New Race was probably an Armenoid branch of the Indo-Europeans.[1168] They may have been characteristically brachycephalic, big boned and fair-skinned, whereas the Mediterraneans are dolicephalic, small boned and brown-skinned. The "Hamitic" founders of Egyptian as well as of Ubaid Sumer belonged to the earlier Mediterranean type.

Interestingly, the most common evidence of sacrificial victims in ancient Egypt are of retainers killed to accompany the dead pharaoh in his journey into the other world. The earliest instance of retainer sacrifice occurs from the Naqada II (Gerzean) period (ca. 3500-3200 B.C,), which coincides with the arrival of the Armenoid branch of the Indo-Europeans who acted as a stimulus to the high cultures of Sumer and Egypt.

The newcomers may possibly be related to the "Beaker" folk, who were widely dispersed in Europe as well as in North Africa in the late chalcolithic era (corresponding to Danube III, ca.2500 B.C.).[1169] The "Beaker" folk are brachycephalic[1170] and interred in a contracted position in graves aligned in a north-south axis rather than the east-west axis followed by the preceding Corded Ware folk.[1171] The beaker folk seem to have been effective traders as well as warriors, the graves of the latter being especially richly supplied with funerary goods.[1172] Cremations too were performed by this community and may have been reserved for the upper classes or castes, since cremations in Moravia are seen to be especially furnished with beakers.[1173] Though it is uncertain where this type originated, Childe believes that they too were of "East Mediterranean stock"[1174] Lahovary too placed their ultimate origin "in eastern

[1167] See G.E. Smith, *The Ancient Egyptians*.

[1168] The Indo-Europeans are traditionally divided into three branches, the Mediterranean, the Alpine and the Nordic. Of these, the Nordic, or Āryan, is represented by Japheth in the biblical Table of Nations. We see that the Indo-Europeans are not identical to the Āryans since they include the Alpine "Armenoid" type identifiable with the Uruk Sumerians.

[1169] See G. Childe, *Dawn*, pp.222-8; cf. R.J. Harrison, *The Beaker Folk*.

[1170] See K. Gerhardt, *Die Glockenbecherleute*; cf. R.J. Harrison, *op.cit.*, pp.160f.

[1171] See G. Childe, *op.cit*, p.226; cf. R.J. Harrison, *op.cit.*, p.51.

[1172] The Beaker folk seem also to have been associated with the ritual monuments of Britain including those at Stonehenge and Avebury (see R.J. Harrison, *op.cit.*, pp.94ff.).

[1173] *Ibid.*, p.55.

[1174] See G. Childe, *op. cit.*, p.227.

Anatolia".[1175] The Beaker folk may perhaps be more accurately identified with the Alpine or Armenoid branch of the Indo-Europeans.[1176]

This Armenoid type seems to have, already in the fourth millennium B.C., entered the Nile Delta from Palestine and Syria, but, as Petrie points out, the type is equally present in Libya and could have entered Egypt from the west as well. In fact, Petrie notices family resemblances between the "new race", as he calls them, and the Libyans, Palestinians, Amorites, as well as the earliest inhabitants of Mycenae, Cyprus and even central Italy. Crete in its Neolithic period seemed to Sir Arthur Evans to be "an insular offshoot of an extensive Anatolian province".[1177] The name of the legendary king Minos of Crete is cognate with Manu/Menes and this may be due to the arrival of the "Armenoid" Egyptians from the Delta, or from farther west, in Libya, in the period immediately following the Neolithic.[1178]

The arrival of the new race is dated by Petrie to around 3200 B.C., that is, the time of the Uruk culture, the rise of which is also, as we shall see, dependent on the infusion of newcomers into a more indigenous Mesopotamian society. As in Mesopotamia, the arrival of the "New Race" in Naqada coincides with the emergence of a greater complexity of social organisation.[1179]

In Mesopotamia, the Uruk culture (from ca. 3500 B.C.) is significantly different from the earlier Susaite culture of the Ubaid period, and we may detect the arrival of the Armenoid, proto-Alpine founders of Sumerian culture in this period. It must be noted also that the earliest Uruk tablets are from both Kish and Uruk proper,[1180] which suggests an extensive north-south migration of the new Sumerians. But the fact that the Sumerian king-list begins its postdiluvian section with the establishment of a kingdom at Kish in the north, which is more likely proto-

---

[1175] See N. Lahovary, op.cit., p.22. However, he suggests that they most probably moved to the British Isles from Iberia.

[1176] The Alpine type is said to have the same round skull as the Beaker folk except that it has a rounded occipital bone whereas the Beaker type has a flattened occipital bone (see R.J. Harrison, op.cit., p.160).

[1177] Quoted in G. Childe, Dawn, p.17. Evans also pointed out the similarities between the cod-pieces of the ancient Libyans and those of the early Bronze Age Minoans (see S. Hood, The Minoans, p.30f).

[1178] See G. Childe, op.cit., p.19; cf. Hesiod, Catalogues of Women and Eoiae, 74: "(Minos) who was most kingly of mortal kings and reigned over very many people dwelling round about, holding the sceptre of Zeus wherewith he ruled many."

[1179] See T. Wilkinson, Genesis, p.185.

[1180] See J. Bottero, Mesopotamia, p.70.

Dravidian and proto-Akkadian, suggests that the political ascendancy of the Sumerians in Uruk was a gradual one, beginning with political accomodation with the original inhabitants of the north and ending with a final establishment of independence at Uruk.

The cuneiform system of writing emerges in the Uruk period and is transmitted in a simplified form to Elam. That the Sumerians were clearly the founders of the system of notation and writing which developed in the south is made clear by the fact that only Sumerian has the phoneme-values required to make the word for Enlil intelligible.[1181] The first numerical tablets found at Uruk are from the Uruk IV period, whereas those in Elam date from the following Uruk III period,[1182] showing that the transmission of writing to Elam was relatively late. The earliest tablets also give evidence of a sexagesimal system of measurement along with four other systems varied according to the objects being measured,[1183] whereas the Elamites used mostly just the decimal system.[1184] The Sumerians seem to have been responsible for both the administrative excellence attested by their invention of writing and the urban civilisation that the Uruk culture, which begins Sumerian civilisation proper, represents.[1185]

A noteworthy difference that is evident between the Ubaid and Uruk cultures is their respective customs of interment, with the former favoring an extended posture of the corpse and the latter a flexed.[1186] We have noted that the Beaker folk of Europe also favoured this form of burial. It is to be noted that, while the skulls found in the graves of the Ubaid period are all dolicocephalic and "Mediterranean", those of the subsequent Uruk culture are mixed, showing at first a "predominance of brachycephali" which is gradually replaced by dolichocephali.[1187] The brachycephalic skulls of Ubaid signal an Armenoid race, belonging either to the Alpine physical type or to the Uralic,[1188] but the new race must have been assimilated into

---

[1181] *Ibid.*, p.80.

[1182] See H. Nissen, P. Damerow, R.K. Englund, *Archaic Bookkeeping*, p.5

[1183] Thus discrete objects were measured mostly in the sexagesimal system whereas land measures were recorded through the Gan2 system (*ibid.*, pp.27,43,138,131).

[1184] *Ibid.*, pp.93-5, pp.75-7.

[1185] See G. Algaze, *Uruk World-System*.

[1186] See J. Oates, "Ur and Eridu", p. 42; cf. the same flexed position in the Naqada graves studied by DeMorgan (see G.E. Smith, *op.cit.*, p.89)

[1187] See H. Frankfort, *op.cit.*, p.9. The recurrence of dolicephalic types suggests a successful absorption of the new brachycephalic type by the indigenous population.

[1188] It is possible to detect a mingling of proto-Āryan peoples with Ural-Altaic elements in a slightly later period, i.e., in the late Yamnaya culture (ca.2000 B.C.), which reveals a practice of skull deformation in infancy that was indulged in later, in the Iron Age, by the

the older population.

The language of the Sumerians may be a form of the original proto-Dravidian/Hurrian language modified by that of the new stock, either Alpine Indo-European or Uralic. The pictorial representations of the early Sumerians reveal markedly Anatolian, "Hittite" noses, and the Sumerian language, both the Main Dialect and Emesal, may have contributed to proto-Hittite itself.[1189] We have seen that the Cretan peoples too may have been related to the Anatolian and the Uruk Sumerians.[1190]

The Dravidians who settled in South India seem to be have been originally related to the Sumerians. In the Tamil *Kallatam* of the 10th century A.D., Skanda/Muruga, or Subrahmanya ('perfect brāhmanhood'),[1191] is said to have bestowed the Vedic knowledge on the sage Agastya, who then transmitted this wisdom to "South India" having crossed the "Vindhya" mountain range. It is possible that the sage Agastya (also called Maitravaruni since he was born of the Vedic gods Mitra-Varuna),[1192] is actually a reference to Akkad,[1193] and the transmission of Vedic wisdom to "South India" a modern rendering of the traditional memory of a migration of proto-Akkadians from northern Mesopotamia to the Uruk region of southern Mesopotamia. The reference to the "Vindhya" mountain range suggests that this immigration proceeded from a region north-east of Kish, since there are no high mountains south of Kish. The fact that Agastya is said to have crossed the "Vindhya" mountains in order to reach Uraga suggests that the Kish dynasties included the earliest peoples who arrived from farther north and these we have suggested may have been proto-Dravidian or Hurrian. The presence of a king with the Sanskrit-like name Ūsîwatar (possibly from (Skt.) vishva=universal) in the 13th dynasty (established at Kish) of the Sumerian king-list[1194] also points to a continuing proto-Indic element in the earliest royal lineage of Mesopotamia.

Mongoloid Huns (see J.P. Mallory and V.H. Mair, *Tarim Mummies*, p.239).

[1189] Cf., in this context, C. Autran, *Sumérien*, p.169: "sous le rapport langue, Sumer représente, en tout cas, l'un des éléments qui, en des temps fort anciens, ont concuouru à la formation de l'indo-européen, qu'il est, par suite, un temoin archaiaque de l'un des dialects pre-indo-européens essentiels".

[1190] See above p.264.

[1191] The name "Subrahmanya" is first attested in Sanskrit in the Baudhāyana Dharmashāstra (600-200 B.C.) and in Tamil in a poem by Cēntanār *Tiruvicaippa* II,3 (9th-10thc. A.D.)

[1192] *Brhaddevata* 30; *Rāmāyana* VII,57.

[1193] See above p.115. According to the Sumerian King-List, Akkad is said to have been founded by Ur-Zababa (see T. Jacobsen, *op. cit.*, p.111).

[1194] See T. Jacobsen, *ibid.*, p.109.

Agastya is said to have learned the "difficult language" of the Tamils from either Muruga or directly from Muruga's father Shiva.[1195] The reference in Kālidasa must therefore be to a time when the Uruk Sumerians (proto-Tamils) were still somewhat alien to the Akkadians. What is curious, however, is that the Vedic knowledge typically associated with the Āryans was itself conveyed to Agastya (Akkad) through the god of the Dravidians. Muruga himself is characterised by his affiliation with mountans and hunting, his typical weapon being the spear, 'vel'. According to Zvelebil, he represents "the Dravidian speakers who 'descended' from the mountains of Southern Iran (Zagros)."[1196] These Dravidians "finally moved eastward as well into the plains of southern Panjab, the Indus Valley, and finally "down south" throughout the peninsula".

The Dravidians of the ancient Near East may have been proto-Tamils as distinguished from the earlier proto-Dravidians. We have seen that the literary references to the sage Agastya and his spiritual instruction of the Tamils suggest that the proto-Tamils are related to the Sumerians of Uruk. Their contemporaneity with the Armenoid rulers of Uruk is suggested also by an episode in the Sanskrit poem of Kalidāsa (5th c. A.D.), *Raghuvamsha* (VI,59ff.) which refers to Agastya's being the officiating priest of a Pāndya (Tamil) king who is the contemporary of Aja (the grandfather of the Ikshvāku king Rāma), and to the capital of the Pāndya king as being not Madurai, as one would have expected if the scene were set in South India, but rather "Uraga",[1197] which seems to refer to the Sumerian Uruk itself, though this would push the origins of the Uruk dynasty to before the fourth millennium B.C., which traditionally marks the start of the Kali Yuga, since Rāma is said to have been born already at the beginning of the Treta Yuga.[1198] Whatever the chronology of the extant literature may be in relation to that of the Yugas, Aja himself seems to be represented in the Sumerian king-list as Aka,[1199] of the first dynasty of Kish, which preceded the foundation of Uruk. One of the extant Sumerian histories related to "Gilgamesh and Agga" too refers to the initial supremacy of Kish and the north under the king Agga, son of Enmebaraggesi, who demands the submission of Gilgamesh in Uruk.[1200]

[1195] See K. Zvelebil, *Tamil Traditions*, p.24.

[1196] *Ibid.*, p.79.

[1197] See G.S. Ghurye, *Indian Acculturation*, p.31.

[1198] See above p.142.

[1199] The "centum" quality of Sumerian is also evident in the Sumerian word for "eye", "igi", which is closer to the Germanic "Auge" than to the Sanskritic "aksha".

[1200] See J.B. Pritchard, *ANET*, pp.44-7. In the Sumerian King-List, Aka is a king of the

The first rulers of Kish may have been proto-Akkadians related to the Ikshvākus, since Ikshvāku itself seems to be identical to Akshak[1201] in the Sumerian King-List.[1202]

If the "solar" Ikshvāku dynasty of the Indian king-lists be representative of the Kish/Akshak civilisation, the other "lunar" dynasty derived from Manu's daughter Ilā, the Aila, may well denote Elam.[1203] These northern Mesopotamians and Elamites may have imparted their spiritual wisdom to the Sumerians of Uruk, whose political ascendancy seems to have been established in the south. Both the Aila [Elamite] and the Ikshvāku [Kish] dynasties are derived from Manu, the proto-Dravidian king (*BP*, VIII,24). If we were to draw up a tentative scheme of first beginnings, we may imagine Noah/Manu as representing an enlightened proto-Dravidian/Hurrian group which branched off into Semitic groups which flourished first in the northern and Elamite mountainous regions and later in northern Mesopotamia, while an Armenoid Indo-European group (perhaps related to proto-Tamil) spread first through north-westerly areas of the Near East and then entered Mesopotamia from the north to finally establish their political supremacy in Uruk.

The original Vedic system of esoteric wisdom elaborated by the proto-Hurrians/Dravidians may have been conveyed, through the mediation of proto-Akkadians, to the Armenoid-proto-Tamil group which had consolidated their power in Uruk as the so-called Sumerians. However, the fact that the historic evidence of the entrance of the modern Dravidians (whom we may call Tamils, to distinguish them from the proto-Dravidians) into South India is of relatively recent date, perhaps around the thirteenth century B.C., means that there are only a few dim hints of the Near Eastern origins of the Dravidian peoples in the earliest archaeology and literature of South India. Nevertheless Lahovary believed that the ancestors of the Dravidians emigrated from Mesopotamia to India already sometime in the course of the fourth millennium.[1204]

---

first dynasty (at Kish), though Gilgamesh follows apparently later in the second dynasty (at Uruk) after the fall of Kish (see T. Jacobsen, *op.cit.*, pp.85, 89-91).

[1201] Akshak was later called Upi (Gk. Opis) and may, like Kish, have been situated in the southern vicinity of modern Baghdad.

[1202] See T. Jacobsen, *Sumerian King-List.*, p.107. The first king of Akshak is recorded in the King-List as Unzi, though there was perhaps an earlier ruler called Zuzu (*ibid.*, p.181), who is the only historically verifiable king of Akshak. The first Akshak dynasty may have ended by 3400 B.C. (see *RLA* I:64).

[1203] It may be noted, in passing, that the Edda ('The Deluding of Gylfi') too records the first human beings as a girl called Embla and a boy called Ask.

[1204] See N. Lahovary, *op.cit.*, p.16.

Lahovary also notes the important linguistic fact that central and western Dravidian, such as Kannada and Telugu, seem to have remained closer to Basque and the ancient non-Aryan languages of southern Europe than Tamil and Malayalam. "At the same time, lexical and even morphological corresondences with Semitic have been retained in several central Dravidian idioms which are lacking in South Dravidian",[1205] which confirms the north-south route of the Dravidian migration into India, and dismisses any theories of an indigenous Indian origin of the Dravidians.

The Tamil tradition of the arrival of Agastya in the Tamil lands is that the sage Agastya first travelled to the Ganges and obtained from her the river Kaveri to irrigate the south of India.[1206] Then he went to Rishi Jamadagni[1207] and got from him his son Trnadhumagni and from Rishi Pulastya his sister Lopamudra and together they travelled to Dvaraka where he collected eighteen of the ruling Vaishnavite Vrshni family as well as the classes called Velir and Aruvalar. Accompanied by these immigrants, he moved south clearing the forests of the south and settling in Podiyil in the south of the Western Ghats. Trnadhumagni was later called Tolkappiyar and wrote the famous grammar called *Tolkappiyam*.

The Buddhist traditional literature maintains that Agastya travelled to the Tamil country (the kingdom of Damila) and settled in Kaveripattana, the capital of the Cholas the the mouth of the Kaveri. According to the Buddhistic work *Manimekalai*, Agastya carried the water that later flowed as the Kaveri in his water-vessel and let the water flow as a river at the request of the Chola king Kandama in the capital Kaveripattanam. The work also refers to Agastya as "the ascetic of rare austerity of the Malaya". This may be a reference to the Podiyil hill in the Brahmanical literature about Agastya, and ultimately back to the Armenian Mt. Ararat associated with Manu, who also is said to have practised austerities on the same Mt. Malaya.[1208]

The earliest archaeological evidence (ca. 1200-80 B.C.) of the entrance of the Tamils into South India is from dolmen burial sites in Adichanallur (similar to those in Palestine and Cyprus), where some of the finds such as golden "mouth-pieces", bronze representations of cocks and spear-heads may be related to the worship of Muruga/Marduk/Ninurta.[1209] The megalithic graves of the Madurai district dating from around 1000 B.C.

[1205] *Ibid.*, p.372.

[1206] See S. K. Aiyangar, *Some Contributions*, Ch.II.

[1207] Jamadagni is a descendant of the sage Bhrigu.

[1208] See above p.145.

[1209] See K. Zvelebil, *op.cit.*, p. 75f.

also reveal resemblances to the early Iron Age graves of the Caucasus and Sialk Necropolis B.[1210]

The Dravidians of South India seem to have been principally characterised by their Shaivite devotion to Muruga. The earliest textual references to Muruga from the Dravidian Sangam literature of the first three or four centuries A.D. bear witness to a Dionysiac god who is capable of infusing women with love-sickness and possessing his devotees in a frenzy.[1211] In the Tamil lexicon, *Tivakaram*, dating from the 8th century A.D., we find a full-fledged religion of Muruga/Marduk among the Tamils since it lists all the titles of the god.[1212]

[1210] See B. and R. Allchin, *op.cit.*, p.230.

[1211] See K. Zvelebil, *op.cit.*, p.78.

[1212] *Ibid.*, p.73.

XIII.

EGYPTIAN RITUALS

The Hamitic religious tradition centred on temple worship was originally not accepted as orthodox by the Āryans who followed the Vedic tradition. The *Manusmriti* (III,152) records the aversion of the Āryan brāhmans to the temple priests who followed the Āgamic tradition: "Doctors, temple-priests, meat-sellers and such should be excluded from the sacrifices to the gods and manes". Heesterman has noted the relative lack of importance of the priestly office in ancient Greece and Iran too.[1213] He attributes the rise of the priesthood to the development of the temple cults in the ancient Near East. In ancient Iran, the development of the priestly estate was probably due to the imperial patronage which developed the cult of the fire-temple. Cyrus the Great is credited with having organised the magi.

In general, the Āgamic, or Tantric, tradition is considered as characteristic of the present degenerate age, Kaliyuga. The *Mahānirvāna Āgama* and other Āgamas state that Smriti and Purāna were predominant in the Treta and Dvāpara ages respectively while the Tantra is principal in the Kaliyuga. Similarly the *Tārapradīpa*, Ch.1, says that in the Kaliyuga the Tantrika and not the Vaidika Dharma is to be followed. In the Satya (Krita) age Vaidika Upasana [meditation on the Vedas] prevailed. In the Dvāpara there were both Smriti and Purāna. The Tantra Shastra was taught at the end of Dvāpara and the beginning of Kaliyuga.

However, the temple traditions were also derived from the Vedic. Indeed the foundations of the temples of Uruk are said to have been laid by the "Seven Sages" themselves in the *Epic of Gilgamesh*, I. And the

---

[1213] J.C. Heesterman, *Broken World*, p.184.

temple rituals are based on the same cosmological understanding that informs the Vedic fire-rituals. The temples were built according to divine geometric plans. They symbolised the Primeval Hill and the pyramids which were introduced in the Third Dynasty of Egypt and modified in the Fourth Dynasty were the Heliopolitan version of this Hill.[1214] According to the solar significance of all religious worship in Egypt, the foundation of the temple too was laid at night by the king.[1215] He oriented the axis of the temple following the position of the Great Bear. After the foundation-stone was laid, the sanctuary of Ra and the other divine statues in the temple were consecrated with fire by the king. The king was thus clearly the life of the temple as well as of the entire land.[1216] As Sauneron noted, the kings' earthly responsibility was "To maintain the universal order, assuring the divine religion and giving its laws to men".[1217] Priests performed religous rituals only in lieu of the king and always in his name.[1218] Since the statue housed in the sanctuary of the temple was believed to be an incarnation of the deity, it was necessary for the priests to undergo ritual purifications before assuming their religious role, including the shaving of their bodily hair and the hair on their head, as well as circumcision.[1219] There seem to have been at least four classes of priests led by a high priest who, in Thebes, was called "the first prophet of Amon in Thebes".[1220] Those who took care of the temple and its statues were called by the Greeks 'stolists', which term may correspond to the Egyptian 'chendjouty' or the 'priest of the private clothing'.[1221] Other officiants included scribes, astrologers and interpreters of dreams.[1222]

The significance of re-birth in the Āryan fire-rituals, further, underlies the temple rituals of the Hamitic peoples as well. As many scholars have suggested,[1223] the funeral of the dead king observed as the re-enactment of the Osiris myth, and the celebration of the dead king's rise as the sun,

---

[1214]   See H. Frankfort, *op.cit.*, p.152f. At Hermopolis, the Primeval Hill was conceived of as an island, the Isle of Flames, that stood in a lake (p.154).

[1215]   See A. Moret, *Du caractère religieux*, pp.131ff.

[1216]   *Ibid.*, p.176.

[1217]   S. Sauneron, *The priests of ancient Egypt*, p.33.

[1218]   A. Moret, *op.cit.*, p.179.

[1219]   S. Sauneron, *op.cit.* p.37.

[1220]   *Ibid.*, p.61.

[1221]   *Ibid.*, p.63.

[1222]   *Ibid.*, pp.63-71.

[1223]   See, for instance, A. Moret, *op.cit.*; H. Frankfort, *Kingship and the Gods*, Ch.10, J. Ste. Garnot, *L'hommage aux dieux*, Première partie, Ch. second; J. Assmann, *Aegypten*.

were essentially the same ceremony as that performed in the induction of cult images in Egypt.[1224] Before the coronation of the new king the dead king was worshipped as the dormant Osiris who would be resurrected as Horus the Younger.[1225] The essential aspect of this identification was the revival of the solar force in Osiris. When Osiris died, his soul took refuge in the Eye of Horus but Seth attacked this too and this is the explanation of eclipses and the daily setting of the sun.[1226] However through sacrifice, the eye is recovered, as PT 179 suggests:

> What thou [the dead king] hast eaten is an eye; thy body becomes filled with it.
> Thy son Horus separates himself from it for thee so that thou mayest live thereby ...[1227]

The resurrection of the dead king is represented as the rise of the sun in PT 920b-923:[1228]

> Pepi [the dead king] ascends to Heaven.
> Pepi embarks on this boat of Re.
> Pepi commands for him (Re) those gods who row him.
> All the gods are jubilant at the approach of Pepi,
> Just as they are at the approach of Re,
> When he emerges at the Eastern side of Heaven,
> In peace, in peace ...

It is as Horus the Younger that the new king recalls Osiris to life after the death of the old king. The new king's coronation was indeed a celebration of the solar resurrection, as PT 752-64 declares:[1229]

> Thy son stands (as a king) on thy throne, equipped with thy aspect, and does what thou wert formerly accustomed to do at the head of the living, by order of Re the Great God and his enthronement

---

[1224] It is not surprising that Egyptian temples were called "eternal horizons" and tombs "houses of eternity" (see A. Moret, op.cit., p.186).

[1225] For an interesting account of the funeral and coronation rites, as well as of the sacred drama depicting the solar transformation of Osiris into Horus that was enacted before the coronation according to the Memphite theology, see H. Frankfort, op.cit., Chs.10,11.

[1226] See A. Moret, op.cit., p.157.

[1227] See H. Frankfort, Kingship, p.112.

[1228] Ibid., p.118.

[1229] Ibid., p.113.

represented an "apparition" of the solar force,[1230] first as lord of Upper Egypt (representing Heaven) and then as lord of Lower Egypt (representing Earth).[1231] The order of the consecration ritual in the Theban period began with the purification, anointment and presentation of the king to the gods. Then the ruling king or the god presented the king to the courtiers, and the crowns of Upper Egypt and Lower Egypt were received by the new king from the hands of the god. Finally the king made donations to the gods.[1232]

The consecration of the pharaoh was followed by regular reenactments of some of its rituals during the Opet festival, which ensured the continued flourishing of the royal "ka" which granted the king his divinity. The Sed festival was a royal jubilee celebrated normally after thirty years of a pharaoh's reign during which the king renewed his rule of the two kingdoms of Upper Egypt denoting Heaven and Lower Egypt denoting Earth. In the second major ritual of the Sed festival, the king ran across a field along the two axes formed by the cardinal points.[1233] The text declares:

> He runs crossing the ocean and the four sides of Heaven, going as far as the rays of the sun-disk, passing on the Earth, giving the field to its mistress.[1234]

This is clearly a dramatisation of the sun's majestic course through the universe which the king imitates in a country combining, as it were, Heaven and Earth. At the end of the ceremony the king shoots an arrow to each of the four cardinal points and he is enthroned four times.

From the Old Kingdom onwards, the kings of Egypt had statues of themselves erected which were preserved in special places until their death and, on the death of a king, his statue was taken by the priests into a special shrine to serve as the statue of Osiris. As in Sumer, the statue was considered as a living being that is "born".[1235] After seventeen days of

---

[1230] The same expression was used for the appearance of the pharaoh at public functions and for sunrise (see H. Frankfort, *op.cit.*, p.148).

[1231] See W. Barta, "Untersuchungen", pp.47,49; cf. p.69 above.

[1232] See A. Moret, *Du caractère religieux*, p.76.

[1233] This is similar to the chariot race run during the royal consecration in ancient India (see above p.235).

[1234] See H. Kees, *ZÄS* LII, 68ff; cf. H. Frankfort, *op.cit.*, p.86.

[1235] See E. Otto, *Mundöffnungsritual*, II, p.30, p.35f.

embalming and burial rituals for the king, the statue underwent a mouth- and eye-opening ritual during which it was transformed into the son of Osiris, Horus, the living sun-god.

The rituals related to the installation and worship of deities in temples are closely related to the consecration of the king. It should be noted, however, that, in pre-dynastic times, the ritual of vivification of statues seems to have been limited to divine statues and not to royal ones.[1236] However, the divinisation of kings that became characteristic later on is certainly of great antiquity, and indeed the worship of the gods was itself generally led by the king and only deputed to priests since he could not personally officiate at all the temple rituals conducted throughout his kingdom.

The image was an iconic incarnation of the solar deity and the priests, as Sauneron pointed out, sought "to preserve, infused in a statue, a part of the divine all-powerful, visible even in life and in the movements of the universe".[1237] The installation of the image of a deity in an Egyptian temple involving "the opening of the mouth and eyes" of the image is first attested from the Old Kingdom in the tomb of Metjen, an official of the fourth Dynasty (ca. 2600 B.C.) A fragment from the sun-temple built by Nyuserre of the fifth Dynasty (ca. 2400 B.C.) also refers to the "fashioning and opening of the mouth". It may be noted that the forked blade called "peseshkaf" used in this ritual seems to derive from the forked flint blades found in the Badarian period (5000-4000 B.C.).[1238]

The earliest documentary evidence of the ritual, however, is that of the ritual of Amun-Re in Pap. Berlin 3055 (Dynasty XXII, ca.945-730 B.C.).[1239] The ritual is also well observed in the grave of Rekhmire (TT 100).[1240] In Egypt, more clearly than in Sumer or India, we see the original solar significance of the rites of the Indo-Europeans since they are clearly dramatisations of the death and resurrection of Osiris. The ritual of mouth- and eye-opening takes place in the workshop. Even as the statute is being cut out of the stone-block the priest enacts the role of Osiris/ the rising Horus by first assuming a "sleep" in which he "sees" his father

---

[1236] *Ibid.*, p.1.

[1237] See S. Sauneron, *The Priests of Ancient Egypt*, p.90.

[1238] Such as, for instance, UC 10244; see above p.262.

[1239] See H. Roeder, "Mundöffnung", p.36; cf. D. Lorton, "The theology of cult statues", p.131.

[1240] See N. de G. Davies, *The Tomb of Rekh-mi-Re'*. Mouth-opening was performed on mummies as well as on statues, and mummies were dressed and fed after vivification just as divine statues were (see A. Moret, *op.cit.*, p.164).

in all his forms.[1241] This is clearly the inspiration for the sculpted statue. After the finished statue is washed with water, natron and incense, a bull representing Seth is slaughtered and the 'sem' priest presents the statue with the foreleg and heart of the slaughtered bull. The priest declares while doing this: "Accept the one who has damaged your Horus eye [the sun]; I bring you his heart".[1242] The fore-leg of the bull [imbued with still warm vital energy][1243] represents the regenerative force [perhaps even a phallic one],[1244] while the heart represents intelligence or self-consciousness [ātman]. The mouth is then touched with the thigh of the bull, the priest declaring: "I have opened your mouth with that which damaged your Horus eye".[1245] The mouth is also touched with several artisan's implements, when the priest comments that it is the "ore that emerged from Seth, the adze of iron-ore".[1246] One implement that was particularly important was the netjerty, another name for the peseshkaf[1247] derived from the word "netjer" meaning "god".[1248] Finally, the mouth is touched with the little finger of the sem priest himself. The priest clearly acts the role of Horus, for he says, "Who has smitten my father?"

After the mouth-opening, the statue is decked in royal clothes and insignia as part of its investiture. In the dressing process, nine or ten types of cosmetics and oils were applied to the face and eyes of the statue to give it a good complexion and fragrance and then endowed with sceptres and the double crown.[1249] When the statue is crowned, it is made to undertake its solar circuit through the universe.[1250] Then it is purified with incense and other libations as part of its divinisation. The perfume in particular is supposed to bind the statue (or the personality that it represents) with the gods, while the libations serve to quicken its limbs.[1251] Finally, it is fed

---

[1241]   See H.W. Fischer-Elfert, *Die Vision von der Statue*, p.7.

[1242]   See H. Roeder, *op. cit.*, p.49.

[1243]   *Ibid.*, p.64n.

[1244]   Cf. the use of "thigh" for the procreative power in *Gen.* 46:26, *Ex.* 1:5, *Judges* 8:30.

[1245]   *Ibid.*, p.50.

[1246]   *Ibid.*, p.51.

[1247]   The peseshkaf itself is used in real life to cut the umbilical cord, which emphasises the birthing process that the statue undergoes (see A.M. Roth, "Fingers, stars and the 'opening of the mouth'").

[1248]   The term "netjer" is in all probability related to the Sanskritic word, "nakshatra", for "star".

[1249]   See A. Moret, *op.cit.*, p.166.

[1250]   *Ibid.*, p.162.

[1251]   See H. Roeder, *op. cit.*, p.41f.

by the king and then installed in the naos, or shrine, which is the darkest room in the temple. According to E. Otto, a final litany was added later at the end of the ritual to identify the statue now as the "Horus-eye".[1252]

In the daily ritual of awakening the god, which repeats that which infuses life into the statue in the workshop where it was formed, the sleeping god stands for the dead Osiris.[1253] The priest first enters the cella and lights a fresh fire. It must be noted, however, that in ancient Egypt the religious ceremonies were normally performed only by the pharaoh, who alone could enter the sanctum. A high priest could do so only if delegated by the pharaoh. The priest thus entered with bowed head (whereas the pharaoh entered upright) and with his hand before his mouth indicating subservient respect.[1254] The statue is awakened by letting in the light by opening the double door of the shrine. The moment the sun reached the horizon, the face of the god was unveiled since the cult statue, like the sun which it incarnates, is now being reborn. The priest says "I bring you your heart in your body, set in its place, as Isis brought the heart of her son Horus to him, set in its place, and vice-versa, and as Thoth brought the heart of Nesret to her..." We have already noted the significance of the heart in these rituals. This dependence of the Egyptian rituals on the solar cosmology is perhaps an indication of the greater antiquity of the Egyptian compared to the Indian temple culture, since the patterns of "archana" of the latter do not reveal this relationship so clearly.[1255] The statue is then anointed with honey: "it binds for him [Amun] his bones, it joins for him his limbs", which is a reference to the dismembered body of Osiris as well as to the materials of which the image was made. Then the god's ba (manifesting virtue) and sekhem (power) are infused into it. Then Maat infuses its ka (vital force) into it: "she places her arms around you, so that your ka will exist through her, your daughter, having formed you and you having formed her". Then there are references to the opening of the mouth: "You open your mouth that you might speak with it".

After the deity has been aroused from its "sleep", it is washed, anointed, clothed and fed. The water for the purificatory rites is taken from a sacred well like the abzu in the Sumerian temples. The anointing of the forehead of the statute with fragrant oils symbolises the formal infusion of divinity into it. After a libation offering, the statue is replaced

---

[1252] See H.W. Fischer-Elfert, *op. cit.*, p.7.

[1253] See A. Moret, *op.cit.*, p.157.

[1254] This rule seems to have been observed in Mesopotamian temples as well, as the evidence of the Babylonian Hammurabi stele suggests.

[1255] See below p.302.

in the naos and the priest closes the doors of the naos. The priest then leaves, walking backwards and sweeping away his footprints as he does so.

The morning service was followed by services at mid-day, when the sun was at its zenith, and in the evening, when it set.[1256] Other protective rituals were performed throughout the day in order to repel the dangers posed to the solar deity by Seth, the murderer of Osiris, or the serpent Apop who opposes the solar force Re. Indeed these rituals were performed mainly to sustain the solar force as represented by Re and Osiris. Every four or five days, the statue of the god was taken out in a procession through the village placed in a ship representing the solar barque and carried on the shoulders of priests. During this ceremony the common people had an opportunity to approach the statue for oracular signs that would help to allay their various distresses.[1257]

[1256] See S. Sauneron, *The Priest of Ancient Egypt*, p.88.

[1257] *Ibid.*, pp.90-96.

XIV.

MESOPOTAMIAN RITUALS

I n the Sumerian tradition, the first temple was in Eridu (6th millennium B.C.) and dedicated to Enki (Akkadian Ea). In the Hymn to Nanna in UET VI/1 67 we learn that Enki, as the lord of the sweet waters of the abzu, is the source of all purity in the temple. The text mentions the washing and anointing of the statue of Nanna in the abzu room.

In the early stages of the Mesopotamian temple cult, according to S.H. Hooke, "the place where the image of the god was housed and the priest was consulted might be a very small and humble affair, indeed nothing more than a mud and reed hut. We have a representation of such a simple shrine on the well-known pictographic tablet from Kish".[1258] The significance of reed as the material of which the ship of life is made has been noted above and we remember that the latter is symbolic of Earth itself.[1259] The Keš temple hymn describes the temple as a representation of the universe itself:

> Temple, whose platform is suspended from heaven's midst,
> Whose foundation fills the Abzu,
> Whose shadow covers all the lands.[1260]

[1258] See S.H. Hooke, *Babylonian and Assyrian Religion*, p.47.

[1259] See above p.138.

[1260] See A.W. Sjoberg and E.W. Bergman, *Sumerian Temple Hymns*, p.176.

Later arose temple complexes with many structures for different deities. The Akitu was a special temple used for the New Year Festival.[1261] Within the Sumerian temple were three important sacred areas, the adytum, or the sanctuary wherein the statue of the deity was installed, the abzu, which must have been a temple tank for purificatory purposes, and the du-ku or holy mound, which represents the primordial phallic mountain from which the sun emerges. In the bilingual text VR50 and 51 for instance, the sun-god Shamash is addressed thus:

> Shamash, when you come out of the great mountain,
> When you come out of the great mountain, the mountain of the springs,
> When you come out of the *duku* where fates are determined,
> When you come out of the [place] where heaven and earth are connected,
> from the foundation of heaven to [this] place.
> The great gods will present themselves before you for judgement,
> The Anunnaki will present themselves to you for decisions.[1262]

The tower of the Sumerian temple took the form of a stepped pyramid like the Dravidian gopuram, and the ziggurat of the temple at Eridu, Eunir, is said to have "grown high [uniting] heaven and earth". The ziggurat at Ur had trees planted on it to make it resemble a "mountain". So it is clear that the ziggurat represents the mountain from which the sun emerges. As in India, where the shikhara is considered the font of the gods, the Sumerian temple is also referred to as "the place where the gods began their life". In the *Poem of Erra*, I,150, the Sumerian mešu tree is called the "flesh of the gods". Indeed the Sumerian term for god, 'dingir', whose cuneiform form is an ideogram for the sky-god, An, may be related to the Indic "deva" which also originally referred to shining celestial forces. The mešu tree is a symbol of Ninurta who, in *Lugal e* (I,310), is called "the great meš tree". Since the tree represents Earth, it is not surprising that the name Ninurta itself means "lord of Earth". Indra too, as we have seen, is identified with the ashvattha tree,[1263] and is equally a phallic figure.

The first ziggurat temple is evidenced in the Ur III dynasty (21st century B.C.) in the Nanna Ekishnugal temple in Ur. The ziggurat represents the "heavenly mount" "whose peak reaches the heavens, whose

---

[1261]   See S. H. Hooke, *op. cit.*, p.48.

[1262]   See E. Jan Wilson, "Inside a Sumerian temple".

[1263]   See above p.81.

foundation is based in the clear abzu" (Hymn to Bel).[1264] We know that
Enlil was often called "Kurgal" meaning "the great mountain", just as Shiva
too was called Parvatha (Mountain) and his consort Pārvathi. That this
ziggurat is identical to the phallic Tree of Life as well is made clear by the
Gudea cylinder (A XXI, 22) which declares that the temple is erected "like
the gishgana tree of the abzu".[1265]

The ziggurat of Babylon, the Etemenanki, had seven stages perhaps
representing the seven "continents" of the Iranian cosmology or "islands"
of the Indian which stand for the planets into which Earth is divided.[1266]
The Uruk temple itself was constructed with seven inner divisions
representing the same seven "continents" or "islands". Uruk too is, with
the same religious symbolism, called a city with seven constituent parts.[1267]
"Sumer" is also probably the name of the "primordial hill" of the central
island of Earth through which the solar force of the universe emerges
since Sumer is called "the great mountain, the land of the universe" in
Enki and the World-Order, l.192. Indeed, in India, Sumeru ('Holy Meru')
is a name of the Mt. Meru in BrdP I,ii,15,42.[1268]

As in India, the temple is built on a "mandala", as the following
instruction makes clear: "Hast du einen Tempel zu bauen, so beginnst
du zur Zeit des Neujahrsfests … vor Sonnenaufgang zeichnest du den
Grundriß des Tempels auf den Erdboden."[1269] The colouring of the temple
structure also followed the sacred tricolor pattern of white, red and
black representing the sattvic, rājasic and tāmasic energies among the
Indians.[1270]

In Assyia, the king presided over the construction and reconstruction
of temples.[1271] The foundation of temples was especially important and the
king cast the first brick. When the temple was finished, the king blessed
the temple and the whole country that it symbolises. The king then invited
the god in the form of his statue to enter the temple. The god was married

---

[1264] Ibid, p.59.

[1265] Ibid., p.62.

[1266] See above pp.46,143.

[1267] See K.-H. Golzio, op.cit., p.19f.

[1268] The names of the other lands around Sumer – Ur, Meluhha, Dilmun, Elam-Marhasi, and Martu – which Enki blesses in the poem of "Enki and the World-Order" may have similar cosmological significances.

[1269] See A. Schott, "Das Werden", p.305 (cf. Herodotus, I, 98, on the temple of Ecbatana).

[1270] This was noted, for example, in the excavations of the temple tower of Dur-Sarrukin (see A. Jeremias, Handbuch, p.178; cf. p.150n above).

[1271] See R. Labat, op.cit, Ch.III.

to his consort-deity and installed in the temple along with other members of his family and retinue. All Assyrian kings were considered the son of some deity and therefore of divine race, and their presence in the palace was as esoteric as that of the deity in the temple.[1272]

In the early period of the city-states, the city ruler, ensi (Akk. ishshakku) exercised the double function of priest-king, whereas later the priestly function, that of the urigallu, became detached from the stately.[1273] This priority of the ensi is similar to that of the pharaoh in Egypt, who alone could enter the sanctum of the temple with upright head.[1274] In Assyria too, according to an Assyrian ritual text (VAT 10112, KAR 146), it was the king who fed the gods, and this custom may have been derived from Sumerian tradition.[1275] There were in Babylon and Assyria, three kinds of priests, kalû priests (responsible for the musical services), mashmashu/ishippu (responsible for the rituals and incantations) and bārû (who served as seers and advisors to the king).[1276] The king often performed the role of ishippu priest.[1277] As in Egypt and India, the temple idol of the deity seems to have served as a representation of the sun, whose birth and life are sustained by the temple priests. The temple rituals were numerous and were divided into daily, monthly and annual ceremonies.[1278] The annual festivals included that of the New Year and the divine marriage. In addition there were rites related to the Lunar Eclipse and the consecration of the kettle-drum.

All temples excavated in Assyria and Babylon "possessed a central court and a cella or chamber in which there was a niche and pedestal for the statue of the god".[1279] The most important element in the temple was of course the idol of the deity. The idol was first "created" and then "infused with life" in a "mis pi" or mouth-washing (mis-pi) ritual followed, on the second day, by a mouth-opening (pit-pi) and eye-opening ceremony.[1280]

[1272] Ibid., p.364.

[1273] See S.H. Hooke, op.cit., p.50.

[1274] See above p.275.

[1275] See R. Labat, op.cit., p.139.

[1276] The bārû priests correspond most closely to the brahman priests in India, while the kalû correspond to the udgātr and the mashmashu to the adhvaryu priests (see above p.249).

[1277] See R. Labat, op.cit., pp.143,147.

[1278] For a comprehensive survey of the temple rituals see M.J.H. Linssen, The Cults of Uruk and Babylon.

[1279] See S.H. Hooke, op.cit., p.48.

[1280] Although the mouth-washing rituals are attested from Neo-Sumerian times and the

The statue is considered to be born in the temple workshop. As C. Walker and M.B. Dick point out, "In fact, the Sumerian title of the ritual, 'For washing the mouth' may allude to the action of the midwife as she cleanses and opens the breathing passage of the newborn at birth."[1281] The ceremony is constituted of three stages, of which the first is a pre-liminal stage in which the statue is physically isolated from both the temple workshop (bit mummi) and the human workers who crafted it. This separation, which takes place at sunset, will enable its rebirth as a god the following morning. In the second, liminal, stage, the statue undergoes its divine gestation. The womb-like tamarisk trough is filled with the river's fructifying "semen". The tamarisk trough is placed on the bricks of the Birth-goddess.[1282] The invocation of sets of nine deities recalls the nine months of gestation.

The image is then taken to the river, representing the watery domain of Ea and presented to its "father" Ea and integrated into the community of gods. Then it is taken to an orchard with a magical circle of reed huts and tents. The image is placed on a reed-mat looking towards the sunrise. This marks the end of the first day's rites, during which twelve mouth-washings are administered to the idol.

On the second day, the idols of Ea, Šamaš, and Asarluhi (Marduk), all representing the solar force, are placed on the thrones in the reed-huts and they are requested to activate the vital functions of the idol. Special care is taken to emphasise the fact that the god was not made by human beings and the craftsmen's hands are indeed symbolically "cut off" to prove this. The origin of the statue's wood is considered to be the Tree of Life itself. At this juncture, the rituals called pit-pi, or mouth-opening, and eye-opening, take place. While the mouth-washing ceremonies are designed for the purification of the idol from contamination, the mouth-opening ceremony is to activate its vital functions. Thus it is stated that a statue that has not had its mouth opened "does not smell incense, does not eat food and does not drink water".[1283] Mouth-opening was normally performed with syrup, ghee, cedar and cypresses, sometimes even salt or flour.[1284] The priests in charge of the mouth-washing ceremony and other

mouth-opening rituals from Middle-Babylonian times, it is possible, as Berlejung suggests, that they date from an earlier period since the incantations are written in Sumerian (see A. Berlejung, "Washing the mouth", p.48).

[1281] See C. Walker and M.B. Dick, "Induction", p.68.

[1282] The brick is the brick structure in which a woman lay for her labour (see W. Lambert and A.R. Millard, *Atrahasis*, p.153).

[1283] Incantation (tablet 3), in C. Walker and M.B. Dick, *op.cit*. p.70.

[1284] See *RLA* X, 'Pit pi and Mïs pi', p.580.

purificatory rituals were the ishippu priests. The king too often assumed this role in Assyria.[1285]

It is important to note that, as Berlejung points out, in the 'washing of the mouth' and 'opening of the mouth' rituals, "the first stage of the ritual is dominated by the presence of Ea,[1286] while the second stage shows Šamaš[1287] involved to a far greater extent".[1288] This reinforces the impression that all the temple-idols essentially represent the solar deity that was born in the Abyss.

In the third, post-liminal stage, the statue, which has now been reborn as a god, is reintroduced into the temple, as if it were a new-born child, as the directions to the priests reveal:

> You take the hand of the god and the incantation "The feet sprinting over the ground, the feet sprinting over the ground" [and] the incantation "As he walked through the street" all the way to that god's temple you recite. At the door of that god's temple you make an offering. You take the god's hand and make him enter ...[1289]

The priest is instructed to take the hand of the god and first introduce him to his father Ea, as well as to the other gods, his brothers. Then the god is made to enter the temple and is seated in his cella, from where it will rule as the bond between heaven and earth. The statue is finally purified with water from the trough and its garments, jewellery and divine paraphernalia are presented to it at night.

Apart from being awoken daily and fed with meals, the image was also taken out of the temple on special festival days and paraded through the city and countryside.[1290] A damaged statute was considered a dead god and its successful repair and mouth-washing were equivalent to a resurrection. A statue that could not be repaired was wrapped in a linen cloth along with some precious metals and thrown into the river, where it returned to its father Ea. Apart from these rituals, the Sumerian temple traditions also included a rite wherein the supplicant took the hand of

---

[1285] See R. Labat, op.cit., p.145.

[1286] Ea corresponds to Osiris and Varuna/Agni.

[1287] Šamaš corresponds to Horus the Younger, Āditya/Sūrya.

[1288] A. Berlejung, The Image and the Book, p.50.

[1289] See C. Walker and M.B. Dick, op.cit., p.83.

[1290] See S. Pollock, Ancient Mesopotamia, p.187.

the deity of a particular temple. This is exemplified in the Great Hymn to Nabû where the supplicant asks Nabû to exalt him.[1291]

The consecration of the divine image was very similar to the consecration of the king in Mesopotamia as well as in Egypt. Both these sorts of rituals may have derived from the consecration of the king exemplified in the Rājasūya ritual among the Āryans. It is true that the divine nature of the kings of Mesopotamia is less distinct than in Egypt and the divine determinative is evidenced only in the case of Naram-Sin of Akkad (ca. 2190-2154 B.C.) and the kings of the following Third Dynasty of Ur (and, later, the Japhetic Kassites).[1292] Under Shu-Sin of Ur the kings who used the royal determinative were treated like gods.[1293] The Assyrians and Neo-Babylonians did not follow this royal custom. However, the Mesopotamian royal consecration reveals the same solar nature of the king as in ancient Egypt. As has recently been studied by Ambos and Berlejung, a Babylonian text dating from the first millennium B.C.[1294] relating to the royal consecration ritual (bīt salā' mê) depicts the king undergoing a nocturnal "imprisonment" before he is invested with the royal insignia. As Ambos notes

> Der König galt als das Ebenbild des Šamaš. Indem der König am Abend der Rohrgebäude durch den westlichen Eingang betrat und am Morgen in der östlichen Tür seine Insignien vor der aufgehenden Sonne empfing, vollzog er auf diese Weise die Bahn der Sonne nach. Des Nachts über hielt sich die Sonne in der Unterwelt auf, und so besitzt auch das Rohrgefängnis in der Steppe einen Unterweltscharakter.[1295]

The ritual begins with a nocturnal procession of the king into the temple and ends the following morning in his palace. This is clearly in imitation of the sequence of the birth of the sun from the dark underworld into which the solar force has been impelled by the storm-force.[1296] Berlejung has also rightly remarked on the similarity between the royal consecration and the consecration of idols:

[1291] See W. von Soden, "Der grosse Hymnus an Nabû".

[1292] See H. Frankfort, *Kingship*, p.224; cf. R. Labat, *op.cit.*, p.368.

[1293] See H. Frankfort, *op.cit.*, p.302.

[1294] The texts related to this ritual include Tablets K 6818 , 8696, 9276+etc and BM 82963 und 64358+ (all from the 1st millennium B.C.). The ritual may date back originally to the second or third millennium B.C. (see C. Ambos, "Das 'Neujahrs'-Fest", p.2).

[1295] See C. Ambos, *op. cit.*, p.6; cf. W. Sallaberger, "Ritual, A" in *RLA*, XI, p.426.

[1296] See Ch.III above.

Wenn die Beschwörungen für den König und das Kultbild eine ähnliche Erscheinungsweise skizzieren, dann läßt sich schließen daß die Kultbilder möglichst königlich, der König möglichst göttlich wirken sollte, so daß er auf diese Weise zum Abbild der göttlichen Herrschaft geriet.[1297]

The divinisation of kings in Mesopotamia is confirmed in a Middle Assyrian text from around the time of Tukulti-Ninurta (1220-1150 B.C.) that has been studied by K.F. Müller, where the king is led to the Assur temple on a throne borne on the shoulders of royal officials preceded by priests who shout "Assur is king!"[1298] The king's sceptre is also that of Shamash, the sun-god, who is the god of justice.

Another important ritual that highlights the divinisation of the king was his sacred marriage and sexual union with the "goddess", archetypally Inanna, who was the consort of Dumuzi the sun-god. Indeed, the kings of Mesopotamia (en's) typically called themselves "spouse of Inanna".

Since Dumuzi is "killed' in the underworld and resurrected, his subsequent union with Inanna signified the revival of dead vegetation as well as of human life. The sacred marriage ritual may have served as a fertility rite.[1299] The hymns celebrating this ritual indeed declare the fertilising power of Inanna. In the Shulgi hymn known as Shulgi X (from the Third Dynasty, ca. 2090-40 B.C.) the goddess also grants the king as "his destiny" sovereignty, or "the shepherding of all the land" (since Dumuzi was traditionally represented as a shepherd).[1300]

However, the full significance of this ritual may have been the more spiritual one of the sexual rites performed in the Indic Shaiva Tantra that express the union of the Purusha and Prakrti (Nature).[1301] The sacred marriage ritual in Mesopotamia was probably performed in a chapel on the summit of a ziggurat. This would be an indication of the major purpose of the sacred marriage as devoted to the creation of the sun, since it is the sun that arises from atop the mountain represented by the ziggurat. According to Frankfort, the sacred marriage was part of the New Year's Festival in which a god captive in the underworld (Enlil-Marduk)

[1297] A. Berlejung, "Die Macht der Insignien", p.33f.

[1298] K.Fr. Müller, "Das assyrische Ritual", p.50; cf. R. Labat, *Le caractère religieux*, p.83.

[1299] See S. H. Hooke, *op.cit.*, p.60.

[1300] See R.F.G. Sweet, "Another look", p.96; cf. D. Frayne, "Notes", pp.15-16; also P. Steinkeller, "On Rulers, Priests and Sacred Marriage", p.136.

[1301] See below p.313.

was liberated by his son (Marduk-Ninurta),[1302] just as Osiris was liberated by Horus Jr.[1303] The liberated god emerges from a mountain as the sun.[1304]

It is not clear if the king actually engaged in sexual intercourse with a high priestess during this ritual, though Herodotus (I,181,5) refers to a sacred prostitute dedicated to the god Marduk: "The Chaldeans also say – although I do not believe them – that the god enters the temple in person and takes his rest upon the bed" on which she waits alone in the shrine. In an Aramaic New Year's ritual in Demotic script which reflects a Babylonian religious tradition, the king and the "goddess" are described as having sexual intercourse. Some scholars have suggested that the "goddess" was probably represented by her idol.[1305] But it is more probable that the "goddess" was an actual hierodule, rather like the Indian devadāsi who, at her initiation, underwent a marriage in the temple with an emblem of the deity and then, as part of her sacred office, regularly offered sexual favours to the king as representative of the deity as well as, in some cases, to other male devotees.[1306] The original ritual of the sacred marriage in Mesopotamia then may have involved a real ritual coupling between the king representing Dumuzi and the hierodule, or priestess, representing Inanna. This would explain the salaciousness of the rumours reported by Herodotus as well as of the lyrics associated with this rite in Sumerian literature.[1307] In Indian temples nowadays, the devadāsi system has been abolished and the sacred marriage is enacted only between the idols of the god and his consort.[1308] In the Sumerian literature, the solar significance of the entire ritual is highlighted by the description of the royal couple after their union: "The king like unto the sun sits beside her".[1309]

[1302] The Assyrian king (H. Frankfort, *op.cit.*, p.324) was represented as "Ninurta who avenged his father", a description that is exactly similar to that of Horus Jr. (see above p.97).

[1303] See H. Frankfort, *op.cit.*, pp.317ff.

[1304] *Ibid.*, p.323.

[1305] So, for example, R.F.G. Sweet, *op.cit.* and P. Steinkeller, *op.cit.*

[1306] See F. Apffel-Marglin, *Wives of The God-King*, cf. K. Chakrabothy, *Women as Devadasis.*

[1307] See Y. Sefati, *Love Songs*, p.225.

[1308] See below p.304.

[1309] See E. Chiera, *Sumerian Religious Texts*, No.1, Col.V, 18ff; cf. H. Frankfort, *op.cit.*, p.295.

XV.

TANTRIC INDIAN RITUALS

Although the extant Indian temples are of a relatively recent date, compared to the Mesopotamian and Egyptian cultures which exhibit temple worship from at least the sixth millennium B.C., the spiritual significance of the sacred rituals of Egypt and Sumer can be fully understood only through a study of the Indian tradition of Tantra, based principally on texts called Āgama, or '[sacred] tradition'.

Āgama represents the religious tradition which came to the fore in India in the age of temple building, though, as its name implies, it certainly draws on very ancient sources of sacred ritual. The delineation of the discipline of bhakti (devotion) in the *Bhāgavata Purāna* may have been one of these sources, and the schools of yoga another. In the *Bhāgavata Purāna* VII,5,23-24, for instance we note the following steps listed as means of attaining to the deity, in this case, Krishna: 1) *shravana* ("listening" to the scriptural stories of Krishna and his companions), (2) *kīrtana* ("praising," usually refers to ecstatic group singing), (3) *smarana* ("remembering" or fixing the mind on Vishnu), (4) *pāda-sevana* (rendering service), (5) *archana* (worshiping an image), (6) *vandana* (paying homage), (7) *dāsya* (servitude), (8) *sākhya* (friendship), and (9) *ātma-nivedana* (complete surrender of the self).

The Āgamas are constituted of four stages, starting with Charya (selfless conduct and service) and Kriya (esoteric worship and the construction of temples and sculptures) and proceeding to Yoga (spiritual concentration) and Jnāna (supreme knowledge). There is no focus on fire-worship in the Āgamas. The four aspects deal with, first, the rules relating to the observance of religious rites, second, rules for the construction of temples and for sculpting, third, yoga and mental discipline, and, finally, philosophical knowledge. The lowest form of Āgamic practice therefore is that of temple worship and the highest the supreme knowledge of the Supreme Being.

The Āgama texts are normally constituted of speeches made by Shiva to Pārvati, whereas the texts that contain speeches made by the latter to her consort are called Nigama. Yamala texts involve the worship of united deities. The Āgamas are written in Sanskrit using the South Indian Grantha script rather than the Devanāgari. The Āgama texts are divided into three types, Tantra (Sattvaguna – or based on the quality of Sattva), Yamala (Rajoguna – or based on the quality of Rajas) and Damara (Tamoguna – or based on the quality of Tamas). There were originally 64 divisions for each of the three divisions Ashvakranta, Rathakranta, Vishnukranta.[1310]

Although drawing on the Vedic tradition, Āgama claims to supersede it. As Flood points out, "The mainstream tantric texts of the Pancharatra and Shaiva Siddhanta maintain a close proximity to the vedic tradition and prescribe a whole way of life that incorporates vedic rites of passage [samksaras] ... along with the supererogatory tantric rites of their tradition".[1311]

Āgama considers the universe as a whole whose every single part bears an influence on the others. Thus a system of sympathetic magic was developed out of it in which the final aim of the spiritual adept (sādhaka) is to transform, within his consciousness, his own person as well as cult-objects and rites into that which these phenomena essentially are. Every god is indeed represented by a 'bija' or seminal mantra which embodies the essence of the god. Thus the syllable 'ram' betokens Agni, 'dam' Vishnu, 'horum' Shiva, etc. And the ultimate aim of Tantra, called 'Siddhi' or spiritual perfection, is a practical realisation of the Upanishadic equation of the individual ātman with Brahman ("tat tvam asi"/that art thou).

Men in general are classified according to the predominance of the tāmasic, rājasic, or sāttvic elements in them, as pashu (animal), vira (heroic) or divya (divine), this classification roughly corresponding to the vaisya, kshatriya and brāhmanical castes among the Vedic Āryas. There are only two life-stages (āshramas) recognised by the Āgamic tradition, those of householders and ascetics, for both brāhmans and non-brāhmans, "though the particular practices of the Vipras [brāhmans] and other castes vary" (*Mahānārayana Tantra*, Ch.8).

[1310] See 'Arthur Avalon' (Sir John Woodroffe), *Shakti and Shakta,* Ch.4.

[1311] See G. Flood, *The Tantric Body,* p.38.

Āgama is divided into Vaishnava (215 in all), Shaiva (28) and Shakta Āgama (77). The Shakta Āgama tradition is normally called Tantra, though Tantra is often used to describe the Vaishnava and Shaiva traditions as well. The term "tantra" itself is derived from the root "tan" which means "to extend", a concept that we have already encountered in connection with the Vedic concept of sacrifice.[1312]

1: Vaishnava Āgamas

Vaishnava Āgamas are divided into Vaikhānasa and Pāncharātra Āgamas. Vaikhānasas may have been the first group of professional temple-priests and are more Vedic in their affiliation. Indeed, they are also called Vaidikāgama and Shruthāgama. The principal Vaikhānasa text is the *Vaikhānasa Sūtra* from the 4th c. A.D.

The Vaikhānasas, like the Āryan brāhmans, consider the grihasthya as being the best stage of the Hindu's life, and worship at home as more important than worship at the temple. The domestic rituals are motivated by the desire for attainments and spiritual benefits (sakshepa), whereas temple worship is merely the duty of the priest (nirakshepa) to help the fulfilment of the desires of the worshippers at the temple. In general, a person who accepts money for the performance of rituals is looked down upon by the Vedic brāhmans.

Vaikhānasas are devotees of Vishnu and consider Vishnu in four principal forms as Achyuta (the immutable aspect), Satya (the static aspect of the the deity), the Purusha (the principle of life), and Aniruddha (the irreducible aspect). The absolute form (nishkala) of Vishnu in the universe is contemplated by the worshipper along with the Vishnu form in his own body, and then the worshipper transfers this spirit into the immovable idol (dhruva bheru). The large immovable image in the temple represents Vishnu's nishkala form, and is ritually placed in the sanctuary and consecrated. The smaller moveable images in the temple represent the sakala forms that represent the manifest emanations of the divinity.

Pāncharātra is a later form of Vaishnava worship associated with Rāmānuja and his teacher Yāmuna (ca. 918-1038 A.D.), who wrote the *Āgamaprāmānya* in defence of the Pāncharātra tradition.[1313] In the Pāncharātra, yajnas are less valued than idol-worship whereas, in the Vaikhānasa tradition, idol-worship is only a development of the yajnas.

[1312] See above p.17.

[1313] For an interesting study of Pāncharātra Tantrism, see G. Flood, *The Tantric Body*, pp.99ff.

Also, among the Southern Indian Pāncharātra followers, more Tamil hymns are recited and more festivals are organised involving all sections of the community. Shūdras and ascetics are given an important role in the performance of rituals. Although Vaikhānasa is generally considered to be the first and principal Vaishnava Āgamic tradition, Abhināvagupta (ca.975-1025 A.D.), however, maintained that the Pāncharātra is superior to the Vaikhanasa since it is meant for the spiritually advanced.

THE PĀNCHARĀTRA DOCTRINE OF DIVINE MANIFESTATION

According to the *Jayākhya Samhita* written before the 10th c. B.C. and based on Samkhya philosophical categories, the Absolute Being (Brahman) is equated with the personal being of Vāsudeva (Vishnu). From Vāsudeva emanate lower forms as vyūhas. The description of the transformations of the ultimate reality in this work is worth noticing for its spiritual insight into the Purusha cosmology of the Vedas and Purānas:

> Having a hundred-fold radiance of fire, sun and moon, Vāsudeva is the Lord, the truth of that [absolute], the supreme Lord. Agitating his own radiance through his own energy (tejas), the Lord whose form is light manifests the god Achyuta, like lightning, O Brahman. [Then] that Achyuta of firm radiance spreads his won form, depending on Vāsu as a wisp of cloud [depends] on the summer heat. Then shaking himself he [in turn] produced the god Satya, whose body is shining, as the ocean [produces] a bubble. He is called the light mode of consciousness who produces himself by means of himself [as the god] called Purusha who is great, an unending stream of light. That supreme Lord is [in turn] the support of all the [lower] gods, their inner controller,[1314] as the sky [is the support] of the stars. As a fire with its fuel sends forth a mass of sparks, O twice-born, so the Supreme Lord, who is yet desireless, [sends forth manifestations].[1315]

We see that the Pancharātra employs the same hypostases of Aniruddha, Achyuta, Satya and Purusha that the Vaikhānasas also do.

After the initial ideal creation comes a lower material phase characterised by Māyā Shakti along with the cosmic body of Purusha. During this phase emerge the individual souls "contaminated by the dust of beginningless karmic traces ... and to which they return during the

---

[1314] Antaryāmin (see below p.293).

[1315] Quoted in G. Flood, *op. cit.*, p.102.

periodic destruction or reabsorption of the lower creation".[1316] From Māyā then emanates Prakrti, the material creation which emanates from the Mahat (the Great). From the Mahat, in turn, is generated the Ahamkāra (the Ego) and thence the mind (for dealing with worldly transactions), the five senses, the five organs of action, the five subtle elements and the five material elements (space, air, fire, water and earth). The individual soul is wrapped in these Shakti emanations and entrapped in them. Liberation consists in the extraction of the soul from its Shakti envelope.

The Pāncharātra, much like the Vaikhānasa, maintains that the deity manifests himself in five-fold manner, as Para, Vyuha, Vibhava, Antaryāmin (or Aniruddha), and Archa. The first four detail the process of divine emanation from macrocosm into microcosm. The last two are the manifestations of the lord within humans and in idols.

Para is the first immanent manifestation of the Lord. This is the "best of the Purushas", "the highest Light". The *Padma Tantra* describes the Lord as dividing himself and becoming with one half the Vyuha Vasudeva and with the other Nārayana, creator of the primal waters. This Para is adorned with nine ornaments and weapons which represent the principles of the universe.

Vyuha is the process of emanation itself marked by the appearance of six gunas in Nārāyana and his consort Lakshmi. From Vāsudeva [corresponding to Achyuta] emanates Samkarshana [Satya], in whom jnāna and bala are manifested. From Samkarshana emanates Pradyumna [Purusha] bearing aishvarya and vīrya. From Pradyumna emanates Aniruddha bearing shakti and tejas. Vishnu's Vyuha forms as Vāsudeva, Sankarshana, Pradyumna and Aniruddha are identified with Krishna, his elder brother, his son and his grandson respectively, who together constitute a complete body of divine power.

Avatāra (descent) is the next manifestation of the Lord, also called Vibhava (human manifestation). All the avatāras spring from Aniruddha, or some from Vāsudeva and the others from the other three vyuhas. The supreme Being however remains transcendent and indifferent to the manifestation.

Antaryāmin is Aniruddha as the inner ruler of all souls seated in the lotus of the heart.

Archa is an inanimate object which is duly consecrated and possessed of miraculous power when the shakti of Vishnu descends into it. It is used as an object of daily worship since the devotee feels the very presence of God in it.

[1316] *Ibid.*

The rituals detailed in the *Jayākhya Samhita* are interesting for the yogic complexity they point to in the divine worship that is to be undertaken by an adept.[1317] The rituals consist of 1. purificatory ablutions (snāna), 2. purification of the elements within the body (bhūtashuddhi), 3. divinisation of the body through imposing mantras upon it (nyāsa), 4. internal worship of the deity (antara-yoga) performed in the mind, 5. external worship of the deity (bahya-yoga) with offerings. The aim of the rituals is to allow the adept to purify the physical or elemental body (bhautika sharira) and induce the soul to ascend from the heart through the body (and simultaneously through the cosmos) to the Lord Nārāyana located at the crown of the head. As Flood observes:

> As in the final dissolution of the cosmos, when each element or category retracts into its source, so in the daily ritual of the adept this process is recapitulated within the adept's body … each of the elements is visualised in a certain way, associated with particular symbols, and as pervading a particular part of the body in a hierarchical sequence. Each element is in turn symbolically destroyed in the imagination through being absorbed into its mantra and into its energies (shakti) of the powers (vibhava) or subtle elements (tanmatra) which gave rise to it.

The adept imagines the soul leaving his body through the crown of the head (brahmarandhra) and at the same time rising through the spheres of space, the stars, lightning, the sun and the moon in the macrocosm. The Lord seated at the crown of the head is visualised in his supreme body (paravigraha) as a mass of radiance standing within a circle of light. We may understand this as the Brahman of the original cosmology that informed the religion of the Indo-Europeans.[1318] The joy that arises from this vision is the supreme energy of Vishnu (parāvaishnava shakti) and results in a stage of higher consciousness (samādhi).

The next step, after transcending the subtle elements along with the gross body, is for the adept to "burn" the latter with the fire arising from his feet that is generated by the power of his mantra. Then all that remains is a pile of ashes fhat is washed away by a flood of milky water arising from his meditation. At this point,

---

[1317] This account of the rites prescribed in the Jayakha Samhita is derived from G. Flood, *op.cit.*, p.106ff.

[1318] See above p.49ff.

With the universe [of his imagination] filled with the ocean of milk, a lotus emerges out containing Nārāyana, whose essence is his mantra ... The [adept's] body is purified, freed from old age and death and has the appearance of pure crystal and the effulgence of a thousand suns and moons. Having purified his body thus, his soul enters the inner lotus[1319] of this subtle body through the aperture of the Absolute from which it had earlier vacated its residence.

We note in this description of the adept's enlightenment, the emergence of the light above the lotus of Earth that characterises the manfestation of Brahman.

The adept is now ready to perform the divinisation of his own body through imposing mantras upon it, followed by mental sacrifice (mānasayāga) and external sacrifice (bāhyayāga). The divinisation of the adept's body is undertaken through the imposition of mantras upon it by touching the various parts of the body while reciting the appropriate mantras.[1320] When the adept is thus fully divinised he is identified with Nārāyana and his ego is transformed into the absolute subjectivity of Vishnu. He can say at the end of this process, "I am the Lord Vishnu, I am Nārāyana, Hari, and I am Vāsudeva, all-pervading, the abode of beings, without taint".

In the internal worship that follows, the adept seeks to establish the supreme Lord within his heart, which is envisaged as a throne. The adept visualises the hierarchical cosmos in the forms of the deities located within his own body. First he situates the power of Earth on his penis, above that the fire of Time, then the Tortoise incarnation of the Lord bearing the insignia of Vishnu, the discus and the club. Above that are situated the cosmic snake, Ananta, and, above Ananta, Prithvi, the Earth-goddess. Above her, at the navel, is located an ocean of milk from which arises a white lotus. On this lotus are situated the sun, moon and fire. Above these is the throne of being upon which rests Garuda, the solar vehicle of Vishnu, and the boar Varāha. The area from the navel to the heart is divided into five sections and the adept finally worships the mantra-throne in the heart.

We note the similarity that this ritual of divinisation bears to the description of the fire-altar as representative of the Purusha in the Vedic Agnicayana ritual. As Brajalal Mukherji has pointed out,[1321] there are

---

[1319] i.e. heart.

[1320] As Gonda points out (*Religionen* II, 47), there are Vedic precedents for these tactile rites (for example, in *SB* III,1,3,25); cf. below p.296.

[1321] In 'Arthur Avalon' (Sir John Woodroffe), *op. cit.*, 'Note to Ch.IV'.

indeed many similarities beween the rituals of the Āgamic tradition and those of the Vedic:

> The worship in both Vaidik and Tantrik rites begins with Acamana, which is a form of ablution in which certains parts of the body are touched with water .... They purify themselves by uttering some Mantras as Bijas while contemplating the Deities of certain parts of their bodies and touching such parts with their fingers ... They make use of certain sounds for removing unclean spirits, e.g., Khat, Phat, Hum ... They attribute a Deity to each letter in a Mantra ... They make gestures with their fingers as part of their religious rites ... and locate the Devatas of particular sounds in particular parts of their bodies ... in performing the Acamana they sacrifice unto themselves conceiving that they are part and parcel of the Great Brahma.

The external worship (pūja)[1322] consists of the drawing of a mandala in which is housed the deity. The presence of Nārāyana as well as of other deities is invoked through mantras and visualisation. The deity is then installed in the mandala and incense and food are offered to it. This is followed by the chanting of mantras and fire-offerings (homa) into the kunda.

The non-initiated devotee in the Pāncharātra tradition adores the Vibhava form of the Lord, the incarnation of the deity, as Rāma, etc., in the temple and then moves on to the worship of His more subtle Vyuha forms.

THE SACRED STRUCTURE OF TEMPLES

Temple worship, like fire-worship, is based on yogic knowledge. We have seen that the major focus on Agni is on its creative solar form and on the preservation of the solar force. In temple worship, the deity whose idol is adored is daily created and sustained exactly as the fire is aroused after its nightly rest and put to sleep at the end of the evening Agnihotra sacrifice.[1323]

The Āgamic texts hold the view that japa (chanting of mantras), homa (offerings made into the sacred fire), dhyāna (meditation), archa are the four methods of approaching the divine. Archa, however, is considered the most comprehensive of the āgamic practices. Already in the 5th century

---

[1322] See below p.308.

[1323] See above p.246f.

B.C., Panini mentions the term 'archa', and Patanjali (2nd c. B.C.), the commentator on Panini's *Ashtādhyāyi*, mentions both immoveable and moveable images such as those in temples. The focus on temple worship seems not to have started in India earlier than around the 4th century B.C. The earliest extant temples in India, from around the 3rd c. B.C., are hewn out of rock or in caves on mountainsides. As George Michell points out, the sanctuary, which must be small and dark,[1324] is like a cave itself and we may reasonably conjecture that this is the reason why the early temples were cave temples. One of the earliest constructed temples is the Buddhist temple built by the Emperor Asoka in Bodhgaya in the 3rd c. B.C.

We have noted that the Vedic sacrifices do not involve idolatry and the only idol mentioned in the *SB* is the gold man that is placed within the fire-altar.[1325] However, it should be noted that the Āgama texts on temple worship use Vedic mantras in their Tantric rituals. For instance, the *Bodhayana Shesha Sūtra* and the *Vishnu Pratishtha Kalpa* combine *Grihya Sūtra* rules with Tantric practices to outline the rites for the installation of Vishnu images, etc. The *Grihya Sūtras* however do not include the Prāna Prathistāpana ritual (infusing life into the idol) which is taken from Tantra, and the latter is combined, as in Egypt and Sumer, with the ceremony of "opening the eyes of the deity with a needle".

There are clear similarities between the structure of the Vedic fire-altars and that of the temples. The Gārhapatya fire is represented in the temple by the vedika platform. The cella where the icon is placed is called a garbhagriha (womb chamber), and we may remember that Agni, and the Vedic sacrificer himself, were considered to undergo a rebirth in the course of the sacrifice. Also, the plinth of the temple is adorned with sculptures of men, horses and other animals which beings correspond to those of the five heads buried in the foundation of the Vedic altar.[1326] The axis on which the temple is built is identical to that of the sacrificial post, yupa, in the Vedic altar which SB III,vii,1,25 describes as rising from the underworld to the heavens. The stambha of the Vedic fire-altar may have later been transformed into the more graphic Shiva Linga of Hindu temples, for Shiva is also called Sthanu or pillar, the *axis mundi*. As Snodgrass points out,

---

[1324] Cf. the reference to the shrine in Dravidian mythology above p.137.

[1325] See above p.229.

[1326] See S. Kramrisch, *The Hindu Temple*, I, 146-7.

Its axial nature is further indicated by its location within the Hindu temple, where it is positioned on the perpendicular that centres the building and emerges through the finial, a conformation that is mirrored in the cosmophysiology of man, in whom Tantric Yoga places a linga at the centre of each of the cakras that are superimposed one above the other along the vertical axis formed by the spinal column.[1327]

The Āgama texts relating to temple worship include yoga methodology since they consider temple architecture as imitative of the human body and locate the six chakras within the temple structure. Following yogic correspondences, the muladhara chakra is identified with the platform for the sacrificial food offerings, the svadhishthana with the flagpole, the manipura with the vahana or vehicle of the god, the anahata with the mahamandapa or assembly hall, the vishuddha with the antarala or corridor between the mandapa and the cella, the ajna with the cult image, and the brahmarandhra with the amalaka stone.[1328]

Temples are built on a mandala representing a supine Vāstu-Purusha oriented according to the course of the sun.[1329] The mandala is designed on the basis of astrological calculations, and orientated according to the course of the sun.[1330] The Purusha in the mandala is based on a legend recounted in the *Mayamata*, of Brahma's creation of a man who grew to such monstrous proportions that his shadow fell on the earth as an eclipse. So Brahma called the ashta dikapalas, the eight gods of the cardinal directions, and with their help overpowered the Purusha by holding it fast against the earth. Brahma jumped on the central portion of this creature while forty four other gods pinned down the other parts. It is clear that the legend of Brahma and the Vāstu-Purusha used to explain this mandala is a Purānic variation of the Vedic account of the formation of the Cosmic Man, or Purusha, which coincides with the emergence of the supreme Light and Consciousness of Brahman. The Vāstu Purusha then was made

---

[1327] A. Snodgrass, *The Symbolism of the Stupa*, p.169.

[1328] See K.-H. Golzio, *op.cit.*, p.127f.; cf. H. v. Stietencorn, *Ganga und Yamuna*, Wiesbaden, 1972, 92-4.

[1329] There is a reference to the Vāstoshpati already in RV VII,54,1-3, though the Lord of the House was represented in Vedic rituals by a firm post that was worshipped by the priests (see H.T. Bakker, "Human sacrifice", p.181).

[1330] See G. Michell, *The Hindu Temple*, p.72.

to serve as the foundation of sacred structures. The presiding gods of the several directions are as follows:

North-east – Īshvara
East – Aditya
South-east – Agni
South – Yama
South-west – the Manes, ancestors
West – Varuna,
North-west – Vāyu
North – Kubera
Centre – Brahma

The *Shilpa-prakasha* (9ᵗʰ-12ᵗʰ c A.D.) describes the parts of a temple as the parts of the foundational god, Mahāpurusha, whom it incorporates. The *Agni Purana* LXI, 19-27, too, declares that the temple is the body of the Purusha, so that the door of the temple is the mouth of the Purusha and the image is his life. We may remember that, in the Vedic fire-altar, the kunda is considered its "mouth".[1331] The centre of the mandala, the brahmasthana, is the most sacred part of it since it denotes the navel of the Purusha whence the universe, or the Mt. Meru which serves as the universal axis, emerged. The spires of Hindu temples, as well as the pyramidal structures of Egypt, are representations of this phallic axis of the universe. When a mandala is divided into an odd number of squares, or ayugma, its centre is constituted by one module or pada, when divided into an even number of sqauares, or yugma, its centre is constituted by a point formed by the intersection of the two perpendicular central lines. The former is considered sakala, or manifest, the latter nishkala, or unmanifest. The sakala mandala is used for shrines of gods with form (sakalamūrthi) and to peform yajnas. The nishkala mandala is used for the installation of idols without form (nishkalamūrthi) and for especially auspicious performances. The *Shandilya Upanishad* describes the different forms of the supreme deity:

from the formless Brahman, three forms (or aspects) arose, (*viz.,*) nishkalā (partless,) sakalā (with parts), and sakalā-nishkalā (with and without parts). That which is satya, vijñāna and ānanda, That which is actionless, without any impurity, omnipresent, extremely subtle, having faces in every direction, undefinable and immortal—that is His nishkalā aspect. Maheśvara (the great Lord) who is black and yellow

---

[1331] See above p.240.

rules, with avidyā, mūlaprakrti or māyā that is red, white, and black, and that is co-existent with Him. This is his sakalā-nishkalā aspect. Then the Lord desired (or willed) by his spiritual wisdom (thus): May I become many?; may I bring forth? Then from this Person who was contemplating and whose desires are fulfilled, three letters sprang up. Three vyāhrtis, the three-footed Gāyatrī, the three Vedas, the three devas, the three varnas (colours or castes) and the three fires sprang. That Supreme Lord who is endowed with all kinds of wealth, who is all pervading, who is situated in the hearts of all beings, who is the Lord of māyā and whose form is māyā—He is Brahma. He is Vishnu: He is Rudra: He is Indra: He is all the devas: He is all the bhūtas (elements or beings): He only is before: He only is behind: He only is on our left: He only is on our right: He only is below: He only is above: He only is the all. That form of him as Dattātreya, who sports with his Śakti, who is kind to his devotees, who is brilliant as fire, resembling the petals or a red lotus and is of four hands, who is mild and shines sinlessly—this is His sakalā form.

The garbhagriha, or womb-chamber where the idol of the deity is placed, is a square cella where the idol is, as it were, born. Only the priests are allowed into this chamber. There is an ambulatory around the inner chamber for the worshippers' circumambulation of the image of the deity. The steeple of the dome above the sanctuary is called shikhara (summit) and represents Mt. Meru, which, as we have seen, represents the central mountain of the matrix of Earth atop which the sun arises.[1332] At the peak of the shikhara is an amalaka stone resembling a lotus bloom which represents Earth crowned by the light of Brahman.

The traditional North Indian style of temple has a beehive-shaped tower, while the Dravidian temple has a tower consisting of progressively smaller storeys as in the Sumerian ziggurat. In the Nāyak residence built in 1600 in Thanjavur, for example, the two high towers have seven layers and are said to represent the Meru Mountain.[1333] The erotic sculptures adorning some of the temples of central India are linked to the importance of "kāma" (love) and "mithuna" (sexual union) in Shaktism as well as, earlier, in the Vedic yajna.[1334] For Kāma is considered as the root of the universe and the universe is to be reabsorbed into its root through

---

[1332] See above p.45.

[1333] *Ibid.*, p.110.

[1334] See below p.310.

desire.[1335] The temple also has a hall held on pillars for meditation, prayer or sacred dances. The temple tank is outside the temple and used for purificatory purposes.

Temple building was governed by the strictest rules of divine geometry. In the Shāstras and Āgamas, the physical form of the temple is identified with "the laws that govern the movements of heavenly bodies".[1336] The *Mayamata*, an architectural text from the Chola period (11th c. A.D.), proclaims that "If the measurement of the temple is in every way perfect, there will be perfection in the universe itself". The plan of the temple is a square which is divided into 64 or 81 smaller squares, each representing a specific deity.

These squares are related to yantras, which are specific geometric shapes representing the energies of the devatas, for each devata has his or her own yantra. One of the most important of the yantras is the Lalitāshrichakra which consists of a red point in the middle of a small white triangle and other red and blue triangles within a circle.[1337] This circle is surrounded by an eight-leaved and a sixteen-leaved lotus. Outside the three circles which contain these two lotuses are three yellow rectangles. So the point is enclosed thus in nine spaces which represent the different forms of the spirit, senses, and matter which cover the centre, which is the union of Shiva and his consort, Lalithā. The adept sinks mystically into this yantra, identifies himself with the nine spaces and realsies the goddess who is at the centre in indissoluble union with Shiva. Thereby he reaches the source of the universe which is also a salvation and immortality.

THE DIVINISATION OF THE TEMPLE-IDOL

The divinisation of the king in ancient India has already been noticed in the rite of anointing of the Rājasūya rituals. In the Tantric tradition, the king's role as a warrior is allied to the shakti of the Goddess which is bestowed upon the king during his consecration.[1338] The divinisation of the king is closely related to the divinisation of statues in the temple worship which forms an important part of the Āgama tradition. The

---

[1335] See G. Flood, *op.cit.*, p.86.

[1336] See G. Michell, *op. cit.*, p.73.

[1337] See J. Gonda, *Religionen*, II, p.48.

[1338] *Ibid.*, p.57.

chief elements in the construction of a temple are said to be its sthala (location), teertha (ford or tank) and mūrthi (idol). Of these the idol is the most important. Indeed, the idol is the centre of the temple, which is, as it were, an outgrowth of the icon. Idol worship is, as we have seen in the discussion of the divine manifestation in the Pāncharātra system, of special yogic significance since it allows the devotee to more easily apprehend the formless and quality-less divinity by detaching himself from his own form and quality in the process of admiring those of the idol. Thus, through his adoration of the idol, the devotee is gradually freed from his own ego.

Just as in yoga the deity (devata) is invoked into the body of the devotee, in Tantric archana the divinity is invoked into an idol. The traditional Hindu temple worship or pūja includes four elements, sankalpa (declaration of the time, place and purpose of the worship), tarpana (satisfaction of the deity through an offering of milk or other sweet liquid), pūja (invocation of the deity and worship), and phala (the result of the act of worship). The actual process of worship of the deity is called archana, which begins with invocations to the deity, the vivification of the idol, dhyāna (meditation on the divinity), āvāhana (invocation of the divinity through specific mudras or gestures), sixteen upachāras (homages) to the idol,[1339] offerings to the idol, and visarjana (departure of the idol on its procession to a body of water where it is submerged).

As in Egypt and Mesopotamia, the consecration of the idol of the deity is of the greatest importance. In the yajashāla, where mostly only men officiate, a brass pot is used which is transformed into an embryo-like body. The brass pot is considered the skeleton, the strings wrapped around it the veins, the yellow and red powder smeared on it the blood and other essential fluids, the cloth tied around it the skin, the coconut on it the head, and the leaves around it its hair. The pot ceremony effects what Waghorne calls

a transfer of disembodied powers from various sources through the medium of the fire to the pots, which act as a transitional body that is then "poured" into the image-body [i.e. the body of the statue]. The powers originate from the holy words chanted by the priests, that is,

---

[1339] These are 1.offering a seat to the deity, 2. offering water to wash the feet of the deity, 3. offering water to wash the hands of the deity, 4. offering water to drink, 5. offering honey, 6. giving a bath to the deity, 7. pouring water over its head, 8. making the deity sit down, 9. offering clothes, 10. offering the holy thread, 11. offering jewellry, 12. offering a vibhuti, or the sacred mark, 13. offering fragrant sandalwood paste, 14. offering turmeric rice, 15. offering a flower garland, 16. chanting the 108 names of the deity.

by their own controlled breath. Power also comes from the raw food, "natural" substance offered to the murti, and then returned to the fire.

The enlivening of the statue with holy water from pots takes place in a ritual lasting for forty eight days and then it is brought to the temple where it is the object of a mahākumbābhishekam.[1340] 108 pots are used to bathe the image with holy water. The pots used for this ceremony are like the earth in whose soil the seed germinates, or like the womb in which the embryo grows. After this the idol has to be purified in a ritual called vigraha sodhana, whereby the statue is purified to make it a suitable vehicle for the divinity. It is placed in water for a night, or sometimes three or even five nights. Then it is cleaned with kusha grass and smeared with honey and clarified butter to heal it of any wounds that it may have suffered during the sculpting.[1341] What is interesting to note is that the enlivening of the image takes place in a yajashāla which is outside the temple just as the birthing process of the image in Sumer and Egypt takes place in a workshop outside the temple. The birthing process is overseen by men while women perform the nurturing functions.

Some Āgama texts such as the *Bhagavat-pratishthadarpana* which follows the *Shaivāgama-prayoga-chandrika*, prescribe eight rites that will give the body of the idol its divine allure. It is first immersed in water to acquire water in its body, then in milk to acquire its skin, then in grains for its muscles, in a silken garment for its fat, in a woollen garment and a tiger-skin for its bone-marrow, in nine precious stones for its bone, in flowers for its semen, and finally in a bed to acquire the proportion, grace and charm of "a sixteen-year-old youth".

The image once installed in the temple is bathed by women in milk (pālābhishekam) and rose water. Then they dry it and clothe it. This is followed by a rite called prāna pratistha in which the statue is infused with divinity. This rite of infusion of life into the idol is also called jīva-nyāsa, or. After it is enlivened, the idol is made to lie on its back facing the east [that is, in the direction of the rising sun] and put to sleep. In the morning it is awakened and fed.

An important ceremony related to the installation of a statue, and one that is normally performed after the installation of the statue on its pedestal, is that called "netronmilana" or opening the eye.[1342] First, the

---

[1340] See J.P. Waghorne, "The Divine Image", p.237.

[1341] Or perhaps of the contamination that it has received at the hands of the sculptor, since the latter tended to be of the shudra caste (see J.J. Preston, "Apotheosis and destruction", p.21).

[1342] See S.K. Ramachandra Rao, *Āgama Kosha*, Vol.9: 'Consecrations', pp.53ff.

master of ceremonies covers the idol with a fresh cloth and dips a golden stylus covered with cotton wick into a golden bowl containing dye, and reciting the Vishnu Sūkta, paints the right eye, and then, reciting the Purusha Sūkta, the left eye. The dye represents earth, the bowl the sun, the stylus the moon. The six details painted on the eye correspond to the mandala which is formed of the five primary elements (mahābhūti – space, air, fire, water, earth). Then a brass bowl containing clarified butter, curds, honey and milk is placed on a heap of grains and the deity is allowed to behold this. Next, with a sharp-pointed stylus of gold, the lines of the eye-lashes are etched, then the white of the eyes, then the pupil, and finally the iris. This done, the sculptor is dispensed with. Then its two eyes and a third in the forehead of the statue are sprinkled. Only then is the idol revealed to the public. It is given a bath in a pancha-gavya mixture constituted of five products of a cow, as well as in eight kinds of earth, and in water. Finally, it is adorned with garments and ornaments. After mantras are chanted before it to render it fully divine, it undergoes further rituals of installation which may include even a marriage rite.[1343] In fact the marriage of the idols of Shiva and his consort Meenakshi is still celebrated in a major festival in Madurai.[1344]

Although the creation of a divine idol involves careful artistic and spritual direction, it is possible, as J.J. Preston points out, that the task of sculpting a statue of a deity may have originally been undertaken by shūdra artisans. In fact, only after the statue is completely sculpted is it taken out by brāhman priests to be bathed. However, once the statue is installed in the temple, mostly only brāhman priests conduct the daily worship of the deity.[1345]

The statue of the principal deity is worshipped four times a day, at sunrise, noon, sunset and midnight.[1346] The daily rituals begin with the purificatory rites of the priests themselves and the reverential opening of the door of the sanctuary. The main rite is the awakening of the deity who is considered to be asleep and thus unmanifest. Hymns are recited to invoke the deity to inhabit the image. When this occurs, the image is bathed, dressed and anointed with oils, camphor and sandalwood, and garlanded, with flames moved before its face. It is then offered refreshments of various cooked foods. After many circumambulations

---

[1343]   See M.-L. Barazer-Billoret, B. Dagens, V. Lefèvre (ed.), *Dīptāgama*, Pondicherry: Institute français de Pondichéry, 2007, II, p.12f.

[1344]   See W.P. Harman, *The Sacred Marriage*.

[1345]   See J.J. Preston, *ibid*.

[1346]   See G. Michell, *The Hindu temple*, p.63.

around the image, the priest then closes the sanctuary door - when the deity is considered to be once again asleep. We see therefore that the process of the creation of the idol and of its adoration closely resembles the creation of the sun from the sacred fire of the yajna.

Since many people were not admitted into a temple in ancient India, the image was occasionally taken out in a chariot, or "ratha", in a procession, just as the Egyptians paraded their divine statues in barques. The use of a barque or ratha for the procession of the idol is derived from the conception of the solar barque or chariot. The risen sun of our system is borne through the heavens as if in a boat. Hence the early Egyptian depictions of the sun in a solar barque. This barque is substituted with a chariot among the Indians and the occasional ceremonial transport of the statue of a deity from outside Egyptian and Sumerian and Hindu temples in processions among the public, either in a barque or a chariot, is a mimetic representation of the circuit of the sun. We may observe in passing that the Egyptian burial of ships as well as the Scandinavian and Anglo-Saxon, and also the burial of chariots from the time of the Andronovo culture of 2000 B.C. to the Celts of the Iron Age, are similarly related to the conception of the deification of kings since the king is a representative of the solar energy and undergoes, on his death, an apotheosis.

Most of the consecratory processes detailed above may be observed in the major temple festival of Dravidian India called the kumbābhishekam[1347] (or samprokshanam as it is called in the case of Vaishnav temples), which is performed at the foundation of a temple or once every twelve years after its initial establishment. The rituals of this festival are undertaken only by highly experienced priests after years of training in the Āgamic rites. The ceremonies last for several days beginning with the pūja and homa for the Vāstu Purusha, the presiding deity of the site where the shrine is to be constructed. Mantras and homas continue to be offered, the latter in the several homa kundasin. A large number of pots containing holy water which is energised by yogic meditations and mantras are placed in front of the vatgasalasm.

The enshrinement of the principal image of the temple is performed with a Netronmilana (or Nayanomilana) ceremony for the "opening of the eyes". A yantra, normally a sheet of copper or gold with symbolic diagrams, is placed at the centre of the sanctum. This is followed by the Ashtabandha ritual in which the yantra is smeared with a special paste made out of eight ingredients such as powdered conch, lac, whitestone,

---

[1347] Kumba means 'pot' and abhishekam 'consecration'.

etc., mixed with butter or oil. Then the stone idol (vigraha) is placed on it. Finally the Prāna-pratishta, or the ceremony of infusing life into the image, is performed. After several other pūjas and yajnas, the priests carry the pots around the temple enclosures (prakaras) and then pour the water in them over the image as a kumbābhishekam. Now the image is a living deity and fit for worship. The holy water is poured also over the vimāna kalasas above the sanctum and over the gopura kalasas by priests standing on scaffolds. Pūjas are then performed for the goddesses and lesser deities in the smaller sanctums in the temple.

2: *Shaiva Āgamas*

The Shaivāgama consists of four different schools, the Shaiva, Pashupata, Soma and Lakula. Of these, the Shaiva is said to have had three branches: Vāma, Dakshina and Siddhānta. The Vāma branch includes Kapala, Kalamukha and Agora, the Dakshina branch includes Kashmir Shaivadarshanas, Svachanda Bhairavam, etc., making up a total of 18 Āgamas.

Of the Dakshina branch, Kashmir Shaivism is mostly monistic in its metaphysics and its principal exponent is Abhināvagupta (10th century A.D.), author of the *Tantraloka*. Other texts include the *Shiva Sutras* of Vāsugupta (ca. 875-925) and Jayaratha's 12th century commentary on the *Tantraloka*.

Kashmir Shaivism considers Shiva as the only Reality and infinite Consciousness. By his own will and energy (Shakti) he appears as the phenomenonal universe. Shakti has five qualities, chit, ānanda, ichcha, jnāna, and kriya. To this is added māyā, or the agent of phenomenal manifestation, which in turn gives rise to five kanchukas - kala (power), vidya (knowledge), rāga (attachment), kāla (time) and niyati (space). One of the major doctrines developed by Vāsugupta is that of spanda, or vibration, which is manifest as a sound within the divine consciousness, rather like the Vedic Vāk.[1348] The individual soul is essentially the pure consciousness of Shiva and must strive towards a recognition of its real divine self, as in Shankara's Advaita Vedantic philosophy. One key feature of this school is 'krama' meaning progress wherein the stages prior to spiritual realisation are understood in a monistic-dualistic (bhedābhedopāya) manner, though the underlying metaphysical doctrine remains monistic. In the 8th century A.D., Somānanda developed the

---

[1348] See above p.57.

notion of 'pratyabhijña' or a spontaneous recognition of the self that arises without any preparatory training.

The Shaiva Siddhānta branch[1349] was most probably a Kashmiri school in its original form, for Satyajothi Shivāchārya (ca. 7th century) is a well-known Siddhānta scholar from Kashmir who is extensively quoted in the pre-Meykandar Shaiva texts. The Siddhānta doctrines of the Kashmiris were continued in southern India by Aghorashiva of Chidambaram (12th century), who is considered one of the most authoritative representatives of southern Indian Siddhānta. Indeed, from the 12th century, the school is evidenced only in southern India. In the 13th century, Meykandar, who is famous for his treatise *Sivajnānbodham*, formulated a dualistic form of Siddhānta based on Aghorashiva's.

The Siddhānta Āgamic texts, which number 28, are said to have been authored by the Seven Sages themselves who received them from the five faces of Shiva. Thus the Sadyojata face of Shiva revealed the Kamika, Yogaja, Cintya, Karana and Ajita. These were taught to the Rishi Kaushika. The Vamadeva face gave rise to Dipta, Sukshuma, Sahasra, Amsumat and Suprabheda, and taught them to the Rishi Kashyapa. The Aghora face revealed Vijaya, Nisvasa, Svayambhuva, Agneya (or Anala) and Vira, and gave them to the Rishi Bharadvaja. The Tatpurusha gave rise to Raurava, Mukata, Vimala, Chandrajnana and Mukhabimba (or Bimba), and taught them to the Rishi Gautama. The Isana face revealed Prodgita, Lalita, Siddha, Santana, Sarvokta, Parameswara, Kirana and Vatula to the Rishi Agastya.

According to another tradition, Shiva revealed the Āgamas to Pārvati and Nandi, the bull that serves as Shiva's vehicle and assistant. Parvati revealed it to her son Lord Muruga, while Nandi, for his part, revealed it to his eight disciples, Tirumalar, Patanjali, Vyaghrapada, Sanatkumar, Sivayogamuni, Sanakar, Sanadanar and Sanandanar, all of whom are given Tamil names, though these may be Tamil forms of Sanskrit ones. For instance, Tirumular, who propounded a monistic Shaivite doctrine that is redacted in his yogic compendium, *Tirumantiram*, is considered by some to have lived in the third millennium B.C., even though the actual redaction of this work may have been made only as late as the 8th century A.D.

Ten of the 28 Shaiva Āgamas are classified as Shivabedha and are dualistic, whereas the other 18 texts belong to the Rudrabedha division and are dualistic-non-dualistic. The 12th century *Kamikāgama* of the Shivabedha class is the Āgama most widely followed in Tamil Shaiva

---

[1349] For an excellent study of Shaiva Siddhanta see G. Flood, *op.cit.*, pp.120ff.

temples, because of the availability of Aghorashiva's commentary (paddhati) on it.

For the followers of Shaiva Siddhānta, as for the Vaishnavas, worship of Shiva is graded through charya, external worship such as cleaning the temple, offering flowers, etc., kriya, which is internal worship related to the actual rituals, yoga, seeking identity with Shiva and jnāna, or wisdom in which the devotee and Shiva are one. The Shaivāgama texts on pūja, such as the 17th century *Pūjaprakāsha* of Mitramishra make clear that the devotee must purify himself internally so that he becomes similar to the deity he is about to worship since "only Śiva may worship Śiva".[1350] The yogic rituals of Shaiva Siddhānta are based on texts such as the *Svachhanda-tantra*, *Mrgendra-tantra*, and the *Kāmikāgama*. Another principal ritual text is the *Somashambu-paddhati* of the 11th c. A.D.

Shiva is understood in Shaiva Siddhānta as the totality of all, consisting of three perfections: Parameshvara (the Personal Creator Lord), Parashakti (the substratum of form) and Parashiva (Absolute Reality which transcends all). Souls and world are identical in essence with Shiva, yet also differ in that they are evolving. A pluralistic stream arose in the middle ages from the teachings of Aghorasiva and Meykandar. For Aghorasiva's school (ca 1150), Shiva is not the material cause of the universe, and the soul attains perfect "sameness" with Shiva upon liberation. Meykandar's (ca 1250) pluralistic school denies that souls ever attain perfect sameness or unity with Shiva. Thus some followers of the Shaiva Siddhānta system maintain a distinction between the self, the Lord and the universe. The Lord is considered as the Pati, or Lord of animals, the soul as Pashu, or an animal, and the bonds of the universe are called pāsha. The bond is constituted of five components – egoism (anava), action (karma), illusion (māyā), the illusory universe, and the power of concealing reality. Siddhānta recognises three types of souls, sakalas are those that have become free from all the three pasas, vijnanakalas are those that have freed themselves from māyā and karma, and pralayakalas are those that would become free from māyā only when Shiva withdraws his entire māyā-shakti finally into himself as a part of the dissolution of the worlds. Indeed, the soul's bond within the universe can be broken only by the grace (prasāda) of Shiva whereby the soul is able to become like the Lord, though ever remaining distinct from Him, for Shiva alone is always free (anādimukta).

The unfolding universe is made up of 36 tattvas (the constituents of matter and of the incarnate soul) which allow the soul to experience the

---

[1350]   See A. Michaels, *Hinduism Past and Present*, p.243.

results of their actions. Through ritual reabsorption of the tattvas, the soul may be liberated. The first ideal manifestation of the Shiva-tattva is called Bindu, the next Māyā, which produces the mixed creation and the last is Prakrti tattva which produces the lower categories of Nature described in the Samkhya.

The initiation rites of the Shaiva Siddhanta system interestingly include a ritual called vishesa-dīkshā whereby the guru transports the soul of the disciple into the womb of the goddess Vāk, consort of Shiva, who has been installed in the fire. The disciple is then reborn from her, exactly as the Vedic sacrificer is reborn during the fire-rituals studied above. Vāk here is Aditi, consort of Varuna/Vishnu in the underworld and gives birth to Agni, the underworld form of the sun which later emerges in our universe as Āditya.[1351] So the process of rebirth in the Shaiva Siddhanta is essentially identical to that of the sun.

In the next ritual, nirvāna-dīksha, the master installs in the body of the disciple the totality of the subtle elements of the cosmos. He then envisages himself as entering the central channel of the disciple's body through the aperture at the crown of the head and going down to the chakra at the heart. Next, the master leaves the disciple's body by the same route taking his disciple's soul as well as the subtle constituents of the universe with him. He brings the soul and the universal elements into his own heart through the aperture at the crown of his own head, and finally emits them from there establishing the disciple's soul and the subtle cosmos on a cord that symbolizes the spinal cord of the disciple. These are purified by the master on the cord and then replaced in the disciple's body as in a new birth.

These major rituals are then followed by daily (nitya karman) rites which burn up the remaining karma in the disciple so that, at death, he may achieve final liberation.

3: Shakta Āgamas

Shakta Āgamas, which may have originated in Bengal, and are generally called Tantras, consider Shiva's consort, Shakti, as the supreme deity. Shakti is the divine energy of Becoming while Shiva is the divine Being. Shakti is therefore regarded as the real power of all creation, maintenance and destruction. It is maintained that from the divine Shakti emerges first a Bindu or mystic drop which calls to life the diverse components of the universe. Shakti creates through her power of Māyā the multiplicity

---

[1351]   See above pp.95ff.

of the phenomenal world. The mystic seed-syllables used in Tantrism are considered as forms of Shakti and are called "mātrkā's" in yantras.

Shakta Tantra divides spiritual development into seven stages. The first four stages are constituted of the lowest stage of Vedic sacrifices, followed by the Bhakti stage practised by the Vaishnavites, and the highest stage of the Jnānamārga (the path of knowledge) followed by Shaivites. The fourth stage is called Dakshināchāra (the right-sided, or male) which leads the sādhaka into the nature of the Devi and makes him a shakta. These first four stages are together called "pravrtti", an emergence from the eternal maternal womb. As in the Vedic sacrifices, the adept has to undergo a "dīksha" and obey his guru to the last moment of salvation. Indeed the dīksha consists in the transference of the vital force of the guru into the adept.

The following three stages are termed 'nivrtti'. During these the sādhaka seeks to neutralise his newly acquired powers in such a way that he realises a universal life. The fifth stage is called Vāmachāra (the left-sided, or female) and aims at the self-destruction of the powers of pravrtti. Vāmachāra tantras are considered to be non-Vedic since they include ritual practices involving meat-eating and sexual union. The sixth stage is called Siddhāntachāra which aims at freeing one from darkness and all the bands in order to establish the universe in macrocosm and microcosm. The seventh stage is called Kaulāchāra, where the adept prepares his own funeral rites. At this stage the adept has gone beyond time and space, having acquired gnosis, Brahmagnāna, and the great mother, Shakti, dwells in his heart.

Since stress is laid on the shakti (energy) of the divinity and this shakti is characterised as female, personified as the consort of Shiva, women are in this tradition given a much more important role as images of the great goddess, and they serve as teachers as well. Also, unlike in the Vedic society, widows are allowed to remarry and the practice of sati is forbidden.[1352] Generally, unlike in the Vedic system, there is much less focus on asceticism in Shakta Tantra, which rather emphasises the female principle.

The Smārta literature (i.e. the Dharmashāstras) had given more emphasis to brahmachārya, while sexual union was permitted only to the grihastha and that only for reproduction. As Flood suggests, the brāhmanical tradition focussed on dharma (social responsibility), artha (material and political prosperity), kāma (pleasure within the bounds of social responsibility) and moksha (salvation). The Shakta

---

[1352] See *Mahānirvāna Tantra* 1,79-80.

Tantric tradition, on the other hand, stresses kāma in such a way that bhoga (pleasure) becomes identified with yoga and bhukti (pleasure) with mukti (salvation).[1353] In the secret nocturnal rite called Shrichakra indiscriminate coitus takes place to recreate the marriage of Shiva and Shakti. The Panchatattva rites involve the use of mada (alcohol), matsya (fish), mamsa (meat), mudrā (grains) and maithuna (coitus). But these rites are not entirely unbridled orgies but rather aim to control the instincts so that carnal activities are given a cosmic, divine dimension. This has precedents in Vedic religion as well, as, for instance, in *BAU* VI,4.

Ch.29 of Abhināvagupta's *Tantraloka* details the 'kula prakriya' rite which involves the unorthodox consumption of meat, alcohol, fish and the performance of ritual sex.[1354] However, as Flood points out, the *BAU* (IV,3,21) too describes the realisation of the self as the Absolute in sexual terms, while the *Chāndogya Upanishad* (II,13,1-2) identifies Vedic recitation itself with the sexual act. As Brajalal Mukherji also pointed out,[1355]

> All Vedic yajnas are based on the idea that Maithunikarana leads to spiritual happiness. Sexual intercourse is Agnihotra (*SB* XI, 6,2,10). Maithunakarana is consecration (*SB* III, 2,1,2, etc.) ... [Yajnas] direct the observance and performance of Maithuna as a religious rite or part of a religious rite ... and they direct that Mantras are to be uttererd during the observance of this rite ... One of the articles of faith of the Vaidik people therefore was that sexual union led the way to bliss hereafter and must be performed in a true religious spirit to ensure spiritual welfare, wanton indulgence being severely deprecated ...

We have noted the dramatic performance of copulation between the king's wife and the dead horse in the Ashvamedha sacrifice and may reasonably suppose this to have been a part of the original Purushamedha as well. However, it is important to observe here that, in the Vedic sacrifice, the stress is always on the phallus and its power to create the sun as well as our ordered universe, whereas in the Shakta Āgama the female aspect of coition is given special stress.

According to Mukherji, many of the other aspects of Tantra are also derived from the Vedas themselves:

[1353] See G. Flood, *op.cit.*, p.82.

[1354] *Ibid.*, p.154ff.

[1355] In 'Arthur Avalon' (Sir John Woodroffe), *Shakti and Shakta*, 'Note to Ch.IV'.

The Vaidik people performed their Somayajnas and Haviryajnas which included the Sautramani, with libations and drinks of intoxicating liquor ... The Vaidik people used to offer to their Devatas at their sacrifices animal and vegetable food ... They offer animal sacrifices ... which include the horse, goats, sheep, oxen ... and human beings (*TB* III,4,1). They believe that by performing animal sacrifices the sacrificer ransoms himself ... or wins all theseworlds ... The animal is the sacrificer himself (*AB* II, 2,1). They direct by special rules in what manner the animal should be killed, cut and offered (*AB* II,6; *SB* III, 8,1,15) ... and believed that offering animal sacrifices to the Devatas was one of the means whereby bliss hereafter could be attained.

The deities worshipped, too, are the same:

In the Yajnas the Vaidik people principally worshipped 1. Saraswati to whom animals are sacrificed and who is the same as Vak or Vagdevi, who became a lioness and went over to the Devatas on their undertaking that to her offerings should be made before they were made to Agni (*SB* III,5,1,21) ... 2. Mahadeva, another form of Agni in all his eight forms ... 3. Rudra, 4. Vishnu, 5. Vinayaka, 6. Skanda, 7. the Lingam on whom they meditated during the daily Sandhya worhsip and who is the same as Shambhu riding on a bull, 8. Shiva ... 9. the cow whom they called Bhagavati and also 10. Indra, Varuna, Agni, Soma, Rudra, Pushan, the Ashvins, Surya and some other deities. For the purpose of attaining eternal bliss they worshipped Ratridevi (*SVB* III,8) and this Ratridevi is described as a girl growing into womanhood who bestows happiness ... The portion of the Ratri Sukta which is included in the Khila portion of the *Rigveda* (*RV*,25) calls Ratri Devi by the name of Durga. ... The *Brihaddevata* II,79, mentions that Aditi, Vak, Sarasvati and Durga are the same ... The principal Devi of the Veda is Sarasvati, who is called Nagna in the Nighantu, expressing nudeness and also referring to that age of a woman when womanhood has not expressed itself.

And he adds:

The worship of the Lingam is foreshadowed by the Vaidik deity Vishnu Shipivishta (*RV* VII, 1001, etc., *Nirukta* V,2,2).

Further, some of the rituals associated with the construction of the Vedic fire-altar are repeated in Tantric ones:

> One of the [Tantric Yantras] is a triangle within a square (*Mahanirvana Tantra*, 5) and this can be traced back to the rules for the preparation of the Agnikshetra, or the Fire Altar of the Vaidik people (*SB* VI,1,1,6). Another curious circumstance in connection with the altar is that both in the Vaidik and the Tantrik ritual the heads of five animals are used in its preparation (*SB* VI, 2,1,5-8).

Indeed, Āgamic practice also includes sacrifices which are called yāga, rather than yajna, and are mostly impersonal, in the spirit of the bhakti cult of the *Gita*. As Biardeau points out, "le 'sacrifiant' du culte agamique – qui est toujours, par la force des choses, un notable, au moins local – se rapproche ainsi beaucoup plus au roi que du maître de maison ordinaire".[1356] This suggests that the Tantric sacrifices retain the public significance of the early sacred rituals of the Indo-Europeans rather more than the rituals of the later Vedic Āryans, which tended to be more domestic, and exclusive, affairs. Indeed, already in the 9th c. A.D., Jayantha Bhatta, a Kashmiri philosopher of the Nyāya school, maintained that the Shaiva Āgamas do not contradict the truths offered in the Veda, being pervaded by Upanishadic teachings about liberation, and do not go against the caste system. Rather, they only add new rituals.[1357]

Shakta Tantra, like all Tantric systems, is closely related to Kundalini yoga since Kundalini represents Shakti while the Purusha is located in the Sahasrāra lotus in the crown of the head. In Shakta Tantra, as in the Vaishnav Pāncharātra, the deities are identified within the adept's body. However, in the Shakta system, within the calyx of the heart (lotus) are visualised Shiva and his consort locked in sexual union indicating the non-differentiation of consciousness and the phenomenal world.[1358] The ritualised sexual acts performed in Shakta Tantric rituals reflect this union of Shakti and Shakta. As Flood points out, in the ecstasy of this union, the body of the adept becomes filled with an awareness of its equivalence to the cosmos and its identity to Shiva, the supreme subject of consciousness, which is "inseparable from his energy and containing within it the totality of manifestation". Here again we note that the enlightenment offered by

---

[1356]   See M. Biardeau, *op.cit.*, p.139.

[1357]   Jayantha however was against the Buddhist Tantrists since they were indeed opposed to the caste system. See G. Flood, *op. cit.*, p.51.

[1358]   Shiva is envisioned within the heart as united with his consort Uma also in the *Kaivalya Upanishad*.

Shakta Āgama is described in terms of the union of male and female principles, or in the terminology of the Samkhya philosophy, of Purusha and Prakrti, whereas, in the other Āgamas, the Vedic image of the Purusha is located by itself in the heart and the highest Bliss is the Light of Brahman to be attained at the crown of the head.

Yoga

The tantric yogic method of achieving cosmic consciousness, that is, Brahman, as well as of transcending the cycle of births, is detailed in the *Kundalini Upanishad* [derived from *KYV*]. This method is particularly related to the Shakta Tantric tradition since it considers the process of the elevation of the Kundalini to the soul as the rise of Shakti to Shiva. The Kundalini is the psychic energy which runs through the human body from the fundament upto the crown of the head, where is to be found the seat of the highest form of spirit:

> Ch.I, 2. Mind is formed out of wind ... Intellect is formed out of fire. Chitta [the sub-conscious] is formed out of water. Ego is formed out of earth.
>
> ...
>
> 11. The Kundalini should pass through the Svadhishthana Chakra [in the genitals], the Manipura Chakra in the navel, the Anahata Chakra in the heart, the Vishuddha Chakra in the throat, and the Ajna Chakra between the eyebrows.

Articles 55-60 detail the rousing of the Kundalini through the control of the internal winds of the body:

> 61. The Kundalini pierces through the Brahmagranthi formed of Rajas.
> 62. Then the Kundalini goes up at once through Vishnugranthi to the heart. Then it goes through the Rudragranthi and above it to the middle of the eyebrows.
> 63. Having pierced this place, the Kundalini goes up to the Mandala [sphere] of the moon. It dries up the moisture produced by the moon in the Anahata Chakra, which has sixteen petals.

Articles 64-66 describe in greater detail the rise of the Kundalini to the mandala of the moon. The Upanishad then continues:

69. The Kundalini then goes to the seat of the Sahasrara. It gives up the eight forms of the Prakriti: earth, water, fire, air, ether, mind, intellect and ego.

70. After clasping the eye, the mind, the Prāna and the others in her embrace, the Kundalini goes to Shiva and, clasping Shiva as well, dissolves herself in the Sahasrara.

71. Thus Rajas Sukla, or the seminal fluid which rises up goes to Shiva along with Marut or Vāyu. The Prāna and Apāna which are always produced become equal.

...

86. Then the Kundalini Shakti is happy with Shiva in Sahasrara Kamala, the thousand-petalled lotus. This should be known as the highest Avastha.

Ch. II. describes the Khechari Vidya which exhorts the adept to chant the sacred syllables of this mantra twelve times every day in order to be free of the illusions of Māyā:

19. Khechari Bija ['seed' syllable][1359] is spoken of as Agni encircled with water. It is the abode of the devas, or the khecharas.

...

27. The seven syllables Hrim, Bham, Sam, Pam, Pham, Sam and Ksham constitute the Khechari Mantra.

Articles 28-31 describe the cutting of the *frenum lingui* whereby the tongue is induced upwards into the head and (Arts. 32-41) the tongue finally reaches the Brahmarandhra [at the crown of the head]:

42. Then the yogi perceives the entire universe in his body as not being different from the Ātman.

Ch. III. introduces the Melana Vidya which focusses on the attainment of Pratyagātma, the simultaneous resolution of the microcosmos and the macrocosmos into the Supreme Self:

30. During the states of waking, dreaming and dreamless sleep, the Vijnana Atma which dwells in this body is deluded by Māyā.

...

[1359] A "bija" ("seed/seminal") syllable is a vocal source of the phenomenal world, since "Vāk" (sound/speech) is one of the earliest forms of the manifesting Soul, Ātman, arising from Viraj, the primal Waters (see above p.32f).

35. Pratyagātma is in the Dahara (Ākāsha or the ether of the heart). It obtains when the worldly wisdom, Vijnana, is destroyed and diffuses itself everywhere and, in an instant, burns the two sheaths, Vijnanamaya and Manomaya. Then it is He Himself who shines within. It shines like a light within a vessel.

At the same time, the universe too is absorbed into the universal Self:

23. Through the absorption of their respective Upadhis, or vehicles, all these in turn are absorbed in the Pratyagātma – the 3 aspects of consciousness, Vishva, Taijasa, and Prajna in man, the 3 in the universe, Virat, Hiranyagarbha and Ishvara, the egg of the universe, the egg of man and the seven worlds.

The Upanishad further specifices these aspects of the microcosm and macrocosm:

28. The first three aspects of consciousness refer to the gross, subtle and Karana bodies of man. The second three aspects of consciousness refer to the three bodies of the universe.
29. In his formation, man is and appears as an egg, even as the universe is and appears as an egg.

The absorption of the material bodies of man and the universe into the Self results in pure Being:

24. Heated by the fire of Jnāna, the egg is absorbed with its Karana, or cause, into Paramātman, or the Universal Self. It becomes one with Parabrahman.
25. ... That alone remains which is the Being-ness or Sat ...

A person who attains this state of beatitude in this life is called a Jīvanmukta, and a Jīvanmukta who abandons his body ultimately is a Videhamukta:

36. Till sleep and death the muni who contemplates thus should be known as a Jivanmukta.
    ...
38. Such a person attains Videhamukti when he gives up even the state of Jivanmukti.

39. No sooner does the body wear off than he obtains the emancipation in a disembodied state, Videhamukti.
40. After that, That alone remains. That is the soundless, the touchless, the formless, and the deathless.
41. That is the Rasa, the Essence. It is eternal and odourless. It is greater than the great. It has neither beginning or end. It is the permanent, the stainless and the decayless.

However, the *Tejobindu Upanishad* (derived from the *KYV*), Ch.4, describes the Jīvanmukta as one who has abandoned all association with his corporeal self and rests in the Self as Brahman. The Videhamukta, on the other hand, has renounced even this identification and rests as pure consciousness and ineffable bliss.

The *Dhyānabindhu Upanishad* too describes the process of the rise of the jīva from the Kundalini through the chakras. The minute description of the chakras, the nervous system and the jīva within it are worth quoting in detail:

Mūlādhāra is the first chakra. Svādhishthāna is the second. Between these two is said to be the seat of yoni (perineum), having the form of Kāma (God of love). In the Ādhāra of the anus, there is the lotus of four petals. In its midst is said to be the yoni called Kāma and worshipped by the siddhas. In the midst of the yoni is the Linga facing the west and split at its head like the gem. He who knows this is a knower of the Vedas. A four-sided figure is situated above agni and below the genital organ, of the form of molten gold and shining like streaks of lightning. Prāna is with its sva (own) sound, having Svādhishthāna as its adhishthāna (seat), (or since sva or prāna arises from it). The chakra Svādhishthāna is spoken of as the genital organ itself. The chakra in the sphere of the navel is called Manipūraka, since the body is pierced through by vāyu like manis (gems) by string. The jīva (ego) urged to actions by its past virtuous and sinful karmas whirls about in this great chakra of twelve spokes, so long as it does not grasp the truth. Above the genital organ and below the navel is kanda of the shape of a bird's egg. There arise (from it) nādis[1360] seventy-two thousand in number. Of these seventy-two are generally known. Of these, the chief ones are ten and carry the prānas. Idā, Pingalā, Sushumnā, Gāndhārī, Hastijihvā, Pasha, Yaśasvinī, Alambusā, Kuhūh and Śānkhinī are said to be the ten. This chakra of the midis

---

[1360] Nādis are channels through which cognitive currents flow and they are concentrated at the chakras.

should ever be known by the yogins. The three nādis Ida, Pingalā and Sushumnā are said to carry prāna always and have as their devatās, moon, sun and agni. Idā is on the left side and Pingalā on the right side, while the Sushumnā is in the middle. These three are known to be the paths of prāna.[1361] Prāna, Apāna, Samāna, Udāna, and Vyāna; Naga, Karma, Krkara, Devadatta and Dhanañjaya; of these, the first five are called prānas, etc., and last five Naga, etc. are called vāyus (or sub-prānas). All these are situated (or run along) the one thousand nādis, (being) in the form of (or producing) life. Jīva which is under the influence of prāna and apāna goes up and down. Jīva on account of its ever moving by the left and right paths is not visible. Just as a ball struck down (on the earth) with the bat of the hand springs up, so jīva ever tossed by prāna and apāna is never at rest. He is knower of yoga who knows that prāna always draws itself from apāna and apāna draws itself from prāna, like a bird (drawing itself from and yet not freeing itself) from the string (to which it is tied).

... Parameśvarī (viz., kundalinī śakti) sleeps shutting with her mouth that door which leads to the decayless Brahma-hole.[1362] Being aroused by the contact of agni with manas and prāna, she takes the form of a needle and pierces up through Sushumnā.[1363]

Jnāna

The highest stage of the Āgamic system is Jnāna, or perfect knowledge of divinity. This is the philosophical counterpart of the more practical disciplines of yoga and the jnāna sections of the Āgamic texts contain various discussions of cosmogony and the individual self. Similar to the precepts of the Vedānta, that is, of the Upanishads, the jnāna doctrine of the Āgamic schools is one which aims at achieving identity with Shiva. According to the *Tirumantiram,* of Tirumalar, in charya, the soul forges a kindred tie in "God's world" (salokya), in kriya it attains "nearness" (samipya) to Him, in yoga it attains "likeness" (sarupya) with Him and finally, in jnāna, the soul enjoys the ultimate bliss of identity (sayujya)

[1361] Breath.

[1362] Brahmarandhra.

[1363] The form of the kundalini is the same as that of the ouroboros serpent evidenced in the mythology of the ancient Egyptians and Mithraists, though the latter mostly represents the macrocosmic serpent that surrounds the universe and protects the dormant solar force Osiris (see above p.102).

with Shiva.[1364] The Siddhi who has become one with the deity sheds blessings on mankind even while remaining in his body.

[1364] See the summary of Jnāna Yoga in the 'Bhagavad Gita' given above (p.172f).

EPILOGUE

We see that the highest stages of both the Vedic and the Āgamic systems are clearly marked by ascetic attempts to transcend this earthly life. However, the later Brāhmanical tradition seems to have favoured asceticism rather less than the Āgamic. The *Baudhāyana Dharmasūtra,* for instance, is rather critical of renunciation since ascetics do not reproduce. The *Manusmrithi* also stresses that the four stages are all equally necessary for a brāhman or twice-born man. The *Yājñavalkya Dharmasūtra* (V.115) and *Vishnu Dharmasūtra* (II.235) further stipulate fines for feeding ascetics at festivals, while Manu (VIII,363) places a similar fine on conversations with female ascetics. This is undoubtedly because renunciation was in the original Vedic tradition reserved to men of the higher castes. and only later, in the Kali Yuga, did the Tantric tradition permit all castes and even women to engage in it.[1365]

Apart from the yogic and jnāna stages, the Āgamic systems are also generally more pragmatic than the Vedic, which stress the notion of self-sacrifice and rebirth rather more strenuously – even during the rituals practised by householders, in the form of temporary abstinence, for instance. The more dramatic rituals of human sacrifice originally practised by the Āryans were obviously even more severe in their requirements. The original solar significance of all these rituals too is clearer in the dramatic representations of the Āryans than in the Hamitic temple rituals, though the Egyptian and Mesopotamian rites are more infused with solar symbolism than the Indian tantric ones. This suggests the relative lateness of the later Hindu tradition.

The Āryan sacrifice was originally restricted to the high-born, who had a more precise understanding of the seriousness of their spiritual aims. We have noted also in our study of the Vedic sacrifices that it was originally the king who was divinised as the solar force, while brāhmans too, in the course of their several sacraments, constantly

---

[1365] See above p.156.

remind themselves of their solar identity.[1366] In the kriya rituals of the Āgamic householder, on the other hand, the notion of sacrifice is relatively obscured in the attempt to approximate the worshippers, without distinction of caste, to the deity. The deity too is given an anthropomorphic representation in the Āgamic tradition through idols that are divinised in the course of their manufacture and installation. Thus, while the Vedic rituals focus on the solar force contained within the ritual fire and venerate its embodiment primarily in spiritually eminent personages such as the king and the brāhman, the Āgamic rituals worship this force as embodied equally in idols and in all human worshippers. The role of the brāhman himself as the 'magus' and master of the fire rituals as well as of the ancient Āryan society in general is certainly diminished in the religions of the Hamitic peoples, where the king is endowed with a greater spiritual glory than even the priests, as we have noted in the case of Egypt and Sumer.

It is clear that it was the Hamitic Āgamic tradition, with its elaborate temple structures and sacred music- and dance-forms, that gave rise to the later Hindu culture of India just as it did, in the west, through Egypt and Anatolia, to the powerful Humanism of Graeco-Roman civilisation that was able to reject the iconoclasm of the Jews who imported the Christian religion[1367] into Europe in favour of a finer expression of its higher spiritual conceptions. Thus we observe, for instance, the identification of Jesus with Helios, the solar force, in early Christian art, as in the pre-Constantinian necropolis under St. Peter's basilica. Further, the tantric emphasis on the correspondences between the macrocosm and the microcosm finds a continuation in the west from the Hellenistic period onwards and especially in the theurgical works attributed to 'Hermes Trismegistus'.[1368]

[1366] See above p.214f.

[1367] For the Indo-European origins of Christianity itself, see T. Harpur, *The Pagan Christ* and A. Jacob, *Ātman*, pp.191ff.

[1368] The rediscovery and propagation of the Hermetic system in the Renaissance were principally due to Marsilio Ficino (1433-1499), who translated the Hermetic corpus, as well as the works of Plato and the Neoplatonists, into Latin and headed the Platonic Academy of Florence founded by Cosimo de Medici (1389-1464). It is interesting that some of the major discoveries in early modern science were made by those who were influenced by Ficino's Neoplatonic and Hermetic veneration of the sun, which he termed "the lord of the sky, which rules and moderates all truly celestial things" (see A. Voss (ed.), *Marsilio Ficino*, Berkeley: Atlantic Books, 2006, p.192). For instance, Copernicus was encouraged in his heliocentric theory by the Hermetic dictum that the sun was a visible god (*On the Revolutions of the Heavenly Spheres*, Amherst: Prometheus Books, 1995, p.25) and William Harvey viewed the human heart as a microcosmic sun, "the starting point of life and the sun of our microcosm, just as the sun deserves to be styled the heart of the world" (*Movement of the Heart and Blood in Animals: An Anatomical Essay*, tr.K. Franklin,

Among the Christian Desert Fathers who began their ascetic orders in Egypt at the same time that Neoplatonism established itself there, we find the use of pscyhosomatic practices similar to the yogic. In particular, the tradition of Hesychasm (stillness), which may have had its origin among the Desert Fathers in Egypt and flourished in Palestine and Cappadocia in the sixth century and was officially accepted into the Eastern Orthodox Church in the fourteenth century, emphasises a yoga-like withdrawal of the senses and a focus of thoughts inwards into the soul with the aid of the "mantric" chanting of the "Prayer of the Heart" or "Jesus Prayer". The aim of this mental ascesis is a unification of the individual soul with the Holy Spirit. The quest to experience the divine "light" stressed by the Byzantine hesychast St. Gregory Palamas (1296-1359) of Mt. Athos also bears a similarity to yogic and tantric enlightenment.

Although there is clearly a more exoteric approach to spiritual practices in Tantrism in comparison to the Vedic ethos, both the the fire-rituals of the Āryans Indians and the psychosomatic religious practices of the Hamites are equally derived from the original yogic understanding of the full macrocosmic dimension of the microcosm and from the concentration of the brāhmans who instituted the original religion of the Indo-Europeans on Brahman as the magical power of manifestation of the Supreme Soul, Ātman. As such, we may be justified in considering them together as the supreme paradigm of the spiritual perfection of the Indo-European mind.

Oxford: Blackwell, 1957, p.59). On the transformation of the mediaeval "magical" worldview into early modern science, see J. Hannam, *God's Philosophers: How the Medieval World Laid the Foundations of Modern Science*, London: Icon Books, 2010.

APPENDIX

HYMNS TO THE SOLAR FORCE

Ātman

RGVEDA X,129

1. Then was not non-existent nor existent: there was no realm of air, no sky beyond it.
2. What covered in, and where? and what gave shelter? Was water there, unfathomed depth of water?
3. Death was not then, nor was there aught immortal: no sign was there, the day's and night's divider.
4. That One Thing, breathless, breathed by its own nature: apart from it was nothing whatsoever.
5. Darkness there was: at first concealed in darkness this All was indiscriminated chaos.
6. All that existed then was void and formless: by the great power of Warmth was born that Unit.
7. Thereafter rose Desire in the beginning, Desire, the primal seed and germ of Spirit.
8. Sages who searched with their heart's thought discovered the existent's kinship in the non-existent.
9. Transversely was their severing line extended: what was above it then, and what below it?
10. There were begetters, there were mighty forces, free action here and energy up yonder.

PURUSHA
Atharva Veda, Bk.X,2

1. Who framed the heels of Purusha? Who fashioned the flesh of him? Who formed and fixed his ankles?
   Who made the openings and well-moulded fingers? Who gave him foot-soles and a central station?
2. Whence did they make the ankles that are under, and the knee-bones of Purusha above them?
   What led them onward to the legs' construction? Who planned and formed the knees' articulations?
3. A fourfold frame is fixt with ends connected, and up above the knees a yielding belly.
   The hips and thighs, who was their generator, those props whereby the trunk grew firmly stablished?
4. Who and how many were those Gods who fastened the chest of Purusha and neck together?
   How many fixed his breasts? Who formed his elbows? How many joined together ribs and shoulders?
5. Who put together both his arms and said, Let him show manly strength?
   Who and what God was he who set the shoulderblades upon the trunk?
6. Who pierced the seven openings in the head? Who made these ears, these nostrils, eyes, and mouth,
   Through whose surpassing might in all directions bipeds and quadrupeds have power of motion?
7. He set within the jaws the tongue that reaches far, and thereon placed Speech the mighty Goddess.
   He wanders to and fro mid living creatures, robed in the waters. Who hath understood it?
8. Who was he, first, of all the Gods who fashioned his skull and brain and occiput and forehead,
   The pile that Purusha's two jaws supported? Who was that God who mounted up to heaven?
9. Whence bringeth mighty Purusha both pleasant and unpleasant things,
   Of varied sort, sleep, and alarm, fatigue, enjoyments and delights?
10. Whence is there found in Purusha want, evil, suffering, distress? Whence come success, prosperity opulence, thought, and utterance?

11. Who stored in him floods turned in all directions, moving diverse and formed to flow in rivers,
    Hasty, red, copper-hued, and purple, running all ways in Purusha, upward and downward?

12. Who gave him visible form and shape? Who gave him magnitude and name?
    Who gave him motion, consciousness? Who furnished Pūrusha with feet?

13. Who wove the vital air in him, who filled him with the downward breath?
    What God bestowed on Purusha the general pervading air?

14. What God, what only Deity placed sacrifice in Purusha?
    Who gave him truth and falsehood? Whence came Death and immortality?

15. Who wrapped a garment round him? Who arranged the life he hath to live?
    Who granted him the boon of speech? Who gave this fleetness to his feet?

16 Through whom did he spread waters out, through whom did he make Day to shine?
    Through whom did he enkindle Dawn and give the gift of eventide?

17. Who set the seed in him and said, Still be the thread of life spun out?
    Who gave him intellect besides? Who gave him voice and gestic power?

18. Through whom did he bedeck the earth, through whom did he encompass heaven?
    Whose might made Purusha surpass the mountains and created things?

19. Through whom seeks he Parjanya out, and Soma of the piercing sight?
    Through whom belief and sacrifice? Through whom was spirit laid in him?

20. What leads him to the learned priest? What leads him to this Lord Supreme?
    How doth he gain this Agni? By whom hath he measured out the year?

21. He, Brahma gains the learned priest, he Brahma, gains this Lord Supreme.
    As Brahma, Man wins Agni here Brahma hath measured out the

year.

22. Through whom doth he abide with Gods? Through whom with the Celestial Tribes?
Why is this other called a star? Why is this called the Real Power?

23. Brahma inhabits with the Gods, Brahma among the Heavenly Tribes.
Brahma this other star is called. Brahma is called the RealPower.

24. By whom was this our earth disposed? By whom was heaven placed over it?
By whom was this expanse of air raised up on high and stretched across?

25. By Brahma was this earth disposed: by Brahma is sky arranged above.
Brahma is this expanse of air lifted on high and stretched across.

26. Together, with his needle hath Atharvan sewn his head and heart.
And Pavamāna hovered from his head on high above his brain.

27. That is indeed Atharvan's head, the well-closed casket of the Gods.
Spirit and Food and Vital Air protect that head from injury.

28. Stationed on high, Purusha hath pervaded all regions spread aloft and stretched transversely.
He who knows Brahma's cattle, yea, the fort whence Purusha is named,

29. Yea, knows that fort of Brahma girt about with immortality,
Brahma and Brāhmas have bestowed sight, progeny, and life on him.

30. Sight leaves him not, breath quits not him before life's natural decay,
Who knows the fort of Brahma, yea, the fort whence Purusha is named.

31. The fort of Gods, impregnable, with circles eight and portals nine,
Contains a golden treasure-chest, celestial, begirt with light.

32. Men deep in lore of Brahma know that Animated Being which
Dwells in the golden treasure-chest that hath three spokes and three supports.

33. Brahma hath passed within the fort, the golden castle; ne'er subdued,
Bright with excessive brilliancy, compassed with glory round about.

RGVEDA X,90

1. A thousand heads hath Purusha, a thousand eyes, a thousand
   feet.On every side pervading earth he fills a space ten fingers
   wide.
2. This Purusha is all that yet hath been and all that is to be;
   The Lord of Immortality which waxes greater still by food.
3. So mighty is his greatness; yea, greater than this is Purusha.
   All creatures are one-fourth of him, three-fourths eternal life in
   heaven.
4. With three-fourths Purusha went up: one-fourth of him again
   was here.
   Thence he strode out to every side over what eats not and what
   eats.
   ...
11. When they divided Purusha how many portions did they make?
    What do they call his mouth, his arms? What do they call his
    thighs and feet?
12. The Brahman was his mouth, of both his arms was the Rājanya
    made.
    His thighs became the Vaiśya, from his feet the Śūdra was
    produced.
13. The Moon was gendered from his mind, and from his eye the
    Sun had birth; Indra and Agni from his mouth were born, and
    Vāyu from his breath.
14. Forth from his navel came mid-air the sky was fashioned from
    his head, Earth from his feet, and from his car the regions. Thus
    they formed the worlds.
15. Seven fencing-sticks had he, thrice seven layers of fuel were
    prepared,
    When the Gods, offering sacrifice, bound, as their victim,
    Purusha.
16. Gods, sacrificing, sacrificed the victim these were the earliest holy
    ordinances.
    The Mighty Ones attained the height of heaven, there where the
    Sādhyas, Gods of old, are dwelling.

Yajna

ATHARVA VEDA, BK. XIX,6

9. In the beginning rose Virāj: Purusha from Virāj was born.
    As soon as he was born he spread westward and eastward o'er the earth.
10. When Gods performed the sacrifice with Purusha as their offering.
    Spring was the butter, summer was the fuel, autumn was the gift.
11. That sacrifice, first-born Purusha, they hallowed with the sprinkled Rains.
    The Deities, the Sādhyas, all the Vasus sacrificed with him.
12. From it were horses born, from it all creatures with two rows of teeth.
    From it were generated kine, from it were goats and sheep produced.
13. From that great general sacrifice Richas[1369] and Sāma hymns were born;
    Therefrom the metres were produced: the Yajus had its birth from it.
14. From that great general sacrifice the dripping fat was gathered up:
    It formed the creatures fleet as wind, and animals both wild and tame.
15. Seven fencing-logs had he, thrice seven layers of fuel were prepared.
    When, offering sacrifice, the Gods bound as their victim Purusha.
16. Forth from head of the high God seven-and-seventy bright beams
    Sprang into being, of the King Soma produced from Purusha.

RGVEDA X,130

1. The sacrifice drawn out with threads on every side, stretched by a hundred sacred ministers and one,—
    This do these Fathers weave who hitherward are come: they sit beside the warp and cry, Weave forth, weave back.
2. The Man extends it and the Man unbinds it: even to this vault of heaven hath he outspun it.
    These pegs are fastened to the seat of worship: they made the Sāma-hymns their weaving shuttles.

[1369] The verses of the Rgveda.

The Creation of the Vedic Hymns and Metres

RGVEDA X,130 (CONTINUED)

3. What were the rule, the order and the model? What were the
    wooden fender and the butter?
    What were the hymn, the chant, the recitation, when to the God
    all Deities paid worship?
4. Closely was Gāyatrī conjoined with Agni, and closely Savitar
    combined with Usnih.
    Brilliant with Ukthas, Soma joined Anustup: Brhaspati's voice by
    Brhati was aided.
5. Virāj adhered to Varuna and Mitra: here Trishtup day by day was
    Indra's portion.
    Jagatī entered all the Gods together: so by this knowledge men
    were raised to Rshis.
6. So by this knowledge men were raised to Rshis, when ancient
    sacrifice sprang up, our Fathers.
    With the mind's eye I think that I behold them who first
    performed this sacrificial worship.
7. They who were versed in ritual and metre, in hymns and rules,
    were the Seven Godlike Rshis.
    Viewing the path of those of old, the sages have taken up the
    reins like chariot-drivers.

The Solar Force in the Underworld

HYMN TO OSIRIS
Book of the Dead (Papyrus of Ani)[1370]

You are a Great One whose strength is mighty, and your son Horus is
your protector; he will remove all evil which is on you. Your flesh is knit
together for you, your members are recreated for you, your bones are
reassembled for you ... Rise up, Osiris; I have given you my hand and have

[1370] *The Egyptian Book of the Dead, the Book of Going Forth by Day*, tr. R.O. Faulkner, p.133.

caused you to stand up living forever. Geb has wiped your mouth for you ... Your mother Nut has put her arms about you that she may protect you, and she will continually guard you, even you the high-born ...

Happy are you, O Osiris! You have appeared in glory, you have power, you are a spirit ... Re rejoices over you and he is well disposed towards your beauty. You have seated yourself on your pure throne which Geb, who loves you, made for you; you receive him in your arms in the West in the Bark of Re, together with Horus who loves you. The protection of Re is your safeguard, the power of Thoth is behind you, and the incantations of Isis pervade your members

Soma

RGVEDA IX,86

1. Born like a youngling he hath clamoured in the wood, when he, the Red, the Strong, would win the light of heaven.
    He comes with heavenly seed that makes the water swell: him for wide-spreading shelter we implore with prayer.
2. A far-extended pillar that supports the sky the Soma-stalk, filled full, moves itself every way.
    He shall bring both these great worlds while the rite proceeds: the Sage holds these who move! together and all food.
3. Wide space hath he who follows Aditi's right path, and mighty, well-made food, meath blent with Soma juice;
    He who from hence commands the rain, Steer of the kine, Leader of floods, who helps us hence, who claims our laud.
4. Butter and milk are drawn from animated cloud; thence Amrta [nectar of immortality] is produced, centre of sacrifice.
    Him the Most Bounteous Ones, ever united, love; him as our Friend the Men who make all swell rain down.
5. The Soma-stalk hath roared, following with the wave: he swells with sap for man the skin which Gods enjoy.
    Upon the lap of Aditi he lays the germ, by means whereof we gain children and progeny.
6. In the third region which distils a thousand streams, may the Exhaustless Ones descend with procreant power.
    The kindred Four have been sent downward from the heavens: dropping with oil they bring Amrta and sacred gifts.

7. Soma assumes white colour when he strives to gain: the
    bounteous Asura knows full many a precious boon.
    Down the steep slope, through song, he comes to sacrifice, and he
    will burst the water-holding cask of heaven,

8. Yea, to the shining milk-anointed beaker, as to his goal, hath
    stepped the conquering Courser.
    Pious-souled men have sent their gift of cattle unto Kakshīvān of
    the hundred winters.

9. Soma, thy juice when thou art blended with the streams, flows,
    Pavamana, through the long wool of the sheep.
    So, cleansed by sages. O best giver of delight, grow sweet for
    Indra, Pavamana! for his drink.

RGVEDA IX,86

3. Like a steed urged to battle, finder of the light; speed onward to
    the cloud-born reservoir of heaven,
    A Steer that o'er the woolly surface seeks the sieve, Soma while
    purified for Indra's nourishment.

4. Fleet as swift steeds, thy drops, divine, thought-swift, have been,
    O Pavamana, poured with milk into the vat.
    The Rshis have poured in continuous Soma drops, ordainers who
    adorn thee, Friend whom Rshis love.

5. O thou who seest all things, Sovran as thou art and passing
    strong, thy rays encompass all abodes.
    Pervading with thy natural powers thou flowest on, and as the
    whole world's Lord, O Soma, thou art King.

6. The beams of Pavamana, sent from earth and heaven, his ensigns
    who is ever steadfast, travel round.
    When on the sieve the Golden-hued is cleansed, he rests within
    the vats as one who seats him in his place.

7. Served with fair rites he flows, ensign of sacrifice: Soma advances
    to the special place of Gods.
    He speeds with thousand currents to the reservoir, and passes
    through the filter bellowing as a bull.

8. The Sovran dips him in the seain and the streams, and set in
    rivers with the waters' wave moves on.
    High heaven's Sustainer at the central point of earth, raised on the
    fleecy surface Pavamana stands.

9. He on whose high decree the heavens and earth depend hath

roared and thundered like the summit of the sky.
Soma flows on obtaining Indra's friendly love, and, as they purify him, settles in the jars.

10. He, light of sacrifice distils delicious meath, most wealthy, Father and begetter of the Gods.
    He, gladdening, best of Cheerers, juice that Indra loves, enriches with mysterious treasure earth and heaven.

11. The vigorous and far-seeing one, the Lord of heaven, flows, shouting to the beaker, with his thousand streams.
    Coloured like gold he rests in seats where Mitra dwells, the Steer made beautiful by rivers and by sheep.

12. In forefront of the rivers Pavamana speeds, in forefront of the hymn, foremost among the kine.
    He shares the mighty booty in the van of war: the well-armed Steer is purified by worshippers.

13. This heedful Pavamana, like a bird sent forth, hath with his wave flowed onward to the fleecy sieve.
    O Indra, through thy wisdom, by thy thought, O Sage, Soma flows bright and pure between the earth and heaven.

14. He, clad in mail that reaches heaven, the Holy One, filling the firmament stationed amid the worlds,
    Knowing the realm of light, hath come to us in rain: he summons to himself his own primeval Sire.

15. He who was first of all to penetrate his form bestowed upon his race wide shelter and defence.
    From that high station which he hath in loftiest heaven he comes victorious to all encounters here.

16. Indu hath started for Indra's special place and slights not as a Friend the promise of his Friend.
    Soma speeds onward like a youth to youthful maids, and gains the beaker by a course of bundred paths.

17. Your songs, exhilarating, tuneful, uttering praise, are come into the places where the people meet.
    Worshippers have exalted Soma with their hymns, and milch kine have come near to meet him with their milk.

18. O Soma, Indu, while they cleanse thee, pour on us accumulated Plentiful, nutritious food,
    Which, ceaseless, thrice a day shall yield us hero power enriched with store of nourishment, and strength, and Meath.

19. 19 Far-seeing Soma flows, the Steer, the Lord of hymns, the Furtherer of day, of morning, and of heaven.

Mixt with the streams he caused the beakers to resound, and with the singers' aid they entered Indra's heart.

20. On, with the prudent singers, flows the ancient Sage and guided by the men hath roared about the vats.
Producing Trita's name, may he pour forth the meath, that Vāyu and that Indra may become his Friends.

21. He, being purified, hath made the Mornings shine: this, even this is he who gave the rivers room.
He made the Three Times Seven pour out the milky flow: Soma, the Cheerer, yields whate'er the heart finds sweet.

22. Flow, onward, Soma, in thine own celestial forms, flow, Indu, poured within the beaker and the sieve.
Sinking into the throat of Indra with a roar, led by the men thou madest Sūrya mount to heaven.

23. Pressed out with stones thou flowest onward to the sieve, O Indu, entering the depths of Indra's throat.
Far-sighted Soma, now thou lookest on mankind: thou didst unbar the cowstall for the Angirases.

24. In thee, O Soma, while thou purifitedst thee, high-thoughted sages, seeking favour, have rejoiced.
Down from the heavens the Falcon brought thee hitherward, even thee, O Indu, thee whom all our hymns adorn.

25. Seven Milch-kine glorify the Tawny-coloured One while with his wave in wool he purifies himself.
The living men, the mighty, have impelled the Sage into the waters' lap, the place of sacrifice.

26. Indu, attaining purity, plunges through the foe, making his ways all easy for the pious man.
Making the kine his mantle, he, the lovely Sage, runs like a sporting courser onward through the fleece.

27. The ceaseless watery fountains with their hundred streams sing, as they hasten near, to him the Golden-hued
Him, clad in robes of milk, swift fingers beautify on the third height and in the luminous realm of heaven.

28. These are thy generations of celestial seed thou art the Sovran Lord of all the world of life.
This universe, O Pavamana, owns thy sway; thou, Indu, art the first establisher of Law.

29. Thou art the sea, O Sage who bringest alf to light: under thy Law are these five regions of the world.
Tlou reachest out beyond the earth, beyond the heavens: thine

are the lights, O Pavamana, thine the Sun.

30. Thou in the filter, Soma Pavamana, art purified to support the region for the Gods.
The chief, the longing ones have sought to hold thee fast, and all these living creatures have been turned to thee.

31. Onward the Singer travels o'er the fleecy sieve, the Tawny Steer hath bellowed in the wooden vats.
Hymns have been sung aloud in resonant harmony, and holy songs kiss him, the Child who claims our praise.

32. He hath assumed the rays of Sūrya for his robe, spinning, as he knows bow, the triply-twisted thread.
He, guiding to the newest rules of Holy Law, comes as the Women's Consort to the special place.

33. On flows the King of rivers and the Lord of heaven: he follows with a shout the paths of Holy Law.
The Golden-hued is poured forth, with his hundred streams, Wealth-bringer, lifting up his voice while purified.

34. Fain to be cleansed, thou, Pavamana, pourest out, like wondrous Sūrya, through the fleece, an ample sea.
Purified with the hands, pressed by the men with stones, thou speedest on to mighty booty-bringing war.

35. Thou, Pavamana, sendest food and power in streams, thou sittest in the beakers as a hawk on trees,
For Indra poured as cheering juice to make him glad, as nearest and farseeing bearer-up of heaven.

Indra

RGVEDA IV, 26

1. I was aforetime Manu, I was Sūrya: I am the sage Kakshīvān, holy singer.
Kutsa the son of Ārjuni I master. I am the sapient Uśanā behold me.

2. I have bestowed the earth upon the Ārya, and rain upon the man who brings oblation.
I guided forth the loudly-roaring waters, and the Gods moved according to my pleasure.

3. In the wild joy of Soma I demolished Śambara's forts, ninety-and-
    nine, together;
    And, utterly, the hundredth habitation, when helping Divodāsa
    Atithigva.
4. Before all birds be ranked this Bird, O Maruts; supreme of falcons
    be this fleet-winged Falcon,[1371]
    Because, strong-pinioned, with no car to bear him, he brought to
    Manu the Godloved oblation.
5. When the Bird brought it, hence in rapid motion sent on the wide
    path fleet as thought he hurried.
    Swift he returned with sweetness of the Soma, and hence the
    Falcon hath acquired his glory.
6. Bearing the stalk, the Falcon speeding onward, Bird bringing
    from afar the draught that gladdens,
    Friend of the Gods, brought, grasping fast, the Soma which be
    had taken from yon loftiest heaven.
7. The Falcon took and brought the Soma, bearing thousand
    libations with him, yea, ten thousand.

RGVEDA X, 89

1. I will extol the most heroic Indra who with his might forced earth
    and sky asunder;
    Who hath filled all with width as man's Upholder, surpassing
    floods and rivers in his greatness.
2. Sūrya is he: throughout the wide expanses shall Indra turn him,
    swift as car-wheels, hither,
    Like a stream resting not but ever active he hath destroyed, with
    light, the black-hued darkness.
3. To him I sing a holy prayer, incessant new, matchless, common to
    the earth and heaven,
    Who marks, as they were backs, all living creatures: ne'er doth he
    fail a friend, the noble Indra.
4. I will send forth my songs in flow unceasing, like water from the
    ocean's depth, to Indra.
    Who to his car on both its sides securely hath fixed the earth and
    heaven as with an axle.
5. Rousing with draughts, the Shaker, rushing onward, impetuous,
    very strong, armed as with arrows

[1371] The early form of the sun (see above p.208).

Is Soma; forest trees and all the bushes deceive not Indra with
their offered likeness.

6.   Soma hath flowed to him whom naught can equal, the earth, the
heavens, the firmament, the mountains,—
When heightened in his ire his indignation shatters the firm and
breaks the strong in pieces.

7.   As an axe fells the tree so he slew Vrtra, brake down the
strongholds and dug out the rivers.
He cleft the mountain like a new-made pitcher. Indra brought
forth the kine with his Companions.

8.   Wise art thou, Punisher of guilt, O Indra. The sword lops limbs,
thou smitest down the sinner,
The men who injure, as it were a comrade, the lofty Law of
Varuna and Mitra.

9.   Men who lead evil lives, who break agreements, and injure
Varuna, Aryaman and Mitra,—
Against these foes, O Mighty Indra, sharpen, as furious death, thy
Bull of fiery colour.

10. Indra is Sovran Lord of Earth and Heaven, Indra is Lord of waters
and of mountains.
Indra is Lord of prosperers and sages Indra must be invoked in
rest and effort.

11. Vaster than days and nights, Giver of increase, vaster than
firmament and flood of ocean,
Vaster than bounds of earth and wind's extension, vaster than
rivers and our lands is Indra.

12. Forward, as herald of refulgent Morning, let thine insatiate arrow
fly, O Indra.
And pierce, as 'twere a stone launched forth from heaven, with
hottest blaze the men who love deception.

13. Him, verily, the moons, the mountains followed, the tall trees
followed and the plants and herbage.
Yearning with love both Worlds approached, the Waters waited
on Indra when he first had being.

Skambha, the Phallic Universe

ATHARVA VEDA, X,7

4. ... Who out of many, tell me, is that Skambha to whom with longing go the turning pathways?

5. Whitherward go the half-months, and, accordant with the full year, the months in
    their procession?
    Who out of many, tell me, is that Skambha to whom go
    seasons and the groups of seasons?

6. Whitherward yearning speed the two young Damsels, accordant, Day and Night, of different colour?
    Who out of many, tell me, is that Skambha to whom the Waters take their way with longing?

7. Who out of many, tell me, is that Skambha,
    On whom Prajāpati set up and firmly stablished all the worlds?

8. That universe which Prajāpati created, wearing all forms,
    the highest, midmost, lowest,How far did Skambha penetrate within it? What portion did he leave unpenetrated?

9. How far within the past hath Skambha entered? How much of him hath reached into the future?
    That one part which he set in thousand places,—how far did Skambha penetrate within it?

10. Who out of many, tell me, is that Skambha in whom men recognize the Waters,
    Brahma,
    In whom they know the worlds and their enclosures, in whom are non-existence and existence?

11. Declare that. Skambha, who is he of many,
    In whom, exerting every power, Fervour maintains her loftiest vow;
    In whom are comprehended Law, Waters, Devotion and Belief

12. Who out of many, tell me, is that Skambha
    On whom as their foundation earth and firmament and sky are set;
    In whom as their appointed place rest Fire and Moon and Sun and Wind?

13. Who out of many, tell me, is that Skambha

He in whose body are contained all three-and-thirty Deities?

14. Who out of many, tell me, is that Skambha.
In whom the Sages earliest born, the Richas, Sāman, Yajus, Earth,
and the one highest Sage abide?

15. Who out of many, tell me, is the Skambha.
Who comprehendeth, for mankind, both immortality and death,
He who containeth for mankind the gathered waters as his veins?

16. Who out of many, tell me, is that Skambha,
He whose chief arteries stand there, the sky's four regions, he irk
whom Sacrifice putteth forth its might?

17 They who in Purusha understand Brahma know Him who is
Supreme.
He who knows Him who is Supreme, and he who knows the Lord
of Life,
These know the loftiest Power Divine, and thence know Skambha
thoroughly.

18. Who out of many, tell me, is that Skambha
Of whom Vaishvānara became the head, the Angirases his eye,
and Yātus his corporeal parts?

19 Who out of many, tell me, is that Skambha
Whose mouth they say is Holy Lore, his tongue the Honey-
sweetened Whip, his
udder is Virāj, they say?

20. Who out of many, tell me, is that Skambha
From whom they hewed the Richas off, from whom they chipped
the Yajus, he
Whose hairs are Sāma-verses and his mouth the Atharvāngirases?

21. Men count as 'twere a thing supreme nonentity's conspicuous
branch;
And lower man who serve thy branch regard it as an entity.

22. Who out of many, tell me, is that Skambha
In whom Ādityas dwell, in whom Rudras and Vasus are
contained,
In whom the future and the past and all the worlds are firmly set;

23. Whose secret treasure evermore the three-and thirty Gods
protect?
Who knoweth now the treasure which, O Deities ye watch and
guard?

24. Where the Gods, versed in Sacred Lore, worship the loftiest
Power Divine
The priest who knows them face to face may be a sage who knows

the truth.

25. Great, verily, are those Gods who sprang from non-existence into life.

Further, men say that that one part of Skambha is nonentity.

26. Where Skambha generating gave the Ancient World its shape and form,

They recognized that single part of Skambha as the Ancient World,

27. The three-and-thirty Gods within his body were disposed as limbs:

Some, deeply versed in Holy Lore, some know those three-and-thirty Gods.

28. Men know Hiranyagarbha as supreme and inexpressible:

In the beginning, in the midst of the world, Skambha poured that gold.

29. On Skambha Fervour rests, the worlds and Holy Law repose on him.

Skambha, I clearly know that all of thee on Indra is imposed.

30. On Indra Fervour rests, on him the worlds and Holy Law recline.

Indra, I clearly know that all of thee on Skambha findeth rest.

31. Ere sun and dawn man calls and calls one Deity by the other's name.

When the Unborn first sprang into existence he reached that independent sovran lordship; than which aught higher never hath arisen.

32 Be reverence paid to him, that highest Brahma, whose base is Earth, his belly Air, who made the sky to be his head.

33. Homage to highest Brahma, him whose eye is Sūrya and the Moon who groweth young and new again,

Him who made Agni for his mouth.

34. Homage to highest Brahma, him whose two life-breathings were the Wind,

The Angirases his sight: who made the regions be his means of sense.

35. Skambha set fast these two, the earth and heaven, Skambha maintained the ample air between them.

Skambha established the six spacious regions: this whole world Skambha entered and pervaded.

36. 36. Homage to highest Brahma, him who, sprung from Fervour and from toil,

Filled all the worlds completely, who made Soma for himself

alone.

37. Why doth the Wind move ceaselessly? Why doth the spirit take no rest?
Why do the Waters, seeking truth, never at any time repose?

38 Absorbed in Fervour, is the mighty Being, in the world's centre on the waters' surface.
To him the Deities, one and all betake them. So stand the tree-trunk with the branches round it.

39. Who out of many, tell me, is that Skambha.
To whom the Deities with hands, with feet, and voice, and ear, and eye.
Present unmeasured tribute in the measured hall of sacrifice?

40. Darkness is chased away from him: he is exempt from all distress.
In him are all the lights, the three abiding in Prajāpati.

41. He verily who knows the Reed of Gold that stands amid the flood, is the mysterious Lord of Life.

42. Singly the two young Maids of different colours approach the six-pegged warp in turns and weave it.
The one draws out the threads, the other lays them: they break them not, they reach no end of labour.

43. Of these two, dancing round as 'twere, I cannot distinguish whether ranks before the other.
A Male in weaves this web, a Male divides it: a Male hath stretched it to the cope of heaven

44. These pegs have buttressed up the sky. The Sāmans have turned them into shuttles for the weaving.

The Rising Sun

RGVEDA IV,27

1. 1. I, as I lay within the womb, considered all generations of these Gods in order. A hundred iron fortresses confined me but forth I flew with rapid speed a Falcon.

2. Not at his own free pleasure did he bear me: he conquered with his strength and manly courage.
Straightway the Bold One left the fiends behind him and passed the winds as he grew yet more mighty.

3. When with loud cry from heaven down sped the Falcon, thence hasting like

the wind he bore the Bold One.

Then, wildly raging in his mind, the archer Kŕśānu aimed and loosed the string to strike him.

4. The Falcon bore him from heaven's lofty summit as the swift car of Indra's Friend bore Bhujyu.

Then downward hither fell a flying feather of the Bird hasting forward in his journey.

RGVEDA IX, 10.

1. Like cars that thunder on their way, like coursers eager for renown,
   Have Soma-drops flowed forth for wealth.
2. Forth have they rushed from holding hands, like chariots that are urged to speed,
   Like joyful songs of singing-men.
3. The Somas deck themselves with milk, as Kings are graced with eulogies,
   And, with seven priests, the sacrifice.
4. Pressed for the gladdening draught, the drops flow forth abundantly with song,
   The Soma juices in a stream.
5. Winning Vivasvān's glory and producing Morning's light, the Suns
   Pass through the openings of the cloth.
6. The singing-men of ancient time open the doors of sacred songs,—
   Men, for the mighty to accept.
7. Combined in close society sit the seven priests, the brother-hood,
   Filling the station of the One.
8. He gives us kinship with the Gods, and with the Sun unites our eye:
   The Sage's ofrspring hath appeared.
9. The Sun with his dear eye beholds that quarter of the heavens which priests
   Have placed within the sacred cell.

Horus

HYMN TO RA: "ADORATION OF RA WHEN HE RISES ON THE EASTERN HORIZON OF HEAVEN"

... *Homage to you*, Harmachis.[1372] It is Khepri who creates himself. How beautiful is your rising on the horizon, when you bring dawn to the earth by your radiance. All the gods rejoice when they see you as king of heaven.

The Lady of the Hour is established on your head, her uraei of the south and north on your brow.

She has made her place in front of you, and Thoth abides at the front of your boat to destroy all your enemies.

Those who are in the netherworld come forth in homage to you, to see that beautiful image.

I have come before you; may I be with you to see your Disk every day. May I not be imprisoned, may I not be turned away.

May my limbs be renewed when I see your beauties like all your honored ones, because I am one of your noble ones on earth.

I have arrived at the land of eternity, and I have attained the land of of infinity; indeed you have commanded it for me, my lord.

The Osiris [scribe] Ani, true of voice in peace, true of voice, *calls out, He says, homage to you w*hen you rise on your horizon as Ra, resting on Truth.

You sail over heaven, and every face sees you as you travel, hidden from their faces.

You show yourself [in] the morning and in the evening [every] day. The Evening Boat is vigorous under your majesty, and you illuminate [all] faces.

[Your] golden flame[?] is not known; your beams are not described in writing.

The lands of the gods see you, and the lands of Punt account you hidden.

You make yourself alone; the Sem-priest opens his mouth; your form is on the Celestial Waters.

May he go in the same way that you go, ceaselessly like your majesty, in a short time. [You] advance, far across the River of Millions of

---

[1372] Harmachis is Horus of the Two Horizons, that is, of the east as well as of the west.

Years, in a hundred thousand little moments, which you have made. You have set; you have finished the hours of night. Likewise you have travelled; you have finished it according to your laws, giving dawn to the earth.

You give yourself to your work as Ra; you rise on the horizon.

As for the Osiris scribe Ani, true of voice, *he says,* he praises you when you shine, and he speaks to you when you rise.

You bring morning to exalt your forms, and you ascend to magnify your beauties.

Advancing, you fashion your limbs in gold; he who is without his birth gives birth as Ra, rising in the sky.

May you let me reach the sky of eternity and the territory of the favored ones; may I be united with the noble and perfect glorified souls of the underworld; may I come forth with them to see your beauties when you rise and in the evening when you go to your mother Nut.

You turn your face to the west, and my arms are raised in acclamation of your setting in life; indeed, it is you who who is eternally praised when you set in the Celestial Waters.

......

As for the Osiris scribe Ani, true of voice, *you will come forth* to the sky; you will sail over the substance of heaven; you will join with the stars.

Hymns will be made for you in the boat; you will be called in the Morning Boat.

You will see Ra in his shrine, and make his disk to set every day.

You have seen the Inet-fish in its forms on the stream of turquoise; you have seen the Ibdu-fish in its time.

The evil one becomes downfallen when he prepares my mutilation, and his backbone is pierced.

The being of Ra is as a good breeze, drawing on the Evening Boat to its arrival.

The sailors of Ra rejoice for the Lady of Life, and her heart is sweet when she overthrows the enemies of her lord.

You have seen Horus on the lookout post, Thoth and Maat at his sides. All the gods rejoice when they see Ra coming in peace to make the hearts of the glorified souls live ...

Mithra

MIHIR YASHT IV

12. …We sacrifice unto Mithra, the lord of wide pastures, … sleepless,
    and ever awake;
13. Who first of the heavenly gods reaches over the Hara,[1373] before
    the undying, swift-horsed sun; who, foremost in a golden array,
    takes hold of the beautiful summits, and from thence looks over
    the abode of the Aryans with a beneficent eye.
14. Where the valiant chiefs draw up their many troops in array;
    where the high mountains, rich in pastures and waters, yield
    plenty to the cattle; where the deep lakes, with salt waters, stand;
    where wide-flowing rivers swell and hurry towards Ishkata
    and Pouruta,[1374] Mouru and Haroyu, the Gava-Sughdha and
    Hvairizem;[1375]
15. On Arezahi and Sawahi, on Fradadhafshu and Widadhafshu,
    on Wouru-bareshti and Wourujareshti, on this bright karshwar
    of Xwaniratha, the abode of cattle, the dwelling of cattle, the
    powerful Mithra looks with a health-bringing eye;
16. He who moves along all the karshwars, a Yazata[1376] unseen, and
    brings glory; he who moves along all the karshwars, a Yazata
    unseen, and brings sovereignty; and increases strength for victory
    to those who, with a pious intent, holily offer him libations.
    For his brightness and glory, I will offer him a sacrifice worth
    being heard …

MIHIR YASHT XVIII.

70. We sacrifice unto Mithra, the lord of wide pastures, …. sleepless,
    and ever awake;
    Before whom Verethraghna, made by Ahura, runs opposing

[1373]   Hara Berezaiti is the mountain range in Airyanam Vaejah and Mt. Hara (Persian Alburz) is its highest peak .

[1374]   Uncertain.

[1375]   Mouru is perhaps Marv (Margiana), Haroya Herat, Gava-Sugda Sogdiana, and Hvarizem Khvarizm.

[1376]   Yazata is a being worthy of worship.

the foes in the shape of a boar, a sharp-toothed he-boar, a sharp-jawed boar, that kills at one stroke, pursuing, wrathful, with a dripping face; strong, with iron feet, iron fore-paws, iron weapons, an iron tail, and iron jaws;

71. Who, eagerly clinging to the fleeing foe, along with Manly Courage, smites the foe in battle, and does not think he has smitten him, nor does he consider it a blow till he has smitten away the marrow and the column of life, the marrow and the spring of existence.

72. He cuts all the limbs to pieces, and mingles, together with the earth, the bones, hair, brains, and blood of the men who have lied unto Mithra.

    For his brightness and glory, we offer him a sacrifice worth being heard....

MIHIR YASHT XXIII

88. We sacrifice unto Mithra, the lord of wide pastures, ... sleepless, and ever awake;

    To whom the enlivening, healing, fair, lordly, golden-eyed Haoma offered up a sacrifice on the highest of the heights, on the Haraiti Bareza, he the undefiled to one undefiled, with undefiled baresma, undefiled libations, and undefiled words;

89. Whom the holy Ahura Mazda has established as a priest, quick in performing the sacrifice and loud in song. He performed the sacrifice with a loud voice, as a priest quick in sacrifice and loud in song, a priest to Ahura Mazda, a priest to the Amesha-Spentas. His voice reached up to the sky, went over the earth all around, went over the seven keshwars.

90. Who first lifted up Haomas, in a mortar inlaid with stars and made of a heavenly substance.[1377] Ahura Mazda longed for him, the Amesha-Spentas longed for him, for the well-shapen body of him whom the swift-horsed sun awakes for prayer from afar.

91. Hail to Mithra, the lord of wide pastures, who has a thousand ears and ten thousand eyes! Thou art worthy of sacrifice and prayer: mayest thou have sacrifice and prayer in the houses of men! Hail to the man who shall offer thee a sacrifice, with the holy wood in his hand, the baresma in his hand, the holy meat in his hand, the holy mortar in his

---

[1377] For Vivanghavant as the first to prepare Haoma for the manifest world, see above p.257.

hand, with his hands well-washed, with the mortar well-washed, with the bundles of baresma tied up, the Haoma uplifted, and the Ahuna Vairya sung through.

92. The holy Ahura Mazda confessed that religion and so did Vohu-Mano, so did Asha-Vahishta, so did Khshathra-Vairya, so did Spenta-Armaiti, so did Haurvatat and Ameretat;[1378] and all the Amesha-Spentas longed for and confessed his religion. The kind Mazda conferred upon him the mastership of the world; and [so did the Amesha Spentas] who saw thee amongst all creatures the right lord and master of the world, the best cleanser of these creatures.

MIHIR YASHT XXV

99. We sacrifice unto Mithra, the lord of wide pastures, ... sleepless, and ever awake;
From whom all the Daevas unseen and the Varenya fiends flee away in fear.
The lord of nations, Mithra, the lord of wide pastures, drives forward at the right-hand side of this wide, round earth, whose ends lie afar.

100. At his right hand drives the good, holy Sraosha;[1379] at his left hand drives the tall and strong Rashnu;[1380] on all sides around him drive the waters, the plants, and the Fravashis [1381] of the faithful.

MIHIR YASHT XXXI

123. We sacrifice unto Mithra, the lord of wide pastures, ... sleepless, and ever awake;
To whom Ahura Mazda offered up a sacrifice in the shining Garonmana.[1382]

124. With his arms lifted up towards Immortality, Mithra, the lord of wide pastures, drives forward from the shining Garonmana, in a beautiful chariot that drives on, ever-swift, adorned with all sorts of ornaments, and made of gold.

[1378] The Amesha Spentas.

[1379] See above p.122.

[1380] See above p.122.

[1381] Spirit of the dead or genius that forms the highest, immortal part of an individual's personality (see ERE, p.116-18); see above p.75.

[1382] The highest heaven.

125. Four stallions draw that chariot, all of the same white colour, living on heavenly food and undying. The hoofs of their fore-feet are shod with gold, the hoofs of their hind-feet are shod with silver; all are yoked to the same pole, and wear the yoke and the cross-beams of the yoke, fastened with hooks of Khshathra vairya to a beautiful....

126. At his right hand drives Rashnu-Razishta, the most beneficent and most well-shapen.
At his left hand drives the most upright Chista,[1383] the holy one, bearing libations in her hands, clothed with white clothes, and white herself; and the cursing thought of the Law of Mazda.

127. Close by him drives the strong cursing thought of the wise man, opposing foes in the shape of a boar, a sharp-toothed he-boar, a sharp- jawed boar, that kills at one stroke, pursuing, wrathful, with a dripping face, strong and swift to run, and rushing all around.
Behind him drives Atar, all in a blaze, and the awful kingly Glory.

MIHIR YASHT XXXIV

142. We sacrifice unto Mithra, the lord of wide pastures, ... sleepless, and ever awake;
Who, with his manifold knowledge, powerfully increases the creation of Spenta Mainyu, and is a well-created and most great Yazata, self-shining like the moon, when he makes his own body shine;

143. Whose face is flashing with light like the face of the star Tistrya; whose chariot is embraced by that goddess who is foremost amongst those who have no deceit in them, O Spitama! who is fairer than any creature in the world, and full of light to shine. I will worship that chariot, wrought by the Maker, Ahura Mazda, inlaid with stars and made of a heavenly substance; (the chariot) of Mithra, who has ten thousand spies, the powerful, all-knowing, undeceivable god.
For his brightness and glory, I will offer him a sacrifice worth being heard....

[1383] Goddess of awareness, knowledge.

Shamash

HYMN TO SHAMASH[1384]

Illuminator, dispeller of darkness of the vault of the heavens,
Who sets aglow the beard of light, the corn field, the life of the land.
Your splendour covers the vast mountains,
Your fierce light fills the lands to their limits.
You climb to the mountains surveying the earth,
You suspend from the heavens the circle of the lands.
You care for all the peoples of the lands,
And everything that Ea, king of the counsellors, had created is
entrusted to you
Whatever has breath you shepherd without exception,
You are their keeper in the upper and lower regions.
Regularly and without cease you traverse the heavens,
Every day you pass over the broad earth.
…
You never fail to cross the wide expanse of sea,
The depth of which the Igigi know not.
Šamaš, your glare reaches down to the Abyss,
So that the monsters of the deep behold your light.
…
You are not dejected during the day, nor is your surface darkened,
By night you continue to kindle.
To unknown distant regions and for uncounted leagues
You press on, Šamaš, going by day and returning by night.
…
At your rising the gods of the land assemble,
Your fierce glare covers the land.
Of all the lands of varied speech,
You know their plans, you scan their way.
The whole of mankind bows to you,
Šamaš, the universe longs for your light …

[1384] See W.G. Lambert, *Babylonian Wisdom Literature*, pp.126-138.

PRAYER OF ASHURBANIPAL TO SHAMASH[1385]

O light of the great gods, light of the earth, illuminator of the world-
regions,
... exalted judge, the honored one of the upper and lower regions,
... Thou dost look into all the lands with thy light.
As one who does not cease from revelation, daily thou dost determine
the decisions of heaven and earth.
Thy [rising] is a flaming fire; all the stars in heaven are covered over.
Thou art uniquely brilliant; no one among the gods is equal with thee.
With Sin, thy father, thou dost hold court; thou dost deliver
ordinances.
Anu and Enlil without thy consent establish no decision.
Ea, the determiner of judgment in the midst of the Deep, depends
upon thee.
The attention of all the gods is turned to thy bright rising.
Sūrya

RGVEDA I,115

1.   The brilliant presence of the Gods hath risen, the eye of Mitra,
     Varuna and Agni.
     The soul of all that moveth not or moveth, the Sun hath filled the
     air and earth and heaven.
2.   Like as a young man followeth a maiden, so doth the Sun the
     Dawn, refulgent Goddess:
     Where pious men extend their generations, before the Auspicious
     One for happy fortune.
3.   Auspicious are the Sun's Bay-coloured Horses, bright, changing
     hues, meet for our shouts of triumph.
     Bearing our prayers, the sky's ridge have they mounted, and in a
     moment speed round earth and heaven.
4.   This is the Godhead, this might of Sūrya:

ATHARVA VEDA, XIII,2

1.   Radiant, refulgent in the sky are reared the banners of his light,
     Āditya's, who beholdeth man, mighty in act and bountiful.

[1385]   ANET 386-7.

2. Let us laud him, the whole world's Herdsman, Sūrya, who with his rays illumines all the regions,
   Mark of the quarters, brightening them with lustre, swift, mighty-pinioned, flying in the ocean.

3. From west to east thou speedest freely, making by magic day and night of diverse colours.
   This is Āditya, thy transcendent glory, that thou alone art born through all creation.

4. Victorious, inspired, and brightly shining, whom seven strong tawny-coloured coursers carry,
   Whom Atri lifted from the flood to heaven, thus men behold thee as thy course thou runnest.

5. Let them not snare thee speeding on thy journey: pass safely, swiftly places hard to traverse,
   While measuring out the day and night thou movest—O Sūrya, even Heaven and Earth the Goddess.

6. Hail to thy rapid car whereon, O Sūrya, thou circlest in a moment both the limits,
   Whirled by thy bay steeds, best of all at drawing, thy hundred horses or seven goodly coursers!

7. Mount thy strong car, O Sūrya, lightly rolling, drawn by good steeds, propitious, brightly gleaming,
   Whirled by thy bays, most excellent at drawing, thy hundred horses or seven goodly coursers.

8. Sūrya hath harnessed to his car to draw him seven stately bay steeds gay with wolden housings.
   The Bright One started from the distant region: dispelling gloom the God hath climbed the heavens.

9. With lofty banner hath the God gone upward, and introduced the light, expelling darkness.
   He hath looked round on all the worlds, the Hero, the son of Aditi, Celestial Eagle.

10. Rising, thou spreadest out thy rays, thou nourishest all shapes and forms.
    Thou with thy power illumest both the oceans, encompassing all spheres with thy refulgence.

11. Moving by magic power to east and westward, these two young creatures, sporting, circle ocean.
    One of the pair beholds all living creatures: with wheels of gold the bay steeds bear the other.

12. Atri established thee in heaven. O Sūrya, to create the month.

So on thou goest, firmly held, heating, beholding all that is.

13. As the Calf both his parents so thou joinest both the distant bounds,
Surely the Gods up yonder knew this sacred mystery long ago.

14. Sūrya is eager to obtain all wealth that lies along the sea,
Great is the course spread out for him, his eastward and his westward path.

15. He finishes his race with speed and never turns his thought aside,
Thereby he keeps not from the Gods enjoyment of the Drink of Life.

16. His heralds bear him up aloft, the God who knoweth all that live,
Sūrya, that all may look on him.

17. The Constellations pass away, like thieves, departing in the night.
Before the all-beholding Sun.

18. His herald rays are seen afar refulgent o'er the world of men,
Like flames of fire that burn and blaze.

19. Swift and all-beautiful art thou, O Sūrya, maker of the light,
Illuming all the radiant realm.

20. Thou goest to the hosts of Gods, thou comest hither to mankind,
Hither, all light to behold.

21. With that same eye of thine wherewith thou seest, brilliant Varuna.
The active one among mankind,

22. Traversing sky and wide mid-air, thou metest with thy beams our days,
Sun, seeing all things that have life.

23. Seven bay steeds harnessed to thy car bear thee, O thou far-seeing One,
God, Sūrya, with the radiant hair.

24. Sūrya, hath yoked the pure bright seven, the daughters of the car, with these,
His own dear team, he travelleth.

25. Devout, aflame with fervent heat, Rohita hath gone up to heaven.
He is re-born, returning to his birthplace, and hath become the Gods' imperial ruler.

26. Dear unto all men, facing all directions, with hands and palms on every side extended,
He, the sole God, engendering earth and heaven, beareth them with his wings and arms together.

27. The single-footed hath outstepped the biped, the biped overtakes the triple-footed.

The biped hath outstridden the six-footed: these sit around the single-footed's body.

28. When he, unwearied, fain to go, hath mounted his bays, he makes two colours, brightly shining.
Rising with banners, conquering the regions, thou sendest light through all the floods, Āditya.

29. Verily, Sūrya, thou art great: truly, Āditya, thou art great.
Great is thy grandeur, Mighty One: thou, O Āditya, thou art great.

30. In heaven, O Bird, and in mid-air thou shinest: thou shinest on the earth and in the waters.
Thou hast pervaded both the seas with splendour: a God art thou, O God, light-winner, mighty.

31. Soaring in mid-course hither from the distance, fleet and inspired, the Bird that flies above us,
With might advancing Vishnu manifested, he conquers all that moves with radiant banner:

32. Brilliant, observant, mighty Lord, an Eagle illuming both the spheres and air between them.
Day and the Night, clad in the robes of Sūrya, spread forth more widely all his hero powers.

33. Flaming and radiant, strengthening his body, bestowing floods that promptly come to meet us,
He, luminous, winged, mighty, strength-bestower, hath mounted all the regions as he forms them.

34. Bright presence of the Gods, the luminous herald Sūrya hath mounted the celestial regions.
Day's maker, he hath shone away the darkness, and radiant, passed o'er places hard to traverse.

35. He hath gone up on high, the Gods' bright presence, the eye of Mitra, Varuna and Agni.
The soul of all that moveth not or moveth, Sūrya hath filled the earth and air and heaven,

36. High in the midst of heaven may we behold thee whom men call Savitar, the bright red Eagle,
Soaring and speeding on thy way, refulgent, unwasting light which Atri erst discovered.

37. Him, Son of Aditi, an Eagle hasting along heaven's height, I supplicate in terror,
As such prolong our lengthened life, O Sūrya: may we, unharmed, enjoy thy gracious favour.

38. This gold-hued Hansa's[1386] wings, soaring to heaven, spread o'er a thousand days' continued journey
    Supporting all the Gods upon his bosom, he goes his way beholding every creature.
39. Rohita, in primeval days Prajāpati, was, after, Time, Mouth of all sacrifices, he, Rohita, brought celestial light.
40. He, Rohita, became the world: Rohita gave the heaven its heat.
    Rohita with his beams of light travelled along the earth and sea.
41. To all the regions Rohita came, the imperial Lord of heaven.
    He watches over ocean, heaven, and earth and all existing things.
42. Mounting the lofty ones, he, bright, unwearied, splendidly shining, makes two separate colours,
    While through all worlds that are he sends his lustre, radiant, observant, mighty, wind-approacher.
43. One form comes on, the other is reverted: to day and night the Strong One shapes and fits him.
    With humble prayer for aid we call on Sūrya, who knows the way, whose home is in the region.
44. The suppliant's way, filling the earth, the Mighty circleth the world with eye that none deceiveth.
    May he, all-seeing, well-disposed and holy, give ear and listen to the word I utter.
45. Blazing with light his majesty hath compassed ocean and earth and heaven and air's mid-region.
    May he, all-seeing, well-disposed and holy, give ear and listen to the word I utter.
46. Agni is weakened by the people's fuel to meet the Dawn who cometh like a milch-cow,
    Like young trees shooting up on high their branches, his flames are mounting to the vault of heaven.

Sūrya as Indra, Vishnu

ATHARVA VEDA XVII,1

7. Rise up, O Sūrya, rise thou up; with strength and splendour rise on me.

[1386] 'Hansa' is 'swan', a traditional Vedic epithet of the sun.

Make me the favourite of all, of those I see and do not see.
Manifold are thy great deeds, thine, O Vishnu.

8. Let not the fowlers who are standing ready injure thee in the flood, within the waters.
   Ascend this heaven, leaving each curse behind thee, Favour us: let thy gracious love attend us.
   Manifold are thy great deeds, thine, O Vishnu.

9. Do thou, O Indra, for our great good fortune, with thine inviolable rays protect us.
   Manifold are thy great deeds, thine, O Vishnu.

10. Be thou most gracious unto us, Indra, with favourable aid,
    Rising to heaven's third sphere, invoked with song to quaff the Soma juice, loving thy home to make us blest.
    Manifold are thy great deeds, thine, O Vishnu.

11. Thou art the vanquisher of all, O Indra, omniscient Indra, and invoked of many.
    Indra, send forth this hymn that fitly lauds thee. Favour us let thy gracious love attend us.
    Manifold are thy great deeds, thine, O Vishnu.

12. In heaven and on the earth thou art uninjured, none reach thy greatness in the air's mid region.
    Increasing by inviolate devotion as such in heaven grant us protection, Indra.
    Manifold are thy great deeds, thine, O Vishnu.

13. Grant us protection, Indra, with that body of thine that is on earth, in fire, in waters,
    That dwells within light-finding Pavamana,[1387] wherewith thou hast pervaded air's mid region.
    Manifold are thy great deeds, thine, O Vishnu.

14. Indra, exalting thee with prayer, imploring, Rishis have sat them down in holy Session.
    Manifold are thy great deeds, thine, O Vishnu,

15 Round Trita, round the spring with thousand currents thou goest, round the light-finding assembly.
    Manifold are thy great deeds, thine, O Vishnu.

16. Thou guardest well the four celestial regions, pervading heaven, and earth with light and splendour.
    Thou givest help to all these living creatures, and, knowing, followest the path of Order.

[1387] Soma.

Manifold are thy great deed, thine, O Vishnu.

17. With five thou sendest heat: with one removing the curse thou comest in bright sunshine hither.
Manifold are thy great deeds, thine, O Vishnu.

18. Indra art thou, Mahendra thou, thou art the world, the Lord of Life.
To thee is sacrifice performed: worshippers offer gifts to thee.
Manifold are thy great deeds, thine, O Vishnu.

19. What is based on what is not: the present lies on that which is.
Present on future is imposed and future on the present based.
Manifold are thy great deeds, thine, O Vishnu.
Sate us with cattle of all varied colour. Set me in happiness, in loftiest heaven.

20. Bright art thou, and refulgent: as thou shinest with splendour so I fain would shine with splendour.

21. Lustre art thou, illuming: as thou glowest with lustre so I too would shine with cattle, with all the lustre of a Brāhman's station.

22. Glory to him when rising, when ascending! Glory to him when he hath reached the zenith!
To him far-shining, him the self-refulgent, to him the Sovran Lord and King be glory!

23. Worship to him when he is turning westward, to him when setting, and when set be worship!
To him far-shining, him the self-refulgent, to him the Sovran Lord and King be glory!

24. With all his fiery fervour this Āditya hath gone up on high,
Giving my foes into my hand. Let me not by my foeman's prey.
Manifold are thy great deeds, thine, O Vishnu.
Sate us with cattle of all varied colours. Set me in happiness, in loftiest heaven.

25. Thou for our weal, Āditya, hast mounted thy ship with hundred oars.
Thou hast transported me to day: so bear me evermore to night.

26. Thou for our weal, O Sūrya, hast mounted thy ship with hundred oars. Thou hast transported me to night: so bear me evermore today.

27. Encompassed by Prajāpati's devotion as shield, with Kasyapa's bright light and splendour,
Reaching old age, may I made strong and mighty live through a thousand years with happy fortune.

28. Compassed am I with prayer, my shield and armour; compassed

with Kasyapa's bright light and splendour.

Let not shafts reach me shot from heaven against me, nor those sent forth by men for my destruction.

29. Guarded am I by Order and the Seasons, protected by the past and by the future.

Let not distress, yea, let not Death come nigh me: with water of my speech have I o'erwhelmed them.

30. On every side let Agni guard and keep me; the rising Sun drive off the snares of Mrityu!

Let brightly flushing Mornings, firm-set mountains, and lives a thousand be with me united.

Sūrya as the One

ATHARVA VEDA, XIII,4

1. Down looking, on the ridge of sky Savitar goes to highest heaven.
2. To misty cloud filled with his rays Mahendra goes encompassed round.
3. Creator and Ordainer, he is Vāyu, he is lifted cloud.
4. Rudra, and Mahādeva, he is Aryaman and Varuna.
5. Agni is he, and Sūrya, he is verilyMahāyama.
6. Calves, joined, stand close beside him, ten in number, with one single head.
7. From west to east they bend their way: when he mounts up he shines afar.
8. His are these banded Maruts: they move gathered close like porters' thongs.
9. To misty cloud filled with his rays Mahendra goes encompassed round,
10. His are the nine supports, the casks set in nine several places here.
11. He keepeth watch o'er creatures, all that breatheth and that breatheth not.
12. This conquering might hath entered him, He is the sole the simple One, the One alone,
13. In him these Deities become simple and One
14. Renown and glory, and force and cloud, the Brāhman's splendour,

and food and nourishment.

15. To him who knoweth this God as simple and one.
16. Neither second, nor third, nor yet fourth is he called:
17. He is called neither fifth, nor sixth, nor yet seventh
18. He is called neither eighth, nor ninth, nor yet tenth.
19. He watcheth over creatures, all that breatheth and that breatheth not.
20. This conquering might hath entered him. He is the sole, the simple One, the One alone,
21. In him these Deities become simple and One
22. Devotion and religious fervour, and renown and glory, and force and cloud, the Brahman's splendour, and food and nourishment,
23. And past and future, and Faith and lustre, and heaven and sweet oblation,
24. To him who knoweth this God as simple and One.

BIBLIOGRAPHY

I: Primary Sources

INDIC

Atharva-Veda Samhita, tr. W.D. Whitney, 2 vols., Cambridge, MA: Harvard University Press, 1905.

The Hymns of the Atharva-Veda, tr. R.T.H. Grifffith, 2 vols., Benares: E.J. Lazarus,1895-6.

The Hymns of the Rgveda, tr. R.T.H. Griffith, Benares: E.J. Lazarus, 1889.

The Veda of the Black Yajus School Entitled Taittiriya Samhita, tr. A.B. Keith, Cambridge. MA: Harvard University Press, 1914.

Rigveda Brāhmanas: The Aitareya and Kaušitaki Brahmanas of the Rigveda, tr. A.B. Keith, Cambridge, MA: Harvard University Press, 1920.

The Šatapatha-Brahmana According to the Text of the Mādhyandina School, tr. J. Eggeling, 5 vols., Oxford: Clarendon Press, 1882-1900.

The Taittrīya Brāhmana of the Black Yajur Veda with the Commentary of Sāyanāchārya, 4 vols., ed. R. Mitra, Calcutta, 1859-1870.

W. Caland, "Eine vierte Mitteilung über das Vādhūlasūtra", *Acta Orientalia*, 6 (1927), 2-3,97-241.

Thirty Minor Upanishads, tr. K. Narayanaswami Aiyar, Madras: Vasanta Press, 1914.

Bhagavata Purana, 5 vols., tr. G.V. Tagare, Delhi: Motilal Banarsidass, 2002.

Srimad Bhāgavata: The Holy Book of God, tr. Swami Tapasyananda, 4 vols., Madras: Sri Ramakrishna Math, 1980-82.

Brahma Purana, 4 vols., Delhi: Motilal Banarsidass, 2002.

Brahmanda Purana, 5 vols, Delhi: Motilal Banarsidass, 1984.

Brahmavaivarta Purana, 2 vols., Delhi: Motilal Banarsidass, 2001.

Linga Purana, 2 vols., Delhi: Motilal Banarsidass, 1973.

Maitrāyani Samhita, ed. L. von Schroeder, Leipzig, 1881-6.

Padma Purana, tr. N.A. Deshpande, Delhi: Motilal Banarsidass, 1988-90.

Shiva Purana, 4 vols., Delhi: Motilal Banarsidass, 1970.

S. Shastri, *The Flood Legend in Sanskrit Literature*, Delhi: S. Chand and Co., 1950.

The Mahabharata, 11 vols., tr. P.C. Roy, Calcutta: Datta Bose and Co., 1924-31.

The Bhagavad Gîtâ, tr. K.T. Telang, 1882.

Rāmāyan of Valmiki, tr. Ralph Griffiths, Low Price Publications, 2003.

W. Caland *Das Śrautasūtra des Āpastamba*, Göttingen: Vandenhoeck & Ruprecht 1921.

Āśvalāyana Śrautrasūtra, tr. K. Mylius, Wichtrach: Institut für Indologie Wichtrach, 1994.

The Baudhāyana Śrauta Sūtram Belonging to the Taittirīya Samhitā; a Sanskrit Work on the Vedic Literature, ed. W. Caland, Calcutta: Asiatic Society, 1904-24.

The Śrauta, Paitrmedhika and Pariśesa Sūtras of Bharadvāja, ed. C.G. Kashikar, 2 vols, Poona: Vaidika Samśodhana Mandala, 1964.

H. Oldenberg and F. Max Müller *The Grihya Sūtras: Rules of Vedic Domestic Ceremonies*, 2 Parts, (Sacred Books of the East), 1886-92.

The Laws of Manu, Translated with Extracts from Seven Commentaries, by G. Bühler, Oxford: Clarendon Press, 1886.

The Dharmasūtras: The Law Codes of Āpastamba, Gautama, Baudhāyana, and Vasistha, tr. P. Olivelle, N.Y.: Oxford University Press, 1999.

Mahanirvana Tantra, tr. A. Avalon (J. Woodroffe), 1913.

Dīptāgama, ed. M.-L. Barazer-Billoret, B. Dagens, V. Lefèvre, Pondicherry: Institute français de Pondichéry, 2007.

Āgama Kosha, ed. S.K. Ramachandra Rao, Bangalore: Kalpatharu Research Academy, 1989-.

John Woodroffe, *The Serpent Power, being the Satcakra Nirūpana and the Pāduka Pañcaka*, London: Luzac and Co., 1919.

Translation of the Surya-Siddhanta, a Text-Book of Hindu Astronomy, tr. E. Burgess, New Haven: American Oriental Society, 1860.

Kalhana's *Rājatarangini: A Chronicle of the Kings of Kaśmīr*, 3 vols., tr. M.A. Stein, London: A. Constable and Co., 1900.

Arrian, *Indica in Arrian with an English Translation*, tr. E.I. Robson, London: W. Heinemann, 1929.

R.C. Majumdar, *The Classical Accounts of India*, Calcutta: Firma K.L. Mukhopadhyay, 1960.

S. Shastri, *The Flood Legend in Sanskrit Literature*, Delhi: S. Chand and Co., 1950.

IRANIAN

The Zend-Avesta, Part I, tr. J. Darmsteter, (Sacred Books of the East, Vol.4), Oxford: Clarendon Press, 1880.

The Zend-Avesta, Part II, tr. J. Darmsteter, (Sacred Books of the East, Vol.23) Oxford: Clarendon Press, 1883.

The Zend-Avesta, Part III, tr. L.H. Mills, (Sacred Books of the East, Vol.31), Oxford: Clarendon Press, 1887.

Pahlavi Texts, Part I, tr. E.W. West (Sacred Books of the East, Vol.5), Oxford: Clarendon Press, 1880.

The Nyaishes or Zoroastrian Litanies, tr. M.N. Dhalla (Columbia University Indo-Iranian Series Vol.VI), N.Y.: Columbia University Press, 1908.

W.W. Malandra, *An Introduction to Ancient Iranian Religion: Readings from the Avesta and Achaemenid Inscriptions*, Minneapolis, MN: University of Minnesota Press, 1983.

R.C. Zaehner, *The Teachings of the Magi*, London: George Allen and Unwin Ltd., 1956.

EGYPTIAN

A. Barucq and F. Daumas, *Hymnes et Prières de l'Egypte ancienne*, Paris: Cerf, 1980.

J. Assmann, *Ägyptische Hymnen und Gebete*, Zürich: Artemis Verlag, 1975.

R.O. Faulkner (tr.), *The Egyptian Book of the Dead, the Book of Going Forth by Day*, San Francisco: Chronicle Books, 1994.

E. Hornung, *Das Amduat: Die Schrift des verborgenen Raumes*, 3 vols., Wiesbaden: O. Harrassowitz, 1973-78.

E. Hornung, *Das Totenbuch der Ägypter*, Düsseldorf: Artemis und Winkler, 1990.

E. Hornung, *The Ancient Egyptian Books of the Afterlife*, tr. D. Lorton, Ithaca: Cornell University Press, 1999.

G. P.Verbrugghe and J.M. Wickersham, *Berossus and Manetho, Introduced and Translated: Native Traditions in Ancient Mesopotamia and Egypt*, Ann Arbor, MI: University of Michigan Press, 1996.

MESOPOTAMIAN

A. Annus, *The Standard Babylonian Epic of Anzu*, Helsinki: The Neo-Assyrian Text Corpus Project, 2001.

H. Behrens, *Enlil und Ninlil: Ein Mythos aus Nippur*, Rome: Biblical Institute Press, 1978.

L Cagni, *The Poem of Erra*, Malibu, CA: Undena Publications, 1977.

E. Chiera, *Sumerian Religious Texts*, Upland, PA: Crozer Theological Seminary, 1924.

A. Falkenstein, *Sumerische und akkadische Hymnen und Gebete*, Zürich: Artemis Verlag, 1953.

H. de Genouillac, "Grande Liste de Noms Divins Sumeriens", *RA* 20 (1923), 89-106.

T. Jacobsen, *The Sumerian King-List*, Chicago: University of Chicago Press, 1939.

L. King (ed.), *Enuma Elish: the Seven Tablets of Creation*, London: Luzac and Co., 1902.

M.G. Kovacs (tr.), *The Epic of Gilgamesh*, Stanford: Stanford University Press, 1985.

W.G. Lambert, *Babylonian Wisdom Literature*, London: Oxford University Press, 1960.

W.G. Lambert and A.R. Millard, *Atrahasis*: The Babylonian Story of the Flood, Oxford: Clarendon Press, 1969.

R. Litke, *A Reconstruction of the Assyro-Babylonian God-list An:^{d}A-nu-um and An: anu šá amēli*, New Haven, CT: Yale Babylonian Collection, 1998.

A. Livingstone, *Mystical and Mythological Explanatory Texts of Assyrian and Babylonian Scholars*, Oxford: Clarendon Press, 1986.

K.D. Macmillan, "Some Cuneiform Tablets Bearing on the Religion of Babylonia and Assyria" *BA* 5 (1906).

K.Fr. Müller, "Das assyrische Ritual I: Texte zum assyrischen Königsritual", *Mitteilungen der vorderasiatisch-aegyptischen Gesellschaft*, 41,3 (1937).

M.J. Seux, *Hymnes et Prières aux Dieux de Babylonie et d'Assyrie*, Paris: Éditions du Cerf, 1976.

J. van Dijk, "Die Inschriftenfunde: II. Die Tontafeln aus dem res-Heiligtum" in *XVIII. vorläufiger Bericht über die von dem Deutschen Archaeologischen Institut und der Deutschen Orient-Gesellschaft aus Mitteln der Deutschen Forschungsgemeinschaft unternommenen Ausgrabungen in Uruk-Warka (1959/1960)*, Berlin: Heinrich J. Lenzen, 1962.

G. P.Verbrugghe and J.M. Wickersham, *Berossus and Manetho, Introduced and Translated: Native Traditions in Ancient Mesopotamia and Egypt*, Ann Arbor, MI: University of Michigan Press, 1996

Poebel, *Historical and Grammatical Texts*, Philadelphia: University Museum, 1914.

W. von Soden, "Der grosse Hymnus an Nabû", *Zeitschrift für Assyriologie und vorderasiatische Archäologie*, 61 (1971), 44-71.

PALESTINIAN

Philo of Byblos, *The Phoenician History*, tr. H.W. Attridge and R.A. Oden Jr., Washington, D.C.: The Catholic Biblical Association of America, 1981.

Josephus *Jewish Antiquities in Josephus, with an English Translation*, tr. H.St.J. Thackeray, London: Heinemann, 1926-65.

E.A.W. Budge, *The Alexander Book in Ethiopia*, London: Oxford University Press, 1933.

GREEK

Herodotus, *Histories*, tr. A.D. Godley, 4 vols., London: Heinemann, 1924-28.

Hesiod, *The Homeric Hymns and Homerica*, tr. H.G. Evelyn-White, London: Heinemann, 1914.

H. Diels, *Doxographi Graeci*, Berlin, 1879

Cicero, *De Natura Deorum, Academics*, tr. H. Rackham, London: Heinemann, 1933.

Nonnos, *Dionysiaca*, 3 vols., tr. W.H.D. Rouse, London: Heinemann, 1940.

Plutarch, *De Iside et Osiride*, tr. J.G. Griffiths, University of Wales Press, 1970.

CELTIC AND GERMANIC

Lebor Gabála Érenn: Book of the Taking of Ireland, Parts 1-5, tr. R.A.S. Macalister, Dublin: Irish Texts Society, 1941.

Tacitus, *Dialogus, Agricola, Germania*, tr. M. Hutton, London; Heinemann, 1914.

The Prose Edda of Snorri Sturlusson, tr. J.I. Young, Cambridge: Bowes and Bowes, 1954.

The Poetic Edda, tr. C. Larrington, Oxford: OUP, 1996.

II: Secondary Sources

H.-P. Adler, *Das akkadische des Königs Tushratta von Mitanni*, Kevelaer: Butzon und Bercker, 1976.

G.W. Ahlstrom, *Ancient Palestine: A Historical Introduction*, Minneapolis. MN: Fortress Press, 2002.

G.W. Ahlström, *The History of Ancient Palestine from the Paleolithic Period to Alexander's Conquest*, Minneapolis, MN: Fortress Press, 1993.

S. Krishnaswami Aiyangar, *Some Contributions of South India to Indian Culture*, Calcutta: University of Calcutta, 1923.

G. Algaze, *The Uruk World-System: The Dynamics of Expansion of Early Mesopotamian Civilization*, Chicago: Chicago University Press, 1993.

R. and B. Allchin, *The Rise of Civilization in India and Pakistan*, Cambridge: Cambridge University Press, 1982.

J.P. Allen, *Genesis in Egypt: The Philosophy of Ancient Egyptian Creation Accounts*, New Haven, CT: Yale University Press, 1988.

C. Ambos, "Das 'Neujahrs'-Fest zur Jahresmitte und die Investitur des Königs im Gefängnis" in Doris Prechel (Hrsg.), *Fest und Eid: Instrumente der Herrschaftssicherung im Alten Orient*, Kulturelle und Sprachliche Kontakte 3. Würzburg: Ergon-Verlag, 2008: 1-12.

K. Al-Nashef, "The Deities of Dilmun", in A. Al Khalifa, M. Rice, T. Almoayed (ed.) *Bahrain through the Ages*, London: Routledge and Kegan Paul, 1993.

F. Apffel-Marglin, *Wives of The God-King: The Rituals of the Devadasis of Puri*, Delhi: Oxford University Press, 1985.

B. Arredi, E. Poloni, C. Tyler-Smith, "The peopling of Europe" in *Anthropological Genetics*, ed. M. Crawford, 2007, 380-408.

J. Assman, *Re und Amun : Die Krise der polytheistischen Weltbilds im Ägypten der 18-20 Dynastie*, Freiburg: Universitätsverlag, 1983.

J. Assmann, *Aegypten: Theologie und Frömmigkeit einer frühen Hochkultur*, Stuttgart:E. Kohlhammer, 1984.

C. Autran, *Sumérien et Indo-Européen*, Paris: Librairie Orientaliste Paul Geuthner, 1925.

H.T. Bakker, "Human sacrifice (Purushamedha), construction sacrifice and the origin of the idea of the 'man of the homestead' (Vāstupurusha)", in J.N. Bremmer (ed.), *op.cit.*, 179-228.

W. Barta, *Untersuchungen zur Göttlichkeit des regierenden Königs: Ritus und Sakralkönigtum in Altägypten nach Zeugnissen der Frühzeit und des Alten Reiches*, Münchner Ägyptologische Studien 32 (1975).

A. Bergaigne, *La Religion Védique d'après les Hymnes du Rig-Veda*, Paris: Librairie Honoré Champion, 1963.

A. Berlejung, "Die Macht der Insignien: Überlegungen zu einem Ritual der Investitur des Königs und dessen königsideologischen Implikationen", *Ugarit Forschungen* 28 (1996), 1-35.

A. Berlejung, *Die Theologie der Bilder: Herstellung und Einweihung von Kultbildern in Mesopotamien und die alttestamentliche Bilderpolemik* (Orbis Biblicus et Orientalis), Göttingen: Vandenhoeck & Ruprecht, 1998.

M. Biardeau, *Le sacrifice dans l'inde ancienne*, Paris: Presses universitaires de France, 1976.

S. Bickel, *La cosmogonie egyptienne avant le Nouvel Empire*, Fribourg: Éditions Universitaires, 1994.

C.J. Bleeker, *Hathor und Thoth, Die Geburt eines Gottes: eine Studie über den ägyptischen Gott Min und sein Fest*, tr. M.J Freie, Leiden: E.J. Brill, 1956.

H.W. Bodewitz, *The Jyotistoma Ritual, Jaiminiya Brahmana I, 66-364 (Orientalia Rhenotraiectina*, Vol 34).

C. Bonnet, *Studia Phoenicia*, 7 (1988), 148-55.

J. Bottero, *Mesopotamia: Writing, Reasoning and the Gods*, tr. Z. Bahrani and M. van de Mieroop, Chicago: University of Chicago Press, 1992.

J. Bottero, *Le problème des Habiru*, Paris: Imprimerie nationale, 1954.

Mary Boyce, "On the Zoroastrian temple-cult of fire", *JOAS*, 95/3.

Mary Boyce, *Zoroastrians: Their Religious Beliefs and Practices*, London: Routledge, 1979.

J.N. Bremmer (ed.), *The Strange World of Human Sacrifice*, Leuven: Peeters, 2007.

G.W. Brown, "The possibility of a connection between Mitanni and the Dravidian languages", *JAOS*, 50 (1930),273-305.

E. F. Bryant, *The Quest for the Origins of Vedic Culture: The Indo-Aryan Migration Debate*, Oxford: Oxford University Press, 2001.

E.A.W. Budge, *The Gods of the Egyptians, or Studies in Egyptian Mythology*, 2 vols., London: Methuen and Co., 1904.

E.A.W. Budge, *The Alexander Book in Ethiopia*, London: Oxford University Press, 1933.

J. van Buitenen, *The Pravargya: An Ancient Indian Iconic Ritual*, Pune: Deccan College Postgraduate and Research Institute, 1968.

W. Caland, and V. Henry, *Agnistoma. Description complète de la forme normale du sacrifice de Soma dans le culte védique*. I-II. Paris: Ernest Leroux, 1906-7.

J. Cauvin, *Religions néolithiques de Syro-Palestine*, Paris: J. Maisonneuve,1972.

D. K. Chakrabarti, "The archaeology of Hinduism", in T. Insoll (ed.), *Archaeology and World Religion*, London: Routledge, 2001.

K. Chakrabothy, *Women as Devadasis: Origin and Growth of the Devadasi Profession*. Delhi, Deep & Deep Publications, 2000

J. Charpentier, "The Date of Zoroaster", *BSOS* 3 (1923-25), 747-55

J. Charpentier, *Brahman; eine sprachwissenschaftlich-exegetisch-religions-geschichtliche Untersuchung*, Uppsala: Almquist & Wiksells, 1932.

P. Charvat, *Mesopotamia Before History*, London: Routledge, 2002.

S.B. Chaudhuri, *Ethnic Settlements in Ancient India: A Study on the Puranic Lists of the Peoples of Bharatvarsha*, Calcutta: General Printers and Publishers, 1955.

E. Chiera, *Sumerian Epics and Myths*, Chicago, IL: University of Chicago Press, 1934.

G. Childe, *The Dawn of European Civilization*, London: Routledge and Kegan Paul Ltd., 1961.

U. Chouduri, *Indra and Varuna in Indian Mythology*, Delhi: Nag Publishers, 1981.

A.B. Cook, *Zeus: A Study in Ancient Religion*, 2 vols. in 3, New York: Biblo and Tannen, 1964-5.

R. Cook, *The Tree of Life: Symbol of the Centre*, London: Thames and Hudson, 1974.

S.A. Cook, *The Religion of Ancient Palestine in the Light of Archaeology*, London: Oxford University Press, 1930.

J.S. Cooper, "Sumerian and Semitic Writing in most ancient Mesopotamia", in *Language and Cultures in Contact: At the Crossroads of Civilizations in the Syro-Mesopotamian Realm*, ed. K. van Lerberghe and G. Voet, Leuven: Uitgeverij Peeters, n.d., 61-77.

F. Cornelius, "Erin-Manda", *Iraq* 25 (1963), pp.167-70.

A. Daniélou, *Shiva and Dionysus, the Omnipresent Gods of Transcendence and Ecstasy*, New York: Inner Tradition International, 1984.

N. de G. Davies, *The Tomb of Rekh-mi-Re' at Thebes*, 2 vols., The Plantin Press, 1943.

J. Day, *God's Conflict with the Dragon and the Sea*, Cambridge: Cambridge University Press, 1985

A. Deimel, *Pantheon Babylonicum: Nomina deorum e textibus cuneiformibus excerpta et ordine alphabetico distributa*, Rome: Pontifical Biblical Institute, 1914.

E. Drioton, *Le texte dramatique d'Edfou*, 1948.

Dubois, J.A., l'abbé, *Hindu manners, customs and ceremonies*, tr, H.K. Beauchamp, Oxford, Clarendon Press, 1897.

J. Duchesne-Guillemin, *Religion of Ancient Iran*, Bombay: Tata Press, 1973.

G. Dumezil, "Dieux cassites et védiques à propos d'un bronze du Louristan", *RHA* 52 (1950), 16-37.

P.-E. Dumont, *L'asvamedha: Description du sacrifice solennel du cheval dans le culte vedique*, Paris: P. Geuthner, 1927.

A. Dundes (ed.), *The Flood Myth*, Berkeley: University of California Press, 1988.

M.S.G. Dyczkowski, *The Doctrine of Vibration: An Analysis of the Doctrines and Practices of Kashmir Shaivism*, Albany, NY: SUNY Press, 1987.

M. Eliade, *Shamanism: Archaic Techniques of Ecstasy*, N.Y.: Pantheon Books, 1964.

G. Erdosy, (ed.) *The Indo-Aryans of Ancient South Asia*, Berlin: Walter de Gruyter, 1995.

A. Falkenstein, "Sumerische religiöse Texte", *ZA* 55 (1962), 11-67.

J. Finegan, *Archaeological History of the Ancient Middle East*, Boulder, CO: Westview Press, 1979.

Fischer-Elfert, H.-W., *Die Vision von der Statue im Stein: Studien zum altägyptischen Mundöffnungsritual*, Schriften der Philosophisch-historischen Klasse der Heidelberger Akademie der Wissenschaften, Bd.5, Heidelberg: Universitätsverlag C. Winter, 1998.

G. Flood, *An Introduction to Hinduism*, Cambridge: Cambridge University Press, 1996.

G. Flood, *The Tantric Body: The Secret Tradition of Hindu religion*, London: I.B. Tauris, 2006.

T. Folger, "The real Big Bang", *Discover*, Dec. 2002, 41-46.

E. Forrer, "Stratification des langues et des peuples dans le Proche-Orient préhistorique", *JA* 217 (1930), pp.227-52.

H. Frankfort, *Archeology and the Sumerian Problem*, Chicago: Chicago University Press, 1932.

H. Frankfort, *Kingship and the Gods: A study of Ancient Near Eastern Religion as the Integration of Society and Nature*, Chicago: University of Chicago Press, 1948.

D. Frayne, "Indo-Europeans and Sumerians: Evidence for their linguistic Contact", *CSMS Bulletin* 25 (1993), 19-42.

D. Frayne, "Notes on the sacred marriage rite", *Bi Or* 42, 5-22.

J. Friedrich, "Agniš", *RLA* I, 1-42.

I. Gelb, *Hurrians and Subarians*, Chicago: University of Chicago Press, 1944.

K. Gerhardt, *Die Glockenbecherleute in Mittel- und Westdeutschland*, Stuttgart: Schweizerbart'sche Verlag, 1953.

Aurobindo Ghose, *The Secret of the Veda*, Sri Aurobindo Birth Centenary Library, vol.10, Pondicherry: Sri Aurobindo Ashram, 1971.

G.S. Ghurye, *Indian Acculturation: Agasthya and Skandha*, Bombay: Popular Prakashan, 1977.

K.-H. Golzio, *Der Tempel im alten Mesopotamien und seine Parallelen in Indien: eine religionshistorische Studie*, Leiden: E.J. Brill, 1983.

J. Gonda, *Notes on Brahman*, Utrecht: J.L. Beyers, 1950.

J. Gonda, *Die Religionen Indiens I: Veda und älterer Hinduismus*, Stuttgart, Kohlhammer, 1960.

J. Gonda, *Die Religionen Indiens II: Der jüngere Hinduismus*, Stuttgart: Kohlhammer, 1963.

J. Gonda, *Vedic Ritual: The Non-solemn Rites*, Leiden: E.J. Brill, 1981.

J. Gonda, *Soma's Metamorphoses: The identifications in the oblatory rites of Śatapatha Brāhmana 12,6,1*, Amsterdam: North Holland Publishing Co., 1983.

J. Gonda, *Prajapati's rise to higher rank*, Leiden: E.J. Brill, 1986.

A.R.W. Green, *The Storm-God in the Ancient Near East*, Winona Lake, IN: Eisenbrauns, 2003.

J.G. Griffiths, *The Conflict of Horus and Seth*, Liverpool: Liverpool University Press, 1960.

H.G. Güterbock, "The god Suwaliyat reconsidered", *RHA* 19 (1961), 1-18.

H.G. Güterbock, "Hittite Mythology" in S. Kramer, *op.cit.*, 139-79.

H.G. Güterbock, *Kumarbi*, 'Istanbuler Schriften' 16, 1946.

W.K.C. Guthrie, *Orpheus and Greek Religion: A Study of the Ophic Movement*, London: Methuen, 1952.

V. Haas, *Geschichte der hethitischen Religion*, Leiden: E.J. Brill, 1994.

V. Haas and G. Wilhelm, *Hurritische und luwische Riten aus Kizzuwattna*, Kevelaer: Butzon und Bercker, 1974.

D. Handelman, "Myths of Murugan: Asymmetry and Hierarchy in a South Indian Puranic Cosmology", *History of Religions*, 27, no.2.

J. Hannam, *God's Philosophers: How the Medieval World Laid the Foundations of Modern Science*, London: Icon Books, 2010.

W.P. Harman, *The Sacred Marriage of a Hindu Goddess*, Bloomington: Indiana University Press, 1989.

T. Harpur, *The Pagan Christ: Recovering the lost light*, Toronto: Thomas Allen, 2004.

R.J. Harrison, *The Beaker Folk*, London: Thames and Hudson, 1980.

J.E. Hartley, *The Book of Job*, W.E. Eerdmans Publishing Co., 1988.

J.C. Heesterman, "Reflections on the significance of the Daksina", *Indo-Iranian Journal* 3 (1959), pp.241-58.

J.C. Heesterman, *The Ancient Indian Royal Consecration: The Rājasūya Described According to the Yajus Texts and Annotated*, 's-Gravenhage: Mouton, 1957.

J.C. Heesterman, *The Broken World of Sacrifice: An Essay on Ancient Indian Ritual*, Chicago: University of Chicago Press, 1993.

J. Hehn, *Die biblische und babylonische Gottesidee*, Leipzig: J.C. Hinrichs, 1913.

W. Helck, *Urkunden der 18. Dynastie, Übersetzungen zu den Heften 17-22*,

A. Hillebrandt, *Das altindische Neu- und Vollmondsopfer*, Jena, 1879.

W. Hinz, *The Lost World of Elam*, tr. J. Barnes, London: Sidgwick and Jackson, 1972.

A.M. Hocart, *Kingship*, London: Oxford University Press, 1927.

A.M. Hocart, *Kings and Councillors: An Essay in the Comparative Anatomy of Human Society*, Cairo, 1936.

S. Hood, *The Minoans: Crete in the Bronze Age*, London: Thames and Hudson, 1971.

S. H. Hooke, *Babylonian and Assyrian Religion*, London: Hutchinson's University Library, 1953.

E. Hornung, *Ancient Egyptian Books of the Afterlife*, tr. D. Lorton, Ithaca: Cornell University Press, 1999.

W. Horowitz, "The Babylonian Map of the World", *Iraq*, 50 (1988), 147-66.

F. Hrozny, "Un dieu hittite Ak/Nis", *RA* 18 (1921), 34-36.

M. Hütter, *Altorientalische Vorstellungen von der Unterwelt: Literar- und religionsgeschichtliche Überlegungen zu 'Nergal und Ereškigal'*, Freiburg: Universitätsverlag, 1985.

A. Jacob, "Cosmology and Ethics in the Religions of the Peoples of the Ancient Near East", *Mankind Quarterly* 140, no.1 (Fall 1999), 95-119.

A. Jacob, *Ātman: A Reconstruction of the Solar Cosmology of the Indo-Europeans*, Hildesheim, Georg Olms Verlag, 2005.

T. Jacobsen, *Treasures of Darkness: A History of Mesopotamian Religion*, New Haven: Yale University Press, 1976.

E.O. James, *Origins of Sacrifice: A Study in Comparative Religion*, London: John Murray, 1933.

E.O. James, *The Tree of Life: An Archaeological Study*, Leiden: E.J. Brill, 1966.

M. Jansen, *Die Indus-Zivilisation: Wiederentdeckung einer frühen Hochkultur*, Köln: DuMont, 1986.

P. Jensen, "Adad-Mythus", *RLA,* I: 126.

A. Jeremias, *Handbuch der altorientalistischen Geisteskultur*, Berlin 1929.

H. Junker, "Das Götterdekret über das Abaton", *DAWW* 56 (1913).

W. Kaiser, "Die kleine Hebseddarstellung im Sonnenheiligtum des Neuserre", in *Aufsätze zum 70. Geburtstag von Herbert Ricke*, Schweizerische Institut für Ägyptische Bauforschung und Altertumskunde in Kairo (Beiträge zur ägyptischen Bauforschung und Altertumskunde 12), Wiesbaden, 87-105.

A. Kaliff, *Fire, Water, Heaven and Earth. Ritual practice and Cosmology in Ancient Scandinavia: an Indo-European perspective*, Stockholm: Riksantikvarieämbetet, 2007.

M. Kavoukjian, *Armenia, Subartu and Sumer: The Indo-European Homeland and Ancient Mesopotamia*, tr. N. Ouzonian, Montreal: M. Kavoukjian, 1987.

K.A.R. Kennedy, "Have Aryans been identified in the prehistoric skeletal record from South Asia?" in G. Erdosy (ed.), *op.cit.,*

K.M. Kenyon, *Digging up Jericho*, London: E. Benn, 1957.

L.W. King, *Babylonian Magic and Sorcery*, London, 1986.

J.V. Kinnier Wilson, *The Rebel Lands: An Investigation into the Origins of Early Mesopotamian Mythology*, Cambridge: Cambridge University Press, 1979.

W. Kirfel, *Die Kosmographie der Inder*, Hildesheim: G. Olms, 1967.

F.M.P. Kotwal and J.W. Boyd, *A Persian Offering: The Yasna: a Zoroastrian High Liturgy*, Paris: Association pour l'avancement des études iraniennes, 1991.

S.N. Kramer, *Sumerian Literary Texts from Nippur: In the Museum of the Ancient Orient at Istanbul*, ASOR, 1944.

S.N. Kramer, *Sumerische literarische Texte aus Nippur*, Berlin: Akademie-Verlag, 1961-67.

S.N. Kramer, *Sumerian Mythology: A Study of Spiritual and Literary Achievement in the Third Millennium B.C.*, Philadelphia: American Philosophical Society, 1944.

S. Kramer, "Review of A. Hendel, *The Babylonian Genesis: The Story of Creation*", *JAOS*, 63 (1943), 69-73.

S. Kramer, *The Sacred Marriage Rite, Aspects of Faith, Myth and Ritual in Ancient Sumer*, Bloomington, IN: Indiana University Press, 1969.

S. Kramer and J. Maier, *The Myths of Enki, the Crafty God*, Oxford: Oxford University Press, 1989.

S. Kramrisch, *The Hindu Temple*, Calcutta: University of Calcutta, 1946.

F.R. Kraus, "Nippur und Isin nach altbabylonischen Rechtskunden", *JCS* 3 (1949), 78-80.

P. Kretschmer, "Indra und der hethitische Gott Inaras", *Kleinasiatische Forschungen* I (1930), 297-317.

R. Labat, *Le caractère religieux de la royauté assyro-babylonienne*, Paris: Librairie d'Amérique et d'Orient, 1939.

A.K. Lahiri, *Vedic Vrtra*, Delhi: Motilal Banarsidass, 1984.

N. Lahovary, tr. K.A. Nilakantan, *Dravidian Origins and the West: Newly Discovered Ties with the Ancient Culture and Languages, Including Basque, of the pre-Indo-European Mediterranean World*, Bombay: Orient Longmans, 1963.

W. Lambert, "Studies in Nergal", *Bi Or* 30 (1973), 355-363.

W. G. Lambert, "Three literary Prayers of the Babylonians", *AfO* 19 (1959-60), 47-66.

W. Lambert, "Studies in Marduk", *BSOAS* 47(1984), 1-9.

B. Landsberger, *Three Essays on the Sumerians*, tr. M. DeJ. Ellis, Los Angeles: Undena Publications, n.d.

B. Landsberger and T. Bauer, "Zu neueröffentlichen Geschichtsquellen", *ZA* 37 (1927), 61-98

D. Lang, *Armenia: Cradle of Civilization*, London: George Allen and Unwin, 1980.

S.H. Langdon, *Babylonian Liturgies: Sumerian Texts from the Early Period and from the Library of Asshurbanipal*, Paris, 1913.

S. Langdon, *Tammuz and Ishtar: A Monograph Upon Babylonian Religion and Theology*, Oxford: Clarendon Press, 1914.

S. Langdon, *Excavations at Kish*, I, Paris: Librairie Orientaliste Paul Geuthner, 1924.

S. Langdon and A.H. Gardiner, "The treaty of alliance between Hattusili, king of the Hittites, and the pharaoh Rameses II of Egypt", *JEA* 6 (1920).

P. Lapinkivi, *The Sumerian Sacred Marriage in the Light of Comparative Evidence*, Helsinki : Neo-Assyrian Text Corpus Project, 2004.

E. Laroche, "Recherches sur les noms divins hittites, *RHA* VII, 45 (1946-47).

M.E. Lefebure, *Le Tombeau de Seti I*, Paris, 1886.

G. Leick, *Mesopotamia: The Invention of the City*, London: Penguin Books, 2000.

B. Lincoln, *Death, War and Sacrifice: Studies in Ideology and Practice*, Chicago: University of Chicago Press 1991.

M.J.H. Linssen, *The Cults of Uruk and Babylon: The Temple Ritual Texts as Evidence. for Hellenistic Cult Practice*, Leiden: Styx, 2004.

E. Lipinski, *Dieux et Déesses de l'univers phénicien et punique (Studia Phoenicia* 14 (1995).

D. Lorton, "The theology of cult statues in Ancient Egypt", in M. B. Dick (ed.) *Born in Heaven made on Earth*, 123-210.

A.A. Macdonell, *A History of Sanskrit Literature*, Delhi: Munshiram Manoharlal, 1961.

V. Machek, "Name und Herkunft des Gottes Indra", *AO* 12 (1941), 143-54.

C. Malamoud, "Terminer le sacrifice: Remarques sur les honoraires rituels dans le brahmanisme", in M. Biardeau, *op.cit.*, pp.155-204.

J.P. Mallory and D.Q. Adams (ed.), *Encyclopedia of Indo-European Culture*, London: Fitzroy Dearborn, 1997.

J.P. Mallory and V. H. Mair, *The Tarim Mummies: Ancient China and the Mystery of the Earliest Peoples from the West*, London: Thames and Hudson, 2008.

S. Marakhanova, "A Version of the Origins of the World in Egyptian, Orphic and Gnostic Cosmogonies", in *Ancient Egypt and Kush*, Moscow, 1993.

J. Mellaart, *Çatal Hüyük: A Neolithic Town in Anatolia*, London: Thames and Hudson, 1967.

S. Mercer, *Horus Royal God of Egypt*, Grafton, MA: Society of Oriental Research, 1942.000

A. Michaels *Hinduism Past and Present*, Princeton, NJ: Princeton University Press, 2004.

G. Michell, *The Hindu Temple: An Introduction to its Meaning and Forms*, Chicago: Univeriity of Chicago Press, 1988.

A. Miles, *Land of the Lingam*, London, 1933.

J. Miller, *The Vision of Cosmic Order in the Vedas*, London: Routledge and Kegan Paul, 1985.

M. Molé, *Culte, mythe et cosmologies dans l'iran ancien*, Paris: Presses universitaires de France, 1963.

A. Moret, *Le Rituel du culte divin journalier en Egypte, d'après les papyrus de Berlin et les textes du temple de Séti Ier, à Abydos*, Paris : E. Leroux, 1902.

A. Moret, *Du caractère religieux de la royauté pharaonique*, Paris: Annales du Musée Guimet, Biblioth. d'Études, Vo.15, 1902.

W.M. Mueller, "Der Bündnisvertrag Ramses' II und des Chetiterkönigs", *MVAG* 7 (1902).

K.L. Muttarayan, "Sumer: Tamil of the First Cankam", *Journal of Tamil Studies*, 8 (1975), 40-61.

K. Mysliwiec, *Studien zum Gott Atum*, 2 vols., Hildesheim: Gersternberg Verlag, 1979.

S.L. Nagar, *The Cult of Vinayaka*, N.Delhi: Intellectual Publishing House, 1992.

H. Nissen, *The Early History of the Ancient Near East 9000-2000 B.C.*, tr. E. Lutzeier and K.J. Northcott, Chicago: University of Chicago Press, 1988.

J. Oates, "Ur and Eridu: the Prehistory", *Iraq* 22 (1960), 32-50.

W. O'Flaherty, *Asceticism and Eroticism in the Mythology of Śiva*, London: Oxford University Press, 1973.

H.Otten and M. Mayrhofer, "Der Gott Akni in den hethitischen Texten und seine indoarische Herkunft", *OLZ*, 1965, 11/12, 545-52.

E. Otto, *Das ägyptische Mundöffnungsritual*, 2 vols., Wiesbaden: Harrassowitz, 1960.

U.C. Pandey, *The Cosmogonic Legends of the Brahmanas*, Gorakahpur: Shivaniketan, 1991/2.

E. Pargiter, *Ancient Indian Historical Tradition*, London: Milford, 1922.

A. Parpola, "The Problem of the Aryans and the Soma", in G. Erdosy (ed.), *op.cit.*

A. Parpola, "Human sacrifice in India in Vedic times and before, in J. Bremmer (ed.), *op.cit.*, 157-78.

W.M.F. Petrie and J.E. Quibell, *Naqada and Ballas*, London: Bernard Quaritch, 1896.

J.A. Philip, *Pythagoras and Early Pythagoreanism*, Toronto: University of Toronto Press, 1966.

S. Piggott, *The Druids*, London: Thames and Hudson, 1975.

S. Pollock, *Ancient Mesopotamia: The Eden that never was*, Cambridge: CUP, 1999.

J.J. Preston, "Apotheosis and destruction in Hinduism" in J. Waghorne (ed.) *Gods of Flesh, Gods of Stone*, 9-30.

J. Przyluski, "Inara et Indra", *RHA* V, Fasc.36 (1939), pp.142-46.

A.D. Pusalkar, "Pre-Harappan, Harappan and post-Harappan culture and the Aryan problem", *Quarterly Review of Historical Studies*, 7,4 (1967-8).

S. Quirke, *The Cult of Ra: Sun-Worship in Ancient Egypt*, London: Thames and Hudson, 2001.

C.K. Raja, *Survey of Sanskrit Literature*, Bombay: Bharatiya Vidya Bhavan, 1962.

A.E. Redgate, *The Armenians*, Oxford: Blackwell Publishers, 1998.

E. Reiner, "The Etiological Myth of the 'Seven Sages,'" *Orientalia* 30 (1961), 1-11.

V.G. Rele, *The Vedic Gods as Figures of Biology*, Bombay: D.B. Taraporevala Sons, 1931.

E.A.E. Reymond, *The Mythical Origin of the Egyptian Temple*, Manchester: University of Manchester Press, 1969.

H. Roeder, "Mundöffnung und rituelle Feindtötung: die soziomorphe Definition eines altägyptsichen Vernichtungsopfer", in E. Stavrianopoulou, A. Michaels, C. Ambos (ed.), *Transformations in Sacrificial Practices: From Antiquity to Modern Times*, Berlin: LIT Verlag, 2008, 19-74.

K. Rönnow, "Zur Erklärung des Pravargya, des Agnicayana, und der Sautrâmani", *Le monde orientale*, 23 (1929), 113-73.

A.M. Roth, "Fingers, stars and the 'opening of the mouth': The nature and function of the NTRWJ blades", *JEA* 7 (1993), 57-79.

G. Roux, *Ancient Iraq*, London: George Allen and Unwin, 1964.

G. Rubio, "On the alleged 'Pre-Sumerian Substratum'", *JCS*, 51(1999), 1-16.

R.T. Rundle Clark, *Myth and Symbol in Ancient Egypt*, London: Thames and Hudson, 1959.

M. Rutten, "Les religions asianiques" in M. Brillant and R. Aigrain, *Histoire des religions* IV, Paris, 1956, 1-117.

J. Sainte Fare Garnot, *L'hommage aux dieux sous l'ancien empire égyptien*, Paris, 1954.

W. Sallaberger, "Ritual, A" *in RLA* XI..

M. Sandman-Holmberg, *The God Ptah*, Lund: C.W.K. Gleerup, 1946.

S. Sauneron, *Les Prêtres de ancienne l'Égypte*, Paris: Éditions du Seuil, 1957.

S. Sauneron, *The Priests of Ancient Egypt*, tr. A. Morissett, N.Y.: Grove Press, 1960.

H.A. Schloegl, *Der Gott Tatenen*, Freiburg: Universitätsverlag Freiburg Schweiz, 1980,

H.-P. Schmidt, *Brhaspati und Indra*, Wiesbaden: Otto Harrassowitz, 1968.

P.A. Schollmeyer, *Sumerisch-babylonische Hymnen und Gebete an Šamaš*, Paderborn: Ferdinand Schoeningh, 1912.

H.W. Schomerus, *Saiva Siddhanta: An Indian School of Mystical Thought: Presented as a System and Documented from the Original Tamil Sources*, tr. M. Law, Delhi: Motilal Banarsidass, 2000.

A. Schott, "Das Werden der babylonische-assyrischen Positionsastronomie und einige seiner Bedingungen", *ZDMG*, 88 (1934).

E. Schrader, *Die Keilinschriften und das Alte Testament*, Berlin: Reuther und Reichard, 1903.

M.K. Schretter, *Alter Orient und Hellas*, Innsbruck: AMOE, 1974.

J. Schwab, *Das altindische Thieropfer*, Erlangen 1886.

Y. Sefati, *Love Songs in Sumerian Literature: Critical Edition of the Dumuzi-Inanna Songs*, Ramat Gan: Bar-Ilan University, 1998.

K. Sethe, *Amun und die acht Urgötter von Hermopolis (Abhandlungen der preussischen Akademie der Wissenschaften*, 1929, Nr.4).

M. Sharma, *Fire-worship in Ancient India*, Jaipur: Publication Scheme, 2002.

S. Sharma, *Scientific Basis of Yajnas aAong with its Wisdom Aspect*, ed. A.N. Rawal and tr. H.A. Kapadia, E-book: www.shriramsharma.com.

D. Shulman, "Murukan, the Mango and Ekambaresvara-Siva Fragments of a Tamil Creation Myth", *Indo-Iranian Journal* 21 (1979).

D. Shulman, "The Tamil Flood Myths and the Cankam legend", in A. Dundes (ed.), *The Flood Myth*, Berkeley: University of California Press, 1988, pp.293-317.

R. Simek (tr. A. Hall), *Dictionary of Northern Mythology*, Cambridge: D.S. Brewer, 1996.

P.O. Skjaervo, "The Avesta as source for the early history of the Iranians", in G. Erdosy (ed.), *op.cit.*

G.E. Smith, *The Ancient Egytians and the Origin of Civilization*, London: Harper, 1923.

A. Snodgrass, *The Symbolism of the Stupa*, Ithaca: Cornell University Press, 1985.

W. von Soden, "Der grosse Hymnus an Nabû", *Zeitschrift für Assyriologie und vorderasiatische Archäologie*, 61 (1971), 44-71.

S. Sorensen, *An Index to the Names in the Mahabharata*, London: Williams and Norgate, 1904.

F. Sommer, Review of H. Eheloff, *Keilschrifturkunden aus Boghazköi*, Heft XXX, *OLZ* 1939.

E. Speiser, *Mesopotamian Origins:The Basic Population of the Near East*, Philadelphia: University of Pennsylvania Press, 1930.

E.A. Speiser, *Introduction to Hurrian, AASOR 20, New Haven,CT, 1941.*

Staal, F. *Agni, the Vedic Ritual of the Fire-Altar*, 2 vols., Berkeley: Asian Humanities Press, 1983.

Staal, F. *Rules without Meaning: Ritual, Mantras, and the Human Sciences*, N.Y.: Peter Lang, 1989.

H. Steible, *Die altsumerischen Bau- und Weihinschriften*, Wiesbaden: F. Steiner, 1982.

G. Steindorf, *Aniba*, 2 vols, Service des Antiquités del'Egypte, Glückstadt, 1935-37.

P. Steinkeller, "On Rulers, Priests and Sacred Marriage: Tracing the Evolution of Early Sumerian Kingship," in *Priests and Officials in the Ancient Near East: Papers of the Second Colloquium on the Ancient Near East, The Middle Eastern Culture Center in Japan*, ed. K. Watanabe. Heidelberg: Winter, 1999, 103-137.

H. v. Stietencorn, *Ganga und Yamuna*, Wiesbaden, 1972.

M. Streck, "Das Gebiet der heutigen Lanschaften Armenien, Kurdistan und Westpersien nach den babylonisch-assyrischen Keilinschfriften", *ZA* XV (1900), 272-5.

G.G. Stroumsa, *Another Seed: Studies in Gnostic Mythology*, Leiden: E.J. Brill, 1984.

R.F.G. Sweet, "A New Look at the 'Sacred Marriage' in ancient Mesopotamia", in E. Robbins and S. Sandahl (ed.), *Corolla Torontonensis: Studies in honour of Ronald Morton Smith*, Toronto: Tsar, 1994, 85-104.

M. Tachikawa and M. Kolhatkar, *Vedic Domestic Fire-Ritual: Sthalipaka, its Performance and Exposition*, N.Delhi: New Bharatiya Book Co., 2006.

K. Tallquist, *Akkadische Götterepitheta (Studia Orientalia 7)*, Helsinki, 1938.

E. Tenner, "Tages- und Nachtsonne bei den Hethitern", *ZA* 38 (1929), 186-90.

F. Thureau-Dangin, "An acte de donation de Marduk-Zâkir-Šumi", *RA* 16 (1919).

F. Thureau-Dangin, *Rituels Accadiens*, Paris: Leroux, 1921

Toorn, K. van der (ed.), *The Image and the Book : Iconic Cults, Aniconism, and the Rise of Book Religion in Israel and the ancient Near East*, Leuven: Peters, 1997.

H.W. Tull, *The Vedic Origins of Karma*, Albany: State University of New York Press, 1989.

A. Ungnad, *Subartu* Beiträge zur Kulturgeschichte und Völkerkunde Vorderasiens, Berlin: de Gruyter, 1936.

A. Ungnad, "Ahura-Mazdah und Mithra in assyrischen Texten?", *OL* 1943 No.5/6, 193-201.

H. Usener, *Die Sintfluthsagen*, Bonn: Friedrich Cohen, 1899.

H. Te Velde, *Seth God of Confusion: A Study of his Role in Egyptian Mythology and Religion*, Leiden: E.J. Brill, 1967.

H. Te Velde, "Human sacrifice in ancient Egypt", in J. Bremmer (ed.), *op.cit.*, 127-134.

N. Veldhuis, *A Cow of Sin*, Groningen: Styx Publications, 1991.

J. Vendryes, "Les correspondances de vocabulaire entre l'indo-iranien et l'italo-celtique", *Mémoires de la société de linguistique de Paris*, 20 (1918), 265-85.

G. P.Verbrugghe and J.M. Wickersham, *Berossus and Manetho, Introduced and Translated: Native Traditions in Ancient Mesopotamia and Egypt*, Ann Arbor, MI: University of Michigan Press, 1996.

J. Wackernagel, *Ueber den Ursprung des Brahmanismus*, Basel: Schweighausen, 1877.

J.P. Waghorne, "The divine image in contemporary South India: The renaissance of a once maligned tradition", in *Born in Heaven, Made on Earth*, 211-243.

J.P. Waghorne and N. Cutler (ed.), *Gods of Flesh, Gods of Stone*, Chambersburg, PA: Anima Publications, 1985.

C. Walker and M.B. Dick, "The Induction of the cult image in ancient Mesopotamia", in C. Walker and M.B. Dick, op.cit., 55-122.

C. Walker and M.B. Dick *Born in Heaven:The Making of the Cult Image in the Ancient Near East*, Winona Lake, IN: Eisenbrauns, 1999.

A.J. Wensinck, "The Ideas of the Western Semites concerning the Navel of the Earth", *Verhandelingen der Koninklijke Akademie van Wetenschappen*, XVII (1916), no.1.

A.J. Wensinck, "The Ocean in the Literature of theWestern Semites", *Verhandelingen der Koninklijke Akademie van Wetenschappen*, No.XIX (1918), no.2.

A.J. Wensinck, "Tree and Bird as Cosmological Symbols in Western Asia", *Verhandelingen der Koninklijke Akademie van Wetenschappen*, XXII (1921), no.1.

M.L. West, *The Orphic Poems*, Oxford: Clarendon Press, 1983.

M.L. West, *East Face of Helicon*, Oxford: Clarendon Press, 1997

G. Wilhelm, *Grundzüge der Geschichte und Kultur der Hurriter*, Darmstadt: Wissenschaftliche Buchgesellschaft, 1982.

G. Wilhelm, *The Hurrians*, tr. J. Barnes, Warminster: Aris and Phillips Ltd., 1989.

R.H. Wilkinson, *Symbol and Magic in Egyptian Art*, London: Thames and Hudson, 1994.

T. Wilkinson, *Genesis of the Pharoahs*, London: Thames and Hudson, 2003.

E. Jan Wilson, "Inside a Sumerian temple: the Ekishnugal at Ur" in D.W. Parry and S.D. Ricks (ed.), *The Temple in Time and Eternity*, 1999.

H. Wohlstein, *The Sky-God An-Anu*, Jericho, NY: Paul A. Stroock, 1976.

D. Wolkstein and S. Kramer, *Inanna, Queen of Heaven and Earth: Her Stories and Hymns from Sumer*, N.Y.: Harper and Row, 1983.

John Woodroffe ("Arthur Avalon"), *Shakti and Shâkta: Essays and Addresses on the Shâkta tantrashâstra*, London: Luzac and Co. 1918.

D. Yoshida, *Untersuchungen zu den Sonnengottheiten bei den Hethitern*, Heidelberg: Universitätsverlag C. Winter, 1996.

H. Zimmern, "Biblische und babylonische Urgeschichte", *Der Alte Orient*, II (1901), 3.

H. Zimmern, 'Religion und Sprache' in E. Schrader, *op.cit.*, 343-653.